DATE DUE			

The New Heavens and New Earth

CUSHING STROUT

The New Heavens and New Earth

Political Religion in America

1817

HARPER & ROW, PUBLISHERS

New York, Evanston, San Francisco, London

For Nathaniel, Benjamin, and Nicholas

FIRST EDITION

Designed by Patricia Dunbar

Library of Congress Cataloging in Publication Data

Strout, Cushing.
  The new heavens and new earth.
  Includes bibliographical references.
  1. United States—Religion. I. Title.
BR515.S77   1973   200'.973   73-4128
ISBN 0-06-014171-9

Contents

We are forever struggling to mediate between the bitter opposites, continually recurring, of conscience and external law, morals and expediency, immanence and transcendence, liberty and authority, the heavenly and the earthly which go to make up man. . . . From the consciousness that we can never reconcile them completely nor exhaust their full meaning arises the manly pride in an unending warfare and an unending labor, the need for which will never be wanting to us or to our children's children; for it is the warfare and the toil of life.

—BENEDETTO CROCE

But "unpractical" as he is, the religious man is nevertheless the transfigured rendering of the politician's fairest dream. No politics ever has, no politics ever can, no worldliness ever has, no worldliness ever can, think through or realize to its last consequences the thought of human equality. . . . It is only religion that can, with the help of eternity, carry human equality to the utmost limit . . .

—SOREN KIERKEGAARD

Foreword

The quotations from Croce and Kierkegaard that introduce this volume pay my respects to two very different thinkers who strongly influenced my thinking about history and religion when I was getting my philosophical bearings in the 1940's. Later I found R. G. Collingwood more congenial than either of the others, though both left their mark on my sense of how history and religion ought to be understood. Reinhold Niebuhr did much to remedy the profound lack of a feeling for political life in Kierkegaard's existentialism, and David Riesman and Erik H. Erikson helped me to see the historical uses of sociology and psychology, matters largely ignored by the philosophical tradition of idealism.

I am indebted, as all scholars in American studies must be, to the achievement of my mentor at Harvard, the late Perry Miller, in restoring intellectual excitement and historical depth to the study of American religion. His own conclusion with respect to religious liberty was that "we didn't aspire to freedom, we didn't march steadily toward it, we didn't unfold the inevitable propulsion of our hidden nature: we stumbled into it." I entirely agree with his negations, though I think there was more pattern than the image of stumbling may suggest. I have to disagree sharply, however, with his judgment that Tocqueville's "pages on religion in *De la Démocratie en Amérique* are probably the least perceptive he ever wrote."* Much of this book is a dissent from his conclusion. Miller preferred the American evangelical views of Robert Baird, partly, I think, because Tocqueville was European and Catholic. Neither Baird nor Tocqueville, however, had

* "The Location of American Religious Freedom," *Nature's Nation* (Cambridge, Mass., 1967), p. 155; "From the Covenant to the Revival," *ibid.*, p. 117.

to face the subtle and pressing problems of how to relate the tradition of religious liberty and disestablishment to the more pluralistic realities of the twentieth century.

One of the mailboxes in a Cornell building is stenciled: "Incoming History." Many messages received there in the 1960's, I thought as I passed it recently, are now piling up in the box marked "Outgoing History." The historian who continues his story, as I have done, into the recent past must run the risk of getting his mail caught in transit between the two boxes. One is taught as well as misled by the currents of change. In a country so eager as my own to respond to every shift in the winds of doctrine, the only protection I know is an effort to keep keen one's nose for the difference between a restorative breath of fresh air and the seductive smell of fashionable opinion.

The historians Allan Nevins and William E. Leuchtenburg originally sponsored this book for an envisaged series, which did not survive the death of the senior editor. I am honored by their confidence in allowing me to choose my own topic. My Cornell colleagues Michael J. Colacurcio, David J. Danelski, Michael Kammen, Milton R. Konvitz, and J. Saunders Redding have done me the service of reading portions of this volume and so, with characteristic generosity, has my long-term correspondent at Harvard, David Riesman. Others, as colleagues, students, or friends, have performed various courtesies in connection with this project: Meyer H. Abrams, Joseph Connolly, Richard Dressner, Dr. Howard Feinstein, Thomas D. Hill, Matthew Leone, Richard Rosecrance, and Rabbi George Sobelman. For time, space, and financial support to finish this book I had the good fortune to enjoy a year's fellowship (in both senses) at Cornell's Society for the Humanities, under the direction of Henry Guerlac.

The subtitle "political religion" I owe to my son, Nathaniel. The phrase itself was also used by Lincoln in speaking about the need for devotion to the Republic's laws, but making a religion out of politics is not the same thing as making a politics out of religion, which is the sense of my title. My footnote references will have to do the duty of expressing my indebtedness to the voluminous scholarship of recent decades in making it possible to construct and criticize such a long and complex story.

Ithaca, N.Y.   C.S.

Introduction

Any visitor to Europe immediately encounters impressively visible evidence in the buildings around him of the historical influence of religion. Yet it is in America, where the visible remains of religious influence are seldom impressive, that weekly churchgoing persists at a much greater rate than is characteristic of Western Europe. This phenomenon, familiar to modern sociologists, was first predicted by Alexis de Tocqueville, the most imaginative and subtle foreign commentator on American life in the nineteenth century.

Touring the country in 1831 as a young man, he stored up similar impressions for his masterwork, *Democracy in America*.[1] Centering his attention on the "habits of the heart" and the "character of mind" of the people of the United States, he was especially fascinated, historically and sociologically, with the prestige of religion in America. Like such later historical students of religion as Max Weber and Élie Halévy, he was interested in the secular consequences of religious ideologies. Above all, however, he wanted to understand American religious life in terms of its relation to the grave problems of making a liberal democratic order. "On my arrival in the United States," he explained, "the religious aspect of the country was the first thing that struck my attention; and the longer I stayed there, the more I perceived the great political consequences resulting from this new state of things."[1] Because of his emphasis on the favorable relation between liberty and religion, Tocqueville parted company with most of his liberal contemporaries, who made an antithesis of the two terms.

The editor of the first modern American edition of the *Democracy*, who was worried in 1945 about "popular loyalty" and "unstinted service," cited Tocqueville's thesis on political religion only in the context

xi

of claiming that "a religious view" of man is "the one sure answer democracy has to give to totalitarian materialism."[2] But a skeptical humanist like George Orwell or E. M. Forster may be more antitotalitarian than anyone else, and religious people have been compelled to challenge the demands for loyalty that even democratic states demand. The specifically historical aspect of Tocqueville's thesis is its point about the making and persistence of a particular style of religion— "a democratic and republican religion." Born a Catholic, he became, as he said, *"un libéral d'une espèce nouvelle,"* because he believed that liberty, law, morality, and religious belief—under conditions of legal disestablishment—were symbiotically related.[3] This argument has rarely been confronted directly in America or France.* American historians have done much since the 1930's to recover American religious history, but usually without reference to Tocqueville's case. Sociologists are more likely to cite it, and one eminent political sociologist, Seymour Martin Lipset, has drawn effectively on Tocqueville's sociology of religion in order to orient his own analysis of the founding of the new nation.[4] But even this notable example has not raised critical issues about the limitations of Tocqueville's thesis as history has exposed them.

I have tried to elaborate historically what Tocqueville only sketchily suggested about colonial origins and national founding, to evaluate his argument in the light of later reform movements, and to examine it as well in terms of emerging tensions over religious diversity and the meaning of disestablishment in the United States, conflicts present not only in his time but in our own. I have tried throughout to stay alert to his blindnesses as well as to his insights, for what a sophisticated perceptive foreigner fails to see may also be as important as anything he discovers.

Complaints can easily be drawn up against taking Tocqueville as seriously as I have done: he is really a speculative sociologist rather than a historian, really a prophet of the future, or really only an adviser to his countrymen, and besides he is too long dead and too often quoted in the 1950's by historians who rationalized an obsolete conservative mood. I am very much aware, having elsewhere made the argument myself,[5] that he was always thinking about the shape of the European future when he was discussing America; and I have no in-

---

* A little-known work by Henry Bargy, *La Religion dans la Société aux États-Unis* (1902), emphasized a Puritan civic religion and a morally activist nineteenth-century style in terms close to Tocqueville, but he never cited him.

tention of letting him become, instead of a provocation for my own detailed historical examination, a substitute for it. But it is a help to think in dialogue with Tocqueville in order to keep one's attention fixed on issues of meaning and value, not merely of existence, regarding the themes I have chosen to study.

Many secular-minded historians often forget that their own preference for nonreligious thinking cannot simply be projected backward into the past. Many church historians, for their part, have often spoken on behalf of religious commitments, making special pleas for the nurturing role of their own faith in the making of the country. As a matter of history, the relationship between religion and democracy in American life is profoundly complex. The temptation to oversimplify is very strong. The religious life has its own claims, which are distorted if faith is evaluated only as it serves secular interests. At this level some write as if God were blessed for having produced Americans. Alternatively, others write as if America were blessed for having made God a private foible. But secular life also has its claims, which are distorted if they are evaluated only insofar as they favor or hurt the interests of religion. At this level some write to celebrate America for having produced the triumph of Protestantism or for having made God popular. Others deplore modern life as a backsliding from sectarian morality. None of these polemical stands is favorable to the writing of history. Our present condition calls for much more sophisticated efforts at understanding.

Increasingly, Americans are facing the conflicts in their own society that new recognition of a radical pluralism of belief has brought about. Just how the state and its agencies should be ordered with respect to a society in which religionists, agnostics, and atheists are seen as spokesmen for *legitimate* options is a historic issue bristling with controversy. But the writing of history, which plays no favorites in this battle, will itself help to clarify the realities of the situation. It may remind us as well how genuinely new this position is in the history of the country. It is a situation that calls for historians who are appreciative of the ambiguities in the relations of democracy and religion, which their ardent partisans tend to convert into simple positives or negatives.

These complexities can be bewildering to the most scrupulous historian. "Having made an initial, apparently necessary, distinction between two entities or processes that offer themselves to him as united," as H. Richard Niebuhr has acutely pointed out, "he asks himself whether the relations are those of interaction, or of parallelism, or of epiphenomenalism, or whether indeed he is dealing with two aspects of a more fundamental reality." His difficulties are not made easier by the fact that "none of these patterns suffices for every occasion."[6] This complexity inheres in the subject, for religion may appear as a form of political action, just as democracy may appear as a kind of faith. And the realities to which both address themselves may have little logical relation to either.

To be a historian is to seek to explain in human terms. If God speaks, it is not through him. If He speaks to others, the historian cannot vouch for it. In this sense the historian is necessarily secularist. Yet, with equal force, nothing human is alien to him, and religion, whatever else it may be for true believers, is profoundly human. My own perspective is independent of any doctrinal or institutional form of religion, but my humanism is not militant. It defines itself not as a rival substitute for religion, but rather in the effort to understand religions historically rather than as eternal truth. I have done my best, particularly on the most controversial issues, to take a firsthand and fair-minded long look at the sources, and I have tried to learn from sociologists and psychoanalysts, not merely from historians, theologians, and other more familiarly humanistic students of the subject.

One terminological problem may stir up a flock of contentious pigeons: my use of the terms "religion" and "nonbeliever." Obviously, people who are not self-defined in terms of Protestant, Catholic, or Judaic commitments, for example, do nevertheless have many important beliefs. It has become fashionable for many theologians to call "religious" any ultimate and organized perspective, but the result is to deny the atheist his repudiations and to sweep up so much into the category of religion that it becomes entirely unclear what possibly could be omitted if it pretended to any organization of values or depth of commitment. In this usage "religion" then becomes simply equivalent to moral seriousness.[7] I think it is clearer and less distorting, especially for historians, to use "religion" and "nonbelief" unpejoratively to distinguish those who pray and worship in some envisaged relation to the transcendent and the tradition of some church from those who deliberately choose to do neither.* This distinction does not deny that secular "unbelievers" have their own traditions in the Enlightenment

* Tocqueville referred to himself in 1824 as a nonpracticing believer but in 1843 as *"tout incroyant,"* yet he strongly affirmed some Christian beliefs and in 1859 was given the last rites of a Catholic, though in what spirit has been debated. See Doris S. Goldstein, "The Religious Beliefs of Alexis de Tocqueville," *French Historical Studies, 1* (December, 1960), 379-93.

and its heirs, nor does it forget that they may also be influenced by some values displaced from traditions called "religious." It merely preserves the meaning of "agnostics" and "atheists," my own common company in university life.

There is a similar difficulty about the scope of the word "politics." I am interested here only in the political consequences of religion, but I do not merely mean electoral politics. I include movements whose energy is not given to conventional parties, and I also pay close attention to the Supreme Court of the United States when its work involves it in the political function of finding legal principles to deal with basic questions of public policy bearing on the place of religious conscience and practice in the public order. In general, whoever influentially comes to terms in thought and practice with the task of giving public meaning to how American religious ideas, values, or attitudes relate to political concepts of liberty, equality, community, and justice is a candidate for inclusion in my story.

I do not present this theme as yet another master key, supposedly unlocking the inner secrets of American history, to hang on the chain with the frontier, agrarian-industrial conflict, economic expansionism, abundance, liberalism, conservatism, immigration, or whatever. Master keys are out of fashion, having too Victorian a look, and even their makers nowadays are careful to warn (at least in principle, though not always in practice) that they are good only for some doors some of the time. I am interested rather in reflecting historically on a theme that corrects the common overemphasis on "pragmatism" as definitive of American politics by drawing attention to ideological, theological, and moral elements. Its continuing vitality lies in the fact that the relation of religious faith to the political order is a perennial intellectual and practical problem for which the answers have continually to be rethought in the light of changing conditions. This study arises from a felt need for clarification on that issue, to which I hope historical knowledge and understanding will make an essential contribution.

But we have his promise, and look forward to new heavens and a new earth, the home of justice.

—New English Bible, 2 Peter 3:13

The Puritan Paradox

For Tocqueville the Puritanism of American colonial life was a profound key to all that was most novel, distinguishing, and hopeful in the political life of the New World. Ever since Mencken's mocking contempt for Puritanism as "the haunting fear that someone somewhere might be happy," scholars have worked to counter it with the recovery of an authentic Puritanism which they could understand with sympathetic respect. By 1944, at a time of world war against fascism, the philosopher-historian Ralph Barton Perry, moved by the purpose of "identifying the American cause with the American tradition," used much of the new scholarship in *Puritanism and Democracy* in order to give Puritanism an important part in the "fundamental agreement of mind and purpose by which the United States has played its peculiar role in the modern world."[1] Yet Tocqueville does not even appear in Perry's index. A decade later Louis Hartz deliberately exploited Tocqueville to emphasize the persistence of an American consensus on a liberal individualistic sense of society, making his own variant of Tocqueville's view that the Americans had been able to keep "the notion of private rights and the taste for local freedom" because "they have had no aristocracy to combat." Tocqueville, however, thought "the notion" and "the taste" were derived from an English aristocratic legacy, while Hartz emphasized the persistence of a Lockean outlook, taken as an initial postulate, and he made nothing out of Tocqueville's deep interest in the religious dimension of the story.[2]

By the 1960's, among younger historians there was a mood of revulsion against the stress on moral and ideological consensus that some commentators of the 1950's had extracted from Tocqueville's work, and a consensus was formed among historians that conflict, not agreement, was the key to understanding the American past, as it was a growing feature of their own present. Even so, the work done by many American historians of religion in the 1960's was increasingly committed to showing, as Perry had done in 1944, that Puritans had played a creative role in the making of the English and the American Revolutions. Though they did not cite Tocqueville, they formed conclusions that were profoundly congenial to his own dominant theme in *Democracy in America* about the historical significance of Puritanism for modern developments.* Although forgotten with respect to his historical insights, Tocqueville was being celebrated as a prophetic sociologist for his trenchant forebodings about the dangers of an egalitarian bureaucratic paternalism and of an alienation of the citizen from a sense of political participation and potency. Ironically, these features of the future seemed to be increasingly characteristic of the American present in the eyes of many commentators, who had forgotten that for Tocqueville the American case had valuable safeguards, protecting it from succumbing to many of the evils of the future threatening Europe. In his view the nature of the connection of religion with politics in America was one of the most hopeful auguries for the American future.

Tocqueville thought that Puritanism was "not merely a religious doctrine, but corresponded in many points with the most absolute democratic and republican theories." Yet nothing is clearer than that harshly enforced uniformity of belief and morality and strict restriction of political power to an elite were characteristic of New England Puritanism. How can these facts be reconciled with Tocqueville's assertion that "the external forms of political liberty were introduced into all the colonies almost from their origin"? Tocqueville himself cited many examples of the repressive rigor that Puritans employed in enforcing their own order in laws which he found "fantastic and oppressive." Yet citizens, he observed, played an electing role in political affairs, authorities were made responsible by legal restraints, measures to protect personal liberty and trial by jury were passed, and provision for public education was made compulsory. He tentatively explained the paradox by concluding that New Englanders were as free from prejudice in their politics as they were narrow and dogmatic sectarians in their religion. The historical result is that in their religion there

---

* Such historians would include, for example, Michael Walzer, William McLoughlin, Alan Heimert, Richard Bushman, Timothy Breen, and David Little.

arises "a passive though a voluntary obedience"; in their politics, "an independence scornful of experience, and jealous of all authority."[3]

If Tocqueville had left the problem in this condition, he would have created by this schizoid interpretation far more difficulties than he would have solved. But he then asserted that these two tendencies, "apparently so discrepant, are far from conflicting; they advance together and support each other." What begins as a mere dualism in Tocqueville's account of the matter ends in a dialectical statement that defines a necessary connection as well as a tension. It is possible to use this dialectical form of the problem to understand better the inner spirit of the Puritans themselves, who in his view had been "like a beacon lit upon a hill, which, after it has diffused its warmth immediately around it, also tinges the distant horizon with its glow."[4] Yet Tocqueville uses the paradox more generally to define an ideal situation in which religion is unsupported by "aught beside its native strength," a situation relatively true of America only after the disestablishment of the churches. The differences between Puritan and post-Revolutionary America in his account are thus blurred.

Looking backward is a dangerous game, for if the historian hunts for his ancestors in his predecessors he is all too likely to find them. He then applies to the past that prism favored by Whig historians eager to see the currents of the Puritan past feeding steadily into streams that flowed into the secure harbor of their own enlightened present. In this fashion all the cleavages of the historical past are smoothed out for the sake of a blandly progressive vision of the grand course of history.

This telescoping of history has been trenchantly criticized by the modern English historian Herbert Butterfield, and it is wise to begin with his warning: "If Protestants and Catholics of the 16th century could return to look at the 20th century, they would equally deplore this strange mad modern world, and much as they fought one another there is little doubt that they would be united in opposition to us; and Luther would confess that he had been wrong and wicked if it was by his doing that this liberty, this anarchy had been let loose, while his enemies would be quick to say that this decline of religion was bound to be the result of a schism such as his." This warning forbids us, for example, to ask *to whom* do we owe our religious liberty, as if a grateful posterity should erect a monument to its benefactors, but it does not forbid our asking *how* religious liberty arose. This latter question leads to a consideration of process.

But Butterfield also warns that if we escape the Whig fallacy, we may fall on the other side into the opposite error and conclude that the Reformation did nothing at all. In that case we superstitiously lean upon the metaphor of "a deeper tide in the affairs of men," regarded "as a self-standing, self-determined agency behind history, working to its purpose irrespective of the actual drama of events."[5] This danger is implicit in the Hegelian metaphor of "the cunning of reason" working its own will on the wills of men. Both the Whig fallacy and its opposite seduce the historian into abstracting from the complex mediations of the actual historical process.

Tocqueville himself, for all his emphasis on the importation into America of "a democratic and republican religion," did not fail to notice and deplore the harsh and sweeping controls that Puritans in New England imposed on erring men. Nor was such control peculiar except in degree to New England. Most of the colonial governments enforced uniformity in religion, made church attendance compulsory, reserved political rights for the orthodox, and took strong action against heretics. Whether in Virginia, New Netherland, Delaware, or Massachusetts Bay, whether Anglican, Dutch Reformed, Swedish, or Congregational, the churches held to these purposes.

As a practical policy, in fact, religious toleration was first a Catholic program in Protestant colonial America. The colony of Maryland, for example, predominantly Catholic in leadership though not in population, had more religious freedom than either Virginia or Massachusetts until the Puritans in 1654 overthrew the proprietor's regime and outlawed the Catholics. Before the colonists sailed to the New World, the proprietor of Maryland urged the leaders of the expedition to "treat the Protestants with as much mildness and favor as Justice will permit."[6] Puritans fleeing Anglican Virginia, or Anglicans escaping the wrath of the Massachusetts Bay Colony, found sanctuary in Catholic Maryland. As Puritan power in Maryland waxed, both Protestants and Catholics were compelled for the sake of internal peace to pass an act of toleration that required only belief in Jesus Christ as a condition of citizenship. This degree of toleration was soon lost, however, in the Puritan revolt of 1654, and by 1692 Catholics were compelled to pay taxes for the support of Anglicans, who disfranchised them and forbade them their own schools. In New York when a Catholic became governor in 1683, he sponsored a bill of rights with a policy of toleration similar to Maryland's short-lived one, and it failed only when a German-born Calvinist led a revolt against the government and inaugurated a reign of terror against the Catholics. By 1693 the Church of England was also established in four major counties of New York.

This history can be explained on the ground that Catholic policy was strategic, reflecting a minority position in American life. But the same argument can be given for Puritan opposition to kings and archbishops in England or on the continent. Yet the drive for religious uniformity is not the whole story, as Tocqueville insisted. By his time in the nineteenth century most American religious groups *could* be loosely characterized in his terms as "democratic and republican." Was he merely reading his own present experience of them back into their earlier history? Was he a victim of the Whig fallacy? His argument did not depend upon denying the facts of Puritan coercion of dissenters. He believed that despite this "narrow, sectarian spirit"—indeed, "in strict connection" with it—Puritan political institutions were favorably disposed toward the development of liberal and democratic practices. How can this connection be understood? Not in spite of coercing dissenters did Puritans favor the growth of modern institutions, but indeed "in strict connection with" their repressions.

Max Weber's *The Protestant Ethic and the Spirit of Capitalism* has made familiar the idea of Puritanism as a seedbed for capitalistic individualism, derived from the doctrine of the calling, which required Puritans to labor diligently in the world. Weber was under no illusions about the regulatory aspects of the Reformation, which, "penetrating to all departments of private and public life, was infinitely burdensome and earnestly enforced." Nor did he see the spirit of capitalism, defined as the *rational and systematic* pursuit of profit, predominant among the entrepreneurs of the commercial aristocracy; he found it most characteristically in the aspiring lower industrial middle classes. In contrast to his popularizers, Weber carefully limited his thesis:

. . . we have no intention whatever of maintaining such a foolish and doctrinaire thesis as that the spirit of capitalism . . . could only have arisen as the result of certain effects of the Reformation, or even that capitalism as an economic system is a creation of the Reformation. In itself, the fact that certain important forms of capitalistic business organization are known to be considerably older than the Reformation is a sufficient refutation of such a claim. On the contrary, we only wish to ascertain whether and to what extent religious forces have taken part in the qualitative formation and the quantitative expansion of that spirit over the world.

What interested him was the irrational force that the doctrine of election gave to good works, not as a means of attaining salvation but rather as a method of "getting rid of the fear of damnation." The Calvinist's salvation did not consist, like the Catholic's, in the accumulation of good works to one's credit, "but rather in a systematic self-control which at every moment stands before the inexorable alternative, chosen or damned." It was this discipline which produced the good works that relieved the Calvinist conscience of its anxiety. This psychology of Puritanism favored the development of a rational bourgeois economic life, and its main legacy to the eighteeenth century was "above all an amazingly good, we may even say a pharisaically good conscience in the acquisition of money, so long as it took place legally."[7]

Taken crudely, without Weber's refinements, the thesis would conflict with the fact that Catholic Europe had a highly developed capital organization until the Counter Reformation in Italy and Spain halted it. The great banking families of the Medici and the Fuggers were linked to Catholic powers, and in the beginning Luther strongly protested against monopolists and money-changers. Not burghers but princes and nobles began the attack on the power of the Church. While Calvin supported usury, which in his time merely meant charging interest, he carefully distinguished interest earned by productive investments from interest earned by exploiting the misery of others. Catholics themselves, for that matter, sanctioned usury in foreign-exchange dealings.[8]

The calling of Puritans to worldly business was profoundly ambiguous. It required, as John Cotton put it, "a combination of virtues strangely mixed in every lively holy Christian, and that is, Diligence in worldly businesses, and yet deadnesse to the world; such a mystery as none can read, but they that know it." A Puritan was called to the general vocation of being a saint as well as to a particular work, and the restraints of the first controlled the spirit of the second. Prosperity was for the good Puritan even a source of anxiety, for he could find in adversity a more bracing tonic to sustain him in the stance his creed required. Not until Puritanism had lost its edge did the sins of pride and avarice give way to the sins of sensuality and idleness, as the stress on the relevance of work to the common good gave way to enthusiasm for the possibilities of self-advancement in the New World.[9] Weber himself recognized that the relevance of his thesis was mainly to this aftereffect. The connection between Puritanism and the gospel of work certainly existed, but this linkage does not support an argument about capitalism being the way Puritans thought about society. Their adherence to strict controls on prices and wages was a world away from the laissez-faire theory of a later age. The Puritan work ethic created a tension in the successful businessman between individual effort and social obligations. It animates, for example, Robert Keayne's last will and testament (1653), an apologia for his rise from butcher's boy in England to merchant and judge in Suffolk County, Massachusetts, after being fined for usury, profiteering, and drunkenness, and being censured by his church. Keayne's outraged piety acknowledged the force of the charges; he merely pleaded not guilty in fact.[10]

Puritans were diligently active as well in devising techniques of social organization. In a sense, as Michael Walzer has powerfully argued, they transformed politics into work. Where the feudal world rested on personal loyalty, kinship, neighborhood association, and custom, the Puritan world demanded impersonal devotion to ideas, parties, churches, and states. "Indeed, the new spirit of the Puritans," as Walzer says, "can be defined as a kind of military and political work-ethic, directly analogous to the 'worldly asceticism' which Max Weber has described in economic life, but oriented not toward acquisition so much as toward contention, struggle, destruction, and rebuilding. . . . It is this above all that distinguishes the activity of the saints from that of medieval men, caught up in the unchanging world of tradition, fixed in their social place and loyal to their relatives; and also from that of Renaissance men, pursuing a purely personal ambition."[11]

Calvinism joined represssion and association on an ideological basis. Calvin himself made obedience the major Christian virtue. He accepted all strong power as ordained by God. Ordinary citizens had no right of resistance, even to unchristian rulers. Lay elders held power in the government of the church, but its form was set by the Word itself, not by their devisings. The state should support the church by exiling unrepentant souls who had been excommunicated from the church, and magistrates should enforce subjection to the Word. Lesser magistrates might resist a heretical king out of obligation to their own ordained office, but they should not resort to tyrannicide. This sternly repressive system had one escape valve: conscientious prophets and teachers, armed with "celestial truth," could set themselves against ungodly kings and nations.[12] The way was open for a Puritan preaching that would build up resistance to authority when power was not itself Puritanized.

In England Puritans found themselves in just such a situation. Queen Elizabeth sheltered them in part by allowing them to exist in connection with or alongside of the established Anglican Church. Puritans used this liberty to experiment with "many of the techniques of what came to be called modern politics; the politics of free assembly, mass petition, group pressure, and the appeal to public opinion."[13] They also became canny in the use of illegal underground tactics, more familiar to modern radical movements; for Puritans could not be assimilated to a society whose Tudor and Stuart monarchs aimed at paternalistic absolutism, rather than at the nurture of a godly magistracy, inspired by the "collective watchfulness" of the Puritans. Perpetually anxious over the sinful state of his soul and his society, obsessed by the possibility of his eternal salvation through faith, the Puritan lived in the light of a universe controlled by an omnipotent God who demanded obedience of men, organized according to divine plan in both church and state. Only through a major historical effort could the Puritan realize his goals. His destiny was social discipline, his temper militant, for the Puritan life was a means of controlling the anxiety that his social existence and religious sensibility constantly aggravated. Stern self-control and social control were his watchwords. Nothing could be further from the liberal spirit of self-expression or social tolerance. In England it was, in fact, the Anglicans who first spoke for the tolerance of an easygoing civility, unwilling to make ideological issues out of every dispute of doctrine; practical acceptance of a national church, with all its hypocrites, was a small price to pay for social peace. The Puritan found this amiable laxness the very opposite of his own high seriousness.

Puritan propaganda helped produce, nevertheless, a vernacular public, avid for print and protest, that eventually made possible the seizure of initiative in the state first by Parliament and then by the army. Puritan preachers in England, caught in a semilegal and tensely critical relationship to established power, fostered a highly developed political consciousness. A historian of English Puritanism, William Haller, has made the connection luminous: "Granted such conditions, Englishmen fell into the habit of joining together as they chose or as circumstances might require for their souls' satisfaction with or without benefit of clergy in church, chapel, or conventicle, at home or in exile, in England, in foreign lands, in the American wilderness. Wherever they went, and they presently went everywhere, and however they differed, this they would all know how to do."[14] This English past helps explain that fertile power of associating for common purposes which Tocqueville would later find so impressive in America.

The insurgency of a vernacular public, as Haller has pointed out, also gave force to the doctrine of calling and covenant. Puritans were called to produce godly magistrates and diligent citizens, and their religious doctrine of covenant made easier the later acceptance of social-contract thinking in a secular context. But covenants themselves were not contracts; they were modes of discipline for church and state, ways of binding men to their duties so that their incorrigible tendency toward sinfulness did not run riot. Yet such covenants, ingeniously elaborated from the Bible, as expounded by such English Puritan divines as William Perkins and William Ames, also reassured men that they had a purchase on their world, that the terrifying power of an inscrutable God was not random or vicious. He condescended to bridge the great gap between creatures and their Creator by expressing Himself through covenants.

God in covenant was more like a constitutional monarch than a despot; man in covenant was more like a citizen than a subject. The government of the church was, as the Cambridge Platform called it in 1648, "a mixed Government," incorporating elements of monarchy, aristocracy, and democracy in a Militant Visible Church. Voluntarism was thus implied in Puritan ideology, despite the dogma of divine predestination that made faith itself a product of God's will. Modern readers find Calvinist predestination inconsistent with Calvinist willfulness, as if spiritual determinism should have produced lassitude among the saints. But the Calvinists were enthralled with a vision that made the world dramatically meaningful in cosmic glory, and their own place in the drama was secured by their participation in the system of theological, ecclesiastical, and social covenants. The great drama demanded great actors, and Puritans steeled themselves to play their roles. Stimulated by anxiety, their passion was for control; repressive as it was, their discipline was for men of great energy; and the pursuit of control itself led from the watchful self to the mutual surveillance of the holy commonwealth and the visible church.

In England the chief result of Puritanism would finally be the individual's sense of being chosen and called, rather than the creation of visible saints in both state and church, linked in a holy commonwealth.

The circumstances of the Puritan Revolution, which plunged the country into civil war, left Oliver Cromwell's New Model Army in control of decisive power. In the Army gathered churches of believers, favoring independent rather than presbyterian organization, made up the vast body of saints; and Cromwell himself, on the basis of his Army experience, urged Parliament to support liberty of conscience rather than enforced uniformity. The humanist scholar and parliamentarian lawyer John Selden, the Puritan silk merchant William Walwyn, fond of Seneca and Montaigne rather than of dogmatic theologians, and the fiery democrat John Lilburne, spokesman of London apprentices and the Leveller Party—all could see that enforced religious conformity in the pursuit of an ecclesiastical state was the sure road to bitter social conflict. The Levellers, in fact, would try to turn the Army into an instrument of democratic political and social reform as well as of greater religious toleration, but the Army itself crushed them, leaving itself with sole power to bring peace to England. The erudite John Owen, who addressed a sermon on toleration to the House of Commons the day after the execution of King Charles I, was a harbinger of the future. Magistrates should publicly provide for the gospel, but they should discipline only the more extravagant, scandalous, or vagabond preachers, leaving, for the rest, spiritual remedies for spiritual diseases. This policy, which received Cromwell's favor, was the outcome of a Puritan crusade that originally had quite different aims. The decisive effect of the revolution was to leave the English people permanently divided in religion. "Wherever they went in the world, and they were about to go everywhere," as Haller has said, "their religious alignments and affiliations would reflect not their oneness as a people but their internal differences of rearing, education, class, and nationality."[15] Democratic in neither political nor social terms, the victorious Puritans would nevertheless find themselves accommodating their aspirations to a more tolerant society.

In America, however, toleration would come to have a different history because social space enabled particular churches to become dominant in particular colonies. Freedom of social space enabled the Puritans to pursue their goal of a holy commonwealth, unimpeded by the conflicting interests of other religions and established classes. Puritans did not, as in England, have to win over established elements of the urban merchants and the country gentry; nor did these groups, when of Anglican persuasion, have to contend in Virginia or New York with a polemical Puritan clergy, expanding its power to reach the public through intensive propaganda. Even Quakers, an intransi-gent persecuted *sect* in England, could become a relatively peaceful and stable *church* in Pennsylvania, though still persecuted elsewhere in America. The coercive drive of Puritans for enforced discipline could also manifest itself in the Bay Colony with a consistency impos-sible in England. Whatever their differences, the majority of settlers in America were heirs of the Reformed or Calvinist tradition. Even Anglicanism in America dated from the settlement of Jamestown when the Church of England was almost wholly Reformed in its theological orientation. Perry Miller has remarked of early Virginians that "the quality of their piety, their sense of their relation to God, was so thor-oughly Protestant as to be virtually indistinguishable from the Puri-tan."[16] The laws of pioneer Virginia, for example, heavily penalized idleness, gaming, drunkenness, violation of the Sabbath, and other "ungodly disorders."

The Puritan, wherever he was found, was shaped by an orientation containing paradoxical elements that could impose restraints on con-stituted authority and emphasize noncoercive voluntary decisions, as well as obedient uniformity in thought and action. A recent student of Calvinism points out that William Perkins, whom the American Puritans much admired, would have no difficulty in assenting to Perry Miller's point that for New England Puritans "obedience was no longer to be wrung from subjects by might, but accepted as a spontaneous token." Perkins taught a paradox: "We must be a law to ourselves: we must be voluntaries, without constraint, freely yielding subjection to the will of God."[17] The Puritan church provided an institutional base for the new order of regenerate life, partially made corporate and actual in the society of saints. Such a position, if forced into minority dissent as it was in England with the Levellers, could call the estab-lished aristocratic world into question. In New England, where Cal-vinism was in power, it would show a more authoritarian face, but even there Puritans did not believe that the categories of saint and citizen, of sacred and secular, could be entirely blended in a visible way. Some seemingly godly men were hypocrites, even saints could sin, and there were still boundaries between church and state. The new order of Christian life could never be identified with ordinary life without falling into a fanaticism that no sober Puritan would have countenanced. Even in New England, voluntarism and consent were as real as repression.

The contribution of Puritanism to republicanism was preparatory and even ironic, in view of its peculiar aims, but it was not merely contingent, unrelated to its own characteristic ideas and institutions. "There was nothing inevitable about the transformation the original doctrine would undergo in America," as Stephen Foster has said, "either in 1630 or 1760 or at any point in between." But Foster's conclusion is too skeptical: "The witches' brew that went under the name of Puritan social thought could have spawned almost anything."[18] What came of it was a matter of a mingling of doctrine and American circumstance, of success and failure, of English and Puritan elements, not of deductive logic from theological propositions. Yet it was fateful for America that politics and religion were first profoundly linked by a movement that emphasized voluntary association for chosen impersonal ends, rested on consent in church and state, put legal limits on all power, envisioned a necessary political life for saints, and carefully distinguished between the realms of church and state. For all these reasons Puritans did prepare the way in their own terms for a different ethos more congenial to republicanism and the democratizing of power. Tocqueville distorted the case in Whig style when he made the early emigrants the bearers of "a democratic and republican religion," but he saw correctly that in America "from the beginning, politics and religion contracted an alliance which has never been dissolved."[19] From his own power of generalization he derived a paradox that can be exploited beyond his own findings to illuminate the special character of the Puritan contribution to civil society.

II

The City on the Hill, the Garden in the Wilderness, and the Glorious Revolution

The conception of liberty that John Winthrop, as governor of the Massachusetts Bay Colony, upheld was a moral one. Civil or covenanted liberty was "the proper end and object of authority," but liberty itself was "a liberty to that only which is good, just, and honest." And this liberty was maintained and exercised "in a way of subjection to authority; it is of the same kind of liberty wherewith Christ hath made us free." Yet Tocqueville believed that "the *spirit of religion* and the *spirit of liberty*" were in America peculiarly combined. The result was that in the *moral* world Americans lived in a "passive though a voluntary obedience," while in the *political* sphere they practiced "an independence scornful of experience, and jealous of all authority." The essence of his point was that the two elements did not conflict: "These two tendencies, apparently so discrepant, are far from conflicting; they advance together and support each other."[1]

The examples of this relationship that impressed him most were the New England system of electing executive officials and "the germ and gradual development of that township independence which is the life and mainspring of American liberty at the present day."[2] Appealing to royal charter, freemen of the Bay Colony insisted on the right to participate in the making of the laws. By 1634 they had deputies to represent them in the General Court for legislative actions, and from 1632 to 1684 there were annual elections of the governing magistrates. The townships, furthermore, provided a nucleus around which political life could be organized. Tocqueville was right that the settlers of New England were both "ardent sectarians and daring innovators." The township itself, whose municipal freedom he found so attractive and so lacking on the continent of Europe, was not an English inheritance. It replaced the parishes, boroughs, and manors from which the settlers had come, where church and state were inextricably entwined. "In order to separate them and also do away with archaic forms of land tenure," as Edmund S. Morgan has pointed out, "it was necessary to construct an altogether new kind of unit, a unit which would be a parish without church officers, a borough without aldermen, a manor without a lord."[3]

These units were given legal sanction by the Massachusetts Body of Liberties, drafted in 1641 by Nathaniel Ward, who had ten years' legal training and practice in the courts of London. Instead of accepting John Cotton's suggested adaptation of Mosaic law, later put into effect in the New Haven Colony, the Bay Colony guarded the traditional liberties of trial by jury and due process of law that Englishmen were struggling to protect. While the Body of Liberties made idolatry, witchcraft, and blasphemy, as well as sexual irregularities, capital crimes, it prescribed far fewer death penalties than the laws did in Old England. The Puritan religious imagination was intrinsically disposed to constitutional limitation of power. As John Cotton put it, "there is a straine in a man's heart that will sometime or other runne out to excesse, unlesse the Lord restraine it." Therefore "let there be due bounds set" both to liberty and to authority.[4] By the code of 1650 the townships became the basis of a public school system. Thus Tocqueville felt that his case was proved that in America religion led to knowledge and civil freedom. Living under a monarchy, the colonists had established a "republic in every township."

Tocqueville used the word "republic" in nineteenth-century American terms to stand for a politically expressed majority will as "the common source of all the powers of the state."[5] In this sense, however, the Bay Colony was certainly not a republic. Within five years of its founding in 1630 the rule was established that only professed and examined saints, who proved by public confession in church that the saving faith had come to them, could become full communicants of the church and voting citizens of the state. By this critical merger of church and state a powerful *minority* of the population was the source of power, and it was morally bound to act not in its own interests but according to strict Christian precepts, and for the welfare of a covenanted people with a divine mission. The same system applied to New Haven. But in Hartford the church communicants were examined less strictly and freemen did not have to be saints. The separatist Plymouth Colony probably did not rigorously test its church members until 1648, perhaps not until 1669, but it never made the franchise dependent upon sainthood, although Quakers were refused citizenship. These two colonies, therefore, would appear to prove Tocqueville's point better than the Bay Colony. (But even in Plymouth the town in 1670 disenfranchised nearly a third of the former voters and developed property qualifications for the status of freemanship and the right to vote.) Yet sainthood was not a class privilege. By 1647 some nonfreemen could vote for town selectmen and be jurymen and by 1658 any Englishman over twenty-four whose estate had a certain value (worth at least two horses) could exercise the town suffrage, regardless of sainthood status. Though the economic test was raised later, this arrangement was a democratic one that supports Tocqueville's argument for all its exaggeration. Exact figures are unobtainable, but perhaps half the adult males in the Bay Colony exercised voting power. During 1637–38 in the Bay Colony, for example, 830 adult males, out of an estimated 1,600, chose to exercise the voting privilege that belonged to church members, and probably some 260 more chose not to take advantage of their right.[6]

The Puritan fusion of church and state was never complete; in fact, it confounded contemporaries who imagined that a church-state like Geneva, a state church like England, or a wide separation like Rhode Island were the only alternatives. Puritan thinking in America was on this point original and complex, and would have been a mystery to both St. Thomas and St. Augustine, for whom the state was either natural or corrupt. Nor was it compatible with Richard Hooker's pragmatic Anglican nationalism, which scorned any Biblical model for the state. Church membership in England was broadly inclusive, but loss of it was also tantamount to social deprivation. The excommunicate lost his legal rights and faced fines and imprisonment. Membership in the Bay Colony, by contrast, was narrowly restricted to the saints, but no excommunicated church member lost his civil rights. While magistrates and ministers often consulted on policy, no minister held public office, whereas in England the bishops of the church sat in the House of Lords. Winthrop himself, in defense of his banishment of Anne Hutchinson and her antinomian followers, who included a high proportion of voters having both wealth and office, arose in church to remind the clergy that affairs of state did not belong to their calling. Magistrates imposed taxes for support of the church and treated heresy as a civil crime with civil disabilities, but the churches could respectfully discipline magistrates only on religious issues. If church and state were joined by a "federal" reading of Scripture that provided the "due form" for both, nevertheless each had its separate calling. This complex relationship cannot strictly be called theocratic, for the clergy had only an advisory role. To some degree the ideal of separation between church and state was implicit in this Puritan overlapping of the two spheres in a unique way.

By modern modes of classifying governments, Puritanism was an anomaly. For Puritans the terminology of "democracy" and "aristocracy" was a function of the number who were ruling, not the method of choosing them. In their lexicon, annual elections of representative bodies in church and in state established "aristocracies."[7] John Cotton was anxious to reassure Viscount Saye and Sele, for example, that the Bay Colony Puritans recognized the class of gentlemen by always electing such a person as governor, but the preacher stood firm on his local ground by reminding the nobleman that they could not convert "hereditary honors" into hereditary authority and power: sometimes God did not furnish the posterity of noble families with "gifts fit for magistracy." In Massachusetts only saints could rule the state. But, His Lordship objected, what if "Carnal men" should have been invested by God with "sundry eminent gifts of wisdom, courage, justice, fit for government?" Magistrates might consult with such men, Cotton replied, but they were not ultimately "fit to be trusted with place of standing power or settled authority."[8] The Puritan system, as Cotton explained, was balanced because, like a three-legged stool, its elements (the freemen, the magistrates, and the church) all worked together to maintain one another so that liberty, authority, and purity were assured in their proper spheres. Citizens were not determined by class standing but by piety; rulers were pious gentlemen, yet elected annually by the pious freemen; church and state were separate and yet overlapping. This strange mixture of democracy, aristocracy, and theocracy helps explain the ambiguous legacy that Puritanism left to later generations.

In its seedtime American Puritanism sowed only one wild oat of advocacy for full toleration as a corollary of religious freedom. This heresy of Roger Williams was as passionately Puritan as the outrage of his persecutors, and his contribution to the problem of Puritanism and politics, religion and society, church and state, was as fanatical as anything which Winthrop and Cotton bequeathed to their descendants. Yet the case of Roger Williams is the best evidence for the argument that toleration grew out of Calvinism only when it had been influenced by the radicalism of separatist sectarianism. Congregationalism itself, as practiced in the Bay Colony, was a curious mixture of the two types of religion that Ernst Troeltsch has called church type and sect type. "The Church has its priests and its sacraments; it dominates the world and is therefore also dominated by the world. The sect is lay Christianity, independent of the world, and is therefore inclined towards ascetism and mysticism. Both these tendencies are based upon fundamental impulses of the Gospel." Sociologically, the church type stabilizes the social order and becomes dependent upon the upper classes; the sects, on the other hand, "work upwards from below, and not downward from above." As Troeltsch pointed out, Congregationalism "stood midway" between these types. Baptists, however, represented the radical, lower-class, sect type of Christianity which, through its connections with the English Puritan Revolution, eventually "helped to loosen the connection between Church and State, which made the formation of Free Churches possible, and which helped to Christianize the ethical and social interests of the English people apart from dogmatic compulsion."[9]

It is to this left wing of the Reformation that Roger Williams was first attracted, converting (for a while) to the Baptists, who emphasized the priesthood of true believers voluntarily joined together by adult confession of faith and in righteous detachment from the state. Exiled followers of Anne Hutchinson, under the leadership of William Coddington and John Clarke, founded Newport in 1639 and established a government based on the consent of the majority, practicing full toleration. Williams, three years before, had made Providence another such outpost of freedom, so that Rhode Island even surpassed the later example of William Penn's Quaker colony, where from 1682 all who accepted Christ could hold political power and all who accepted God could enjoy religious freedom. Williams's career had the drama of the "dissidence of dissent."

The son of a shopkeeper, Williams found a patron to support his education at Cambridge, married a wealthy lord's maid, and became a Puritan. In 1630 he left England as a separatist in the same year as Winthrop's expedition. But the Bay Colony settlers were nonseparating Congregationalists who still maintained their sense of belonging to the Anglican Church, for all their dedication to its reformation. This difference would be fateful for later conflict between Williams and Winthrop. As minister at Salem, Williams soon proved to be a contentious and brilliant mind. He read the Bible according to the dangerously metaphorical method of typology, seeing the Old Testament as a mere prefiguration of the New, the heart of the gospel; and he denied the right of the Bay Colony's royal patent to land on the ground that it belonged to the Indians. Not only did Williams voice disturbing doubts about the righteousness of the Puritan covenant with God; he also accused the established clergy of wallowing in "warm and soft and rich seats and saddles," maintained by compulsory taxes. With unusual freedom from ethnic prejudice, he reminded Englishmen proud of their birth and blood that before God they were no better than Indians:

> By nature, wrath's his portion, thine no more,
> Till grace his soul and thine in Christ restore.
> Make sure thy second birth, else thou shalt see
> Heaven ope to Indians wild, but shut to thee.[10]

Banished to the winter wilderness by the Bay Colony, Williams lived with the Indians and compiled *A Key into the Language of America,* adorned with moral and anthropological observations on the life of the savages who had befriended him in his exile. This experience of disillusionment with the established powers nourished his major contribution to the theory of toleration, *The Bloudy Tenent of Persecution* (1644).

To the retrospective eye Williams is an extraordinarily attractive figure, and sympathy has tended to blur the profound Puritanism of his outlook. Protestantism generated a double tradition in Luther and Calvin, stressing with the former the inner experience of second birth as an individual reality, or emphasizing with the latter the social destiny of saints bound together in covenant. The Bay Colony precariously linked both elements together in a church-state of visible saints. But the Puritan method of scrutinizing the Bible as the mode of arriving at faith gave every believer a potential argument against the authority of learned clergymen. How could they step between him and the gospel itself, which God used to bring about His transformation of the souls of men? God was illimitable power, the Great Jehovah. How presumptuous therefore to think that He could be, by enforced religious discipline, commanded "to give faith, to open the heart, to incline the will." Forced worship was necessarily a "stink in God's nostrils," a denial of the Calvinist doctrine of His total sovereignty.

It followed that the true saints must be gathered invisibly. Once, long ago, the primitive church of Christ and his apostles had been a "garden" separated from "the wilderness of the world." Now the garden had become a wilderness in the turbulent changes of history. There was no true apostolic succession, no true church. The restoration of that garden would require that "it must of necessity be walled in peculiarly unto Himself from the world." To claim to be able to organize the saints in a visible church-state was to have churches and magistrates judging each other: "What blood, what tumults, hath been and must be spilt upon these grounds?" To argue that magistrates derived power from popular consent would only make matters worse by subjecting the church to unregenerate men: "And if this be not to pull God and Christ and Spirit out of heaven, and subject them unto natural, sinful, inconstant men—and consequently to Satan himself, by whom all peoples naturally are guided—let heaven and earth judge." This barb, thrown into the face of John Cotton, the Bay Colony's most learned spokesman for the establishment, had behind it the power of Williams's passionate vision of a world of sinners judged by an omnipotent wrathful God. There was no chosen people on earth, as the Israelites had been before Christ's coming; no model "city upon a hill," as Winthrop had called the Bay Colony. There was only a "spiritual Israel" and "they only that are Christ's are only Abraham's seed and heirs." When magistrates and ministers disciplined consciences that were opposed to their own, they claimed to know more than they possibly could. It was impossible that they would not "fight against God in some of them" and "hunt after the precious life of the true Lord Jesus Christ."[11]

The church could only be like a corporation in the city, not the gathering of visible saints in political and ecclesiastical unity. The state was still responsible for peace and order. Baptists, for example, could not legitimately object to militia duty in Providence. Magistrates were like ship commanders who "may judge, resist, compel, and punish" transgressors of the common safety "according to their desert and merits." Quakers, who confused the "inner light" with the historical Christ, thus confounding "clear scriptures with spiritual and mystical illusions," were no less mistaken.[12] Yet they should be fought, as Williams fought them, with ardent debate rather than force. Relatively indifferent to man's political life, Williams separated the church from the state in order to protect his religious conviction that God alone could give authentic grace to erring men.

No Puritan would have disagreed in principle. What made the

difference was the Bay Colony's policy of trying to distinguish as best it could who, in fact, *had* experienced a saving faith. The leaders would have admitted that hypocrites sometimes passed for saints, but only perfectionists would for that reason abandon the vision of a covenanted community of saints set as "a city upon a hill" as an example to the world of the great mission of the Protestant Reformation. Otherwise the saints could not fulfill their duty in this world of living out the full social destiny of Christian man. Williams's position, from this point of view, looked like anarchy. Furthermore, the Puritan leaders had been sorely tried by Williams's betrayal of his penitent promise not to teach against the King's patent to the land or to pronounce the English churches unchristian.

When the governor and his assistants finally brought him to book, the occasion was his public teaching that a magistrate ought not "to tender an oath to an unregenerate man, for that we thereby have communion with a wicked man in the worship of God, and cause him to take the name of God in vain." The corollary of this conviction was Williams's belief that magistrates had no right to enforce any of the first four Commandments. Only the "second table," concerning the family, murder, adultery, theft, perjury, and covetousness, legitimately fell into the social area of magisterial responsibility. Moreover, Williams himself by 1635 had refused to communicate with his own church in Salem unless it would refuse communion with the other churches. The exasperated General Court gave him six weeks to leave, but Williams continued to publicize his views, and the leaders decided to ship him back to England. When Williams refused to obey a warrant ordering him to Boston, a ship was sent to apprehend him; but Williams had fled. His own congregation, which once had defied political interference in the choice of its minister, now turned against him, and a handful of his followers who continued to support him were cast out of church. Winthrop in a private letter advised him to steer his course for Narragansett Bay, free of English claims, and the exile "took his prudent motion as a hint and voice from God."[13]

There is a bust of Williams in the pantheon of international Calvinism in Geneva. Radically premature for New England, he was prophetic of the imminent future in England. In 1644 his published dispute with John Cotton, like Milton's tract on the need for a more liberal divorce law, provoked scandalized English Presbyterians to urge that both screeds be burned. "The collapse of monarchical and ecclesiastical authority and the triumph of the army," as William Haller has remarked, "set all godly souls at last completely free to heed whatever call or revelation they believed had come to them, to commune with one group or another as the spirit moved them or with none at all, a law to themselves in what seemed to many a lawless world." The state would protect all peaceable communions and regard all persecutors as enemies of religion: "Justified by grace within, one could afford to wait as long as necessary for grace to manifest itself as it would in a visible church. Yet one might also at the same time look for regenerate souls to turn up in any company of men not certainly of Antichrist."[14] Outlawed in New England, this conception would be turned to practical advantage by Oliver Cromwell, who, at the final crisis of the Puritan Revolution, could thus find justification for his use of power.

Yet in England toleration did not reach as far as it did in Williams's Rhode Island after he became its leader. Independents like John Owen, vice-chancellor of Oxford, wanted Parliament to settle the upheavals in the English church by establishing a state-supported, tithe-taking institution that would yet allow for considerable religious variations. More radical Independents in the New Model Army wanted to move to Williams's position, and in 1652 Williams himself published a plea to Parliament, on behalf and in the name of Major William Butler, that "no person be forced to pray nor pay, otherwise than as his soul believeth and consenteth." In his own name he rushed to the printers *The Hireling Ministry None of Christ's* to persuade Cromwell and the Independents not to stop short before dealing with this vestige of established intoleration. But Cromwell was occupied with foreign policy and the war with Holland; and the Independents accepted the collecting of tithes. "Radicals like Major William Butler, John Milton, Roger Williams," as one historian has said, "were left to contemplate a revolution that stopped short of completion."[15] Williams returned to America, and England in 1660 returned to monarchy under Charles II, thus ending the Puritan Commonwealth.

After Rhode Island had secured a royal charter in 1663, Williams could boast to a Connecticut friend that His Majesty's grant was made in order to test the experiment "whether civil government could consist with such liberty of conscience."[16] Rhode Island levied civil taxes, for it pleased God, as Williams said, to command tribute "not only for fear, but for conscience's sake." Nor should men complain when the rates were low and "no man that hath a vote in town or colony, but *he hath a hand in making the rates by himself or his deputies.*"[17] Surely men who fell out over land claims, as Rhode Island and Connecticut did over the town of Westerly, could find some "humane and political medicine" to solve their problems. The crucial point was that Rhode Island had liberty of conscience, which made all other issues seem but mere "dishes and bowls of porridge." Williams offered to join Connecticut in a mutual sacrifice of some control of land for peace's sake, but on toleration he held firm: "We must part with lands and lives before we part with such a jewel." If his political policies failed and he too perished, no matter: "It is but a shadow vanished, a bubble broke, a dream finished. Eternity will pay for all."[18]

Ever since Constantine, Christianity's historical fate had been bound up with political repression of men's consciences in the name of orthodoxy. Williams's voice made an extraordinary break with that tradition because he spoke out of a deeply felt Calvinist faith, as Puritan as any in New or Old England. Williams demonstrated, as other Puritans did in England, that a radical Calvinist conscience could inspire as deep a passion for toleration as it could for the holy-commonwealth ideal of John Winthrop. For all his Calvinism, however, Williams broke new ground in his emphasis on the need for civil rulers without religious tests for their competence. He knew that political competence and sainthood were not causally linked, that human society had its own forms of civility that made peace and heresy compatible. To this extent, though like other Puritans he expected the second table of the Commandments to be legally enforced by the state, he opened up the possibility of finding purely human sources of community. On practical grounds alone he could object to the exclusion of English lords, who might have political competence as leaders, merely because they were not saints. But this objection was not at all democratic; his democratic sentiments were entirely religious. Since "not many *Wise* and *Noble* are called, but the *poore* receive the *Gospel,* as God hath chosen the *poore* of the *World* to be *rich* in *Faith*," Williams observed that ordinarily "there may not be found in a true *Church* of Christ (which sometimes consisteth but of few persons) persons fit to be either *Kings* or *Governours*," whose tasks were no less difficult than those of a physician, a ship's pilot, or any army commander.[19] If the poor were much more likely to be good Puritans, then a Puritan state based on the rule of saints would necessarily lack the skills that only the aristocratic class could bring to politics. Seen in this light the Bay Colony Puritans were unrealistic democrats, expecting saints to have political competence to manage their own affairs. The conflict of Williams with Winthrop dramatized the political ambiguity of the Puritan movement. Intolerance was in some respects more democratic than radical toleration in the context of the seventeenth century. Furthermore, the attractiveness of Williams's policy of toleration in the eyes of liberal historians has obscured the fact that in the 1670's, when he was still alive, Rhode Island established Sunday laws creating a citizens' "constable watch" to make sure that no person engaged in "tippling or gaming, or wantonness" or hired labor on the Lord's day.[20] Williams, like other Puritans, did not believe, as moderns do, in distinctions between morality and legality, sins and crimes. To this extent his conception of separation between church and state was a limited one, and the "blue laws" of Rhode Island were not as mild as those of Pennsylvania, where there were many exceptions to Sunday prohibitions.

Williams brought Rhode Island to the position that William Penn's Quaker Colony of Pennsylvania achieved from its outset in 1681 under its charter from Charles II. Puritans persecuted Quakers as mad enthusiasts, bent on subversion, but historically they seem themselves to be part of the Puritan movement, seeking a return to simplicity, to Biblical truth, to covenanted community, and to a personal experience of the transforming effect of the Holy Spirit. Like the Puritans too, Quakers enjoined industry, frugality, and thrift as economic virtues of the Christian, and their history in both England and America proved that if one Quaker foot was solidly planted in the meetinghouse, the other was as stoutly placed in the countinghouse. They differed from the Puritans chiefly in their intense insistence on the nonrational inner light of Christ within the soul, an illumination available potentially to all men. This perfectionist emphasis led Quakers to scorn intellectual theology, learned clergy, and conventional deference to social superiors—much to the scandal of shocked Puritans.

Quakers had fought and served the state with Cromwell, buoyed by their millennialist hopes. But their refusal to take political oaths eventually barred them from the New Model Army, and the failure of the Puritan Revolution to wipe out Rome disenchanted them with Cromwell's leadership. By 1661 they declared themselves pacifists and refused to pay tithes. Yet, when given the chance for power in America, William Penn himself asserted in the preface to the Pennsylvania Constitution of 1682 that "government seems to me a part of religion itself, a thing sacred in its institution and end." Political power was not merely for correction and punishment; it was also "capable of kindness, goodness, and charity," like private societies. It would con-

tinue among men, he prophesied, even during the millennium ush-
ered in by "the coming of the blessed second Adam, the Lord from
Heaven."[21] By 1756, even in America, the Quaker witness against violence, long compromised by legalistic subterfuges, came to a crisis
when the colony faced open warfare with the Delaware and Shawnee
Indians. A majority of Friends conscientiously resigned from office
rather than administer a province at war.

If the Quakers' moral reservations about certain political functions
necessarily troubled their role as politicians, their advocacy of liberty
of conscience gave them a consistency of policy in toleration that only
a Roger Williams had grasped in the seventeenth century. Holding
open meetings in England under the harsh Clarendon Code of Charles
II's first Parliament, Quakers suffered the brunt of English persecution
and learned to steel their consciences behind bars. At the age of
twenty-four, a dozen years before the Holy Experiment was tried in
Pennsylvania, Penn produced *The Great Case of Liberty of Conscience,* inspired by his own experience of prison. Liberty of conscience,
he argued, entailed freedom of assembly on matters of religion that
were "wholly independent" of secular affairs. The real blackness of
the business of persecution was this cruel dilemma: "Must they be
persecuted here if they do not go against their consciences, and punished hereafter if they do?"[22] Force could make a hypocrite; only faith
"grounded upon knowledge and consent" could make a Christian.
Furthermore, persecution was destructive of social peace, prosperity,
and unity. Penn had studied law at Lincoln's Inn, and his training
served him well in 1670 when he was tried for fomenting riot by holding a Quaker meeting in the streets of London. Despite intimidation,
the jury declared Penn and a fellow Quaker not guilty, but Penn was
forced to cite the Magna Charta against the court, which fined and
jailed both prisoners and jury for contempt of its advice. A higher
court reversed the decision and established a notable English precedent
in the defense of the right of the jury to come to its own conclusions.

Penn's commitment to freedom of conscience was well suited to
the community he established in America, where the "Pennsylvania
Dutch" (Germans and Swiss), the Scotch-Irish, Swedes, Finns, Dutch,
and Welsh lived with English Quakers, a prophecy of the pluralistic
society that would later make America distinctive in the Western
world. In this sense Penn's colony was more of a city upon a hill, an
exemplar for others, than New England ever was or could be in its

passion for uniformity. Only bitter experience could teach the Puritans in New England what the Quakers knew as a matter of deepest faith.

In New England the pressure on the Bay Colony for religious freedom would come from the internal opponents of the Mather dynasty and from the English government itself, allied in common cause not for the sake of democracy but against the isolationism of the Bay Colony and the political influence of its clergy. The British imposed a short-lived imperial regime under Sir Edmund Andros as governor of the Dominion of New England, to which New York and New Jersey were later added. Then in 1688 William of Orange landed in England, and "the Glorious Revolution" soon had its local counterpart in Boston. The Protestant succession of William and Mary enabled Increase and Cotton Mather to identify their own outcry against the loss of the colony's charter with a stout defense of good English liberties, as Whigs understood them. The Mathers would, however, have to persuade the English government that Massachusetts could in fact practice as much toleration as now obtained in England under William III. "They would survive and would rule only if they learned, however reluctantly," as Perry Miller has said, "to regard themselves as no more than a majority of Dissenters within the most loyal of all British provinces."[23] The colony would have to extend the franchise, regardless of church membership, to all forty-shilling freehold estates and accept the imposition of a royal governor. In return it would have a charter and an elected lower house with control of the purse. By this exchange the Puritans would learn how to venerate their prescriptive rights as Englishmen, and increasingly they would discover the secular possibilities that lay hidden in the contractual obligations implied by Puritan covenants. Revolution in England sponsored religious freedom and Whig politics in America.

The portent of these developments was the parson of Ipswich, John Wise. The first son of an indentured servant to enter Harvard College, Wise first made his mark by a passionate protest against taxation without representation, as imposed by the Andros regime. Tried and fined, he gained the favor of the Massachusetts Bay Governor, Sir William Phips, and served him as chaplain on a military expedition in Quebec. In the notorious debacle of the witchcraft trials at Salem, Wise appeared as a character witness in defense of the accused. A stout opponent of presbyterian efforts to control congregational churches, Wise found the best spirit of English civil government in the autonomy of local congregations. With "majesty mixed with affability, gravity with facetiousness, charity and severity," he seems to have charmed his admirers as a plain-spoken parson with his feet planted foursquare on New England earth. In *A Vindication of the Government of New-England Churches* (1717), Wise spoke up for congregationalism in a new idiom. His cause was entirely traditional, but his reasoning turned tradition upside down by praising congregationalism for basing itself on democratic principles in accord with natural law and right reason. His tract also gave arguments from the Bible, printed in a separate section, but it mainly rested on the secular reasoning of Baron Samuel von Pufendorf, his "chief guide and spokesman." Indeed, Biblical sanction was historically secondary: God approved what nature and right reason dictated regarding natural liberty, equality, and justice. Wise was not, like the English Levellers, a propagandist for political and social democracy; nor was he, like Roger Williams, an original theologian. But his thinking did mark out the path that Puritans could travel from the Biblical "federal theology" to that fondness for "natural law" and "right reason" which a more self-respecting humanity would indulge in the Enlightenment:

In this Discourse I shall waive the Consideration of Man's Moral Turpitude, but shall view him Physically as a Creature which God has made and furnished essentially with many Enobling Immunities, which render him the most August Animal in the World, and still whatever has happened since his Creation, he remains at the upper-end of Nature, and as such is a Creature of a very Noble Character.

In Wise's book the language of covenant mingled freely with the language of contract. Men contracted to form society, then again to make a particular government. Man in a state of nature was naturally free and equal, and when he first thought of devising a civil body, he naturally turned to the administration of common affairs by common judgment, and so established democracy. Yet Wise restricted his democratic case to church polity, accepting for political life the traditional ideal of "mixed government," best exemplified by the British Empire, a kingdom "most like to the Kingdom of Jesus Christ, whose Yoke is easie and Burden light."[24]

In Wise's thinking a new respect for man's natural competence pushed into the background his "moral turpitude," and the covenant, designed for the control of rebellious unregenerate human nature, became instead a contract, expressing his natural sociability and reasonableness. The state, instead of being a disciplinary institution, presupposed the virtue of its citizens. When Puritanism had done its work, men would be ready for the liberal Lockean state. Increasingly thereafter, Puritan repression would seem incomprehensibly barbarous, its contribution forgotten. "Liberal confidence made repression and the endless struggle against sin unnecessary," Michael Walzer has pointed out; "it also tended to make self-control invisible, that is, to forget its painful history and naïvely assume its existence."[25]

One of the merits of Tocqueville's understanding of Americans was the fact that this connection was not lost on him. A "great austerity of manners" counterpointed American turmoil and restlessness, and the American imagination "even in its greatest flights" was "circumspect and undecided." These "habits of restraint recur in political society," Tocqueville noted, "and are singularly favorable both to the tranquility of the people and to the durability of the institutions they have established." He did not question that this austerity derived from religious faith. For that reason the religion of Americans was "the first of their political institutions; for if it does not impart a taste for freedom, it facilitates the use of it."[26] Strange as it may seem, Sigmund Freud would have agreed with him. "It is just as impossible," he wrote, "to do without control of the mass by a minority as it is to dispense with coercion in the work of civilization." As Philip Rieff has observed, "By 'mass' Freud means not merely the 'lazy and unintelligent,' but, more importantly, those who 'have no love for instinctual renunciation' and who cannot be 'convinced by argument of its inevitability.' "[27] Like the Puritans, Freud knew that the history of self-control was painful and that the social contract exacted a high price. Viewed in this light, it is not so surprising that he named his second son after Oliver Cromwell.

But repression as a theme in Puritanism was modified by a persisting stress on the limits of power. It was not only human nature that needed restraint but government itself, which had to be limited by laws of a fundamental nature that protected citizens in their rights. John Wise's thinking marked the resonance of a segment of Puritan colonial opinion with English Whig polemicists who stressed traditional English liberties and the need for ordinary people to keep a close watch on their rulers. In the early 1720's this form of republicanism was vigorously voiced in the secular journalism of James Franklin and his brother Benjamin, who planted sharp anticlerical barbs in the pages of the *New-England Courant*. In 1721 they published the first American edition of Henry Care's *English Liberties,* which John Wise had drawn on for his own work. The Franklins also republished from England *Cato's Letters,* polemical republican essays by Thomas Gordon and John Trenchard, who tutored many of the future patriot leaders of the Revolution in how to match their respect for traditional liberties with their suspicion of the overbearing designs of rulers.[28]

Wise, the Franklins, and Trenchard and Gordon could all find receptive New England ears because of the local repercussions of the Glorious Revolution of William of Orange. After the overthrow of the Andros regime, when a new governor, council, and lower house were established in Massachusetts Bay by an electorate no longer restricted to the saints,* the colony passed "A Bill for the General Rights and Liberties" that was directed against any future Sir Edmund: no deprivation of liberty or property without due process of law or trial by a jury of peers and no taxation without legislative consent were affirmed as fundamental liberties in language not only reminiscent of English petitions of right but prophetic of American declarations in the Revolutionary era. The Andros regime had failed in its imperial effort but it had succeeded, in a way it surely had not intended, in rousing the colonists to assert their identification with traditional English liberties.[29] In so doing they shifted Puritanism towards a more republican system. But they also nurtured an audience for men whose ideas, however much they were Protestant, did not essentially depend upon Puritan theology, church government, or morality for their derivation or appeal. These new men did not displace the changing Puritans, for if they had done so it would be impossible to imagine how the intercolonial revivals of the mid-eighteenth century could have happened on a popular basis. Instead they signified the growing emergence of a republican tradition that would under the pressure of events draw eclectically on Calvinist and Whig, on clerical and anticlerical, on English and American political traditions.

---

* The governor, however, was royally appointed and the council was only indirectly elected.

III

The Great Awakening and the Rising Generation

One of the major gaps in Tocqueville's knowledge of the American people was his failure to appreciate the role of evangelical piety in the making of its society. A man of sober reason with a Catholic feeling for discipline and order, he looked distastefully on the more emotional and enthusiastic aspects of the religious temper. He did not fail to observe that some Americans manifested "a sort of fanatical spiritualism" in rude camp meetings where "strange sects" endeavored "to strike out extraordinary paths to eternal happiness." But, as with many other travelers, his shock and disdain led him to a dismissing judgment: "Religious insanity is very common in the United States." He could account for it only by seeing such enthusiasm as a minority's inevitable reaction against a major tendency of Americans to busy themselves with "promoting their own worldly welfare."[1]

The recurring wave of revivals from the middle of the eighteenth century to the Civil War was, however, much more important to the mainstream of American history than Tocqueville realized. The evangelical temper nurtured voluntary religious organization, unsustained by state taxes, and thus formed links between pietists and political rationalists that helped prepare the way for the Revolution. In this way pietism reinforces his own theory of American religion.

The Great Awakening of the mid-eighteenth century seemed to its preachers and converts to be a great outpouring of God's grace on the hearts of sinners, transforming their souls and preparing them for some great impending fulfillment of their destiny. To its greatest theologian, Jonathan Edwards, it was a portent of the Millennium which New England could play a leading role in bringing about in advance of the Second Coming of Christ. For the historian, however, the

Awakening is testimony to the rhetorical power of its preachers and the readiness of their congregations for a new style of religiosity. Its long-run effect was to prepare colonials for the separation of church from state in the Revolution.

The Awakening was an international movement in Germany, Great Britain, and America. Wherever it burgeoned, it preached the individual's personal experience of a change of heart in the crisis of conversion as the central meaning of religion. This current of pietism flowed from Holland and Germany into New Jersey and Pennsylvania through such men as Theodorus Jacobus Frelinghuysen and Henry M. Mühlenberg. (It failed, surprisingly, to rouse the Quaker apostles of the inner light because, as so often happens to religious movements, their success had conventionalized their faith and dulled their intensity of feeling. They also repressed the painful memory of their own bitter past in their recoil from the unrespectable new enthusiasts. Moreover, Quakers abhorred Calvinist determinism.)[2] The Scotch-Irish Presbyterian William Tennent conducted a "Log College" in Pennsylvania to train evangelical ministers in the new style, and his son Gilbert became the most powerful preacher of the Awakening in the Middle Colonies. In 1740 he accompanied the great English Anglican itinerant preacher George Whitefield on a tour to Boston, where they made contact with the New England revivalists. They were familiar with German pietist works through the scholarly efforts of the Mathers, and Edwards's report on the Northampton revival of 1734–35 would find its way back to John Wesley. Out of his own revival work in England, Wesley developed the Methodism that would later capture the American frontier. Both Wesley and Whitefield, to complete the circuit, were themselves influenced by Lutheran and Moravian pietists.[3]

In time revivalism would water the soil of all regions in colonial America, though New England produced its only first-class mind of international reputation. It would bring Presbyterianism and Baptism to the South, giving that region an evangelical tradition that would long survive its decline elsewhere. In back-country Virginia a bricklayer in Hanover County, Samuel Morris, read Luther and Whitefield to his neighbors with great effect. Samuel Davies, a graduate of William Tennent's Log College and a New Light Presbyterian, became pastor after visiting Morris's "readinghouses" for the excited crowds. In 1748, Davies widened this wedge by getting licenses to build seven Presbyterian meetinghouses in five counties under the protection of the English Toleration Act. Davies also knew how to whip up popular feeling against "a mongrel Race of Indian Savages and French Papists" in a fervent appeal for volunteers to defend the frontiers after General Edward Braddock's defeat in 1755. The "Fear of Jehovah's Curse" and the "Love of our Country," combined with "humble, broken-hearted" penitence, would work together to provide fighting men with a religion to keep them "incorrupted in the midst of Vice and Debauchery." In North Carolina a convert of the Great Awakening in Connecticut, Shubal Stearns, organized in 1758 the Separate Baptist (Calvinist) Sandy Creek Association, whose members a decade later were the backbone of the Regulator movement in the Piedmont, revolting against the economic inequities of the established government. Devereux Jarratt, one of the few Anglican revivalists in Virginia, cooperated closely with the Methodists in a revival that reached its climax in 1775–76 when the colonies formed their will to revolution.[4]

New England was ready for the ministry of Jonathan Edwards partly because it had already encountered his maternal grandfather, Solomon Stoddard, and before him the Half-Way Covenant. The churches in synod met in 1662 to meet the problem of the growing number of people who, though baptized, did not experience a saving faith. What of their children? Should they be baptized, as earlier children of saints had been, in the confident expectation that they would experience the saving faith? If not, the majority of the population would soon be made up of the unbaptized. The compromise proposed was that nonprofessing members could have their children baptized provided such parents, "not scandalous in life," would externally join in a formal pledge of "solemnly owning the Covenant before the Church." They would not be entitled to vote in church affairs or to share in the Lord's Supper, but they would be subject to church discipline. Although resisted by the laity and the Massachusetts deputies, the practice slowly spread until by the end of the century New England churches commonly instituted collective rites of "owning the Covenant," even including those without previous connection to the churches. The ratio of professing saints to the adult population was, however (at least for three Massachusetts towns recently studied), greater in the period 1670–89 than it had been twenty years earlier, despite plausible fears about the diluting effect of the new compromise.[5] The truly pious may not have declined but even increased, yet once the old pattern was broken, some churches would go further. Solomon Stoddard in Northampton, Massachusetts, decided in 1677 to accept anyone not openly scandalous into full church-membership privileges. After 1700 this radical abandonment of the ideal of a regenerate church of true believers, for the sake of a wider mission to the society, increasingly spread in the Connecticut Valley.

Stoddard himself preached revivals in his own parish, and his rhetorical tactics anticipated those of his grandson. "When Sermons are delivered without Notes," he advised, "the looks and gestures of the Minister, is a great means to command Attention and stir up Affection." Stoddard favored such imagery as the burning lake of fire and brimstone because sinners needed to be aroused by fright to an anxiety over their salvation, for "a mixture of fear and hope makes men diligent."[6] Men could know the supernatural experience of a saving conviction, acquired through grace after strenuous human preparation, because by self-reflection they could intuitively see for themselves the inner action of their minds and so acquire assurance. Conversion, which ought to be the experience of any reputable minister, was a datable event taking place not by degrees but all at once. These themes announced the presence of a preaching style and strategy that would be developed in a modified way by the revivalists of the Awakening. Once the collective owning of the covenant had become a feature of the Half-Way Covenant and once Stoddard's tactic had removed any invidious distinctions between saints and nonsaints in terms of church privileges, it is not surprising that a need would arise for a more authentic religious commitment that could still be widely shared in a communal way. The time for the Great Awakening had come to make true saints on a popular basis, though it would not solve but only create anew the problem of purity in doing its own work.

Jonathan Edwards's leadership in the Great Awakening was one of those notable conjunctions between private needs and public anxieties which characterize the lives of great men. As the only son in a family of eleven children, he must have known that his mother's hopes for a successor to her distinguished father, Solomon Stoddard, rested on him. His own father, learned in Greek, Latin, and Hebrew, was as methodically exacting of his son as he was of himself, and Timothy Edwards had good reason to be both fearful and obstinate in the search for self-control. Brought up in a family shaken by his father's divorce from an unfaithful wife and by two murders committed by the wife's siblings, he was vividly aware of potential disaster. As a minister he prefigured his son's famous quarrel with his congregation by denying communion to his East Windsor flock for more than three years because it would not agree to his censure of a boy who married a girl without her parents' consent. In late adolescence Jonathan Edwards experienced conversion as the total giving away of his self to God. The depth of his awareness of sinfulness in a precarious existence could have been justified by ample evidence in his family's history, and the jealousy and contention of his cousins in opposition to his own pastorate must have been a perpetual reminder of the ordinary depravity of men outside the fellowship of saints united by bonds of holy affections.[7]

By his intellectual talent alone Edwards might have become a scientist or a man of letters in eighteenth-century style, like Benjamin Franklin, but the intensity of his inner life, his capacity to feel the exaltation of sensual joy in the glory of God's immediacy in the constant creation of nature's dappled splendor and the abasement of unworthiness in the soul's potential vileness, fitted him for the family tradition of the ministry. For a solitary young man the church was community, for an ambitious son it was eminence, and for an intellectual and a poet the starkness of Calvinism provided ample scope for his taste for argument and his feeling for form. In the Awakening itself he found an opportunity for leadership that called on all his resources.

Edwards has become commonly known as the greatest of American Calvinists, but it was John Locke who provided him with a modern way of restating an old position. Locke's doctrine of sensations as the source of knowledge was turned by Edwards into a reformulation of the idea of grace. It became "a simple idea" in Locke's meaning, bringing home to the sinner a concrete sensation of the glory and sweetness of grace. Edwards knew grace as a man knows the sweetness of sugar by tasting it. And the vivid terrifying imagery of his sermon "Sinners in the Hands of an Angry God" was a calculated rhetorical effort to use language so as to give the soul the concrete sense of what damnation was like. Man, in his natural state of sinfulness, was hung over a fire like a loathsome spider in God's fingers. Before he was in his teens he had scientifically studied spiders and explained the rainbow according to the great Newton's laws of light. This knowledge was turned to religious ends by a man whose own sense of the glory of God drove him to see the Lord's majesty in the summer thunder, for the beauties of nature were "emanations or shadows of the excellencies of the Son of God." Like light on a mirror, "the refulgence shines upon and into the creature, and is reflected back to the luminary," so that "the beams of glory come from God, and are something of God, and are refunded back again to their original."[8]

Edwards could terrify sinners; but his point was to dramatize the issues by subverting the sinner's complacency: "The bow of God's wrath is bent, and the arrow made ready on the string, and justice bends the arrow at your heart, and strains the bow, and it is nothing but the mere pleasure of God, and that of an angry God, without any promise or obligation at all, that keeps the arrow one moment from being made drunk with your blood." His own faith, far from being morbid, was "a sweet burning" in the heart that came to him on a solitary walk in his father's pasture. It was the sense of "a sweet, and gentle, and holy majesty; and also a majestic meekness; an awful sweetness; a high, and great, and holy gentleness." He could respond adequately to the "entertaining" manifestation of God in the summer's thunderstorms only by chanting his thoughts "with a singing voice." Edwards's preaching of hell-fire was for the purpose of "awakening unconverted persons in this congregation." It contained an implicit promise: "And now you have an extraordinary opportunity, a day wherein Christ has thrown the door of mercy wide open, and stands in calling and crying with a loud voice to poor sinners; a day wherein many are flocking to him, and pressing into the kingdom of God." Damnation was a terrible danger, yet "God seems now to be hastily gathering in his elect in all parts of the land; and probably the greater part of adult persons that ever shall be saved, will be brought in now in a little time, and that it will be as it was on the great outpouring of the Spirit upon the Jews in the Apostles' days, the election will obtain, and the rest will be blinded."[9] Who could resist the sense of crisis, full of hope as well as of fear, that this preaching inspired?

Edwards was a theologian, the most systematic ever produced in New England, as well as a philosopher in touch with the modern ideas of Newton and Locke. His *Treatise Concerning Religious Affections* was properly concerned to distinguish the more bizarre and delusionary effects of the revival from its genuine work. True conversion was no spasm of the muscles, no sudden ecstacy of the spirit. It brought no new revelations, no inspired prophecies—only "a due apprehension" of those things taught in Scripture. The "holy affections" of true grace led "the believer to a lifelong earnestness and diligence" in making "this practice of religion eminently his work and business."[10] Edwards was as far from antinomianism as he was from Arminianism.

Most of the evangelists were not hysterical prophets for hysterics.

That friend of rational morality and Newtonian science, the good doctor Benjamin Franklin, against his own inclination so fell under the spell of Whitefield's preaching that he emptied his pockets into a collection for Bethesda Orphanage in Georgia and admiringly estimated that the preacher's voice, with its musical modulations, could reach from the middle of Market Street in Philadelphia almost to Front Street, a circle that conceivably could hold some thirty thousand spectators.[11] Franklin himself later had a hand in buying ground and building a house where itinerant evangelists might find a pulpit when they were rejected by the regular clergy. (Later, significantly, he would find it useful for meetings of voluntary political associations.) Franklin not only shared Edwards's interest in Locke and Newton, but his own practical humanitarianism led him to approve of Edwards's stress on the diligent good works that conversion entailed, exemplified in the preacher's own later missionary efforts on behalf of the Indians at Stockbridge. Edwards would have called Franklin an Arminian, yet despite this cleavage between them, both men argued that deeds are virtuous not through self-denial but in proportion to the degree of virtuous inclination that motivates them.[12] This position Edwards would later make central to his famous treatise attacking the Arminian doctrine that freedom of the will is essential to moral judgment: man's utter dependence upon God's sovereignty is quite consistent with the ordinary habit of finding particularly blameworthy men who are vicious by natural inclination.

Reasonable men had, however, some justifiable doubts about the revivals. James Davenport, venting his wrath against the unconverted souls of ministers, leading bands of singing saints in the streets, and urging lay preaching, also led a mob at New London, Connecticut, in the public burning of fancy clothes and unregenerate books. Furthermore, Edwards's own uncle in 1735 had cut his throat in a fit of melancholia, and others hysterically spoke of following his example. The defenders of reasonable religion had targets for their charges; and the stage was set for Charles Chauncy's *Seasonable Thoughts* with its parade of antinomian horrors and offenses to an "enlightened Mind," whose rational faculties of Understanding, Judgment, and Will were supposed to be snaffles and curbs for the bloody horse of Emotion. One aspect of the Enlightenment's new rationalism thus confronted in Edwards another devotee of the new knowledge that Locke and Newton had triumphantly established.

The Separates, radical "come-outers" from the organized churches, drew the conclusion that doubting was a sin and that laymen could be ministers. Saints had assurance of grace by inner experience and only saints should comprise a true church. Neither Edwardsian New Lights nor rationalist Old Lights would sanction the Separates, though Edwards came closer to their position when he later demanded a public, sincere, and credible profession of grace as a condition for full church membership. By 1750 too many saints resented him on other grounds to be willing to reopen the issue of commitment in Northampton, and they closed out their pastor instead.

In New England style, he was brought down by his own relatives. Edwards's cousin Solomon Williams supported the Awakening, but he opposed the great Calvinist because Scripture itself commanded, "Judge not, that ye be not judged." There was no sure way of discriminating saints, as Solomon Stoddard had concluded. Stoddard's grandson Joseph Hawley, whose father had cut his throat in the earlier revival, opposed Edwards ostensibly on Arminian grounds, but his motives were more personal than ideological. He later abjectly confessed his own slanderous and conniving role in defeating his cousin. Edwards was ground between two millstones, and he had aided his enemies six years earlier by his own highhandedness in publicizing the names of some youngsters accused of smirking over a midwife's manual, the Puritan youth's substitute for pornography. Hawley had powerful support in a popular village blacksmith and a liberal clergyman whose ordination the Hampshire County association had once opposed with Edwards's backing. The vote against Edwards by a committee of town and parish members was a foregone conclusion. Friends of Edwards hoped to organize a seceding church for him, but he insisted on a second council of advisement, and it urged him to accept a call to Stockbridge in the Berkshires.[13] Ten years after the Awakening had begun, the philosopher of the revival went into exile there as a missionary to the Indians.

The biography of Edwards has its tragic overtones of *hubris,* but the history of the Awakening itself is better understood in the category of irony. Even the New Light–Old Light nomenclature is not what it seems to be, a pointer to a generation gap. The conservative critics of the Awakening spoke for a new rationalism in theology; the radical pietists for an older emphasis on sin and God's wrath in the context of newer techniques of itinerancy and mass preaching. Edwards was thirty when he delivered his great sermon "A Divine and Supernatural

Light, Immediately Imparted to the Soul by the Spirit of God, Shown to be Both Scriptural and a Rational Doctrine," the most compact and eloquent statement of New Light Calvinism and an immediate prelude to his leadership of a revival in Northampton that would serve as a model for the later intercolonial movement. Gilbert Tennent, the leading revivalist of the Middle Colonies among the Presbyterians, was the same age as Edwards, and the fanatical Davenport and the melodious Whitefield were more than a decade younger. But the New Lights had no monopoly on young leaders. The major opponent of Edwards, Charles Chauncy, was two years younger than he was; Jonathan Mayhew, who was even more Arminian in tendency, was four years younger than the radical Davenport. Lemuel Briant and Samuel Webster, who later wrote influential critiques of New Light Calvinism, were only nineteen and twenty-two, respectively, at the height of the Awakening. Almost half of the 114 New England clergymen who officially supported the Awakening in 1743, however, had graduated from an American college more than twenty years before.[14] Both New Lights and their enemies were struggling for control of the future, and what joined them together was a common perception of the saliency of the issues that divided them.

The revivals were in part a strategy well adapted to the history of conflict over ministers' salaries, parish boundaries, and meetinghouse locations and repairs. To increase the number of adult converts was to increase the number of ratepayers that were also church members, who otherwise might be outvoted by the larger constituency of citizens with the legal responsibility to vote on these matters.[15] A public conflict offers satisfactions as well as frustrations, and every polemicist leans on his opponent to clarify and bolster his own role. The Old Lights also provided a vent for anticlerical feeling in general, enabling the New Lights to displace it on to them in particular by casting doubt on the integrity of a ministry without inner experience of Calvinist truths. When enthusiasts pushed the pietist position closer to the antinomian conclusion that inner certainty of grace and future freedom from sin were entirely possible, moderates drew back from a radicalism that might end by subverting all professional and educated ministers.

Critics of the Awakening were scandalized by the encouragement it gave to scorn for unconverted ministers, to the tumults of uninvited itinerants, to the discrediting of conventional clerical credentials and the encouragement of uneducated lay preachers, to the self-righteous schisms of enthusiasts, to the melodramatic torments or ecstacies of the twice-born souls, and to the danger of an antinomian stress on inner assurance, rather than on moral behavior, as the essence of saving faith. A convention of Massachusetts pastors,[16] condemning these errors in 1743, inspired the second convention in which ultimately 114 New England clergymen officially signed their support for the revivals, while warning against lay preaching (but not against exhorting) and usurpation of another pastor's territory in "ordinary cases," a criticism deemed much too mild by fourteen of the signers. This document of moderate support was careful to reject any taint of antinomian stress on the necessity for inner assurance of grace or for conversions only by converted clergy. By 1745, however, on Whitefield's return to New England, at least nine clergymen who had previously supported him joined fifty-four others and the faculties of Harvard and Yale in opposing his influence.[17] Edwards himself would later confess that he had been too lax in the revivals of the 1730's in failing to distinguish true grace from the merely physiological convulsions of the saints in the throes of the second birth. Most revivalists held the line with him: only habitual long-term practice of Christian virtues, not the subjective certainties of an emotional crisis, could prove the true glory of the saints, even though twice-born agonies were necessary.

This pragmatic position was reaffirmed in the twentieth century by William James, whose *The Varieties of Religious Experience* focused on the conversion experience of "the sick soul." James wrote not only out of the example of his dramatically disturbed and converted father but also from his own experience of suicidal depression. It was his point that in such crises the "subliminal self" below the level of ordinary consciousness is a double key that opens doors to inhibitions, hallucinations, convulsions, paralyses, and delusions on the one hand, and to spiritual conversion, saintly obsessions, and "a wider world" of spiritual meaning on the other.[18] Religion, in this view, was deeply engaged with the dynamics of the unconscious that Freud was concurrently analyzing in a systematic theory and therapy.

Certainly there was evidence in the revivals of responses that resemble the hysteria that Freud located on the clinical map. Jonathan Edwards, for example, celebrated the piety of Abigail Hutchinson, a young woman "infirm of body" who was inspired (he tells us) by "a spirit of envy" toward the conversion of another young woman "to do her utmost to obtain the same blessing." Known for her dutifulness as a daughter, Abigail became agonized with doubts precisely on this point. Edwards also reports her to be full of an overwhelming "flow of affection to those whom she thought godly" and also of a morbid longing to die, expressed in pleasure at the idea of worms feeding on her body. One is not surprised to learn that she suffered terribly from an inability to swallow food and eventually died of malnutrition. This pitiful story vividly enough illustrates James's point that "morbid-mindedness" in the "neurotic temperament" may furnish "the chief condition of the requisite receptivity" to "inspiration from a higher realm." But such morbidity was not widespread enough, in all the colonies, to provide the historical key to the Awakening, even if James Davenport did excuse his errors on the grounds of suffering from fever and "the cankry Humor" that a court judged to be "insanity."[19]

James provides a primary historical clue ignored by historians when he notes that "conversion is in its essence a normal adolescent phenomenon, incidental to the passage from the child's small universe to the wider intellectual and spiritual life of maturity." James also notes that commonplace conversions are "kept true to a pre-appointed type by instruction, appeal and example. The particular form which they affect is the result of suggestion and imitation." The late teens and early twenties, as Erik H. Erikson has said in commenting on the age of the converts discussed in James's *The Varieties of Religious Experience,* is a time "painfully aware of the need for decisions, most driven to choose new devotions and to discard old ones, and most susceptible to the propaganda of ideological systems which promise a new world-perspective at the price of total and cruel repudiation of an old one."[20] It is in keeping with this observation that such later influential New Light preachers as Isaac Backus, David Brainerd, Aaron Burr, Samuel Langdon, Joseph Bellamy, Samuel Davies, John Cleaveland, Jacob Green, and Samuel Hopkins should all have been between seventeen and twenty-five at the peak of the Awakening, 1741.* They were essentially products of the movement itself. But, of course, emphasis on the identity-crisis stage does not explain why any particular ideology is adopted rather than another.

Yet the gospel of the twice-born sick soul, as James characterized it, must have a particular appeal to young people because it accentuates and interprets the crises of growth; and it has not been sufficiently

* The average age of New Side Presbyterian active revival ministers in 1740 was 25.38 compared to 58.77 for their Old Side enemies. See William H. Kenney, *George Whitefield and Colonial Revivalism: the Social Sources of Charismatic Authority, 1737–1770* (diss., University of Pennsylvania, 1966), pp. 137–41.

noticed in the historical literature that documents produced by the revivals themselves point to the importance of young converts. The revivalists themselves were candid about the fact that "Youth is ordinarily the time of the more and more powerful stirrings and strivings of the Holy Spirit," and Jonathan Dickinson of New Jersey addressed himself to young people in 1739 because, he said, "I have more hope of them than of others, for it has been a constant Observation that the most that are ever brought to a Saving Interest in Christ, are converted in their youth." Edwards's own revival efforts were first directed in 1734 at the young people whom he organized into "private companies" for the practice of "social religion" after the usual evening lectures. This process was greatly facilitated by the conversion of a young woman, known to be "one of the greatest company-keepers in the whole town," whom many thereafter went to see.[21] The most commonly repeated theme in the various contemporary accounts of the origins of revivals is the lament by ministers that the young people in town are much engaged in "frolicking," "tavern-going," "company-keeping," "night-walking," and other signs of the decay of "family government." Revivalists were worried about the loose living of the younger generation, a perennial American and evangelical theme.

They were also justifiably worried about the failures of the clergy in America, who were often uninspired and uninspiring examples. But beyond these realities the Awakening also drew on a desire for spiritual status. Edwards candidly spoke in 1736 of the power of emulation in the conversion process: "There is no one thing that I know of which God has made such a means of promoting his work amongst us, as the news of others' conversion." Just as Abigail Hutchinson envied the distinction of a celebrated converted young woman and thought her eminence unmerited, so whole towns could be stimulated by the news of mass conversions elsewhere into a competitive rivalry in witnessing to the true faith. Edwards again made the point clearly:

As what other towns heard of and found in this, was a great means of awakening them; so our hearing of such a swift and extraordinary propagation, and extent of this work, did doubtless for a time serve to uphold the work amongst us. The continual news kept alive the talk of religion, and did greatly quicken and rejoice the hearts of God's people, and much awakened those who looked on themselves as still left behind, and made them the more earnest that they also might share in the great blessings that others had obtained.

So were some 300 saved in six months, according to Edwards, and including males in about equal proportion with females, unlike the case in Stoddard's day. The adult population of his town, according to Edwards, was nearly equivalent (in 1736) to the number of church communicants (620, or 200 families) and by his own breakdown of the converted into age categories the revival of 1735 swept up 33 under fifteen years of age and 50 over forty. Thus the majority of the new saints must have been in the bracket from fifteen to forty years of age. He was impressed with the conversion of the old and the children because usually in "stirrings of this nature, the bulk of the young people have been greatly affected."[22]

These figures are helpful in acquiring some quantitative view of one revival in one town, but what of the later more influential and extensive revival of the 1740's, which Edwards himself distinguished from its forerunners? A central document for this event is the *Christian History*, a journal published to celebrate the Awakening in a series of ministerial reports from the colonies, Scotland, and Wales. Whenever ministers speak in this collection of the sociology of their converts, not only in New England but in parts of Pennsylvania and New Jersey as well, they point out that it is "young people" who are "especially" or "chiefly" affected by the revival.[23] Edwards, in his letter to the *Christian History*, was once again helpful about sociology in Northampton. The work of the revival, he asserted, was "almost wholly upon a new Generation; those that were not come to Years of Discretion in that wonderful Season nine years ago, *Children,* or those that were *then Children:* Others that had enjoyed that former glorious Opportunity without any Appearance of favoring Benefit, seem'd now to be almost wholly pass'd over and let alone." He had himself precipitated matters in Northampton by calling together in 1741 a group of people between the ages of fifteen and twenty-six, years that in modern psychological terms largely overlap with the stage that Erikson has identified as the "identity crisis."* In March, 1741, Edwards led a ceremony of public renewal of covenant with all those Christians above fourteen, pledging them to "Honesty, Justice, and Uprightness" in dealing with their neighbors. Collectively they promised to pay their debts, avoid "backbiting," revere the common good, and repress those "Freedoms and Familiarities in Company" which tended to "stir up

* See Appendix.

or gratify a Lust of Lasciviousness." A glimpse of the nonpolitical tenor of the revival is evidenced by Edwards's view that the main influence of the revival on public affairs was to diminish party division in the town over the problem of the "Common Lands," an issue for fifteen years "above any other particular thing." By 1743, however, he lamented, youth had already begun to fall away from the revival spirit, even though it had been "purer" than that of 1735.[24] The fervor of Christian reform was a flickering flame in the rising generation.

Revival preachers were candidly aware that thunderstorms and earthquakes often worked to frighten people into a sudden respect for God's majesty, but they did not put their trust in these circumstantial conversions. They were impressed instead with the effect of their own preaching. It was not merely the terror that could be produced by dramatizing the fallen creature's damnation, as in Edwards's "Sinners in the Hands of an Angry God"; more importantly it was, in *Christian History* editor Thomas Prince's phrase, "this *searching* Preaching that was both the suitable and principal *means* of their Conviction." A preacher such as Gilbert Tennent searched out his hearers' hearts by "laying open their many vain and secret Shifts and Refuges, counterfeit Resemblances of Grace, *delusive* and *damning* Hopes, their utter Impotence, and impending Danger of Destruction: whereby they found all their Hopes and refuges of Lies to fail them, and themselves exposed to eternal Ruin, unable to help themselves, and in a lost Condition." Thus did preachers exhibit the Spirit's power in Boston, until it withdrew its awakening influence by November, 1742, in "a gradual and awful Manner."[25] Divinity worked through the preacher's subtlety in exposing the creature's defenses.

In modern terms it is necessary to conclude from such evidence that the dynamics of the revival were connected with a public rhetoric able to exploit subconscious feelings of guilt and dependency that were weakly defended against by a hedonistic indifference in the young, or that were easily reactivated in older persons who had externally committed themselves to the evangelical framework but had grown conventional in their piety. These dynamics cannot be understood except in terms of a society in which the pressure of religious norms and authority was internalized, even though ordinary behavior often did not match the accepted injunctions. Twice-born Calvinist preaching tapped veins of irrational self-hate and repudiation of others that often make young people an intense mixture of conservative and radical impulses. Even in 1741, adults could be shamed by the sudden idealism of the young, when traditional ideals had lost their luminous application to ordinary life and newer standards had yet to be convincingly discovered. Yet the aim of the revivals was conservative. The preachers characteristically scolded the worldly ways of the young and emphasized the need for restoration of "family government." The revival transcended the family, however, in a public context of high excitement in which the young person's soul was considered to be of momentous value, and it was linked in hope to a collective reformation identified with the emerging meaning of history in a coming millennium on earth that was supposed to be inaugurated by the revival itself.

Resistance, as psychoanalysts call it in reference to their patients, was noticed by Peter Thatcher, minister at Middleborough in Massachusetts, whose church won some 174 new communicants, leaving his flock unusually weighted with males: "Scores, *this Day,* told me of their Hatred of me above any one." He immediately added that it was very affecting "to hear the *young People* crying and wringing their Hands, and bewailing their Frolicking and Dancing, their deriding public Reproofs thereof."[26] The guilt of this hostility against the minister could be eased by confession while the aggression itself could be displaced on to Old Light critics of the process.

The "other-directed" component of this "inner-directed" Calvinism, to borrow David Riesman's familiar terms, was implicit in the mass setting. Edwards noted that in 1741 the acts of conversion were more vividly "visible" than before, "more frequently in the Presence of others, at religious Meetings, where the Appearances of what was wrought on the Heart fell under publick Observation." These public circumstances also brought to bear the power of shame, arising from the gap between one's ego ideals and one's ego, particularly on those already externally dedicated to Christian life, while for the unrecruited and erring young, large meetings were an easier place for confessing guilt than the family pew. Thatcher noted that in his church the revival first affected church members: "Numbers brought to *pray* in their *Families,* to instruct and *catechize* their Children." Thatcher himself had earlier modestly hoped only for the conversion of his own children: "If God gives our Children Covenant-Grace, it's our best Portion." By December, however, he was delighted to discover that he had a general revival going.[27]

The Awakening shattered the standing order of churches in schisms and withdrawals, but it also reinstituted community control and conformity—the repressive side of the story that has been largely omitted from accounts bent on drawing a straight line from the Awakening to the American Revolution. No doubt there were sublimated erotic and hedonistic feelings in the street singing led by James Davenport or in the ecstatic communal joy known to the gracious saints. But it was not freedom from law or society so much as conformity to the censorious pressure of the brethren that followed conversion: "Every church member considered himself his brother's keeper. The most trivial derelictions from duty were noted and reported, and espionage and talebearing encouraged as if they were cardinal virtues. . . . Every man was at the mercy of the 'inward actings' of his neighbor's soul."[28]

The precariously seated clergy made an ally out of youth by evoking, interpreting, and legitimating its inner guilt, its public shame, and its ardent hopes for historical meaning and direction. Christian charity and communal commitment in joyous grace to the expectation of millennial progress, before the Second Coming, guided many lives, but in the mass conditions of conversion the saints must inevitably have been vulnerable to an inner sense of possible fraudulence. In any event the growth in the number of churches in the next decade did not keep up with the growth of the population, except in areas where immigration from Germany and Ireland enlarged the rolls of certain sects.[29]

Begun as a way of restoring clerical prestige and renewing the restraints of the Protestant ethic on the rising generation within the tradition of family government, the Awakening peaked within three years and lost its hold on even Edwards's parish. By 1744 Edwards would find that the sanctions of family government had to be invoked again to quell the restlessness of young people under Puritan restraints. In his "Farewell Sermon," six years later, he reminded his parishioners that he "ever had a peculiar concern for the souls of young people," and he told them that he was sure that his leadership in the campaign of 1744 "for the suppressing of vice among our young people" was what gave so great an offense and made him "obnoxious" to his flock. His last words of advice to his estranged congregation insisted on "family order" as the most important temporal "means of grace" without which all else failed.[30] So did the wheel turn full circle for the greatest leader of the Awakening as he ended his pastorate with the same concerns that had animated the inception of the revivals. Paradoxically, the Awakening had fostered the Separates with their confidence in inner assurance of grace and lay preaching, radical beliefs that Edwards did not share, but it also had produced an influx of saints who would not stand by 1750 for Edwards's demand for a more sincere and credible profession of grace and its active obligations as a condition for full membership. The ferment of the Awakening brewed an indiscriminate laxness about doctrine and discipline as well as a renewed intensity of conviction and closer bonds of community in a covenanted faith.

The Awakening was enmeshed in a net of historical ambiguities. By stressing the necessity for a religion of the heart that was truly experienced and not merely intellectually understood or morally practiced, the revivalists had made an issue out of sincerity that inevitably fostered schisms, contention, and eventual doubts about the authenticity of their own mass influxes to the churches. Devoted to social peace, family government, and stricter moral control over the young, they found themselves forced to challenge public laws that were passed to restrict their own movement. Skeptical of the learned institutions for their harboring of Arminian tendencies and their emphasis on institutional credentials, they were compelled to build their own colleges to produce pietistically oriented ministers. Tending to exalt individual congregations as gathered brethren of true believers, they were led by the technique of itinerancy and by fear of their enemies to organize in denominational associations to foster the influence of their own pietist faith. The Awakening was caught in an irony of history that turned all their original intentions to the service of purposes they had not originally contemplated and only temporarily fulfilled what they had intended.

The immediate effect of the revivals, according to Edwards, was to temper the social conflicts that had previously divided Northampton over the issue of common lands. In this sense the revivalist impulse was profoundly nonpolitical. Yet in more long-range terms it contributed to social conflict and change because of the religious schisms and secessions that it generated. These diversities made the system of legal disestablishment less and less acceptable to newly awakened and highly sensitive consciences. At the same time, New Lights learned to recognize each other across old colonial boundaries, and to this extent congregations moved toward a more collective and organized denominational status that would eventually even make Baptists respectable.[31] When the Presbyterian synods of New York and Philadelphia rejoined in 1758 after the split of 1741, the New Lights enjoyed a decisive majority role. The most influential offshoot of the left-wing Separates movement was the emergence from it of the Baptist leader Isaac Backus, whose sect was deeply and energetically committed to principles of separation between church and state that would put on the defensive the system of legal establishment both in Virginia and in New England. In the aftermath of the Awakening, congregations would be generally enhanced in their powers and many New Lights would support the pleas of many Separates for relief from penalties for nonattendance at the legally supported churches. Increasingly by the middle 1760's, as Richard L. Bushman has elegantly put it, the establishment was becoming "neither an agency of social control nor a symbol of community coherence, but only the religion of the majority."[32] The Awakening had fostered a concern for purity of soul in a popular context that minimized or even discredited the importance of traditional institutional credentials for the clergy, thus favoring laymen's power. Its fissuring effect on the churches had sponsored closer bonds of mutual surveillance among the saints while also weakening their ties to the conventional form of legal support for Christianity. In this respect it promoted the development of what would be recognized in the next century as a voluntary system of Protestant pluralism and legal disestablishment.

Yet the fierce piety of New Light Calvinism was also hostile to secularization of life, and New Lights and Baptists alike would be strong partisans of traditional state enforcement of Puritanical blue laws against the pleasures of a more hedonistic life. The Awakening fostered religious freedom as a civic matter only indirectly and always within Protestant limits that did not include complete separation or secularization. The Awakening witnessed to family order as well as to the religion of the heart, to conformity of soul in Calvinist obedience, as well as to challenges to the standing order. It reproduced, in new form, the ambiguities about freedom and order that had always been implicit in Calvinist religion. With an earnest righteousness and a touchy defensiveness, nurtured by their recent emotional victories over their own guilty self-division, the twice-born, like so many reformers who only want renewal, were the vigorous agents of change. In the resulting more fluid and energetic religious situation, the civil order would increasingly be forced to consider extensive toleration of dissidence as the only way to preserve civil peace.

The Dissenters in England, struggling against Anglican exclusions, were a powerful impetus in pushing American dissent toward greater toleration. When the Connecticut General Assembly passed coercive measures to control the New Lights by restricting ordination to graduates of approved schools, punishing itinerants, and depriving New

Lights of their civil offices, English Dissenters lectured the governor of Connecticut, pointing out that magistrates ought only to have the power to keep the peace. Penalties against enthusiasts, however troublesome they were, would damage the nonconformist cause in England. There even New Lights could seem more rigid than Dissenters should be. The Virginian revivalist Samuel Davies, in London with Gilbert Tennent to collect funds for the College of New Jersey, discovered that English Presbyterians "seemed to think that we were such rigid Calvinists that we would not admit an Arminian into communion." In New York the urbane Presbyterian William Livingston, his polemical wits sharpened on the *Independent Whig,* the journal of English Dissent, would fight for a public college free of royal charter or divinity school. Where Presbyterians, Episcopalians, Anabaptists, Lutherans, Quakers, and Moravians were all zealous for their own tenets, to give any religion a legal preference would only create "a Nursery of Animosity, Dissention, and Disorder." His cogent essays on toleration and separation, broadcast in the *Independent Reflector,* would provide models for debating teams at the College of New Jersey, and James Madison later fondly remembered their "energy and eloquence."[33]

As English Dissenters learned to embrace Locke's defense of religious toleration, so also in America pietists learned the same lesson. Isaac Backus, a product of Puritan New England and the Calvinist Great Awakening, led the way. The death of his father in 1740 plunged his mother into a severe depression from which she was lifted by the enthusiasm of the revivalist fervor of the Awakening. At the age of seventeen the farm boy Backus heard such fiery preachers of the second birth as James Davenport. Soon both mother and son joined with other Separates, who believed in testing for signs of authentic conversion, in lay ordination of preachers by majority vote, and in freedom from regulation by the county ministerial associations. Separates were split about the vexed issue of infant baptism, and Backus was still troubled about it when he married a Baptist. For Baptists the answer was clear: adult baptism and the public testimony of saints were logically related. This voluntaristic theory, earlier held by Evangelical Anabaptists on the extreme left wing of the Reformation, was far from the corporatism of the Puritans, who scorned such "enthusiasm" as subversive perfectionism. Backus struggled to shuck off the remnants of the conservative tradition that had bred him. By 1756, when he was made the pastor of a Baptist church, he had learned to draw for himself and others a sharp contrast between the Old Testament dispensation, with its national church and gospel of works, and the New Testament, with its priesthood of visible saints and gospel of grace.

The pilgrimage of Backus was representative of the struggle that many converts were going through to form a new identity more appropriate to the individualism of American society as it grew out of its Puritan past, dominated by the more organic traditions of the Old World. The internal revolution that the saints had made in England, which brought them to a new toleration and a more voluntaristic position, did not happen in America, where the establishment was weakened by the Awakening and the Revolution was directed against imperial control. When he had wandered in the ecclesiastical wilderness of the Separates, Backus and his followers had suffered the imposition of taxes for religious reasons. Both his mother and his brother had been imprisoned for nonpayment. It was not hard for them to see the connection between this oppression and the "taxation without representation" that the British imposed on the colonies. Backus's vigorous circuit riding and publicizing gave a Calvinist style to the growing Baptist movement, and his whole life was vivid proof that the pietistic Calvinist temper could be deeply devoted to religious liberty. Like the persecuted Evangelical Anabaptists of the Reformation, the Baptists formed a voluntary fellowship of disciples of Christ, but unlike their European forerunners they did not withdraw from the world by refusing to hold office, bear arms, or take political oaths. In America, without a powerful establishment to crush them, they could envisage a much more active role for themselves in a world which was not so hopelessly mired in sin and might even be on the threshold of an imminent millennium. "Nor is it all improbable," announced the New England Baptist Association in 1784, "that America is reserved in the mind of Jehovah to be the grand theater on which the divine Redeemer will accomplish glorious things. . . . If we observe the signs of the times, we shall find reason to think he is on his way."[34]

The Revolution made that belief plausible, but the millennial faith helped make the Revolution popular. The line between the Awakening and the Revolution, however, is not a straight one. Revivalism was divisive, and the pietistic conception of Christianity did not always entail republicanism in politics or resistance to British policy. John Wesley and many of his early Methodist missionaries to America were devout Tories, and a leading opponent of the Revival, Charles Chauncy, would find in theological rationalism a firm basis for devotion to the republican revolutionary cause. The search for connections points toward a more devious process.

The Awakening fissioned belief, and the fissioning favored toleration for lack of a firm consensus on the legitimacy of ecclesiastical authority or the truth of dogma. By this process religiously minded men were moved toward the acceptance of private judgment in religion that English Dissenters, as well as more skeptical and secular men, had embraced on other grounds. The way was thus prepared for a later alliance between Christian believers and American *philosophes* that would transcend the debate during the Awakening between Calvinist pietists and the advocates of "reasonable religion."[35] It was not the inspiration nor the ideology of the Awakening that brought about a historic conjuncture of Christianity and republicanism. It was instead an unintended consequence that many of those who in 1740 spoke of the virtues of family government would in 1776 speak of the vices of British government. But the Awakening had done its ironic part in weakening the legitimacy of an established religious order. By emphasizing family order over the young, rather than ecclesiastical order over the whole society, it was in league with a future that would make all religious groups in America voluntary organizations that were neither withdrawn sects nor controlling churches but denominations. Its Puritanism also conspired with the recurring efforts of later pietists to use the state to impose an evangelical ethic on the larger society. Herald of separation, it was also herald of Puritanical moral reform.

IV

Calvinist Whigs and the Spirit of '76

The American Revolution was in large part the crystallization of a Whig liberalism which men like Franklin, Adams, Jefferson, and Paine spoke for in an idiom that has become classical. Their contributions to the stock of democratic-republican ideas is proof of how much modern liberty owes to the rationalism of the Enlightenment. Deistical or Unitarian rather than Calvinist in their orientation, they had learned to have a justified suspicion of institutional religion as a political force. The Declaration of Independence and the Articles of Confederation, through which the rebels formed their first intercolonial government, make conventional references to "the Supreme Judge of the World," reliance on "Divine Providence," and respect for the "Great Governor of the World." But these documents in no way reflect any distinctive Christian gospel. Only one clergyman, John Witherspoon of New Jersey, signed the Declaration, and none of the famous names of the Revolution were noted for their active work in any religious denomination. The political leaders of this generation of founders were learned in the classics and the secular political philosophy of John Locke, James Harrington, the English Whigs, and Montesquieu, rather than in Luther, Calvin, or Jonathan Edwards. If Tories were Anglican, so, at least nominally, were most of the signers of the Declaration. In the list of grievances that Jefferson drew up in the Declaration of the colonial cause, none refer primarily to religious issues. If the colonials had been dependent for their revolutionary leadership on any single religious group or tradition, there would have been no Revolution.

Yet these caveats do not contradict the point that a historical appreciation of religion in America is necessary in order to understand what happened in '76. Once again the connection is implied in Tocqueville's acute observations, though he himself did not spell out the links with respect to the Revolution. Tocqueville was extraordinarily impressed by the lack of revolutionary zeal in America by comparison with Europe. He attributed it to the prevalence of commercial life, which bred caution and compromise, as well as to the widespread holding of private property, which made most men anxious about sweeping changes that might disturb their possessions. These causes were reinforced by "the singular stability" in America of "general principles in religion, philosophy, morality, and even politics." Indeed, the danger existed that modern men might in the future arrive at such a state of equality, with public opinion pressing "with enormous weight upon the minds of each individual," that they would come "to regard every new theory as a peril, every innovation as an irksome toil, every social improvement as a stepping-stone to revolution, and so refuse to move altogether for fear of being moved too far." He dreaded such a development because it would lead men "to glide along the easy current of life rather than to make, when it is necessary, a strong and sudden effort to a higher purpose."[1]

In the Revolution, however, the Americans made just such a strong and sudden effort to achieve new public aims. Tocqueville noted that "intelligence in New England and wealth in the country to the south of the Hudson long exercised a sort of aristocratic influence, which tended to keep the exercise of social power in the hands of a few." Despite this influence, the Revolution put the United States on a democratic path, for the aristocracy in America "sympathized with the body of the people, whose passions and interests it easily embraced; but it was too weak and too shortlived to excite either love or hatred."[2] Indeed, it produced "the best leaders of the American Revolution." This analysis can be strengthened by reference to what he called "a democratic and republican religion." As Tocqueville implied, religion itself was no barrier to revolution—indeed, it accelerated it.

The contrast with France in this case is particularly evident. Wherever in America the churches did not sympathize with the Revolution, they were too weak in their social control to impede the flow of events. Religious diversity permeated the Middle Colonies, and the undersupplied Anglican Church was never able to cope successfully in the Southern colonies with the difficulties of establishing control over scattered settlements in a large area. Where the Puritan establishment was still influential, the clergy itself became ardent patriots. An outspoken Anglican loyalist of Trinity Church, New York, for example, complained with disgust that he did not know of a single Presbyterian minister "who did not, by preaching and every effort in their power, promote all the efforts of the congress, however extravagant."[3] By 1773 the Catholic leader in Maryland, Charles Carroll of Carrollton, was protesting against the actions of the royal governor and helping to swing Maryland in favor of the patriot party. American loyalists had no bastion of church power to fortify their conservatism. It was therefore unnecessary for political leaders to preach the Revolution, in French style, as a surrogate secular religion.

The clergy itself preached the Revolution as an extension of their religious commitments. The conventional elements of the revival survived unchanged, however, even in the middle of the Revolution. A pietist in New Hampshire, for example, celebrated in 1799 the death-bed gracious joy of a reformed twenty-three-year-old in order to warn the young people of Epping against "Night-walking, gaming, frolicking and wantonness."[4] Edwards would have applauded, but by then for many Americans the Revolution itself was a reformation; and for more than a decade Calvinist preachers had been spelling out the political meaning of Christian life in sermons that moved well beyond the Awakening's stereotyped puritanical obsession with the worldly pleasures of the young. Revivalists were always announcing the failure of their efforts on the very heels of celebrating their successes, and they applied their anxious sense of the waxing and waning of the Spirit to the struggle for independence from imperial control.

The Calvinist clergy, whether pietist or liberal, easily assimilated republican talk of rights, charters, and contracts because they had always been engaged in a theology that emphasized the role of consent in all of man's important relations. Locke himself, for that matter, was the son of a Puritan captain, the protégé of a Puritan colonel, the pupil of an Independent tutor at college, an adviser to one of Cromwell's collaborators, and an exile temporarily among French and Dutch Calvinists.[5] For the liberal Calvinists in America the Lockean emphasis on confidence in man's estate in the state of nature was congenial to their own Arminian tendencies, which the Great Awakening had dramatized. For the evangelical Calvinists, on the other hand, the Awakening had tutored them in the experience of challenging the established order when it sought to suppress the "enthusiasm" of the revivalist party, and they were better prepared than their opponents for the willingness actively to resist repressive laws. Calvinists had traditionally played an important part in public affairs by preaching at election times and on ceremonial fast days and thanksgiving days, when they related their religious ethos to the great events of the time. The nonclerical republicans themselves would find in the clergy valuable sources of support and communication. The Congregationalist Dr. Samuel Cooper, a friend of Franklin and Sam Adams, spoke at meetings of the Sons of Liberty and was chaplain to the General Court in Massachusetts during the Revolutionary years. Cooper, Adams, and John Hancock were at the home of another patriot minister, Jonas Clark of Lexington, the night before the battle at Concord by the rude bridge that arched the flood, where the shot was fired that was heard round the world. English dissenting Whigs were in touch with the liberal Calvinist Jonathan Mayhew; and the pietist Calvinist Nathaniel Niles, who left the ministry after the Revolution, served in two New England legislatures, sat on the bench as a Vermont Supreme Court judge, and was a Jeffersonian Republican Congressman in the 1790's.

The career of John Witherspoon was particularly vivid in illustrating the indirect links that can be found between evangelicals like Gilbert Tennent and Samuel Davies on the one hand and republicans like Benjamin Rush and James Madison on the other. New Light Presbyterian trustees at the College of New Jersey, impressed by the report of Tennent and Davies, called Witherspoon from Scotland as president. In Scotland he had been identified with the minority party in the General Assembly, challenging the system that enabled patrons to force a minister on a parish against the wishes of the congregation. Like Jonathan Edwards, he had publicly condemned some profane antics of young people, naming names to add salt to the wound, and he had been sued for defamation of character, an episode that must have convinced New Lights that he was a true son of the Great Awakening.[6] He had been licensed to preach, in fact, during the very year that the *Christian History* first appeared in New England to celebrate the Awakening.

Witherspoon's decision to accept the call to America was shaped by the persuasive powers of Benjamin Rush, a Philadelphia physician who had gone to school under the evangelicals Samuel Finley and Samuel Davies. As a young man Rush had experienced the conversion that made him "seek the favor of God in his Son." In Edinburgh as a student, he had heard Witherspoon preach and had met spokesmen for the Scottish Enlightenment who woke him to republicanism. Back in Philadelphia, Rush would later lodge John and Sam Adams, as well as inspire and assist Tom Paine in publishing *Common Sense*. The humanitarian doctor and the Presbyterian college president were political allies, marking the overlapping of evangelical and rationalist traditions in a common cause. Witherspoon moderated the division between New Lights and Old, tutored James Madison, signed the Declaration of Independence, served in the Continental Congress, and had the honor of being burned in effigy by the British encamped on Staten Island. He was, said John Adams, "as high a son of liberty as any man in America."[7]

The Tories agreed in highlighting the influence of what they called "the black Regiment" of pastors in fomenting resistance to British policy. Thomas Hutchinson, acting royal governor of Massachusetts, complained in 1770 of the militancy of the clergy, noting that "our pulpits are filled with such dark covered expressions and the people are led to think they may lawfully resist the King's troops as any foreign enemy." The clergy not only served in the army as chaplains, soldiers, or officers, but in New England alone at least sixty-seven of them were active in town committees or provincial or national political congresses and conventions.[8] The clergy kept their popular influence by keeping pace with public events.

At the same time they proved Tocqueville's point about American sobriety by giving to the defense of American liberties a persistent stress on respect for legitimate authority and on the identification of the highest freedom with "whatever is fit, reasonable or good" in relation to the public interest.[9] Anarchy, licentiousness, avarice, and prodigality were the dreaded devils of hell for all American pastors, and they believed in government as much as they hated tyranny. No rebels have been more saturated with respect for traditional morality and civic order, yet without calling for dictatorship or terror; and no enthusiasts for the millennial prospects of the revolutionary future can ever have been as troubled as the Americans were by the special guilts of those who considered themselves a chosen people, addicted to declaring occasions for public fasts and national humiliation. Calvinism, originally elitist and authoritarian, offered themes of constitutional limitations and collective redemption that could be redefined in a post-Puritan world of greater toleration and wider popular participation in government so as to lend the energy of moral passion to the republican cause.

This Puritanical counterpoint in the Revolutionary argument resonated with the outlook of radical Whigs, each reinforcing the other.

When Calvinist traditional jeremiads insisted that the troubles with Great Britain were divine punishment for American moral declension through absorption in pride and prodigality, they provided the people with a Puritanized version of Whig political science, which was also obsessed in secular terms with the threat of luxury to simple republican public virtue. The clergy and the Whigs both preached the Revolution in the belief that patriotism and martial vigor would cleanse the American soul of its impurities and make it capable of supporting a true republic. English Whigs like John Trenchard and Thomas Gordon, writing in the *Independent Whig* and *Cato's Letters,* had already popularized for colonial readers a brisk defense of the Glorious Revolution of 1688 and the house of Hanover against Toryism and High Churchmen. Their crisp, aggressive propaganda for republican rationalism and the right of private judgment in religion and politics identified the common good with the policy of "Protestant free Countries" that knew how to "maintain the People in Liberty, Plenty, Ease, and Security." The highest virtue for them was "Publick Spirit" as an "impartial Benevolence to all Mankind," and they praised religion in so far as it made "universal Love and Benevolence to the whole Creation" a motive for "kind, humane, and affectionate Actions" toward God's creatures.[10] This Protestant republicanism would produce profound echoes in American clergymen who were engaged in formulating a republican Protestantism. Different idioms could meet in the realm of action, puritanizing republicanism and republicanizing Puritanism. A close look at the clerical threads in this fabric of the emerging American republic verifies Tocqueville's sensitivity to the importance of republican religion in the formative years of the nation's struggle to be born.

Searchers for historical continuity have traditionally argued that Jonathan Mayhew, minister of the West Church in Boston, anticipated the later role of the clergy when he chose the centenary of the execution of Charles I in 1649 to affirm the general right of rebellion against tyrants, an obligation consistent with veneration for the traditional jealousy of Englishmen for their constitutional rights. An early rationalist of Unitarian inclination, Mayhew believed that God himself was limited by "the everlasting tables of right reason," and that the people were themselves proper judges of when their princes had overstepped their bounds. But Mayhew was venting a partisan spleen at Anglicans who ritually mourned the death of Charles I, and he was careful to urge upon his audience a pious and dutiful loyalty to the present prince. A recent historian has argued instead that the New Light Joseph Bellamy did "all but proclaim to the people of God the necessity of a civil war," and he finds "the consequences of Bellamy's rhetoric" in eastern Connecticut's opposition to the Stamp Act.[11] But once again the desire to find results in intentions has tortured the documents to produce anticipatory cries.

When Edwards's disciple Bellamy delivered the Connecticut election sermon in 1762 before the General Assembly, he could have had no inkling of the role that New Light Calvinists would play during the Revolution. Applying the pietist ethic of love, he sketched an ideal state, functioning as "one united happy family," which would one day be actualized in the millennium. He also embellished the same ambivalent moral that Puritan jeremiads had long made traditional: although full of satisfaction with the civil and religious arrangements of Connecticut and with "all the good things of this world" its people enjoyed, he was equally sure that sin had entered into the colony, and the hearts of the people were "the source of all our Calamities, Civil, Ecclesiastical and Domestic." To the rulers he therefore urged a stringent campaign to punish and suppress "drunkenness, idleness, and all kinds of debauchery," and in the war on sin he urged that "every Man in the Colony join to stone it with stones, till it is dead." Nothing in his address would have enabled anyone to imagine that in three years the stones would be real ones, thrown by mobs at supporters of the Stamp Act. For Bellamy righteousness *was* happiness, and it was the colony's "present interest to become strictly religious" because it was "the readiest and directest way to become a happy People." All that was different from the Awakening in this effusion was Bellamy's more liberal emphasis on God's "perfect moral Rectitude" as the ground of human esteem and honor for the Deity, whom otherwise we could encounter only to "fear and tremble before him.[12]

Two years after Bellamy's sermon and more than a month after the passage of the imperial Sugar Act, an Old Light preacher in his election sermon to Connecticut's General Assembly went over the same themes in the somewhat different idiom of liberal Calvinism. Also pleading for "disinterested love to our brethren" as the key to the gospel, Noah Welles sought explicitly to link this ethic to patriotism and the willingness "to die for the good of the community." As men grew older, they accumulated "reciprocal dependencies and connexions, and consequently the social obligations thence resulting," so that even self-interest would lead men to patriotism because their own welfare would be "involved in it, and inseparably connected with it." Tocqueville would have been delighted to find in this rationale his own insight that Americans preached the doctrine of "self-interest properly understood" so as to persuade men to care for the general welfare on the ground that it would be of advantage to them. Zeal for "the public happiness" should not be diluted by an "indolent and luke-warm disposition"; on the other hand, Welles warned that "there are hypocrites and impostors, wild enthusiasts and frantic zealots in patriotism and politics, as well as in religion." Welles might have cocked an eye at Bellamy in this reference that recalls the divisions of the Awakening; and whereas Bellamy had idealized the image of the state as a happy, well-ordered family, joined by righteous love, Welles affirmed that "Liberty is the glory of a community, the most firm and unshaken basis of public happiness."[13]

No more than Bellamy, however, did Welles find any fault with the current civic and religious privileges enjoyed in Connecticut. Both preachers defended obligatory financial support on a parish basis for ministers, and both condemned "the litigious disposition" of their people. Like Bellamy, Welles also urged suppression of "immorality, profaneness, intemperance, uncleanness, sabbath-breaking, neglect of public worship, and every other vice." Both of them conventionally condemned tyranny *and* the spirit of discontent. Welles was sure that the colony still tasted "the dear, the delightful sweets of liberty," even though in two weeks a Boston town meeting would denounce taxation without representation and propose united colonial action for the first time in the developing quarrel with the mother country.[14] There was in neither sermon any sound of the firebell in the night, warning of the coming civil conflict over British policy. What both sermons did contain, however, that had bearing on the future was a common stress on the corporate aspects and social relevance of their faith, a theme that would soon have a new political meaning.

It was the Stamp Act that woke the clergy from their parochial slumbers. Three weeks before the Virginia House of Burgesses on May 30, 1765, replied to the imperial measure by passing a resolution affirming that taxation without representation was an affront to "the distinguishing Characteristick of *British* Freedom," the Connecticut colony's election-sermon preacher was still oblivious to the new era.[15] He identified resistance to authority with damnation and assumed that "the quiet enjoyment of life, liberty or property" depended mainly on requiring everybody to pay taxes for support of the clergy and on Christianizing the Indians as a measure of colonial defense against attack from savages.[16] Seven months after this burst of irrelevant conservatism from the establishment, Stephen Johnson, a New Light preacher who had been in his late adolescence during the Awakening, broke out of the pietists' ritualized obsession with "debauchery" as the emblem of sin in a Fast Day sermon in Connecticut that added some powerful new themes to the traditional rhetoric. Johnson made the usual plea for "repentance and reformation, frugality and industry," to redeem a sinful people's lapses, and he displayed pious respect for the Glorious Revolution of 1688 and the illustrious house of Hanover. But he revived the traditional Puritan analogy between America and Israel as "the covenant people of God" to remind his audience that the Biblical people had been brought into "a state of wretched bondage." There was an ominous prophetic note in the irony that the method of enslaving the Israelites was in time "the means of their full and final deliverance; at least prepared and opened the way to it." Johnson also spoke for the future in his insistence that the idea of "passive obedience and non-resistance" was a "doctrine of iniquity" where fundamental rights and liberties were at stake. He cited Locke on the law of nature, "the great law of self-preservation, bound upon us by our Maker," that forbids men to give up their liberties, for they owe to posterity the "birthright inheritance" of English liberties of freedom and property within the balanced system of King, Lords, and Commons. Such a system could not oppress unless its spirit had gone or its structure been corrupted. If the British failed to provide the relief guaranteed by such an inheritance, then the awful prospect loomed of an empire "broken up and ruined."[17] These political themes would soon become the stock in trade of all the revolutionary clergy, and they were also reminiscent of the tracts produced after the overthrow in 1689 of the Andros regime in New England.

Johnson cautiously spoke of resistance to the Stamp Act only in terms of "all lawful, most prudent, and effectual means," but he envisaged a more radical possibility for the colonials:

For the breach of public faith, in the abolition of their charters and privileges, annulling their governments and legal securities, abolishes their oaths of allegiance and connection with Great Britain: And their government being thus dissolved, without any act of theirs, they are absolutely in a state of nature and independency. Should this happen (which I pray God never may) I see not but with all the freedom, and best reason in the world, they might go on much in their old forms, or assume what new ones they please.

Johnson was careful to express trust in the good sense of King and Parliament and to deny that he made any strict parallel with the troubles of Israel and Egypt, but his whole sermon was fired by the warning that it *could* happen here. "We have privileges, civil and sacred, O my brethren and countrymen," he reminded his hearers, "which are worth the *having,* worth the *holding,* at the dearest rate: And which (if need be) it were well, it were good earnings of mortality, to die for."[18]

In eastern Connecticut, New Light laymen were dominant in the lower house of the state. Fiercely opposed to the Old Lights' reluctant acquiescence in the passage of the Stamp Act, they had a long history of opposing Old Light representatives, who had tried to stifle them with repressive legislation during the Great Awakening; and they also brought to their political life the sense of righteous solidarity and enthusiasm that animated their pietist religious experience. A Sons of Liberty mob from a New Light area of the colony successfully forced Jared Ingersoll, an Old Light and colonial agent in London, to abandon his post as distributor of the hated stamps. In opposing the measure, New Lights also saw an opportunity to propose a slate of candidates for the coming election that would depose traditional Old Light control of the council and governorship. By 1766 it was said that in this colony religious principles were a badge of one's political creed: "An Arminian, and a Favourer of the Stamp Act signify the same Man."[19]

In western Pennsylvania, Scotch-Irish Presbyterians found their political opportunity in joining with the wealthy proprietors of the colony against the Quaker-dominated Assembly. It had petitioned for a royal governor to supplant the proprietors, who controlled the governorship and exempted their own land from taxation. The Stamp Act gave the Presbyterians, largely dominated by New Lights since 1758, an angry occasion for attacking the Quaker party and its Anglican allies. The luckless stamp distributor complained that the Presbyterians, in league with the proprietors, had become rebels, "as averse to Kings, as they were in the Days of Cromwell, and some begin to cry out, *No King but King Jesus.*"[20]

Liberal Calvinists tended to be more conservative than New Lights in opposing the Stamp Act, if only because as Old Lights in the 1740's they had defended the stability of the legally established order. Their distaste for "enthusiasm" sensed in the political radicals, who often encouraged mob action destructive of property, a censorious, fanatical temper reminiscent of twice-born men of the Awakening who had once scorned unconverted clergy. When Jonathan Mayhew rejoiced at the repeal of the Stamp Act, he characteristically mingled counsels of humility and moderation with appeals for wakeful attention and praised the "mercantile part in particular" for having "done themselves much honor" in the recent fight for liberty. He was sure that King and Parliament had the "commercial interest of the colonies much at heart" and had the right "to superintend the general affairs of the colonies, whatever we may think of the particular right of taxation."[21] Similarly, Charles Chauncy, who had been Edwards's opponent in the 1740's, emphasized the "commercial good" of repeal of the measure, left it debatable whether the act had been unconstitutional, celebrated the British opposition leader William Pitt rather than local actors against the measure, and condemned the outrages of "Mobish" actions, especially the sacking of Thomas Hutchinson's house.[22] John Tucker, another eloquent voice of the Old Light Calvinists, preached an election sermon in 1771 that left it up to both the rulers and the people to judge of their rights under their civil constitution, while warning against the danger of "the licentiousness among the people" that led men "to despise government"; and he must have had New Lights and their radical political allies in mind when he cautioned against following "political zealots" who sought out heretics in the church and traitors in the state.[23] For all their caution, nevertheless, liberal Calvinists produced the only important contemporary clerical oration on the "just indignation of an enraged multitude" at the murder of five colonials when British troops fired upon a Boston mob that had insulted and stoned them. John Lathrop of Boston's Second Church, preaching six days after the event, not only demanded capital punishment for the guilty as a "law of God" (a position supported by Chauncy two months later), but he also affirmed the right of subjects to "reduce matters to their original *good order,* whatever be the fate of those *wicked men* who for ends of their own would subvert the RIGHTS of the people."[24] A passion for law and order could have its own radical potential in circumstances where British policy was seen as illegal and innovating.

Puritan covenant theology had always been based on a view of human nature rooted in suspicion of its tendency toward depravity. The pietists, for all their political support of the radicals, did not neglect the traditional Puritan emphasis on guilt. But in the covenant of grace itself they could find an analogue with politics. The traditional Christian freedom from the slavery of sin and Satan now had a political reverberation audible in defining "holiness" as that which gives title to "immunities and privileges" of the children of God. If ordinary depraved human nature needed to be held in rein, then the movement for new laws and constitutions could also be seen as a way of protecting oneself against human depravity. Calvinism not only offered doctrines of resistance to illegitimate authority; it offered doctrines for developing new revolutionary governments: "We should leave nothing to human virtue, that can be provided for by law or constitution."[25]

Pietists were fond of a metaphor from Amos: "Let judgment run down as waters and righteousness as a mighty stream." The political logic of this metaphor implied that the state was like a river. If there is corruption in the civil power, then "the same sort of corruption also prevails *among the people,*" just as the bed of a river is the source of the river's contamination. In this view wicked kings were punishment for a wicked people, and the decay of government ultimately went back to the decay of "family government," which was "the foundation of all government; as families are the foundation of peopling the country." Pietist enemies of British policy were therefore drawn inexorably "to look at home, in our hearts and conduct, for the original cause of all the difficulties; and see to it, that the land, from whence the streams originate, is pure." So Ebenezer Chaplin, for example, in his *Civil State compared to Rivers* (1773), found at home the same evils of "usurious contracts," living beyond one's means, and scheming for other men's property without proper compensation that the colonists complained of in the behavior of the British government. Chaplin was content to leave action to the General Court, which would "know better what is to be done"; for his congregation there was the Christian duty of seeking a "new heart." There was, in sum, "a general reformation of every thing sinful to do."[26] If this theme alone had consistently been developed, pietists would have become conservative or apolitical moralists, rather than supporters of the Revolution.

The pietistic ethic of love, however, took an activistic communal form in the social ideal of saintly solidarity among the brethren. Nathaniel Niles in *Two Discourses on Liberty* (1774) developed the implications of this strand in a way that exhibited its political potential. Niles spoke both the new language of contract and the old language of collective guilt, but as a pupil of Joseph Bellamy, in turn a disciple of Edwards, he also saw the state as an extension of the community of saints: "We, and all we have, belong to the community. Whenever therefore the common cause requires it, we should, like Paul, be ready to lay down our lives for the brethren. It is but what we owe to the community." Just as church brethren were joined in discipline, so also were citizens in the state: "Every one must be required to do all he can that tends to the highest good of the state: For the whole of this is due to the state, from the individuals of which it is composed. Everything, however trifling, that tends, even in the lowest degree, to disserve the interest of the state must also be forbidden." Niles drew from this ethic the majoritarian conclusion that the accents of true liberty were "much more likely" to be heard in the voice of the majority, which knows best "the circumstances and exigencies of a state" and is closer to the general interests. Niles thought that "the glorious revolution in favor of the house of Hanover" was "perfectly justifiable" on these principles, but he added to this perfunctory bow to the King a more deeply felt populistic salute to "the lower classes of mankind" from which most saints were drawn, rather than from among the great rulers of history.[27]

For Niles, Christian liberty would "exceedingly sweeten the enjoyment of civil liberty if we can obtain it or soften the fetters of slavery if we shall be forced to wear them." In this sense it was the highest value, yet he affirmed that "no man can be a Christian and not a friend to civil liberty, in the strictest sense." In Calvinism, God elected men who freely gave their hearts to him: "The saint will never be required to do anything irksome or disagreeable because his heart will spontaneously choose to do, whatever his sovereign will choose to command." In such a perfect state "the individuals are all of one mind."[28] The secular analogue of this saintly spontaneous obedience in heaven was loyalty to the majority's interests here below. Calvinism in this New Light republican produced a mutation of populistic Puritanism because he had infused the gospel with a political commitment not intrinsic to it but to his own loyalties to American patriots.

The communal theme in Niles was an evangelical version of a widely shared Whig idealization of ancient Roman virtue and of the eighteenth-century republican belief that a republic is peculiarly dependent upon the public virtue of patriotism. Like the Whigs, Niles feared that republican virtue was a precarious achievement, only he located it, in evangelical-Puritan terms, within God's controversy with a chosen people in need of repentance. Thus Niles ended his discourse on civil liberty by saying that "nothing more than piety and economy," along with some unspecified "prudent and decisive measures," was needed to meet the challenge of the hour. Without active repentance in America, he feared that the oppression of the colonies by the British government might continue as just punishment for such sins as the American enslavement of Africans.[29] The American case hung in the balance between redemption through revolutionary resistance and damnation for accumulated sinfulness. Whigs and pietist Calvinists spoke overlapping but different languages that enabled them to cooperate, but it was the clergy who had learned most from the collaboration by politicizing the gospel to suit the revolutionary case.

"The most radical of democratic theories was derivable, in sum," asserts a recent historian and defender of the evangelical party, "from another, and perhaps the greatest, of the students of John Calvin."[30] This large claim implies a straight line from Calvin and Edwards to Levi Hart, who had studied with Edwards's disciple Joseph Bellamy and married the latter's daughter. It is true that Hart was both Edwardsian and democratic, but the elements of his thought cannot so simply be derived from Calvin's student. What makes him characteristic of the evangelicals in the pre-Revolutionary years is his reworking of traditional themes in the light of Whig values and ideas. Hart's address to the freemen of Farmington, Connecticut, *Liberty Described and Recommended* (1774), was mainly an eloquent attack on the cruelty and barbarity of the slave trade. He urged his hearers to imitate Rhode Island's prohibition of it and so eliminate the glaring inconsistency of corrupting the struggle for American liberty with acquiescence in African slavery. In Edwardsian fashion Hart defined moral volition as "exercises of will" through the "influence of motives" formed with respect to "moral objects," and the theoretical burden of his address was that society, like a trading company, was constituted by each individual's giving his proportion to the common stock so that he became "a good or bad member in proportion as he uniteth to, or counteracteth the interest of the body." Like the radical Whig republicans, Hart believed that the "welfare and prosperity of the society is the *common good*, and every individual is to seek and find his happiness in the welfare of the whole, and every thing to be transacted in society, is to be regulated by this standard." He drew from this maxim a democratic-republican conclusion: "None therefore but the representatives of the whole body, in whom as far as possible, the interest of all ranks is contained, are proper to make laws for the regulation of society."[31]

Hart also linked this corporatism, however, to the eighteenth-century social-contract theory of "mutual agreement" as the basis of society. His originality was to find the fundamental consensual element in the relation between husband and wife: "All the larger circles of society originate from family connection or mutual compact between husband and wife; and mutual compact necessarily implieth certain rules and obligations which neither of the parties may violate with impunity."[32] The passage is interesting because Locke's opponent Sir Robert Filmer had based his monarchical theory on the metaphor of the family: people owed obedience to their governments as children owed obedience to their parents. Puritanism had always been engaged with the image of the family as a metaphor for the state, and the crucial need for the discipline of family government had been deeply involved in the inception of the Great Awakening itself. It was necessary in the context of colonial protest against British policy to redefine the hallowed image of the family so as to emphasize its consensual element. Hart is therefore a good example of how pietistic Edwardsianism was transformed in the pre-Revolutionary years with an infusion of contractualism that Locke and the English Whigs had made commonplace.

The prestige of the idea of liberty was so great among colonials in the 1770's that Hart's Christianity, prophetic of nineteenth-century piety in the abolitionist crusade, was formulated entirely in terms of spiritual freedom. The purpose of his address, he wrote in his introduction, was to speak "to the slaves of sin and satan that they may escape from their bondage, and be made partakers of the glorious liberty of the sons of God." Since civic freedom was the liberty to act for the common good, it paralleled exactly the greater Christian liberty to cherish the general good as an emancipation from the bondage of sinful selfishness. "What is English liberty? What is American freedom? When compared with the glorious liberty of the sons of God?"[33] Pietistic Calvinism also contained elements of conservative Puritan moralism in its stress on family government, but its emphasis on the ethic of benevolence toward the whole and the joyful liberation from sin in the new birth of the twice-born enabled it to develop themes that resonated with republican ideas of public virtue and the central importance of a system of political freedom as a social value. The corporatism of the Puritans was thus given more democratic direction and the libertarian elements of the Christian gospel were brought to the foreground.

Covenant theology had always given disciplined obedience a limited contractual element, but on the eve of the Revolution equality and mutuality as the fundamentals of agreement were given an unusual stress. In this development American Calvinism acquired a democratic thrust that had been only latent in the Puritan elected aristocracy of the saints or in the basically nonpolitical pietism of the Great Awakening, with its characteristic double focus on the social need for conservative moral conformity among the rising generation to Puritan sobriety and on the personal necessity of an individual transformation, emancipating men through grace from the tyranny of sin. If the pressure of the republican cause influenced Calvinists to move in a democratic direction if they would keep pace with their constituency, the emotional and moral energy of Calvinism itself lent popular and vigorous assistance to that cause. As Perry Miller first perceived: "What we today have to grasp is that for the masses this coalescence of abnegation and assertion, this identification of Protestant self-distrust with confidence in divine aid, erected a frame for the natural-rights philosophy wherein it could work with infinitely more power than if it had been propounded exclusively in the language of political rationalism."[34]

The pietists' mingling of contractual theory and a corporate emphasis on the general welfare was not peculiar; it characterized some of their secular allies as well. Commemorating the Battle of Bennington, a Republican orator in 1799 apotheosized the "supreme power" of "the body of the people." They were not party to a contract because their representatives were only deputies of the "absolute will of the sovereign people." He soon lapsed, however, into the language of "social compacts" as constitutive of society and cited "liberty, property and security" as "the great objects of society." Most pleased with the Constitution's rejection of "superstitious establishments of every kind," he reserved his hottest fire for the priestcraft of Catholics, Scotch Presbyterians, English court parasites, and recent American college graduates who produced the "discordant jargon of the present day, about prevailing atheism, and principles of licentiousness in America" in order to discredit the immortal Franklin and Jefferson.[35] This polemic establishes him as a stout deistical liberal democrat. Liberal antirevivalist

Calvinists were also devoted to the inherited political, religious, and economic privileges of the colonies, the contractual theory of government, and a moral emphasis on the virtue of love of country as being peculiarly necessary to free government. Such "enlightened" exponents of the common good, however, could cite the example of Rome and quote Cicero, rather than depend on the pietistic solidarity of the saints.[36] The eclectic political idiom of republicanism, whether pietist, liberal, or Whig, was seldom alert to potential contradictions, but it was effective in mobilizing support for a revolution that bitterly divided the colonies. Propagandizing the people was all the more necessary because so many colonials were reluctant to jettison their profitable ties to the imperial system. Washington's army in 1780 numbered only one thousand greater than the Loyalists who served in British forces.[37] Building local support for the Revolution was a vital task because arousing the people meant the difference between defeat and victory, and the clergy were often closer to the pulse of those whose roots were provincial rather than imperial.

Pietist Calvinists were ideologically prepared for a particularly fierce attack on Tories and their sympathizers. The ethic of love, Nathaniel Whitaker argued in his *Antidote against Toryism* (1777), necessarily implied a "holy abhorrence" to evil. Patriot Calvinists could then turn the Christian ethic into the duty to hate thy Tory neighbor; for just as God "hates sin with a perfect hatred from the essential holiness of his nature," so as men conform to him they must hate those "who seek the hurt of society." True benevolence was hatred of Tories. A favorite theme of the Calvinist clergy was the Biblical curse of Meroz, passed on a people that failed to arm in order to recover liberty. Whitaker proposed keeping a "watchful eye" on "over prudent men" who counseled moderation and tolerance, as his Old Light religious enemies often did. He urged confiscation of the estates of all those who gave aid to America's enemies, exile for those who would be "slaves of power," and physical retaliation on British prisoners of war for any harm done to captured colonials.[38] Whitaker would have these steps taken by government, not by popular mobs, but another Presbyterian New Light, John Murray, not only proposed disenfranchisement for America's internal enemies who used "monopoly and extortion" as their weapons; he pointed to a Biblical precedent translated in modern terms as *"Nehemiah headed a Mob!"*[39] In a Thanksgiving sermon at the end of the Revolutionary War he warned his people of their sinful ingratitude for their political blessings, an impiety demonstrated by the lack of family government, by opposition to Sabbatarian laws, by the ominous growth of profanity, intemperance, adultery, incest, and suicide, and by the prevalent taste for gaming, plays, and masquerades. There is an ascetic strain in most revolutionaries, but in the Americans it was often pietist-Puritan.

The connection between pietist religious ideology and pietist politics is visible in Murray's reminder that church members are pledged to "mutual stipulations to watch over each other for good." Their mutual watching should extend to the dangers of monopoly in land or commerce, or of the slack toleration of Tories returning from exile. Calvinists always supported legitimate authority, so republican saints should "mark the man for a traytor who dares to oppose a just taxation, or refuses to bear his part of it." It was just as necessary for the liberated people to be alert to sedition as it had been for them to be sensitive to encroachments of British power. The New Light concern for the true saints in religion was matched by the New Light concern for the true republicans in politics. When Murray in a flight of communal enthusiasm envisaged the elimination by unanimous consent of all state divisions for the sake of "ONE GREAT REPUBLIC" which would pulse with "ONE HEART AND ONE LIFE," he showed how thoroughly his political ideas represented a displacement of his pietist attitudes.[40] Pietists knew from their own church experience that the brethren, as Whitaker had put it in 1774, were bound to treat every member as a Christian brother "and govern him agreeable to the laws of Christ; and if he refuses to submit, they are bound to reject him as an enemy to the laws and kingdom of CHRIST." Like Edwards, Whitaker would irrevocably lose touch with his parish after the war when, in his own idiom, he failed "to promise heaven to works of natural men" and sought to reinstitute the test of a credible profession of grace for communion privileges.[41]

So long as the clergy could preach the Revolution itself, however, as a "work of reformation" to which "the rising generation" should pay special heed (as the General Association of Connecticut Congregationalists had declared in 1776), they were in vibrant touch with the people. The Continental Congress itself reflected the spirit of Calvinist piety in recommending that states encourage "true religion and good morals" as "the only solid foundation of public liberty and happiness" by suppressing "theatrical entertainments, horse racing, and such other diversions as are productive of idleness, dissipation, and general depravity of principles and manners." Though three states were divided on the resolution, only two flatly opposed it. During the war the Continental Congress declared three Fast Days for prayer and contrition, and from 1777 to the Treaty of Paris six years later it proclaimed the first annual national Thanksgiving Days—a custom carried on by Presidents Washington, Adams, Madison, and Lincoln.[42]

Millenarian glories had once been vouchsafed only to the Awakening's converts, but in 1766 a Sons of Liberty orator had taken Revelations 13 for his text and found the "mark of the beast" as foretold in apocalyptic vision clearly stamped on former prime ministers the Earl of Bute and George Grenville, and on the latter's hated Stamp Act paper.[43] All Calvinists could join in enthusiasm for the national future, tempered by a common tradition of urging repentance and reformation. Only their idioms were different. The liberal Calvinist Samuel Williams, in a local Thanksgiving Day discourse on patriotism in 1774, identified Christianity with a "comprehensive benevolence" essential to republics; and he rejoiced in American traditions of taxation "lodged wholly in our hands," jury trial by peers, security of land tenure, freedom of press, and liberty of conscience. Repentance and self-denial were morally appropriate and politically necessary, yet he could foresee North America as an asylum of liberty for all mankind, a place destined to carry forward further than anywhere else "the perfection and happiness of mankind." Williams's oration in good liberal style celebrated "experiment and observation" in philosophy and government while at the same time cocking a jaundiced Old Light eye at religious enthusiasm and fanaticism for producing "a spirit of *levelism* and fierceness" subversive of church, state, science, and morals.[44] Three years later a fellow liberal Calvinist, Samuel West, in a lengthy application of Biblical prophecy to colonial history, pointed to French and Spanish aid to the American patriots as reasonable and evidential proof of the text that going to Babylon was the way to deliverance.[45]

Pietist Calvinists eagerly pursued the same themes with their characteristic more Biblical fervor. The glorious prospects opened up by the Revolution prophesied "in due time, the universal establishment of the Messiah's kingdom in all its benign efficacy in the hearts and lives of men." So in New York preached the popular John Rodgers, who as a youngster had heard George Whitefield and later studied under the New Light Samuel Blair as a substitute for a college education.[46] Victory over the British convinced George Duffield, New Light chaplain to the Continental Congress in Philadelphia, that here in America "the various ancient promises of rich and glorious grace begin their complete divine fulfillment . . . and with them the fulness of the Gentile world shall flow to the standard of redeeming love; and the nations of the earth become the kingdom of our Lord and Saviour, under whose auspicious reign holiness shall universally prevail, and the noise and alarm of war be heard no more."[47] For such patriots it was not only bliss to be alive in such a revolutionary dawn; it was also agony, for the guilt of backsliding was much greater precisely because of the great things God had done for the American people. Like Samuel West, all American ministers knew the relevant passage in Amos: "You only have I known of all the families of the earth; therefore I will punish you for all your iniquities."[48] Chosen in glory, America was chosen in woe, and in this national and cosmic self-centeredness preachers could keep alive as a continuing anxiety the need for republican virtue no matter what military successes were achieved.

One issue of particular concern to all Calvinists and also influential among secular Whigs was the common fear that the British sought to impose mitered power on America through an episcopate for American Anglicans. In this controversy, the links forged between English Dissenters and their American counterparts were part of the chain which tied the colonies together in a movement to merge civil and religious liberty. The wealthy Thomas Hollis, for example, a descendant of Yorkshire Baptists, reprinted Locke's *Essay concerning Toleration* at his own expense, endowed Harvard College with liberal theological and political books, read the colonial press at the New England Coffee House in London, and publicized the polemical writings of Americans like Jonathan Mayhew, whose face he even had etched for circulation among the Dissenters.[49] Hollis was also close to friends of Franklin who managed the London *Chronicle* and served the Dissenters' cause.

Secular patriots in America also responded to this religious issue. The young Boston lawyer John Adams first broke into the pamphlet war preceding the Revolution with an attack on civil and ecclesiastical tyranny. Hollis read it in the Boston *Gazette* for August, 1765, and thereupon reprinted it, under the title of a "Dissertation on the Canon and the Feudal Law," in the London *Chronicle*. Adams's charge that Great Britain was bent upon "an entire subversion of the whole system of our fathers by the introduction of the canon and feudal law into America" employed a legendary and Whig version of history that transformed the earlier American Puritans into a vanguard inspired by "a love of universal liberty" and a healthy contempt for "the ridiculous fancies of sanctified effluvia from episcopal fingers."[50] The colonial protesters against the Stamp Act were, Adams insisted, true inheritors of the classical republics, Magna Charta, and the heroes of English rebellion against Kings Charles I and James II. American rebels were animated by the spirit of the British constitution and of the inherent rights of human nature itself. Secular and religious strands of ideology were thus woven together in the Whig cause.

The pressure of English Dissenters on Parliament would, in fact, prevent any action to create American bishops of the English church. The fear of Anglican hopes, nevertheless, stimulated the ministers to a propaganda campaign in which the American clergy could join hands and submerge their differences against the common danger. They convinced themselves that they had long enjoyed both civil and religious freedom. From their experience of sustained connections through correspondence and travel with the English Dissenters, the American clergy learned how to mount concerted attacks on any British inclinations toward strengthening the church in America. Men like William Livingston of New York and Charles Chauncy of Boston sustained the Whig cause in vigorous newspaper polemics in the major Northern cities.

Even in the South, where through the Great Awakening Presbyterians had grown in strength, the Anglican cause of an American episcopate had little strength. Anglican laymen were as jealous of their power in the vestries as Congregationalists were of theirs in the parishes of New England. When four Anglican clergymen opposed the episcopate, the House of Burgesses in Virginia applauded them and voted unanimously against the plan. When Jonathan Boucher espoused Filmer's defense of monarchy, he was driven from his pulpit by the wrath of his pastorate. Northern Anglicans found themselves without potent allies. Republicanism in religion throughout the country, except for an ineffective group of Anglicans in the Middle Colonies, prevented any religious differences from frustrating political unity against the new British legislation that was designed to tighten control of the empire.[51]

The contribution of this clerical anticlericalism to the Revolution is manifest in the specific connections between ministers and revolutionaries. In 1766 Jonathan Mayhew suggested to James Otis that the political leaders of the people take a leaf from the book of the ministers' organizations. "It is not safe for the colonies to sleep," Mayhew warned, "for it is probable they will always have some wakeful enemies in Great Britain." Colonials would need men who dared to rock the boat and not the cradle. About to set out for an ecclesiastical council, he wrote that there was an analogy between a "communion of churches" and a "communion of colonies." In this letter lay one germ of the idea of the Committees of Correspondence, of which Sam Adams and others would make such effective use in fomenting the Revolution.[52] The artisan Paul Revere played his part in the ministers' campaign by engraving a copy of "The Mitred Minuet" for the *Royal American Magazine*. His satirical sketch of the signing of the Quebec Act was drawn so as to convict Lords Bute and North of insidious Romanist tendencies, encouraged by Satan himself. In sober fact, the British government, anxious to win the loyalty of French Canadians to the crown, had extended the boundaries of the province to the Ohio and Mississippi Rivers, centralized its government, and given the Catholic Church the right to tithe its own believers. So persuasive was the mingling of the strains of civil and religious liberty in the colonial argument, however, that the Continental Congress accused Parliament of having supported impiety, bigotry, and murder by "establishing" the Catholic Church.

This prejudiced rhetoric scarcely helped the Congress's unsuccessful efforts to woo Canadian Catholics to the American cause. In 1776 Congress sent to Montreal a commission headed by Franklin and including John Carroll, who later became the first Catholic archbishop in America. Worn out by the exhausting trip, Franklin returned to find the colonies well on the road to independence. When he had recuperated, he had a hand in revising Jefferson's draft of the Declaration, which specifically charged the King with "abolishing the free system of English Laws in a neighboring Province, establishing therein an Arbitrary government, and enlarging its Boundaries so as to render it at once an example and fit instrument for introducing the same absolute rule into these Colonies." Jefferson wisely bypassed the Catholic issue, but the Quebec Act had made its mark on the revolutionary mind. Whatever the differences between pietists and liberals, all could agree at the end of the war with the New Light John Murray in commending the "able labours of the ingenious Doctors Mayhew and Chauncy" for repelling the alleged but improbable dangers of mitered power in America.[53]

Men like Patrick Henry and John Adams, radical leaders of the Revolution, had found close connections between the Church of England and Parliamentary tyranny, but they had not foreseen how their own arguments could later be just as persuasively used against the remnants of establishment. Henry first made his reputation as a liberal lawyer by defending a parish sued by its rector for loss of wages incurred through the passage in 1758 of the Two-Penny Act. Designed to alleviate the plight of debtors, it had fixed the price of tobacco used in payment of debts and clerical salaries at a level far below what the clergy could profitably expect of the market price. Adams, similarly, had emerged as a revolutionary agitator through his attack on the alleged danger to the colonies from episcopal canon law. But both patriots would later find themselves viewed as conservatives when New Light Presbyterians and Calvinistic Baptists turned similar libertarian arguments against the remnants of establishment in both Virginia and Massachusetts. The coming of the Revolution promoted this strategy, for in its atmosphere the principles of religious dissenters of New Light persuasion, as Bernard Bailyn has said, "appeared not as deviant claims against what was proper and normal but as legitimate and persuasive proposals, appropriately part of a general effort to realize more fully and universalize the natural tendencies of colonial life."[54] Adams would accordingly be embarrassed by the need for rationalizations of the Massachusetts establishment when, in 1774, Quakers and Baptists, committed to a radical libertarian position, invited delegates from Massachusetts to Carpenter's Hall, Philadelphia, to confront them with Pennsylvania's religious liberty as a standard. They could point out that the Boston Tea Party was a protest against a threepenny tax, the same amount Baptists were forced to pay; and in that same year Jonathan Parsons, a New Light Presbyterian of Newbury, Massachusetts, could make a plea for wider religious liberty in a sermon commemorating the Boston Massacre.

Parsons celebrated Newburyport's freedom, in contrast to other towns in Massachusetts, to pay compulsory ministerial charges at one's own meetinghouse, rather than on a parish basis. He treated "our natural and constitutional privileges" as "a legacy left us by Christ, the purchase of his blood," and pointed to the similarity between Britain's taxing of the colonies and the Massachusetts system of church establishment. What was tainted sauce for the goose of imperial policy was tainted sauce for the gander of establishment. Whereas Roger Williams had founded freedom from establishment on the need to keep the garden of the church pure amid the wilderness of the world, Parsons shifted the argument to an insistence on the need for founding both state and church on common principles of "justice, benevolence and moderation, or there can be no peace." A system of "equal liberties" for all denominations would "naturally tend to beget affectionate union."[55]

An Old Light liberal Calvinist, John Tucker, replied to Parsons by arguing that the only reasonable religious liberty was freedom not from taxation but from being forced to attend a particular denomination or to conform to its rites. He pointed to the acceptance by English Dissenters of a system that also required them to pay support for ministers they might happen to dislike. Tucker sharply distinguished between "civil oppression" and "spiritual tyranny." If the majority determined on a particular policy, consistent with the constitution, then the minority was obligated to accept it. Laws for a multiple establishment were only political measures, aimed at the "good order and welfare of the state," designed to make men "better members of *civil society.*" Tax support for all clergy was on all fours with measures for supporting schools. To this extent the minister was a "civil officer." Tucker also seized on Parsons's assertion that "the sense and meaning of Scripture" could only be known by "confessions of faith." Tucker stressed instead the lack of any infallible interpreters of Scripture and the traditional priority of the Word itself to any interpretation of it. Parsons, he complained, would deny communion privileges according to tests of faith. Reinvoking the thirty-year-old conflicts of the Great Awakening, Tucker concluded that the dogmatic censoriousness of the New Lights was the real cause of New England's lack of internal peace. In an *ad hominem* vein he also accused Parsons of basing his policy on an attempt to line his own pockets through his popularity as a preacher by fattening his congregation with paying believers from other parishes.[56]

Tucker's adroit reply is evidence that the more latitudinarian party was less sensitive to the spiritual rights of believers than were the New Lights, who tended to blur the distinction between church and state out of their passion to extend piety to all the relations of life. In this sense the New Lights spoke in practice for what modern men would judge to be a wider religious liberty, but they did so on the unmodern ground that a common spiritual ethic ought to control both church and state. Parsons, at the same time, was more willing than Tucker to conclude with respect to British policy that "the spirit of Christian benevolence would animate us to fill our streets with blood, rather than suffer others to rob us of our rights."[57]

Some liberal Calvinists moved towards Parsons's position. Samuel West, who believed God could never contradict natural laws by counseling unlimited obedience to magistrates and who democratically affirmed that the "collective body of the state," when properly informed, "is always right," suggested in 1776 that requiring the individual to defray only "the necessary charges of his own meeting" was the best way to "take off some of the most popular objections against being obliged by law to support publick worship, while the law restricts that support only to one denomination."[58] Some New Lights, for their part, rejected the whole idea of congregational authority. In the same year of Tucker's debate with Parsons, Nathaniel Whitaker scored John Wise's famous democratic rationale for congregationalism on the ground that the churches arose out of "God's *appointment,* and not any human covenants." Nor was there any *"explicit* consent or covenant" in colonial obedience to "the common laws of the empire." Whitaker, as a good child of the Awakening, was worried that tying church authority explicitly to covenant would "encourage young people to give a loose to their vanity, being under no restraint from the church, of which they are as truly members and under the same bonds, as those who attend the Lord's supper." Men might well arrange the state to suit their "mutual happiness," but the church was a hierarchical system of authority, and all the fairer in disciplinary issues because of it, like the system of justice in England.[59] Other radical New Lights protested against Whitaker's position, and his argument was proof of the philosophical disarray of his own party and of the irrelevance of concepts of church government as indicators of political position. Americans in '76 were not, as is often suggested, democratic republicans because of their experience of congregational church systems. Most ministers, however, would have agreed with John Murray that historically civil and religious liberty went together: "Between civil liberties and those of religion there is a near and necessary connection; when the one expires, the other cannot survive . . . as religious reformations must generally open the door for the removal of civil distresses, so every step in the struggle for liberty should be measured and governed by the rules of piety."[60]

Many pietists moved beyond the bounds of the New England system of toleration and taxation, but even the radical John Murray branded Baptists in Rhode Island as Anabaptists, stigmatized by the anarchic excesses at Münster back in the 1530's.[61] Furthermore, Baptists and New Lights alike, however critical they were of the New England Standing Order, were themselves supporters of rigid sumptuary legislation and of the enforcement of Sabbatarian and other blue laws. The desire to democratize political policy, to eliminate the slave trade, and to expand liberty of conscience, which the Revolution stimulated, went hand in hand with a clerical willingness to use the state to enforce a narrow morality of traditional Puritan cast. But secular patriots did not themselves cohere on a consistently higher standard of religious liberty. Neither Sam Adams nor Patrick Henry, the most vocal radical advocates of popular revolution, had any qualms about accepting the system of tax support for Christianity that had evolved in Massachusetts and Virginia.

The odd case of Joseph Hawley points up the confusion that still reigned in New England at the end of the Revolution. Recanting his Arminianism, which had made him a leading figure in deposing Jonathan Edwards from his pulpit, Hawley later became a pietist and fervent supporter of the Revolution. When the Constitution of 1780 in Massachusetts required a declaration of Christian faith from officeholders, he consistently refused to serve in the state senate because such a declaration should only be made in church.[62] Hawley's protest was deemed quixotic at the time, but in a few years Virginians would find themselves in a position to legislate Hawley's position into practice. Pietists and rationalists had learned to cooperate in the Revolution for political liberty, despite their inability to agree on religious matters. The success of the American cause would give them a new opportunity to translate their alliance into a fight for a new standard of religious liberty at home.

Tocqueville's emphasis on the Puritan roots of the Revolution does less than justice to the rationalist anti-Calvinists who led it, but their Calvinist allies did play a role in mobilizing local opinion. Furthermore, a recent study of colonial New England towns even goes so far as to argue that "town discipline in the Revolution resembled nothing so much as church discipline throughout the provincial era." Patriots used the techniques of censure, burnings in effigy, and the carting of tarred-and-feathered dissidents in order to expose the Tory heretic to a public view and thus induce his repentance. Tocqueville had devoted a chapter to the importance of the townships, and Michael Zuckerman, 135 years later, has seen the towns as the main actors in the critical step into revolution and later in the formulation and adoption of a new Massachusetts constitution. But where Tocqueville saw "the spirit of liberty" in the towns, Zuckerman, while conceding the nonoligarchical democratic nature of the political participation of the citizenry, sees a smothering communal ethos unable to accept real differences: "The dark demon of Puritan xenophobia still slumbered fitfully; it was dangerous to go beyond the bounds of the substantive sentiments of the society."[63] Tocqueville himself, in discussing the citizen in the towns, noted that "more social obligations were there imposed upon him than anywhere else," and he observed in the 1830's a potentiality for majority tyranny that alarmed him. Where Zuckerman is appalled by the degree of unanimity expressed on major issues in the towns, Tocqueville was impressed instead with the general need, if society is to exist, for "a great number of men" to consider "a great number of things under the same aspect" and to hold "the same opinions upon many subjects."[64]

His image of America, however, had ambiguous elements in it, and the legacy of Puritanism was itself deeply ambiguous. Covenants rooted in suspicion of human nature merged with more confident contracts. The mutual surveillance of the saints over their erring tendencies commingled with constitutionalism; the responsibility of authorities to the true faith was joined with the need for popular participation by citizens in the major institutions of society; the importance of the individual's conversion experience was translated into collective expressions of fidelity to the covenant in order to bring about a society of believers, preparing for a millennial national redemption. Localism and wider bonds of community competed for loyalty. Tocqueville's *Democracy in America* described a dominant political freedom and a lurking despotism of opinion, and he was convinced that colonial origins provided a key to this strange new world. The Puritan background in relation to the Revolution, as modern scholarship has uncovered it, confirms his belief that it offers a historical basis for understanding this paradoxical development.

V

Disestablishment in Virginia: A Symbiotic Alliance

Tocqueville believed that "religions ought to have fewer external observances in democratic periods than at any others." Men living in democratic times, he explained, are "impatient of figures; to their eyes, symbols appear to be puerile artifices used to conceal or to set off truths that should more naturally be bared to the light of day; they are unmoved by ceremonial observances and are disposed to attach only a secondary importance to the details of public worship." He himself firmly believed in "the necessity of forms, which fix the human mind in the contemplation of abstract truths and aid it in embracing them warmly and holding them with firmness," but in "the ages upon which we are entering" it would be important to keep such forms to a minimum so that religion would not become "limited to a band of fanatic zealots in the midst of a skeptical multitude."[1]

Revolutionary America took a long stride into a more democratic age, and many Americans shared the conception of religion that Tocqueville described. Their new state constitutions, except in Maryland, South Carolina, and most of New England, legally disestablished the churches, while still preserving in many states Christian tests for the exercise of civil rights. The leadership for more sweeping separation between church and state came from a group of political thinkers and statesmen who had played an important role in the Revolution. Their own attitude toward religion discounted its corporate visible features, and they were supported by some religious leaders like the Presbyterian John Witherspoon and the Baptists Isaac Backus and John Leland, spokesmen for groups that had previously suffered at the hands of the established order.

This alliance was not just a marriage of convenience. The secular leaders, participants in the Enlightenment's culture of liberal political philosophy, Newtonian science, and classical humanism, still preserved residual connections with Christianity, even when they attacked specific Christian dogmas and practices. Their Christian allies also thought of themselves as friends of the secular ideology of social contract and the natural rights of man. The two groups were symbiotically related, and it was this mutually advantageous alliance that prepared the American scene for that mixture of religion and liberty which so impressed Tocqueville on his tour.

During the Revolution the friends of liberty did not expect the state to be wholly neutral to religion, and they usually took for granted a consensus in support either of Protestantism or of some form of Christianity. The Revolutionary armies had chaplaincies for a variety of faiths, and Congress itself had Anglican and Presbyterian chaplains. During the period of the Articles of Confederation, in 1787, the Northwest Ordinance (promoted by Massachusetts men) reflected the double desire to remove religious barriers to civil rights while at the same time providing for land grants that could be used for the support of both religion and schools, since they were equally "necessary to good government and the happiness of mankind." In the Continental Congress, delegates favoring this support were more than twice as numerous as those opposing, but because of their distribution the supporters could not muster the necessary backing of seven states.[2]

In Virginia the standard of religious liberty was given a new and more radical definition by a decade of dispute following the Revolution. Out of this controversy Jefferson and Madison emerged as victorious spokesmen for a new conception of separation between church and state, a point of view debated with unprecedented depth and clarity. In this still smoldering fire, contemporary advocates seek to bank the ashes of the past in order to warm their own ideological hearths, quarreling in the process with the Supreme Court's judicial prodding of the embers. Virginia's influential Bill of Rights in 1776, antedating the Declaration of Independence itself, asserted an equal right of all "to the free exercise of religion, according to the dictates of conscience." Part of this Madisonian phrasing would eventually find its way into the First Amendment to the Constitution of the United States, where it would remain to puzzle posterity about its meaning. But a decade of controversy gave clear and precise meaning in Virginia to Madison's terms, developed in close collaboration with Thomas Jefferson. While Franklin had a more jesting tone, John

Adams a more puritanical seriousness, and Tom Paine a more angry militancy, all these rationalists linked their ideal of toleration to a shared conception of "enlightened" religion, purified of the corruptions they believed the historic faiths had made in the simple truth. Jefferson wanted posterity to remember him above all for the Declaration of Independence, the University of Virginia, and the Virginia Statute for Religious Freedom. These achievements are organically related: independence of Great Britain, according to the philosophy of natural rights, entailed a new approach to education and to religion. The university would be nonsectarian and secular; the individual's conscience would be free to follow its own bent in religion; believers would support their churches only by voluntary contributions to a pastor of their own choosing. This position makes a deep separation between church and state, cutting the former off from any public money —at least in principle. Does this kind of separation between church and state presuppose a liberal deism? Is it merely the political expression of a type of religion that is not obligatory for those who do not share Jefferson's eighteenth-century religious assumptions?

Scholars have raised these questions from both Protestant and Catholic perspectives. Jefferson's mild rationalism is seen as religiously indifferent in contrast to Roger Williams's passionate Protestantism; alternatively, Jefferson and Madison are accused of a Protestant bias in favor of religion as a private affair, abstracted from institutional embodiment. Thus Perry Miller, the most sympathetic historian of American Puritanism, sees the leadership of the movement for religious liberty as coming from "a rational aristocracy, shot through with deistical beliefs, willing to see any number of religions have their freedom because they believed in none of them. As Nathaniel Ward has said, nothing is easier than to tolerate when you do not seriously believe that differences matter."[3] From this point of view the rationalists are accused of religious cynicism. Father John Courtney Murray, an important defender of limited separation between church and state and a leading liberal Catholic, has argued that a prohibition against *any* official relations between religion and government or against *any* public aid to religion is a sweeping and absolutistic conclusion that can be supported *only* by "a theological premise," the rationalists' idea of religion as a private affair. To base modern policy on this conception is, therefore, to beg the question by assuming the truth of a sectarian position. Concluding that "no establishment" means "no aid" is merely trying to "establish" one religion, that of Jefferson and Madison: "In order to make separation of church and state absolute, it unites the state to a 'religion without a church'—a deistic version of fundamentalist Protestantism."[4]

Certainly the rationalist statesmen did not believe in the traditional Christian religions, but they did have a religion of their own, neither cynical, deistical, nor fundamentalist in any exact sense. Franklin's famous reply in 1790 to Ezra Stiles, president of Yale, who asked the good doctor about his religion, expressed the relaxed, urbane tone of the American *philosophes*:

You desire to know something of my religion. It is the first time I have been questioned upon it. But I cannot take your curiosity amiss, and shall endeavour in a few words to gratify it. Here is my creed. I believe in one God, creator of the universe. That He governs it by His Providence. That He ought to be worshipped. That the most acceptable service we render to Him is doing good to His other children. That the soul of man is immortal, and will be treated with justice in another life respecting its conduct in this. These I take to be the fundamental points in all sound religion, and I regard them as you do in whatever sect I meet with them.

As to Jesus of Nazareth, my opinion of whom you particularly desire, I think his system of morals and his religion, as he left them to us, the best the world ever saw or is likely to see; but I apprehend it has received various corrupting changes, and I have, with most of the present dissenters in England, some doubts as to his divinity; though it is a question I do not dogmatize upon, having never studied it, and think it needless to busy myself with it now, when I expect soon an opportunity of knowing the truth with less trouble. I see no harm, however, in its being believed, if that belief has the good consequence, as probably it has, of making his doctrines more respected and more observed; especially as I do not perceive that the Supreme takes it amiss, by distinguishing the unbelievers in his government of the world with any peculiar marks of his displeasure.[5]

Franklin's charming letter strikes all the notes in the rationalists' philosophy: the notion of a common ground "in all sound religion"; the suspicion of the "corrupting changes" which churches and theologians have made in Jesus's "system"; the doubt of, and indifference to, the divinity of Christ; the identification of worship with "doing good" to other men; the pragmatic reduction of belief from truth to good consequences; the absentee God, who does not punish unbelievers with any "peculiar marks of his displeasure."

Franklin's religion is of a piece with Jefferson's "Bible," in which he edited the gospels so as to recover "the most sublime and benevolent code of morals which has ever been offered to man," an ethic purged of all theological and miraculous elements, yet still related to a humanized version of the life of Jesus. Jefferson believed that his version of the Bible proved that he was "a *real* Christian." He could console John Adams for the death of Abigail by gracefully suggesting the possibility of a future "ecstatic meeting with the friends we have loved and lost," but immortality was not with him an article of deep belief.[6]

Both Adams and Jefferson wrote voluminously to each other in their retiring years, and their correspondence is witness to their fascination with religion as an intellectual issue. In creed they were Unitarians, although Jefferson contributed to the Episcopal Church and Adams preserved from his Puritan ancestors a vivid sense of the persistence of human frailty, irrationality, and invidious emulation—in himself as well as others. While Adams had read the Calvinists and their opponents in a lifetime of omnivorous theological reading, he did not blame Jefferson for finding his entertainment, "the Marbles and Nine Pins of old Age," in Euclid, Newton, Thucydides, and Theocritus. Both agreed, as Jefferson put it, that reasonable men should sweep away "the gossamer fabrics of factitious religion" and "live without an order of priests, moralise for ourselves, follow the oracle of conscience, and say nothing about what no man can understand, nor therefore believe; for I suppose belief to be the assent of the mind to an intelligible proposition." There was revelation enough in the human understanding. If Adams and Jefferson had been on Sinai with Moses and were told that "one was three and three, one," they might have been amazed and terrified by the lightning and earthquakes, they might have been too frightened to speak, they might have been scared into lying, but, said Adams, "We could not have believed it." Let divines "howl, snarl, bite" as they might, saying he was no Christian: "I say Ye are no Christians: and there the Account is ballanced. Yet I believe all the honest men among you, are Christians in my Sense of the Word."[7]

Whatever their political differences, Jefferson and Adams were virtually at one in their religion. In their correspondence it is clear that seventeenth-century theological issues had lost all meaning for them, but they did not have either the indifference of skeptical agnostics or the intellectual boldness of militant atheists. Their religion needed no embodiment in specific churches, nor did it reflect the personal agony of sin and conversion that pietistic evangelicals preached. Both men were religiously sanguine; Hell had no terrors and Heaven was a wished-for possibility, a spur to present action. But if religious hope should turn out to be a fraud, men would never know it. Yet neither man was blind to evil and suffering. They debated the uses of grief, and Adams believed men would learn to acquire from it not "Stoical Apathy" but "Patience, and Resignation, and tranquility." Jefferson thought Adams had "exhausted the subject," adding only that considering the abuses as well as the uses of grief, "we may consider its value in the economy of the human being, as equivocal at least." Too many afflictions "cloud too great a portion of life to find a counterpoise in any benefits derived from its uses." He agreed with Adams that the Cross itself was an "Engine of Grief" that had produced "calamities." Enlightened men could not but shudder at how "knavish Priests" had added "prostitutions" of the original tragedy that would fill "the blackest and bloodiest Pages of human History." With this lament Adams set himself to read twelve volumes of Charles François Dupuis's *L'Origine de tous les Cultes ou Religion Universelle,* while Jefferson, less heroically, contented himself with "the humble achievement of reading the Analysis of his work by Destutt-Tracy, in 200 pages 8 vo [octavo]."[8] Their reading confirmed them both in the need for freedom of conscience.

Large numbers of Americans today, especially among Protestants, would find themselves in considerable agreement with Jefferson and Adams. But to the historian their religion appears not as the universal common sense of the matter but as the historical common sense of the American Enlightenment, already fading in the years when the two aging patriots conducted their dialogue. Their religion was not intellectually powerful or imaginatively exciting, as Edwards's theology was, but it was humane, honest, and informed by prodigious reading. Neither Roger Williams nor Jonathan Edwards ever devoted more than a small fraction of as much hard thought and industrious scholarship to political philosophy, and no men in America had done more than Adams and Jefferson for their country, as men of action with a courageous capacity for innovation. Historians of religion today are inclined to patronize this rationalistic religion, which seems so theologically complacent and commonplace. But they have forgotten that its lack of militancy, except on behalf of freedom of conscience, made it possible for revolutionaries to be much more tolerant of traditional religions than the history of persecution might reasonably have justified. Such men were preeminently fitted for the role of conducting the new nation toward a condition of freedom of conscience in which all the contending religions could find their own place, a position they could not have hewn out for themselves because no sect or church had the power to carry a large majority with it.

Jefferson set forth his theory of toleration in *Notes on the State of Virginia,* a classic of the American Enlightenment. Begun in 1781 as a reply to inquiries about the New World from the secretary of the French legation at Philadelphia, the *Notes* used the occasion to lecture Jefferson's own countrymen on the meaning of religious freedom. In Jefferson's philosophy man is responsible for his conscience only to God, not to government. Political power regulates injurious acts, but religious opinion does no injury: "It neither picks my pocket nor breaks my leg." Only reason can attack error. Just as government cannot establish truth in physics, so it cannot establish truth in religion. "Truth can stand by itself." Furthermore, differences of religious opinion are advantageous because each sect performs the office of censor over the other. Coercion in religion has only served to make "one half the world fools, and the other half hypocrites." Even if a sect should arise "whose tenets would subvert morals," there is a remedy, as New York and Pennsylvania had shown, because good sense "laughs it out of doors, without suffering the state to be troubled with it." The way to silence religious disputes is "to take no notice of them." The spirit of the people would not allow prosecution for heresy, but the spirit of the times "may alter, will alter." The time to act constitutionally is now, because "from the conclusion of this war we shall be going down hill." The people will become absorbed in money-getting and "never think of uniting to effect a due respect for their rights."[9]

Jefferson and Madison formulated their position against the background of a history in which the establishment of a single church had evolved toward a multiple establishment of the major Christian faiths. This type of establishment had developed before the Revolution in New York and during it in Maryland and South Carolina as well. (The latter explicitly established Protestant Christianity.) In Massachusetts, Anglicans, Quakers, and Baptists had been gradually exempted since 1727 from paying taxes for the Congregational town churches, if they could obtain certificates showing they were regularly attending members of their own services. By the Massachusetts Constitution of 1780 dissenting groups were, however, compelled to pay a general tax for the support of "public Protestant teachers of piety, religion, and morality," chosen by the towns. By obtaining certificates dissenters could direct their share of the general taxes to their own church. This pattern was followed as well by New Hampshire and Connecticut. Wherever establishment survived the Revolution, it had become a "multiple" form of "Christian" establishment.

The draft of the Virginia Bill of Rights of 1776, as drawn up by George Mason, originally went only as far as defending "toleration" in opposition to the use of "force and violence" in coercing dissent. This standard did not make freedom of conscience a fundamental right, nor did it prevent legal privileges for religion or political exclusions for religious reasons. James Madison proposed three changes: that "compulsion" be substituted for "force," that "the full and free exercise of religion according to the dictates of conscience" be substituted for "toleration," and that a clause be added which would prevent any men "on account of religion" from enjoying "peculiar emoluments or privileges" or suffering any "penalties or disabilities." These provisions would have separated church from state much further than the legislature was yet ready to accept. Madison had to settle for the inclusion only of his "free exercise" clause, a phrase that was subject to later development as the core of a more extensive separationist theory.[10]

Jefferson was busy in Philadelphia while this drafting was taking place, but he sent on his own proposal, too late to be considered at Williamsburg. He would have protected anyone from being compelled to "maintain *any* religious institution." Madison and Jefferson identified full disestablishment with the free exercise of conscience. It was not enough that the Virginia convention had repealed parliamentary laws restricting religious liberty; heresy was still an offense at common law and the Virginia Assembly had itself in 1705 left on the record a set of statutes fatal to religious freedom, restricting public employment to Trinitarian Christians. Under the new Virginia constitution, the Assembly empowered dissenting ministers to perform marriages and abolished all tithes, but it authorized the Church of England vestries to tax the local parishes for poor relief; it reserved church property for Anglican use; and it postponed the question of levying a general tax for the benefit of all churches. Furthermore, Jefferson failed in 1779 to win passage of a comprehensive set of bills for doing away with the remnants of the landed aristocracy, building a state system of public schools, and definitively separating church and state. Only the laws regulating land inheritance passed. Jefferson was disappointed in his hope that the legislature would accept in principle his definition of religious liberty as freedom from enforced financial support of *even one's own* church and freedom from *any* religious tests for offices of public trust. These may have been "the natural rights of mankind"; they were not that yet in Virginia.[11]

The conservatives had met Jefferson's scheme in 1778 with another. It was premised on the belief that the state should encourage the true faith, that the Episcopal Church should be confirmed in its property holdings; and that the Assembly should allow the incorporation of new churches with similar privileges from the Assembly if they subscribed to beliefs in one God, a future state of rewards and punishments, and the divine inspiration of the Bible, "the only rule of Faith." These proposals effectively established a sort of minimum abstract "Christianity," whereby those major sects that qualified could pay taxes to the churches of their choice. Faced with this collision of views between Jefferson's plan and a general "Christian" establishment, the legislature again postponed its resolution of the fundamental issues. In 1784 they rose again, and the conservatives had the support of a popular Revolutionary leader, Patrick Henry. They now proposed a general tax for support of "some form of Christian worship." If any taxpayer did not indicate a choice among the Christian churches, his money would go to religious "seminaries of learning" within the citizen's county. Quakers and Mennonites could use their taxes for any purpose. In this way public funds might be used not only for the support of churches but also for the support of religious education.[12]

In 1785, the year Jefferson's *Notes on Virginia* was published in Paris, the hard-pressed Assembly voted to have the general assessment bill distributed to a divided people for public discussion. Its powerful supporters included George Washington, John Marshall, and Patrick Henry. James Madison carried the argument to the people through his *Memorial and Remonstrance Against Religious Assessments,* which brought the Jeffersonian principles of religious liberty to bear upon the issues. Madison was once a pupil of John Witherspoon, the Scotch Presbyterian president of the College of New Jersey, and the Virginian had enthusiastically discovered in Witherspoon's syllabus for "Moral Philosophy" the great names of the Scottish Enlightenment: David Hume, Francis Hutcheson, Adam Smith, Thomas Reid, Lord Kames, and Adam Ferguson. From them Madison received what he called his "very early and strong impressions in favor of Liberty both Civil and Religious."[13] Like Madison, Witherspoon also believed that every church should be supported voluntarily by the contributions of its members without help from the taxing power of the state. Madison's chief opponent, Patrick Henry, had gone to church for years in the parish of the Reverend Samuel Davies, a fount of the Awakening in Virginia, successor to Edwards at Princeton, and founder of the Hanover County Presbytery, which had put the whole problem of religious liberty to the Virginia Assembly in 1773. Both religious backgrounds had engendered support for the Revolution and religious liberty. Regarding the assessment bill, however, what might seem marginal differences were actually major differences of public policy.

The critical point was the conception of a church as an organization dependent for its financial support on the voluntary contributions of its members to their own minister. Either pietism or theological rationalism could lead to this conclusion. Jefferson and Madison, in fact, found their religious supporters in those ministers who, like the itinerant Baptist John Leland, saw no contradiction between their pietistic religious convictions and the social theory of rationalism with its emphasis on natural rights and government by compact. Such men could revere Jefferson as one of their greatest heroes, despite his own total lack of pietistic tradition, and so lend their support to Madison's struggle for religious liberty. This merger of rationalists, Baptists, Presbyterians, and Lutherans might have scandalized logicians, but it was a passage of intellectual history of tremendous benefit to the movement for religious liberty. Leland, a Congregationalist of Massachusetts who converted to Baptism in 1774, chose for his epitaph: "Here lies the body of John Leland, who labored to promote piety, and vindicate the civil and religious rights of man." His pamphlet *The Rights of Conscience Inalienable* (1791), aimed at stripping the high-flying churchman of "his legal Robe," was pure Jeffersonianism: "Truth disdains the aid of law for its defense—it will stand upon its own merits."[14]

The conundrum that Jefferson and Madison left to posterity was one they never appreciated: did their policy, as charged, seek to "establish" their own "enlightened" religion under the guise of "disestablishment"? The Baptists and Presbyterians did not think so, either in Virginia or Massachusetts, and Madison as a young man had heard an imprisoned Baptist preach from the window of a jail. In his *Remonstrance* Madison made one major religious assertion: "It is the duty of every man to render the creator such homage and *such only*, as he believes to be acceptable to him; this duty is precedent, both in order of time and degree of obligation, to the claims of civil society."

He did not, therefore, take the position of an atheist or agnostic who has no traffic with any Creator, however defined. Such men might abuse the freedom that Madison would preserve for them, but it would be "an offense against God, *not against man:* to God, therefore, *not to man,* must an account be rendered." This argument presupposed an individual relation to God, unmediated by any human agencies and independent of man's civic life. In this sense it was profoundly non-Catholic and non-Puritan by its separation of the sphere of religion from public life. Roger Williams would have agreed only for the sake of religion itself; Madison wanted to protect society from religion as well. He believed that politically powerful forms of religion threatened civil freedom. Danger lay in "ecclesiastical establishments" because "in no instance have they been seen the guardians of the liberties of the people." Tyrants, in fact, "may have found an established clergy convenient auxiliaries."[15] Therefore, a church defined as a voluntarily supported organization of believers was the only kind of church compatible with a free society. The general assessment bill was also odious because it gave special treatment to Quakers and Mennonites, thus violating equality by its favors as it did by its burdens. It would encourage emigration and discourage immigration, arouse new social animosities and jealousies, and by its unpopularity weaken the prestige of the laws. Not only the individual's conscience but the welfare of society itself demanded full disestablishment.

In this Jeffersonian-Madisonian view a voluntarily supported church is best for both religion and society. Far from being indifferent to religion, these statesmen believed that the liberal state needed its own style of religious expression. No doubt it was a style especially congenial to Unitarians and Baptists, but while the number of Baptist churches was second only to that of Methodist churches by 1850, Unitarianism flourished only in New York and New England. Clearly, other factors were much more important than this partiality in accounting for the varied prosperity of religions in America.

The Jeffersonian-Madisonian view was not secularist in the sense of considering all religions mere superstitions or socially harmful. If it was secular in Father Murray's sense of assuming "the social irrelevance of religion," it was precisely the social relevance of established religion, as a potential threat to civic freedom, that led Jefferson and Madison to what Father Murray deplores as "the exclusion of religion from the secular affairs of the City and its educational system, its relegation to the private forum of the conscience or at best to the hushed confines of the sacristy."[16] However we evaluate this narrowing of religion's sphere of action, the fact is that the visible, corporate, socially relevant religion of the Episcopal Church did not propose the degree of religious freedom that Jefferson and Madison provided for all citizens. The defeated assessment bill of 1784 did not reach so far in its lack of discrimination between religions as to provide equality for non-Christians as well. While it did not discriminate among Christians, it would have excluded from its privileges Jews, agnostics, and atheists. Whatever implicit religious bias the Jeffersonian-Madisonian conception of religious liberty may have contained, it was certainly more impartial than any conception then alive in their society. Locke himself did not tolerate atheists or Catholics; Roger Williams's colony excluded Catholics from the franchise; and even Pennsylvania, which alone had not penalized Catholics and whose state constitution was otherwise the most liberal of all, demanded that officeholders accept the whole Bible as divinely inspired. Jefferson's Statute for Religious Freedom, finally passed in January, 1786, by a large majority of the Assembly, preserved to each believer "the comfortable liberty of giving his contributions to the particular pastor whose morals he would make his pattern, and whose power he feels most persuasive to righteousness." It also detached civil rights from any dependence upon "our religious opinions." In his *Autobiography* Jefferson noted that some legislators wanted the act to say that Christ was "the Holy Author of our religion," and the great majority voted down this suggestion as proof that they meant the bill "to comprehend, within the mantle of its protection, the Jew and the Gentile, the Christian and Mahometan, the Hindoo, and infidel of every denomination."[17] Virginians had raised a new standard of religious liberty.

The ardent devotees of the Age of Reason in America, precisely because they could put secular interests ahead of religious differences and were not closely bound to any organized religion, were the only group who, on an intercolonial basis, could speak clearly for a new standard of religious liberty. The vast majority of the people by the end of the colonial era, though many attended religious services and were much more literate in the Bible than their counterparts today, were not, strictly speaking, members of any organized church. If the rationalists presupposed a religion without much semblance of ecclesiastical structure, they reflected the religious condition of most of the inhabitants. Even so, the ideal of a Christian state was deeply imbedded in many American minds, and the general assessment bill lost by the slim margin of only three votes. Madison and Jefferson had won a precarious battle on a local issue, not a national victory for a new standard of separation. And their own religious position was still the faith of only a few *philosophes*.

The alliance between pietists and rationalists for separation of church and state was not always untroubled. Jefferson and Madison were fearful that their cherished project for a state university might become a religious monopoly or an arena for theological warfare. They primarily respected republican virtue, not intellectual diversity, and the University of Virginia was for them, as Jefferson put it, "a vestal flame" for inspiring Whiggism. For religious education they relied on inviting theological seminaries to locate nearby, on building up an impressive library of theological writings, and on providing Sunday services in the Rotunda by rotating pastors. For his first appointment to a professorship Jefferson invited Thomas Cooper, a republican who was also a philosophical materialist, scandalizing a stiff opposition led by John Holt Rice, a Presbyterian clergyman, editor, and promoter of the first Southern graduate seminary for clerical training. Rice and his followers valued religious principles and habits as being "unspeakably more important than genius and learning." They supported Jefferson's plans for the university only because they hoped to establish church-endowed theological chairs, compulsory worship, and Bible instruction. Their clamor against Cooper forced his resignation, and Jefferson won their support for his conception of the university only because Rice decided that by supporting it Presbyterians could better infiltrate it. The Presbyterians favored a state-wide public-school system even more than Jefferson did when he felt that his pet project for a university was threatened; and it is worth noting that New England, where religious establishments survived into the nineteenth century, produced a strong system of public education long before disestablished Virginia ever did. Yet Jefferson had to sacrifice Cooper to gain Presbyterian support, and the tension between religious orthodoxy and the secular sciences would plague American higher education for many years to come.[18] By 1792 even Virginia would pass a Sunday law, forbidding ordinary labor, business, or recreation on the Sabbath—explicit testimony to the power of the evangelical impulse even in a state where the rational republicans had scored such notable victories.

In Massachusetts, Baptists pressed hard for wider separation between church and state, but even they gladly accepted a Christian test oath for public office and acquiesced in laws to compel church attendance and Sabbath observance. The Constitution of 1780, although it never obtained the legally required two-thirds majority, made all males pay religious taxes to the majority religion of each town or parish, thus in practice favoring the Congregationalists. Though the courts at first granted relief to protesting Baptists, they reversed themselves later and decided that all churches had to be incorporated and obtain special certificates in order to be exempted from paying to support the majority's religion.[19] New Hampshire was even more explicit in affirming in its Constitution of 1783 that morality and piety were "rightly grounded on evangelical principles" as the "greatest security to government."[20] It provided for public support of Protestant clergy and restricted eligibility for service in the state legislature to Protestants. The standards of rationalists and pietists, made luminous by the Jeffersonians and the Baptists, were clearly not national. The eminent gentlemen sitting in the Constitutional Convention at Philadelphia in 1787 would have to decide if they should be.

VI

Disestablishment in "a Compound Republic"

Tocqueville's reflections on America focused on what seemed to him as a Frenchman to be a paradox. In the United States of 1831 the spirit of religion and the spirit of freedom "reigned in common over the same country." Surprisingly, the relation existed through disestablishment, not in spite of it. Therefore, he concluded, in the future, as communities became more democratic, it would become "more and more dangerous to connect religion with political institutions."[1] Americans today do not agree on what separation of church and state should mean in terms of the connections between religion and society. They disagree, in fact, with a passion. Those who advocate closer connections between political power and religious groups tend to do so for the sake of organized Christianity, in defiance of Tocqueville's warning. Those, on the other hand, who argue for mutually exclusive relations between church and state tend to do so for the sake of Jews and nonbelievers. In this debate both sides appeal for confirmation to the Founding Fathers.

Did the framers of the First Amendment agree among themselves more than contemporary Americans do? Does the First Amendment provide an unambiguous or a viable solution to the problem of separation? Tocqueville did not discuss these questions, taking for granted the degree of separation he encountered in America. However blurred, it was clearer and wider than anything prevailing in Europe. Yet if his theory of the symbiotic relation between religion and democracy in America is correct, we would expect to find that the Amendment did not prevent that relation, but nurtured it. Does the record actually support such a conclusion?

The historian's difficulty in settling the question is due to the nature

91

of his evidence. Records of Congressional motions and votes do not often enough give the reasons for which proposals were made and accepted or rejected. The long sequence of changes by committees in the wording of the relevant clauses in the First Amendment itself casts doubt on any clear and precise interpretation of their meaning. If a consensus was achieved, incompatible views may have been reconciled by a formula ambiguous enough to satisfy different positions. The record shows that no easily found agreement existed; it was hammered out by repeated efforts at phrasing. Eight state senators from Virginia felt that the First Amendment fell short of Virginia's own Jeffersonian standards, though the majority of the state's convention voted to accept it. Perhaps the majority was reassured that such objections were groundless; or perhaps it wanted what it got because it could not get what it wanted.[2] It is certain, at least, that Madison, who played the most important part in winning the battle for the ten Amendments constituting the Bill of Rights, was later clear in his own mind about what *he* thought the debatable clauses meant. But that is not evidence for others' understanding of them, either in the Congress or among the people at large. The problem is partly obscured by a fog of ambiguity that cannot be entirely dissipated. If such matters are difficult, they are also, "like the name Achilles assumed when he hid among women, not beyond all conjecture."

At least regarding the Constitution itself there was near unanimity in the Convention at Philadelphia in voting for the clause that prevents any religious tests for federal officeholding. That agreement was easily purchased because the Constitution left any other religious issues to the states themselves, which varied in their arrangements from New England's general tax support of religion to Virginia's voluntarism. But Antifederalists, who feared that the new government would be too powerful, demanded a Bill of Rights as the price of ratification. Presbyterians and Baptists generally feared that the Constitution did not provide sufficient safeguards for religious freedom, and they had earlier been the chief supporters of James Madison in the struggle for religious liberty in Virginia. Madison, as a major architect of the Constitution, was its chief defender before the people in Virginia. He himself was compelled to win back the dissenting groups by a commitment to a Bill of Rights, which he had not favored in the Convention itself. Ironically, Patrick Henry, who had opposed Madison in the Virginia conflict over the general assessment bill in support of religion, now charged the new government with being a danger to civil liberties. Madison, as he explained with elegant precision in *The Federalist*, believed in a stronger central government and in remedies for the evils incident to republican government, but he insisted that the new system was "a compound republic," not a tyranny, and that the remedies were all consistent with the spirit of republican government itself.

"A dependence on the people is, no doubt," Madison argued in *The Federalist*, "the primary control on the government; but experience has taught mankind the necessity of auxiliary precautions." These safeguards included the separation of executive, legislative, and judicial powers; the division of the legislature into two branches, differently organized; a qualified executive veto; the checks of states and central government against each other; and the protection of minority rights in both civil and religious affairs by the "multiplicity" of interests and sects which an "extended republic" covering a large territory could provide. The new government was "wholly popular" in its fundamental principle, even though it was a representative republic rather than "a pure democracy" like Athens. "In the extent and proper structure of the Union, therefore," Madison summed up, "we behold a republican remedy for the diseases most incident to republican government."[3] This secular conception of republicanism owed something to Locke, James Harrington, and Montesquieu, but much more to American experience and the need for compromises that the Convention had imposed. It resulted in a new and articulate theory of popular republicanism designed for a large country, and it self-consciously broke with the traditional precepts of European political theory with its idealization of constitutional monarchies incorporating "mixed" principles of government, or, alternatively, of small city-state democratic republics.

Madison at the Convention and in *The Federalist* relied on the multiplicity of sects to protect religious freedom. Yet in Virginia he had tirelessly fought for the statute of religious freedom that Jefferson framed in memorable phrases. Writing Madison from Paris, he was anxiously concerned about the Convention's failure to append a bill of rights. Madison replied that he feared that "the rights of conscience in particular, if submitted to public definition, would be narrowed much more than they are likely ever to be by an assumed power." Later he explained to another correspondent:

Notwithstanding the explicit provision contained in that instrument for the rights of conscience, it is well known that a religious establishment would have taken place in that state, if the legislative majority had found as they expected a majority of the people in favor of the measure; and I am persuaded that if a majority of the people were now of one sect, the measure would still take place and on narrower ground than was then proposed, notwithstanding the additional obstacle which the law [Statute of Religious Liberty] has since created.[4]

Madison was afraid that spelling out religious liberties would narrow them because he did not think a majority would hesitate to pass a general assessment bill if it had the power, no matter what Jefferson had said in his statute. But with the new government covering such a large territory there would be no need to be alarmed about the formation of such a majority. Sheer diversity would prevent such action on a national basis. Jefferson and Madison through their correspondence, however, came to believe that a declaration of rights would give political truths the character of fundamental maxims and so educate the people. A bill of rights would also furnish a text whereby both state legislatures and the federal courts could "try" the acts of the federal government. Furthermore, politics made amendments advisable. In Virginia, Patrick Henry was accusing Madison of having ceased to be a friend to religious liberty. Baptists were alarmed. Madison gave his assurance to them that he thought the First Congress should recommend a bill of rights, *"particularly the rights of conscience in the fullest latitude."*[5]

Madison carried the burden in the House of collating the suggestions of various states and factions for amendments. In this process he added one of his own, declaring that no *state* should violate the equal rights of conscience, freedom of the press, or trial by jury in criminal cases. This provision went further than any state convention had proposed, and the Senate ultimately rejected it. Whatever Madison managed to win for the rights of conscience, therefore, would apply only as a protection against actions of the federal government. Further application would come only in the twentieth century when the Supreme Court, ruling through the Fourteenth Amendment, gradually implemented Madison's idea of making certain essential rights apply as well to state governments.

Madison's Congressional proposal for religious freedom once again transcended Patrick Henry's position, as it had in the struggle for Virginia's statute of religious freedom. The Virginia ratifying convention had suggested Henry's position that no particular religious sect or society ought to be favored or established by law in preference to others. This standard did not forbid government support for religion, provided the aid did not favor any particular sect. Madison asked Congress to give a much broader guarantee: "The civil rights of none shall be abridged on account of religious belief or worship, nor shall any national religion be established, nor shall the full and equal rights of conscience be in any manner, or any pretext, abridged." This wording, given Madison's known views, obviously went beyond merely prohibiting a national church. A Connecticut member of the House challenged Madison out of fear that "a support of ministers or building of places of worship might be construed [by federal courts] into a religious establishment." Madison's reply was soothing: "He believed that the people feared one sect might obtain a preeminence, or two combine together and establish a religion to which they would compel others to conform. He thought if the word 'national' was introduced it would point the amendment directly to the object it was intended to prevent."[6]

Madison said he did not know "whether the words are necessary or not," but they had been required by some of the state conventions who feared national power. His language suggests a fairly narrow meaning to "establishment," implying enforced conformity to an orthodoxy. He withdrew his suggestion, in any case, for fear the word "national" might offend Antifederalists. At the same time the House passed a new proposal, made by Samuel Livermore of New Hampshire, which asserted that "Congress shall make no laws touching religion, or infringing the rights of conscience." This wording would appear to be as broad as any that Madison himself might wish. Livermore also supported Madison by framing a second proposal designed to prohibit *states* from "infringing the right of conscience."[7] The House accepted both resolutions. So far, Madison was winning.

Livermore himself was a staunch member of one of three Episcopalian churches in a Congregational state. The New Hampshire Constitutions of 1784 and 1791 allowed towns to tax for support of the churches, and minorities could in practice obtain their share of taxes when and if their status was recognized by the towns. This system, generally favoring Congregationalists, lasted as late as 1819, and restriction of public offices to Protestants was still hotly debated in 1876. Yet this conservative state, in its convention of 1788, called to consider the new federal Constitution, had voted under Livermore's leadership to recommend an amendment on religious freedom exactly like the sweeping one that he later proposed in Congress. New Hampshire men must have accepted such broad language because it kept Congress from "touching" religion in New Hampshire. Any sweeping separation on the state level would have affronted the vast majority in Livermore's state. (As late as 1816, a Methodist state senator in New Hampshire could get only three votes for a measure providing that no person should be compelled to make a contract for support of any church.)[8]

Livermore's radically inclusive wording of the clause limiting Congress was, however, rephrased by Representative Fisher Ames from Massachusetts to read: "Congress shall make no law establishing religion, or to prevent the free exercise thereof, or to infringe the rights of conscience." It is ironic that this wording, very close to the First Amendment itself, was proposed by a man for whom, in Emerson's phrase, "the word 'liberty' was like the word 'love' in the mouth of a courtesan." Ames was rather cynical about Madison's struggle for a bill of rights, but Madison accepted the wording anyway. The Senate was not satisfied. It threw out the Livermore proposal affecting the states, and it reduced the Ames resolution to a ban of Congressional establishment of "articles of faith or a mode of worship." The House in turn found this too narrow and proposed a conference committee with the Senate. The Senate conference committee included the Catholic Charles Carroll of Maryland, and Madison himself chaired the House committee. The House, following instructions, agreed to accept the Senatorial form of other Amendments on condition that the Senate approve the conference committee's new wording on religion: "Congress shall make no law respecting an establishment of religion or prohibiting the free exercise thereof." The Senate agreed to the condition; the deed was done.[9]

But just what *was* done in the long debate from June 8 to September 25, 1789? The word "respecting"—perhaps a broadening of meaning —had been inserted in Ames's proposal; his last clause, against "infringing the rights of conscience," had been eliminated. The rest remained. No minutes exist to show what went on in the conference committee's thinking. One thing is clear: the states were free to do whatever *their* constitutions permitted. Madison felt that he had won a victory in the bargain with the Senate. But he had lost what was to him "the most valuable Amendment in the whole list," the one limiting action by the states. He may have sweetened this disappointment by seeing more in the final Amendment than his colleagues did. He believed, in fact, that it fully incorporated his own theory of separation. No doubt "establishment" meant more than fixing a national creed. The Senate did not get House approval on that narrow meaning. On the other hand, the House had finally dropped from Madison's, Livermore's, and Ames's resolutions the prohibition against laws "infringing the rights of conscience"—perhaps a concession to those who would not go so far as to protect nonbelievers as well as believers, a guarantee that Jefferson and Madison had won in the Virginia battle. The Connecticut Representative whose objections had led to Livermore's motion had been worried that the Amendment might "patronize those who professed no religion at all."[10] It is impossible now to say just how far the balance was tipped on Madison's side of the argument. The fairest inference would be that the difficulty in getting an agreement meant that the full and precise implications of the First Amendment, respecting Congressional action in the field of religion, could *not* be spelled out if men were to come to agreement. The balance struck must have been ambiguous enough in its details to close the gap that had grown during the long hot summer of 1789.

Madison, at least, had no doubts. For him disestablishment meant no political connections whatever with religion. In 1811, as President, he vetoed a grant of land to a Baptist church on the basis that the First Amendment forbade the use of federal funds for the use and support of religious societies. He even disapproved of the appointment of chaplains to Congress. Yet he himself, before the passage of the First Amendment, had served on a committee setting rules for the election of chaplains to Congress, an inherited practice that became entrenched in American mores. Furthermore, the First Congress, which passed the Bill of Rights, voted that President Washington recommend to the people a day of thanksgiving and prayer. Though Jefferson as President scrupulously refused to do so, Madison himself later followed Washington's tradition, taking care, however, to make his Presidential proposals merely recommendatory.[11] History transforms the deeds of the makers of history. For all his heroic labors and keenness of mind, Madison did not carry the country along with Virginia's sweeping separation of churches from the state: indeed, the country in some degree carried him.

Madison was right for his foreseeable future about his original belief that libertarians could safely rely on the extent of the union and the diversity of sects to prevent any national legislation comparable to that which his enemies had proposed for Virginia in the general assessment bill. To that extent, if he *had* won a "victory" in the First Congress, he had won it where he did not really need it. And he had lost it in the states where he did need a victory if his principles were to prevail. The question of the use of the Congressional taxing power to aid religions on an equal basis would not clearly come before Americans until the nature of the religious population had dramatically changed in the twentieth century. That issue did not have to be specifically and unambiguously faced in 1789 because everyone knew that the tax power was so used only in a few states, and most people in the union as a whole did not belong to any church, however much they read the Bible or attended sermons.

The residual ambiguity of Madison's halfway victory in 1789 has one advantage for his posterity. It leaves some of the issues about the relation of disestablishment to free exercise, and of both to political power, open to debate on grounds of historic developments and present actualities, rather than upon legalistic convictions about the exact intent of the First Congress. The temptation to enlist the Founding Fathers in one's own cause is perennial and irresistible. But history sometimes has a way of refusing to give clear answers unless it is prompted. That small margin of doubt, which a scrupulous refusal to prompt reveals, can be used to foster present possibilities.

Even if Madison had won everything he wished for in principle, he would have left a legacy that contemporaries could not inherit without modification. His theory of absolute separation as a corollary of the free exercise of religion had the defect of containing a theological premise that only some religious groups can accept. In this sense his theory of separation in practice would produce the paradox of favoring churches whose traditions stress individualism and fear of the state. Evangelical Baptists and Lutherans had supported Jefferson and Madison in their struggle for separation in Virginia because both the pietists and the rationalists believed that man's relationship to God was prior to society and government. In Madison's own language: "It is the duty of every man to render the creator such homage and *such only,* as he believes to be acceptable to him; this duty is precedent, both in order of time and degree of obligation, to the claims of civil society."[12] This rationalist and evangelical theory was, however, not shared by all Americans, especially not by those Protestants belonging to religious factions that profited from close connection with the state. The Madisonian theory was at variance as well with the practice of the states, whose early reports are full of cases in which decisions of the courts assumed that Christianity was itself part of the common law inherited from England.[13]

Whatever the First Amendment was intended to mean, it could not aid religious libertarians as a check against state actions until twentieth-century justices of the Supreme Court of the United States had incorporated some of its elements into the Fourteenth Amendment, ratified in 1868, which is applicable to the states. Yet the Madisonian vision of religious liberty could influence the states insofar as men outside of Virginia were inspired by it. In Maryland, for example, a devout Scotch Presbyterian and Jeffersonian, Thomas Kennedy, stoutly battled as a legislator for eight years to provide equal political rights for Jews in the states. Six months before Jefferson's death on July 4, 1826, Kennedy's efforts to revise the restrictive state constitution came to fruition and Jews were soon elected to office. But Maryland also illustrated the tenacity of the tradition of identifying political rights with theistic religious beliefs because even its Constitution of 1867 stipulated a declaration of belief in the existence of God as a condition for officeholding, and this barrier was not removed until the Supreme Court of the United States invalidated it a century after the outbreak of the Civil War.[14] Madison's principle of religious liberty was not fully realized in Maryland until 172 years after ratification of the First Amendment.

Madison's colleagues at Philadelphia were not prepared to substitute his clear principles for the mixed pattern that prevailed in the states. They went along with him to guard against the danger that Congress in exercising some granted power, such as taxation, might meddle in religious matters; but while they set a national barrier against the possibility of discriminatory taxation on behalf of any church, they also set one against Congressional interference with local efforts to foster religious enterprises. Americans absorbed the First Amendment's clauses on separation and free exercise so that they were compatible with a dominant belief that separation was also in some ways a linkage, that liberty and Christianity were close friends, and that a federal union entitled even nonbelievers to hold office at the national level, while permitting states to restrict full political rights to Protesants. Neither pietists nor Jeffersonians could have been fully satisfied with the results. A modern Supreme Court majority would tend to forget this point when it looked backwards at the original understanding

through the eyes of the Fourteenth Amendment and with an individualistic, noninstitutional attitude toward religion that would have been
quite congenial to Madison and his evangelical supporters.

Tocqueville hit on the probable truth about a majority of the
American people in 1789 when he described "the natural state of
men" in an age of "indifference":

> But if the unbeliever does not admit religion to be true, he still considers
> it useful. Regarding religious institutions in a human point of view, he
> acknowledges their influence upon manners and legislation. He admits
> that they may serve to make men live in peace and prepare them gently
> for the hour of death. . . . On the other hand those who continue to
> believe are not afraid openly to avow their faith. . . . As they do not
> consider the society in which they live as an arena in which religion is
> bound to face its thousand deadly foes, they love their contemporaries
> while they condemn their weaknesses and lament their errors.
>
> As those who do not believe conceal their incredulity, and as those who
> believe display their faith, public opinion pronounces itself in favor of
> religion: love, support, and honor are bestowed upon it, and it is only by
> searching the human soul that we can detect the wounds it has received.[15]

Tocqueville was justified in thinking that he had found a lasting
consensus on the sensitive issue of the place of religion in relation to
the public order because the Catholic priests with whom he talked in
America were as convinced as the Protestants of the benefits of separation in contrast to European establishments. By the time of the publication of his first volume, even Massachusetts had abandoned the
policy of direct use of the tax power to support religion. The legal
diversity on this issue, which the First Amendment had comprehended
in 1789, had been narrowed. To Tocqueville it suggested the important principle that religion in America prospered because "it restricts
itself to its own resources."[16] Pietists and liberal rationalists shared this
principle, but they had not fully carried the country with them. Inevitably, church and state being actual historical institutions, their
relations could not be absolutely discriminated and controlled by clear-
cut principles. As a comparative judgment, however, in relation to
Europe or to the American Puritan past, Tocqueville's point is persuasive. For all the ambiguities that were hidden in the somewhat
enigmatic and remarkably laconic phrasing of the First Amendment's
religious guarantees, it did mark a new departure in the practical embodiment of a higher national standard of religious liberty. But the
federal nature of the union, as "a compound republic" in Madison's

terms, meant that it also confirmed a varied legacy that included Virginia republicanism and post-Puritan survivals of Protestant establishment in New England. Not until the mid-twentieth century would the question of the meaning of the settlement of 1789 regarding the religious clauses be reopened to widespread sharp and angry debate.

VII

Popular Revivals, the Art of Associating, and Majority Tyranny

Tocqueville believed that "equality of condition" leads men in two directions. Distrusting traditions and forms, men exercise a Cartesian independence of mind that trusts only in private judgment. At the same time their sense of social equality tends to expose them to an overwhelming sense of their own insignificance and weakness, in contrast with the great mass of their fellows. Consequently, faith in public opinion becomes "a species of religion, and the majority its ministering prophet." "In the principle of equality I very clearly discern two tendencies," he concluded; "one leading the mind of every man to untried thoughts, the other prohibiting him from thinking at all." Furthermore, social equality disposes each member of the community "to sever himself from the mass of his fellows and to draw apart with his family and his friends, so that after he has thus formed a little circle of his own, he willingly leaves society at large to itself." This kind of "individualism" (which he called "a novel expression" for "a novel idea") is especially prevalent, he argued, at the outset of the construction of a democratic society upon the ruins of an aristocracy.[1] The bitter feelings resulting from the class tensions of revolution nurture both a dependence upon private judgment and a social withdrawal into a small circle of family and friends.

Tocqueville in these comments was prophesying the outlines of a possible future, and the experience that suggested it to him was based not so much on his American visit as on his journeys to England and his observations of Normans under the bourgeois July Monarchy of Louis Philippe in France.[2] He carefully distinguished the case of the United States from the darker outlines of his projected future society. Model-building is a characteristically modern scientific technique, and

Tocqueville's method is sophisticated in using it. But he was also a prophet, and for him the "ideal type" was a possible and dangerous European future. In this light the American example was mainly useful because of the demonstration it provided of the variety of safeguards that could be developed against the threat of "democratic despotism" in which men withdrew from the public order into a "virtuous materialism" that sapped ambition, pride, and the common will to take social action on large problems.[3]

The Americans had protected themselves from the potential evils of social equality in several ways. Two of these were related to the role of American religion in both its passive and its active aspects. In Tocqueville's view the skeptical intellect in America was restrained by the hold of Christianity on the public mind as "a religion which is believed without discussion." If this dominance put severe limits on intellectual freedom, it also made for a moderation and stability in democracy that political institutions alone, under majority rule, could not guarantee. The Americans protected themselves from the civic indifference of "individualism" because they "carried to the highest perfection the art of pursuing in common the object of their common desires and have applied this new science to the greatest number of purposes." This talent for forming voluntary public associations was essential; without it, the feeble power of the individual in democratic society would render men helpless, dangerously vulnerable to relapse into barbarism. For this reason the Frenchman, who at first found it incredible and ridiculous that in the United States "a hundred thousand men had bound themselves publicly to abstain from spirituous liquors," concluded by finding nothing more deserving of the attention of his fellow countrymen than "the intellectual and moral associations of America." The Americans proved the truth of a general principle that "if men are to remain civilized or to become so, the art of associating together must grow and improve in the same ratio in which the equality of conditions is increased."[4]

Tocqueville visited America at a time (1831–32) when the Methodists and the Baptists were on their way to becoming the majority religions in America and by 1850 they far surpassed their nearest rival, the Presbyterians, in number of churches. Tocqueville failed to notice, however, how the process of evangelizing the frontier provided important evidence for his observations. Not only did these religious sects provide illuminating examples of voluntary associations, but they also dramatized the limitation on individual private judgment by a dogmatic Christianity that found social expression in a rigorous discipline of church members. Insofar as Methodists and Baptists shared the tendency of sects to form societies of the like-minded, they fostered as well that "tyranny of the majority" which Tocqueville originally lamented in America. During his nine-month visit he had found less "independence of mind and real freedom of discussion" in America than in any other country. These conformist tendencies were "as yet but slightly perceptible in political society"; their unfavorable influence was mainly on "the national character."[5] To offset them Tocqueville found "mitigating" influences in the power of local government, the prestige of lawyers, and the educative institution of trial by jury, but these examples show that he was thinking mainly of political causes and effects. If the effects were as yet confined to national character, however, rather than to political society, then his stress on unlimited legislative power in the states as the source of the difficulty was misplaced.

Tocqueville believed that if a legislature could be prevented from being "the slave of its passions," the executive provided with a proper share of authority, and the judiciary made independent, "a government would be formed which would still be democratic while incurring scarcely any risk of tyranny."[6] These conditions, he felt, did exist on the national level because the Founding Fathers, as Madison carefully explained in *The Federalist,* had established them. They shared the same reservations that Tocqueville felt about the omnipotence of legislatures, and they both expressed their fears in a republican spirit by preferring federalism and the separation of powers to the traditional idea of a "mixed government." Social power superior to others had to be placed somewhere, Tocqueville believed, and he accepted the coming of democratic institutions as a historical necessity. What alarmed him was that faith in public opinion would become "a species of religion."

More than he realized, it was, in fact, a species of organized religion in Jacksonian America that produced a faith in the majority as its "ministering prophet." This religious factor played its historical part in fostering in America that dialectic of private judgment and dependence upon the mass which Tocqueville saw as central to democratic society in principle. In this respect his sociological model of an egalitarian society coincided with the actual historical case of the United States. Always sensitive to the social importance of religion in the New World, he nevertheless did not clearly see how it linked "the tyranny of the majority" with his observations on the significance of voluntary associations. He had been told of three-day camp meetings of Methodists among the pioneers of Michigan; he had learned in Cincinnati that the Methodists prevailed in the Mississippi and Ohio Valleys; and he had heard in Montgomery, Alabama, that Southern religion was, because of the Methodists, more exalted and fanatical than in the North. Exploring the northern region of the Michigan Territory with his friend Gustave de Beaumont, Tocqueville had spent two weeks on the frontier, keeping account of all the types he met. "Hardly a phase of pioneering, hardly a significant aspect of the westward movement escaped their attention," as the historian of his journey has said; "inn-keepers, farmers, fur-traders, half-breed hunters, and full blooded Indians: all were encountered by the two friends, and their appearance in this habitat vividly described. Only the circuit-riding Methodist is missing."[7] It was a near miss.

The Scotch-Irish Presbyterian James McCready, with three congregations on the Gaspar, Red, and Muddy Rivers, inaugurated the mass revivals of the second Great Awakening at the turn of the century in the frontier region of Kentucky and Tennessee. From there the revivals spread to the Western Reserve, Georgia, and the Carolinas; to Virginia, Maryland, Delaware, and Pennsylvania; and on to New York, New England, and even Canada. In the first few years of the great camp meetings Presbyterians, Methodists, and Baptists united in a common effort to reap the harvest of converted souls, but sectarian rivalry was too strong for this ecumenical effort to survive. By 1825 the camp meeting itself had become virtually an exclusively Methodist technique, though never officially acknowledged or supervised by the central governing body of the church. Methodist revivalism fitted the circumstances of frontier life in doctrine, organization, and technique. Itinerant preachers, drawn from the rank and file but selected and regulated by the central administration, spread the gospel of experienced grace and zealous moral endeavor into the backwoods settlements. In Methodist theology man was dependent upon God's grace, but He made it continuously possible for sinful men to respond to the call by making the decision for faith whereby they might become redeemed through God's recognition of their growth toward perfection through the discipline of their new life. The hard-pressed, self-educated circuit rider, traveling on horseback for a month or more to cover his territory, preaching a sermon a day for a mere hundred dollars a year, often sick and the butt of frontier toughs, was the hero of this movement, which consumed many of its evangelists after a dozen years of such punishing work. A frontier saying summed it up in terse eloquence: "There is nothing out today but crows and Methodist preachers."

In the camp meeting frontier religion found its characteristic expression. Gathered in homemade tents, for several days thousands of families would eat, drink, sing, shout, pray, and cry together. Seated on rude benches in front of the platform built for a battery of preachers, the frontiersmen were convicted of their sins, warned "to flee from the wrath to come," and exhorted to pray for the anxious souls who sat on the "mourners' benches" awaiting their second birth in the crisis of conversion. Hucksters pitched their wares at the sidelines; whiskey poured from the smuggled-in kegs, where the toughs who had come to jeer guzzled freely, fought, or found a woman. Respectable girls and their swains courted as they could; sometimes sexual and religious anxiety nourished each other as hysterical women tore open their blouses in their excitement and fell into erotic postures; and often hundreds of pioneers fell stricken to the ground, jerked spastically, or even barked like dogs in their agony.

> Sinners through the camp are falling;
> Deep distress their souls pervade
> Wondr'ring why they are not rolling
> In the dark infernal shade.[8]

The Negroes with their own tents, benches, and preachers, segregated as usual, added their singing and clapping to the din. Flickering fires at night, thunderstorms, even earthquakes gave a theatrical support to the frontiersman's superstitious susceptibility, and the ritual of mass joining of hands linked people together in warm fellowship and mutual defiance of the hazards, the rigors, and the monotony of frontier life. It was a jamboree and an awesome rite, a family picnic and a religious crisis, one community under God, temporarily indivisible, with free will and heavenly justice for all.

As it became institutionalized and moved eastward, the camp meeting naturally became more sedate, more regulated, more conventional. But even in its earlier more barbaric style, the meeting was the prelude to a commitment, not merely a temporary release of tension. Methodists put converted souls on probation for months before their full acceptance into the church, and the Methodist discipline itself was a system of mutual surveillance and watchfulness much like that practiced by the early seventeenth-century Puritans. All growing sects of this period—Presbyterian, Baptist, and Quaker as well as Methodist—took membership seriously as a way of life, enforced by marrying within the faith and by trials for breach of discipline. The Elkhorn Baptist Association of forty churches, for example, expelled 183 out of 2,442 members in 1803 for breach of discipline.[9] The sinner could suffer organized condemnation not only for drunkenness, lechery, gambling, swearing, or fighting, but also for abusing his power or neglecting his duties regarding his family, property, or trade, as well as in his church affairs. If the crisis of conversion was experienced collectively in the camp meeting, so also the regenerate's commitment was to a collectively regulated individual and social discipline. "Each one seemed to be the insurer of the other's reputation," wrote an early Methodist, "and felt himself as responsible for his upright character as though he was his special guardian; hence, everything that indicated, in the slightest degree, a departure from the path of holy rectitude, would at once awaken the liveliest apprehensions and interest on the part of the rest."[10]

The frontier was not the legendary school of individualism but the actual setting for a mass religious experience and a community morality. The anxious soul on the mourner's bench was submitting his inner self to the scrutiny of the others who prayed for him; and when he found relief in decision it was in the submission of his inner self and social behavior not only to God but to His believers and their way of life. This submission contained within it the Puritan paradox of a calling that prescribed diligence and individualistic striving for self-control and self-betterment within a setting that established social as well as religious meaning for the individual's efforts. "Their inner direction, in short," as a recent sociological student of Protestant pioneers has observed, "was partly (and only partly) conformity to peer control."[11]

Nothing could be a better example of Tocqueville's paradox of social equality with its double tendency toward private judgment and dependence upon the mass. The Methodist sinner was fiercely democratic. Circuit riders were told by the *Discipline:* "Do not affect the gentleman. You have no more to do with that character than a dancing master. A preacher of the gospel is the servant of all." The strength of the circuit rider lay in his own closeness to the folk he served, and neither Baptists nor Methodists had any use for theological training of ministers, a refinement they scorned for its aristocratic implications.

At the same time preachers exhorted their flocks: "Go work in God's vineyard. *Go work today*. To postpone is ruin, to neglect is death."[12] This emphasis on works, which Benjamin Franklin so familiarly linked with skeptical deism and worldly success, was joined in the Methodist mind with evangelical enthusiasm and the discipline of the church. Franklin's utilitarian ethical temper and practical humanitarianism illustrated Tocqueville's point that the Americans followed the principle of "self-interest rightly understood"—that is, "an enlightened regard for themselves constantly prompts them to assist one another." In this way Americans become disciplined "in habits of regularity, temperance, moderation, foresight, self-command; and if it does not lead men straight to virtue by the will, it gradually draws him in that direction by their habits."[13] This latter-day secularized Puritanism was characteristic of the middle-class men of the East, but Tocqueville did not appreciate the force of the evangelical spirit of the calling on the less established classes in the newer states and frontier territories. Baptists and Methodists in the early nineteenth century exhibited, indeed, many of the characteristics of what twentieth-century people think of as the emotional religion of lower-class Negroes in store-front churches, as dramatized by James Baldwin in *Go Tell It on the Mountain*.

Frontier religion was also inclined to a petty moralistic exaggeration of trivial pleasures into major sins, but seen in their actual setting some of these indulgences were barbarous traits of a bellicose people that swilled whiskey in staggering quantities. If Methodist discipline was repressive, it was partly because it had so much raw vitality to civilize. Although aggressively anti-intellectual in its preference for a self-taught lay ministry (in contrast to the Wesleys' own learning and artistic interests), it did after 1830 support private and public colleges and universities. By 1860, Methodists had founded thirty-four permanent colleges, second in number only to the Presbyterians, who traditionally trained a scholarly ministry.[14] Peter Cartwright, a hardy self-taught circuit rider from the age of eighteen and a presiding elder at twenty-three, bitterly condemned divinity-school trained ministers, but as a member of the Illinois legislature, he introduced the first bill for the establishment of a state college and later helped found two Methodist colleges. With their widely circulating religious newspapers and book sales the Methodists were agencies of literacy to an undeveloped people, and it is no anomaly that one of the leading founders of the Chautauqua organization in 1874 was a Methodist bishop.[15]

Yet the camp meeting itself was, in part, a compensation for the aesthetic starvation that popular Protestantism itself accentuated by its hostility to all forms of art except gospel songs. In this sense Methodism's major technique for successful growth was made necessary by needs that its own rigid moralism aggravated. The excesses of some of the more hysterical scenes in the early days testify to a desperately needed outlet for emotional excitement. In England, much less democratic and much richer in social rituals of all kinds, the camp-meeting technique never won acceptance. When Lorenzo Dow tried to establish it there with the help of two English Methodists, they were expelled for their pains in promoting such "highly improper" activities.[16]

Social equality in America, however, was sharply limited by racial prejudices. The frontiersman, knowing that his soul was equal before God with any graduate of an Eastern theological school, knew just as well that he was better than Indians and Negroes. The test of the power of Protestant Christianity on public issues involving despised minorities was the fate of the Indian and the slave. Dedicated Baptists, Methodists, and the American Board of Commissioners for Foreign Missions (Congregational and Presbyterian) had set up missions in Cherokee country, exchanging schooling of children for the privilege of preaching the faith. Both of the leading native chiefs were active Protestant converts. Samuel Worcester, a missionary from the American Board, learned the syllabary that Sequoia had invented for the Cherokees as an aid to spreading literacy, and set up a press to print the Bible and the Indian constitution in the Cherokee national newspaper. He worked with Elias Boudinot, a full-blooded Indian educated at Andover Theological Seminary and in Litchfield, Connecticut, where he had scandalized the pious community by marrying a white woman. But Georgia had ceded its public lands to the federal government on the premise that in time the Indians would be removed. Senator Theodore Frelinghuysen of New Jersey, a member of the Bible, Tract, Sunday School, Temperance, and Foreign Missions societies, demonstrated to the Senate for six hours his extraordinary powers of eloquence on behalf of the Cherokees, and the secretary of the American Board, Jeremiah Evarts, so powerfully established their legal case, determined by treaties with the United States, that Chief Justice John Marshall himself gave it the accolade of being "the most conclusive argument he had ever read on any subject whatever."[17]

Harassed by Georgia laws drafted to get them out, the missionaries who had publicly defended the Cherokees were arrested and offered the choice of an oath of allegiance to the state or prison. Worcester chose prison. The Supreme Court, stonily ignored by President Jackson, upheld the Indian claims without effect. The American Board, under pressure not to aggravate the Southern nullification crisis, persuaded Worcester to accept a pardon in 1833. By now Boudinot, disillusioned with the prospects of federal help, recommended parleying for removal, thus opening himself to the charge of treason to his people.[18] In the winter of 1838–39 most of the Cherokees were forced to migrate to Oklahoma under Army escort, with a fourth dying on the way. The whole missionary program east of the Mississippi was sabotaged by land-hungry states. Even Isaac McCoy, a Baptist missionary who had effectively worked with Indians in Michigan, supported this tragic expropriation of tribes rapidly progressing in educational development.

But missionary enthusiasm for converting Indians was doomed to founder anyway on the unrealistic assumption that Protestant metaphysics, ethics, and social values were universal truths, which enlightened Indians would embrace once they had been shown the light of the gospel. What the missionaries might have done, despite their anthropological innocence, was to prevent Indian removal, but on that issue they were divided and undone by their own assumptions of cultural superiority, which political men believed with unhesitating ruthlessness.

Frontier religion was not powerful enough to mold the culture on racial issues to a higher standard, for all the efforts of individual preachers. Only the Quakers made antislavery testimony a disciplinary requirement. Methodist deacons could be Negroes, in principle, and itinerants were forbidden to marry slaveholders, but Southern Methodists, bending to the pressure of their culture, expressed gratitude to Peter Cartwright for bettering the commercial value of their servants by curing them of the habits of getting drunk, stealing, and breaking the Sabbath.[19] Soul-saving by preachers was also money-saving for masters, and admitting the Negroes into segregated galleries of white churches was also a prudent way to keep their religious enthusiasm within safe bounds, especially after slave rebellions had struck fear in the masters' souls. The forming of Negro churches was therefore often the result of resentment against this paternalistic integration. The division of the races into distinct churches and conferences showed itself among Baptists and Methodists at a much earlier date than among Presbyterians and Episcopalians, even though Baptists were readier than any other group to extend the privilege of ordination to colored

preachers. It was always possible for the churches to persuade themselves that in order to bring their missionary message to the Negro soul
they had to conciliate slaveholders. Evangelicals could argue further,
in Lutheran style, that the highest freedom was from sin and the worst
slavery was bondage to lust, regardless of the social condition of men.[20]
Just as they passionately believed in separating church from state, the
evangelicals could by analogy expediently separate their religion from
the larger society.

Yet Western evangelicals felt strong party ties. The Methodist *Western Christian Advocate* counseled those planning to attend an annual
conference camp meeting in 1839:

Should we at table spend twenty minutes in discussing the merits of Van
Buren, Clay, and Harrison, and their claims to the presidency, or in debating the comparative viciousness of "Whiggism" or "loco Focoism"
would any good result from it? For Christ's sake let us avoid these themes,
and not introduce them among people who seek our society, not to reform
their politics, but to save their souls.[21]

The advice was necessary because camp-meeting attenders were, in
fact, inclined to link their religion and their politics. Baptists and Methodists alike were more likely to be drawn to the party of Jackson out
of an affinity for the gospel of the common man in both politics and
religion. At a Democratic convention in Illinois in 1860, Cartwright
joked, "I have waged an incessant warfare against the world, the flesh,
and the devil and all other enemies of the Democratic party."[22]

By encouraging popular participation in religious organizational life,
the evangelical sects were training grounds for popular participation in
the organizational work of politics that Jacksonians invited.[23] A man
who had learned to speak his faith before others could also learn to
voice his politics in public. The "Jacksonian persuasion," with its ideological contrast between the "productive" hardworking humble people
who labored by the sweat of their brow, in contrast to those who derived their profits from a "speculative" economy, overlapped the evangelical code of simplicity and plainness for true believers. Jacksonians
believed that no specialized intellectual training made men fit for being the people's representatives, and evangelicals made the same assumption about their own ministry. If General Jackson harbored no
love for Indians or Negroes, his prejudices were widely shared on
the frontier in the South and West. If the Jacksonians were in fact
more deeply attracted by speculative practices and the temptations of

an expanding capitalism than their ideology would suggest, so also the evangelicals' morality cultivated a work ethic that advised men to better themselves through diligent application to the business of their calling. Like Jefferson, the Jacksonians were also strong defenders of separation between church and state, a position that had demonstrated its appeal for Baptists and Methodists in the Virginia struggle over the establishment. Furthermore, the Federalists and Whigs who opposed Jefferson and Jackson were often closely linked with the old Standing Order in New England. It is an old political rule that "the enemy of my enemies is my friend."

One of the best illustrations of the connection between popular Western religion and the politics of Jacksonianism is the religious revival, led by the Baptists, that flared up in Kentucky as the panic of 1819 hit the region. A meeting was called in Frankfort, as in other places all over Kentucky, to deal with the despair of the people. Held in a church, the assembled penitents confessed to "extravagant importation and consumption of foreign luxuries" as well as to "extravagant speculations." The banks, they charged, had tempted them to this acquisitiveness, particularly the national Bank of the United States. Pledging themselves to frugality and industry, they demanded that the banks suspend specie payment and issue moderate amounts of paper money to ease the currency shortage. Furthermore, the legislature should be convened in special session to pass stay laws for debtor relief. The Baptist preacher who chaired the meeting was a close friend of Richard M. Johnson, later a popular Jacksonian Senator and Vice-Presidential candidate for the Democrats in 1836. Johnson earned his candidacy by his spirited defense in 1829 of complete separation between church and state in opposition to those Puritan Protestants who urged halting the transportation of the mails on Sunday, and the Congressional reports on the same theme were written by a Baptist preacher. Johnson himself was a country Baptist who had promoted and subscribed to a new branch of the Bank of the United States and borrowed heavily from its parent, plunging himself into a morass of disastrous business schemes. In debt and out of favor with the prominent bankers, he turned to the people at large for support by promoting the Kentucky Relief Party and later joined in the ill-conceived Jacksonian assault on that "monster," the Bank of the United States.[24] The ambivalence in the evangelical doctrine of the calling between economic self-advancement and social discipline overlapped the Jacksonian ambiguity that embraced eager participation in a burgeoning capitalism and a guilt-stricken nostalgia for the simplicities of Jeffersonian principles.

Jacksonian ideologues were usually Jeffersonian rationalists rather than evangelical pietists, but the power of the alliance between pietists and rationalists had already proved itself in American politics. Both groups had a fear of strong central government linked in Hamiltonian style with the interests of an economic and social elite. Statistics cannot prove the connection between evangelical popular Protestantism and politics, but they are at least suggestive. By 1850 there were more Methodist churches than any other in twenty of the thirty states. Not even the Baptists came anywhere near them. All fourteen of the states that gave popular majorities to both of Jackson's administrations were in this Methodist group, except for Georgia and Missouri, where the Baptists by 1850 had the largest number of churches. Delaware and Maryland, also in the Methodist group, voted against Jackson only by the narrowest of margins. In the states that gave large majorities to Jackson's opponents in both presidential elections (Massachusetts, Connecticut, Vermont), the Congregationalists, legatees of Puritan establishment, still had the largest number of churches in 1850.[25] These figures suggest a resonance between religious and political identities.

Tocqueville believed that social equality led men to "seek for the sources of truth in themselves or in those who are like themselves."[26] This point has direct relevance to the Methodist conquest of the frontier through the camp-meeting experience of the sinner's discovery of his own self-transformation before the eyes of his fellow pioneers. In milder form the same process was at work in the East, particularly in Oneida County, New York, where migratory Yankees also experienced uncertainty and displacement. Here Charles G. Finney played the important role of institutionalizing the revival for the business and professional classes. His career provides a window on the process by which traditional Calvinism was transformed into a much less intellectual and much more optimistic and complacent religion, cut to fit the figure of his audience. As a result, old connections between revivalist religion and Democratic politicians were rubbed out.

Born a Connecticut Yankee and named for the hero of a sentimental novel, Charles Grandison Finney was the spokesman for a sentimental religion in a sentimental age, the most successful winner of souls north of the Ohio and the Potomac, a public figure as vivid as Daniel Webster. As a young lawyer in Utica, New York, Finney played the cello and sang in a Presbyterian church choir, occasionally enjoying an argument with his minister, whose doctrines puzzled him. Surely, Finney felt, faith lay in one's own power, not God's. In 1821, after praying in the woods, Finney returned to his law office and dissolved into tears, feeling the Holy Spirit descend upon him, "like a wave of electricity . . . waves and waves of liquid love." He wept aloud "the unutterable gushings" of his heart; overflowing, he carried the good news to his neighbors in an orgy of prayer and fasting.[27] Local ministers offered to pay his way to Princeton for theological training, but Finney wanted none of it. His power in making converts was, however, too great an asset to be neglected; the Presbyterians suppressed their qualms and licensed him to preach. In 1824 the Female Missionary Society of the Western District in New York commissioned this imposing man, over six feet tall with the eyes of a stage hypnotist and the timing of an actor, to spread the good tidings.

Finney came on the scene when revivalism was already a thundering success on the frontier and a commonplace of Eastern college life. In the East the revival technique was now a conservative instrument. Jonathan Edwards's grandson Timothy Dwight had turned Yale College into an engine of reaction primed to fire on deism, infidelity, Jefferson, and the French Revolution, with sedate revivals as the major weapon. The ministry was an escape from the farm for Lyman Beecher, who fell under Dwight's spell. The new conservative political uses of revival preaching were illustrated by the fact that Beecher made his reputation by prophesying God's terrible vengeance for the sin of dueling, which had recently led the Jeffersonian Aaron Burr to kill the Federalist Alexander Hamilton. Burr was of evangelical Calvinist background, son and namesake of Edwards's predecessor as president of the College of New Jersey; his victim was a deistical skeptic. But Hamilton believed that Christianity had conservative political uses for controlling the lower classes, and heirs of the Puritans agreed with him, particularly when they benefited from legal establishment. In Litchfield, Connecticut, Beecher turned to revivalism as a tactic in the fight to preserve the Congregational establishment. Called to Boston in 1826, Beecher found the Unitarians fashionable in educated society. Their growth was spurred by a state court decision that gave parishes of Unitarian believers legal control of churches whose small core of members were Congregationalists. Beecher began "inquiry" meetings with assistants to probe the souls of the doubtful so that he might individually direct his own muscular preaching at them and save them from defection to Unitarianism.

The rigor of the old Calvinism that Edwards had preached was giving way to a more accommodating system that softened the idea of man's dependence upon a totally sovereign God who elected whomever he pleased without reference to human striving. At Yale, Nathaniel W. Taylor was Dwight Professor of Didactic Theology in the Divinity School from 1822 to 1857. Taylor was convinced that Edwards's theology was defective in his treatment of moral agency and free will. In *Man, A Free Agent without the Aids of Divine Grace* Taylor maintained that the very meaning of sin depended upon man's natural capacity for freedom of choice. Certainly men *would* sin: "The very birth of a human being is an event which involves the certainty of entire moral depravity, without the supernatural interposition of God to prevent it." But infants *could* not sin until they became moral agents, whenever that might be. Preaching to the Connecticut clergy in Yale Chapel in 1828, he redefined Calvinism and exhorted his audience to "throw all the guilt of sin with its desert of wrath, upon the sinner's single self. Let us make him see and feel that he can go to hell only as a self-destroyer."[28] This doctrine, considered by some Calvinists to be a betrayal of Edwards, provided a theological basis for restless men like Lyman Beecher, who were doers rather than thinkers. The occasion was made ripe for Finney.

Finney brought to the East the Western techniques of protracted meetings and the "anxious seat," a lawyer's capacity to speak to professional men, and an indifference to the subtleties of theological issues. So armed, he made Calvinism over in a style borrowed from Methodists to suit the temper of his audience. In his *Lectures on Revivals of Religion,* a training manual on how to organize a revival, Finney defended his variation from the old Calvinists:

When I entered the ministry, there had been so much said about the doctrine of election and sovereignty, that I found it was the universal hiding place, both of sinners and of the church, that they could not do anything, or could not obey the gospel. And wherever I went, I found it indispensable to demolish these refuges of lies. And a revival would in no way be produced or carried on, but by dwelling on that class of truths, which hold up man's ability, and obligation, and responsibility. This was the only class of truths that would bring sinners to submission.

It was not so in the days when President Edwards and Whitefield labored. Then the churches in New England had enjoyed little else than Arminian preaching, and were all resting in themselves and their own strength. These bold and devoted servants of God came out and declared these particular doctrines of grace, Divine Sovereignty, and election, and they were greatly blessed. . . . And they dwelt on them so long, that the church and the world got intrenched behind them, waiting for God to come and do what he required *them* to do, and so revivals ceased for many years.[29]

Finney's explanation betrays his expediency. A new emphasis was needed for a new situation, and the price of that change was the shucking off of doctrinal distinctions in theology: "All ministers should be revival ministers and all preaching should be revival preaching; that is, it should be calculated to promote holiness." But who then would indoctrinate the church? "Strange! Do they not know that a revival indoctrinates the church faster than any thing else? And a minister will never produce a revival, if he does not indoctrinate his hearers." Now, however, the doctrine was the technique; the technique, the doctrine. Conversion was neither a protracted agony nor a discipline: "Some of the best Christians of my acquaintance were convicted and converted in the space of a few minutes."[30] Finney dealt in a product that a modern public-relations man might call "instant Calvinism, easy to take, just shake before using."

The New England establishment fought Finney at first, sensing in his preaching an appeal to popular feeling which might be as subversive of the Standing Order as Methodists and Baptists had proved to be. But just as the Whigs learned to steal Jacksonian thunder by associating their candidates rhetorically with log cabins, as opposed to the alleged silver spoons of their opponents, so also did the Congregationalists and Presbyterians confer with Finney and finally join him. By 1832 Lyman Beecher was defending Finney as an exemplar of Nathaniel Taylor's "New Divinity" at Yale. Beecher soon went west to become president of Lane Theological Seminary in Cincinnati, where "Old Light" Presbyterians filed charges of heresy against him for his abandonment of the doctrines of human depravity and inability. Beecher emerged unscathed by talking out of both sides of his mouth, asserting with unblushing casuistry that original sin was "involuntary," but yet did not "force the will" to evil, though it descended from Adam "by natural generation, through all the race."[31] The line between the traditional Calvinism and the New Divinity was smudged by putting new views in a language that smacked of traditional doctrines.

Finney believed that he "had a right to expect the Holy Spirit to cooperate with us" by granting grace. A persisting skeptic was merely a hardhearted good-for-nothing who had the temerity to defy Heaven and the preacher's will. Any doubting Thomas must have been horrified at this clear sign of his own stubborn malignancy, proof of the very charges which the preacher, with blazing eyes and a rough tongue, drew up against him. Doubtful souls were singled out by name so that all the congregation could fasten their attention on God's hardened enemy and "break him down" to contriteness. But even Finney could not engineer revivals indefinitely. By 1828 one of his most influential converts, Theodore Weld, wrote him that his revivals had become "matters of such everyday commonness as scarcely to throw over you the least tinge of solemnity."[32] After a brief pastorate in New York City, Finney gave his lectures on the methodology of revivals and followed Beecher west to become president of Oberlin College.

It is impossible to determine how many converts Eastern revivals actually made, but it is likely that those most attracted were those who, like Finney himself, had already come under the influence of the churches. Many must have attended for the satisfaction of watching others go through the same process that had affected them, reconfirming them in the rightness of their own membership. The whole emphasis of the preachers was on the easiness of conversion if the sinner only responded to the assaults of their preaching. Theological discipline was eroded to a point that washed away all intellectual barriers to acceptance. Little was left of traditional Calvinism except the conventionally thrilling imagery of the burning lake of hell. The individual sins which preachers condemned were reassuringly familiar and minor indulgences—smoking, drinking, gambling, dancing, fashionable dress, theatergoing, and novel reading. There was nothing in their sermons to disturb small-town Puritanism. After 1830, Lane Seminary and Oberlin College would become hotbeds of abolitionism, but Finney segregated his churches and never made slavery the basic issue of his sermons. His audiences were respectable citizens, and the convert could feel that he was joining them in a socially acceptable way.

Revivalism had become an institutionalized technique. It had obvious tactical purposes at a time when the days of the politically privileged Standing Order were numbered. Baptists and Jeffersonians suc-

ceeded in separating church and state in Connecticut by 1818, in
New Hampshire by 1819, and in Massachusetts by 1833. This political
change put all churches on an equal footing whereby they had to support themselves without the aid of compulsory taxation. Voluntarism
in religion was necessary, and Finney's style of religion was ideally
designed to suit the case. Lyman Beecher finally reconciled himself to
this shift in the status of religious groups by concluding that "by voluntary efforts, societies, missions, and revivals, they exert a deeper
influence than ever they could by queues, and shoe-buckles, and cocked
hats, and gold-headed canes."[33] The old churches had now come to
accept the standing that the Baptists, Methodists, and Unitarians demanded as a matter of principle.

Revivalism in the Puritan churches of New England in the second
Great Awakening had begun as a defensive alliance of Federalists and
the established clergy against deism, Jeffersonianism, and the French
Revolution. It ended by dragging its converts, if not kicking and
screaming, then sighing and weeping, carried along by Finney's "waves
and waves of liquid love," into the voluntaristic pattern of a new age.
Latter-day Puritans were not Jacksonians; indeed, the Yankee counties of western New York, where Finney first made his mark as a
reaper of souls, was a strong Whig area. The Presbyterian revivalist
Albert Barnes of New Jersey, who believed that evangelical techniques
exactly suited "the active, hardy, mighty enterprise of the nation,"
found in the response of merchants in 1840 to "Tippecanoe and Tyler
too" a vibrating of hearts "with a common emotion from Bangor to
New Orleans." Why should there not be, he asked, "as deep common
feeling on the subject of religion?" Finney's lawyerlike, respectable,
and nontheological pietism easily blended with regional, ethnic, class,
and party loyalties. The linkage of patriotism and Christianity (which
Tocqueville had noted) was a favorite Whig ideal, and it might be
voiced even by rationalistic lawyers who had no trace of Finney's style
of piety. A case in point is Chancellor James Kent of New York. In
The People v. *Ruggles* (1811) Chief Justice Kent, a skeptical Whig
who believed in religion only as a restraint on others, upheld a stiff
fine against the blasphemous utterance of the barfly Ruggles on the
ground that the common law protected Christianity: "The people of
this State, in common with the people of this country, profess the general doctrines of Christianity. . . ."[34]

The formerly Puritan churches were committed to a traditional
moral stewardship over the Yankee emigrants to the newer states, and

they found in revivalism a new technique for executing their conservative mission as heirs of the old established order. The American movement for home missions, Bible and tract societies, and the Sunday school paralleled the British evangelical alliance of merchants, bankers, and members of Parliament. In the years between 1780 and 1830 they had practiced philanthropy and moral surveillance of the community in order to counteract the secular revolutionary rationalism that had marked the French Revolution. British moral leaders, like William Wilberforce and Hannah More, were well known to their American counterparts, who freely borrowed their tractarian techniques. British evangelicals hoped to humanize the poor, and keep them in their place at the same time, by sending representatives of the middle and upper classes among them to distribute Bibles and improving tales to teach the lessons of conversion, benevolence, and contentment. By 1816 a "united front" of American evangelicals, especially from the Presbyterian and Congregational churches, was launched to bring merchants, bankers, and clergy together in a national effort to make sentimental Protestantism the cultural law of the land before "superstitious" Catholics and frontier "barbarians" had corrupted a vulnerable people.

By 1834 a convention in New York City of these heirs of the old established churches had so perfected their talents for organization that they could schedule meetings of twenty-two societies in one five-day period as a feast for the morally strenuous. Baptists and Methodists were hard pressed to compete with this potent combination of social prestige, financial power, and organizational skill. "What is the church, but the collective body of Christ's disciples?" asked a new-style Presbyterian. "And what the conscience and faith of the church, but the conscience and faith of her individual members? What then are the duties of the church, but the duties of the individuals who constitute it?"[35] This voluntarism, which so impressed Tocqueville on his visit to America, was a threat to those churchmen who wished to preserve tighter clerical control of laymen, traditional discipline, and revered doctrine, but it had the future on its side. Out of this lay and clerical alliance emerged the teetotalist "temperance" movement that gave so many pious Americans a strong taste for intemperate moralizing and good works.

The humanitarian crusaders in the Jacksonian era characteristically came from this milieu of Sunday-school teachers, ministers, and missionaries. They discovered and attacked certain social evils, whether the condition of the deaf and dumb, the insane, and the blind, or the vices of liquor, prostitution, and slavery, with a transforming concern much like that of "convicted" souls who had experienced conversion. It was boasted that the American found his substitute for the arts and sciences of Europe in such practical philanthropic activities. *"Those* would indeed make our country a theater of wonders, to the eye of taste and science," one reformer proudly explained in 1829; "but *these* have dedicated her to the service and glory of God."³⁶

Thoreau saw the connection between religion and philanthropy when he scorned the churches and announced that "he would not go into doing-good because the profession was over-crowded." The energy with which Thoreau and Emerson attacked the conformity and the philanthropy of their day is itself indirect evidence of the force of popular Protestantism in forming a social character attuned to group-mindedness and good works. "Repentance is not a free and fair highway to God," Thoreau protested in his journal. "A wise man will dispense with repentance. It is shocking and passionate. God prefers that you approach him thoughtful, not penitent, though you are the chief of sinners." Emerson's great essay "Self-Reliance" was a sharp thrust against the popular religion of his day: "I tell thee, thou foolish philanthropist, that I grudge the dollar, the dime, and cent I give to such men as do not belong to me and to whom I do not belong." He would go to prison if need be for those with whom he felt some spiritual affinity, "but your miscellaneous popular charities; the education at college of fools; the building of meetinghouses to the vain end to which many stand; alms to sects, and the thousand-fold Relief Societies;—though I confess with shame I sometimes succumb and give the dollar, it is a wicked dollar, which by and by I shall have the manhood to withhold."³⁷ To defend individualism the Transcendentalists spoke in their own religious language against the conformity that popular Christianity engendered.

The political context of this conflict was dramatized by the five trials of Abner Kneeland for blasphemy in Massachusetts, a showdown between the village atheist and the pillars of the community that Sinclair Lewis would have relished. Samuel Gridley Howe, a leading humanitarian reformer, friend of liberal revolutions abroad, and director of the New England Asylum for the Blind, publicly sounded the alarm about the fiery rationalist views of Kneeland, who lectured thousands in Boston's Federal Street Theatre and published gibes against the clergy and the rich, as well as bench and bar. To save the Commonwealth from this reincarnation of Tom Paine, Howe published an article in the *New England Magazine* for 1834–35 exposing this "hoary-headed apostle of Satan" who subverted the state with his heretical opinions on religion, property, marriage, and contraception. Indicted for publishing irreverent jests against the Immaculate Conception and prayer, while affirming his own disbelief in the Universalists' faith in God, Christ, miracles, and immortality, Kneeland was charged with violation of a statute against blasphemy. The law was as recent as 1782, yet the Puritan punishments of pillory and whipping were still provided as possible penalties. Enemies of Kneeland were convinced that those who attended "the Infidel orgies" at the Federal Street Theatre doubly damned themselves by being loyal Jackson men as well. Appropriately enough, a high-ranking member of the state's Democratic Party represented Kneeland before a succession of Whig judges, who were easily intoxicated by this potent brew of atheism, Democrats, and sex.

David Henshaw, boss of the Democratic Party in Massachusetts, took up public defense of Kneeland as a matter of liberty of conscience and freedom of the press. Appealing his conviction to the state Supreme Court, Kneeland assumed the burden of his own defense, pointing out that the obscenity charged was a quotation from Voltaire, that his own "atheism" was really pantheism, and that the blasphemy statute was an unconstitutional invasion of the state's Declaration of Rights. Chief Justice Shaw, a conservative Unitarian and Whig, disregarded these arguments and accepted the previous verdict as proved. As for the Constitutional issue, he leaned on Chancellor Kent's earlier decision that blasphemy was a crime at common law. The one judge who dissented from Shaw's opinion was Marcus Morton, the only Jacksonian on the bench, a man strongly committed to Jefferson's principle of religious liberty as a protection for disbelief as well as for varieties of belief. Certainly Kneeland should not be punished, Morton argued, merely for *"wilfully"* doing what he has a legal right to do."

During the delay of judgment on the verdict, the liberal Unitarian and Transcendentalist Theodore Parker wrote a friend that Abner, "jugged for sixty days," would come out "as beer from a bottle, all foaming, and will make others foam. . . . The charm of all is that Abner got Emerson's address to the students [the Divinity School Address], and read it to his followers, as better infidelity than he could write himself."[38] Liberal Unitarians, Transcendentalists, and Baptists rallied to Kneeland's defense with a petition to the governor for pardon on the ground that religion needed no support from penal law. The document bore the names of William Ellery Channing, Theodore Parker, Emerson, Bronson Alcott, William Lloyd Garrison, and other intellectuals of the Bay State, but it had no effect on the governor, Edward Everett, a conservative Unitarian Whig and rival in four elections to Marcus Morton. Politics and religion combined to give more weight to the counterpetition from Massachusetts clergymen. Kneeland served his time and went west to found an unsuccessful utopian community.

What he had proved without realizing it was the truth of Tocqueville's point that in America Christianity was accepted without discussion or inquiry as "an established and irresistible fact." He who would challenge it would find that he had set himself against the massed opinion of the community. Religion in America was mingled with "all the habits of the nation and all the feelings of patriotism, whence it derives a peculiar force." While egalitarian passions moved men to condemn religious forms as "useless and inconvenient veils placed between them and the truth," this activity of "individual analysis" was restrained "within narrow limits" by the immense social pressure of Christianity. Emerson himself discovered these limits when, having found the Lord's Supper a hollow rite he could no longer perform with good conscience, he left his Unitarian Church. Addressing the faculty at the Harvard Divinity School in 1838, he scandalized them with his attack on miracles, historic revelation, and subordination to Christ. The churches, he charged, were conventional: "The village blasphemer sees fear in the face, form, and gait of the minister." Even Emerson's tone, more religiously serious than that of his opponents, did not save him from the Biblical scholar Andrews Norton's charge of preaching "the latest form of infidelity." He was not invited back to the Divinity School for some thirty years.[39]

Tocqueville was impressed with the advantages of the public favor that Christianity enjoyed in America; it saved democratic man from an unrestrained pursuit of private judgment that would "keep his mind in perpetual unrest" and so "prevent him from penetrating to the depth of any truth or of making his mind adhere firmly to any conviction." Ready-made opinions were to this extent "a salutary servitude" because they enabled men "to make a good use of freedom." In this way Christianity in the United States held sway as "a commonly received opinion." But in view of the natural power of public opinion in a democratic country, augmented by the political power of the majority, Tocqueville feared that in the future intellectual authority "may readily acquire too much preponderance and confine the action of private judgment within narrower limits than are suited to either the greatness or the happiness of the human race." Yet, on balance, Tocqueville felt that America had solved the problem well by limiting the scope of religion's influence through disestablishment, by having a minimum of ecclesiastical "forms, figures, and observances," and by producing preachers who, "while they never cease to point to the other world as the great object of the hopes and fears of the believer, do not forbid him honestly to court prosperity in this." In this respect all the Christians in America "look upon their religion in the same light":

All the American clergy know and respect the intellectual supremacy exercised by the majority; they never sustain any but necessary conflicts with it. They take no share in the altercations of parties, but they readily adopt the general opinions of their country and their age, and they allow themselves to be borne away without opposition in the current of feeling and opinion by which everything around them is carried along. They endeavor to amend their contemporaries, but they do not quit fellowship with them. Public opinion is therefore never hostile to them; it rather supports and protects them, and their belief owes its authority at the same time to the strength which is its own and to that which it borrows from the opinions of the majority.[40]

This analysis is remarkably penetrating, but it minimizes the political relevance of religious commitments in America and the close connection between popular Christianity and that conformist social character which so appalled him on his tour. Popular Christianity, which he valued as a safeguard against the danger of atomization inherent in his theoretical model of an egalitarian society, was in American actuality also a source of the "tyranny of the majority." That tyranny, rooted in equality rather than in the "more or less popular institutions which men living under that condition may give themselves," made faith in public opinion "a species of religion, and the majority its ministering prophet."[41] Tocqueville was caught in a conflict between his respect for religion as a source of social cohesion and his fear of the tendencies toward conformity in America.

It is doubtful, however, that social cohesion could be reconciled with intellectual freedom so long as cohesion itself was found in a popular Christianity that was treated as an established fact beyond challenge. That dilemma made the preachers' campaign against "infidelity" as comic as it was hysterical. The point was amusingly proved by a debate in 1829. Alexander Campbell of the fast-growing Disciples of Christ took on the skeptic Robert Owen in an encounter supposed to be won through "reason, argument, persuasion." A thousand people swarmed into a Methodist hall in Cincinnati to hear speeches, lasting as long as twelve hours each, over a period of eight days. Knowing his audience, Campbell concluded by asking the good people to demonstrate that their polite attention was no mark of apathy, but on the contrary an expression of "the meekness and forbearance which Christianity teaches." He then called upon all the assembled people who believed in Christianity, or wished to see it prevail, to signify their feelings by standing up. After this maneuver had brought the crowd to its feet, Campbell asked all doubters and enemies of Christianity to rise. Three arose.

"Campbell, with all his erudition, did not need to waver as he took his part in the era," as Martin E. Marty has pointed out; "he had not failed to appeal to reason. He merely wavered in his faith in reason when it *really mattered*."[42] Campbell's victory over free thought was won before the debate began. What he needed to win from the debate was the respectability for his own antiecclesiastical, antisectarian New Testament gospel that a highly publicized "victory" over "the infidel" could bring him. By the time of his death in 1866, perhaps half a million people were members of the Disciples of Christ; that was the kind of victory he wanted and won. Popular American Christianity was much like that eighteenth-century English club which had as its condition of membership some experience of travel in the Orient. When it was found that certain people whom the club wished to accept had never been to the Orient, the rules were changed so that the condition of membership was "experience in the Orient, or having ever expressed the wish to travel there."

The religious societies did, however, illustrate Tocqueville's principle of the art of associating for civic purpose. They did protect men from that "general apathy" which was "the proper object of our most strenuous resistance" as the gravest danger of all. Whether that was a sufficient gain, as against the conformist tendencies of these associations, Tocqueville did not have to judge because he did not see how closely the art of associating, in this respect, was connected to that "tyranny of the majority" which he blamed for the loss of that "manly candour and masculine independence of opinion which frequently distinguished Americans in former times, and which constitutes the leading feature in distinguished characters wherever they may be found."[43]

Tocqueville recommended American religion as an example to those who looked forward to a republican government "as a tranquil and lasting state," because he thought that a common religious style morally tamed the dangers of majority power. To this extent the absence of critical discussion about Christianity seemed to him "unquestionably good," despite his fears for majoritarian tyranny. James Fenimore Cooper, however, more clearly saw the connections between the Puritan heritage and the nineteenth-century cult of public opinion. He was himself something of an American Tocqueville, without the Frenchman's poise and clearsighted recognition that modern men needed to give up aristocratic advantages for the sake of "the new benefits which equality may supply."[44] Cooper paid his respects to pietism by giving his mythical frontier hero Natty Bumppo an influential spiritual legacy from his pious Christian mother whose cabin door was always open to the Moravian missionaries. Deerslayer, as D. H. Lawrence pointed out, was "a saint with a gun."[45] But Cooper, after seven years of enjoying the civilization of Europe, was disgusted with his countrymen's lack of moral and intellectual freedom, their willingness to let society meddle with the private affairs of individuals. The "pious but exaggerated religionists who first peopled the country" had left an inheritance that reduced men to the state of a "sneaking democrat, who finds it necessary to consult a neighborhood before he can indulge his innocent habits and tastes." Through Mrs. Abbott of the provincial town of Templeton in *Home as Found* (1838) Cooper dramatized an evangelical compound of "piety, censoriousness, charity, proscription, gossip, kindness, meddling, ill-nature, and decency."[46] It was an opening skirmish in a long war waged by American writers against the power of piety.

VIII

Peculiar People in the Land

A democratic people, Tocqueville prophesied, would not "easily give credence to divine missions" and would "laugh at modern prophets" because in such periods men "will seek to discover the chief arbiter of their belief within, and not beyond, the limits of their kind."[1] This forecast would seem to benefit liberal Unitarians, who could say with William Ellery Channing that the idea of God is only an enlargement of "the idea of our own spiritual nature," or favor radically humanistic Transcendentalists, who could say with Emerson that "nothing is at last sacred but the integrity of your own mind." But neither Unitarians nor Transcendentalists carried much of the country with them. The old jests about Unitarianism are not far off the mark: they believed in the fatherhood of God, the brotherhood of man, and the neighborhood of Boston; and he who has been born in Boston does not need to be born again.

All but four of the male members of the Transcendentalist Club, first organized in 1836 at George Ripley's home in Boston, were themselves Unitarian ministers.[2] Although Jefferson expected Unitarianism to become the majority religion in America, by 1850 more than 90 per cent of its churches were located in New York and New England.[3] Liberal religion was a major source of much that was best in American intellectual life, but it was doubly handicapped in extending the scope of its influence. Its mild rationalism seemed to be a badge of the prestigious social and literary establishment of Boston, while the inner rebellion of Transcendentalists, who appealed instead to a poeticized philosophy of spontaneity, instinct, intuition, or imagination, inspired by romantic and literary patterns suggested by Victor Cousin, Words-

126

worth, Coleridge, or Carlyle, was much too radical, idiosyncratic, and sophisticated to attract the popular mind. The triumphant religion in America would be neither rationalistic nor radical, neither genteelly cultured nor sophisticatedly antirational. It would mix liberal, pietistic, and evangelical elements to form an aggressive, anti-intellectual faith that was patriotic and suspicious of subversion—a temper that showed a harsh face to those outside the fold.

But success was never sure or permanent in a mobile society whose proselytizers had to capture public opinion. Any groups that seemed to have some firm cohesion tainted by autocratic, conspiratorial, or morally deviant customs were bound to seem subversive, and their existence provided the others with a meaningful enemy to confirm their own sense of loyalty and group identity. Catholics and Mormons, who clearly did have a faith in the supernatural, were nevertheless deviant enough from the dominant popular majority to become targets of opportunity for their fellow countrymen. Protestants had appropriated the family, the public school, and the republic as their own symbols. When Catholics revered the Pope and celibate priests worked for their own parochial schools, or when Mormons produced their own divine revelation to autocratic prophets who practiced polygamy, they provoked the majority to fierce hostility toward these stigmas of deviation.

In Europe, as David B. Davis has pointed out, "the radical sectarian, while professing faith in liberty of conscience, in the moral autonomy of the individual and in the inevitability of the millennium, after a period of struggle with the powers of darkness, always stood in the position of a heretic condemned and persecuted by the established order."[4] But in America these sectarian ideals were themselves rapidly becoming part of the established order. Thus deprived of the social bond nurtured by opposition to established authority, sectarians found unity instead in combating their common enemies. The popular imagination was nervously titillated by a quasi-pornographic journalism exposing the alleged lecherous iniquities of Catholic priests and Mormon prophets. While ministers noted with alarm the spread of prostitution, divorce, and the lax morality of the cities, the sins of the nation could be symbolically punished in righteous indignation vented at the subversive enemy, who conveniently furnished lurid accounts written by reformed apostates. Contemporary historians, familiar with the American obsession with the more complex issue of Communist conspiracy, have been able to see the emotional dynamics at work in this process.

Fighting Rome, New York legislators with the help of some Catholic laymen passed the Putnam Bill in 1855 to compel lay ownership of all church property, a blow at Catholic bishops struggling with their own laity for control of their churches according to canon law. Nationally, an organization of Protestant ministers sprang up to attack Catholicism as subversive of civil and religious freedom. A midnight mob incited by Lyman Beecher in 1834 burned the Ursuline Sisters convent at Charlestown, Massachusetts, and two churches were put to the torch in Philadelphia during a riot in 1844. Entangled in these conflicts was Catholic resentment of the Protestant atmosphere of the public school, which in Philadelphia provoked a bishop's remonstrance against the use of Protestant Bibles, prayers, and hymns. To avoid violence in New York, after failing to gain a Catholic share of the Public School Society funds, Bishop John Joseph Hughes stationed armed guards around the city's Catholic churches.[5]

That the public schools claimed to be nonsectarian did not make them impartial. That position had first been won by Horace Mann through a struggle in Massachusetts between Unitarians and the old Calvinists. Mann himself had revolted against Edwardsian Calvinism when at the funeral of his brother Dr. Nathaniel Emmons preached on the perils of dying unconverted. Recoiling in horror, Mann later became a Unitarian, and his theory of a nondenominational teaching of a common piety and morality, supplemented by use of the Bible as a text, was itself Unitarian in spirit.[6] He believed it was the "Religion of Heaven" as opposed to the "creeds of men," but, as one of his conservative opponents in the American Sunday School Union pertinently asked, "Who but men are to determine what is 'the religion of heaven'?" This separation of morality from theology was thoroughly characteristic of the Protestant temper of mid-nineteenth-century America. Mann, a typical Protestant reformer who neither drank nor smoked, protected the schools from the charge of being godless at the price of compromise that would soon prove unacceptable to Catholics, who used a different version of the Bible. In 1853 in New York the state Superintendent of Schools, in order to square himself with a previous statute that prohibited the use of public moneys for religious teaching in any schools, had to rule that school prayers could not be required or Catholic pupils compelled to attend if the King

James Version of the Bible was used in class—a position with echoes for New Yorkers more than a hundred years later.*

The ubiquitous humanitarian reformer Samuel Gridley Howe expressed to Horace Mann in 1852 the Yankee doubts about the great influx of Irish immigrants: "So long as these poor creatures came to us only fast enough to be leavened by the little virtue there was in us, so long we welcomed them; but if they are to pull us down instead of our pulling them up we may well cry hold off!" Howe himself was prepared to admit that the process of immigration, taken as a whole, "may be good for humanity" however evil he found it locally, but many of his more militant fellow Protestants were inclined to assume the right "to partition off God's earth and say here shall be Saxon and here shall *not* be Celt. . . ."[7]

Catholics themselves in Europe had recently propagandized against an alleged international conspiracy against thrones and altars supposedly hatched by freethinking Masons, French *philosophes,* and revolutionary Jacobins; New England Protestants had then heartily joined in the propaganda in order to paint the Jeffersonians and their Democratic Clubs in the black colors of treason. This clerical campaign reflected Puritan defensive attachment to the privileges provided by establishment of the church in New England.[8] Now after Puritan Protestants had become committed to the voluntarism that disestablishment had forced upon them, they posed as defenders of freedom against an autocratic Catholicism. The common ingredient here was that American Catholics were now mainly found in the camp of New England's old political enemy, the Democratic Party. Prejudice against immigrants reinforced religious prejudice against Catholics and political prejudice against Democrats.

This Protestant defense of American liberties against an imagined conspiracy from abroad, directed by "the feudal potentates of Europe," as Lyman Beecher called them, did not, however, have much success at the polls outside of local offices in New England and the border states. A lukewarm nativist like ex-President Millard Fillmore received a popular majority in no state and only one electoral vote when, as leader of the American Party, he ran in 1856 on a platform constructed so as politically to disable immigrants and Catholics.[9]

---

* The occasion that prompted the case involved punishment of a Catholic child for refusing to memorize passages from the Bible. See R. Freeman Butts, *The American Tradition in Religion and Education* (Boston, 1950), pp. 135–37.

Other issues were more significant, and a rigid ideological party, as Madison had predicted in *The Federalist,* could not in an extended republic achieve a political majority. Know-Nothingism mainly succeeded in freezing American Catholics in a defensive, suspicious posture with a tenacious loyalty to the party that was the enemy of its enemies.

Although Tocqueville wrote before the major influx of Catholic immigrants into America, he was right in pointing out that while American Catholics are not "forcibly led by the nature of their tenets to adopt democratic and republican principles," they are "not necessarily opposed to them; and their social position, as well as their limited number, obliges them to adopt these opinions." His own experience led him to say that American Catholics were "the most republican and democratic class in the United States," an exaggeration that loyalty to the Democratic Party would not justify.[10] Massive immigration brought to the cities a peasantry that clung to conservatism in both religion and politics as a rock of stability in a bewildering new world. For most of the nineteenth century, in fact, the Catholic in America had little influence on shaping liberal values or principles. Yankee intellectuals, who could afford to take the risk of social radicalism by the security of their own native roots, did not see, however, that this option was denied to recent immigrants from European villages. In this situation only Yankee converts, like Orestes A. Brownson, could champion a more active and critical role in both the Church and society for American Catholics. This passive conservatism of the ordinary Catholic was the despair of reformers from churches that strongly emphasized lay participation as the American Way. The victory of the bishops over the laymen in the trusteeship controversies heavily underlined this difference of religious traditions.[11]

The Mormon experience of persecution was much worse than the Catholic, though it is hard to remember now because Mormon respectability has become so accepted that a Mormon was a contender for the Republican Presidential nomination in 1968. It is no accident that Mormonism, a religion invented on American soil, was conceived in the area of western New York where prosperous rural Yankee emigrants from New England had been subjected to the excitements of the Finney revivals and the murder of a renegade Mason, William Morgan. Mormonism drew from both Protestant doctrines and Masonic rituals. The leaders, Joseph Smith and Brigham Young, were both born in Vermont. Young belonged to a family of Methodist lay preachers, and Smith's mother had impressed her boy with her father's account of his "extraordinary" conversion to Presbyterianism. The boy, unable to decide what was right, held off from joining his parents' decision to enter the Presbyterian Church; he soon reported visitations from the angel Moroni, who brought news of a book, written upon gold plates, giving an account of the former inhabitants of this continent and the fullness of the true gospel as delivered to them, along with two magic stones that conveniently enabled the reader to translate the plates.

The Book of Mormon, published in 1830 as a revelation supplementing without contradicting the Bible, and covering the years 600 B.C. to A.D. 421 on the North American continent with prophecies of the coming Messiah and the great apostasy to follow, treated all the controversies of the day with a fertile imagination. Alexander Campbell of the Disciples of Christ in his contemporary review of the book noted that it dealt with "every error and almost every truth discussed in New York for the last ten years." Its range covered a host of issues: "infant baptism, ordination, the trinity, regeneration, repentance, justification, the fall of man, the atonement, transubstantiation, fasting, penance, church government, religious experience, the call to the ministry, the general resurrection, eternal punishment, who may baptize, and even the question of free masonry, republican government, and the rights of man."[12]

Like the early Puritans' works, the Book of Mormon in its historical sections links the fate of believers with the Jews and provides a covenant for a New Jerusalem; like the revivalists of Smith's period, it stresses free will, the perfectibility of man, judgment according to one's works, and potential salvation for all with the exception of apostates and persecutors of the Saints. It adds some appealing novelties of its own in its theory of the material perpetuity of the world; its tritheistic conception of a deity who is yet of the same race as mankind, needs them, and develops by his own efforts as they do; and it finds a place for the Indians by defining them as apostate Jews, descendants of the lost tribes of Israel, who will one day be reconverted into friendly whites. Mormons restored as well the mystical practices of visions, faith healing, and exercise of the gift of tongues, and they drew upon the deep-seated adventist expectations of American Protestantism to forecast a Second Coming of Christ who would preside over an American Zion in the West. The founder of the Adventist Church in America, William Miller, had prophesied the Second Coming in 1843–44, and Joseph Smith received his own revelation at the same time that if he lived until eighty-five he would see it himself. Shortly after that time (1890) a Mormon tract announced that the Messiah had come to the Western Indians in the form of Wovoka, a prophet of the Ghost Dance among the Paiutes.[13]

Mormons were as opposed to idleness and to stimulants as much as any revivalist, but they had a refreshingly hospitable attitude toward dancing, the theater, and education. While they accentuated marriage by making its covenant good forever, they qualified or enriched it— depending on one's point of view—by reviving the custom of polygamy as practiced by Old Testament patriarchs. If the origins of Mormonism seem incredible to the modern reader, they are no more so than the story of Christ, to which the murder of Joseph Smith by an enraged mob in 1844 provided believers with a suggestive parallel.

Seen against the Mormons' native background, it is not so surprising that they took the risk of ignoring Tocqueville's prediction that democratic societies would not give credence to divine missions and modern prophets. It is more surprising that Mormonism proved of great appeal to more than eighty thousand European emigrants, especially among the lower class of Britain's cities. Many of them braved the staggering hardships of pushing handcarts across the Rockies to join Brigham Young's state of Deseret in the Salt Lake region of Utah. A recent historian of Mormon emigration from Britain to Utah stresses the appeal to the impoverished workers of a church with living prophets, continuous revelations, a restored priesthood of apostolic authority, and the promise of a millennial kingdom in America.[14] For men like Chester Nimmo's father in Joyce Cary's novel *Except the Lord,* Adventism was the consoling religion of English farm laborers, trapped in bitter poverty; for the urban poor, Mormonism was the good society come to earth in Utah.

The Mormons held out the possibility of an experienced solidarity in community dedication to a godly way of life, a restoration of the early Puritan dream of "a city on a hill with the eyes of all people upon us," a vision that the American democratic republic had itself made real for most of its citizens. But the majority in an "extended republic" on a continental scale was vulnerable to fears of internal subversion by those who followed the inspiration of different visions. The organization of the Mormon utopia was, in fact, an oligarchy, even though its tithing did not support bishops, elders, and deacons, who worked for their living in other callings. Both Smith and Young were heads of the church and also mayor and governor, respectively, of Nauvoo, Illinois, and the Utah Territory. Of thirty-five leaders in top positions of the church in Utah from 1847 to 1877, as many as twenty-one held high office in the church for more than thirty years and eighteen held political office.[15] Mormonism was essentially theocratic, and some of its schismatical groups openly advocated monarchy. Some Mormons objected that Joseph Smith himself reigned secretly in Nauvoo, where he had established a kingdom and a Council of Fifty, and it is at least clear that in 1841 he was elected for life as sole trustee of the church with complete control in principle over its property. "Congregationalism, so much a part of the democratic habits of the converts," as Thomas F. O'Dea has explained, "was important; but however important it may have been, it had to become either the registering of assent to a leadership believed to be divinely inspired or rebellion." Mormonism as it developed became "a democracy of participation and an oligarchy of decision-making and command."[16]

A gathered people, the Mormons provoked violent hostility among the gentiles by their authoritarian organization and their practice, at first in secret and then openly, of polygamy. Their critics claimed to speak for freedom and the rights of women, but in fact it was Mormon conversion of some free Negroes in frontier Missouri that first aroused mob violence against them, though Mormons themselves were never abolitionists and actually believed that blacks lived under the curse of being descendants of Ham. Mobs attacked the office of a Mormon newspaper, which had hinted at the coming doom of slavery and the colonizing of blacks in Africa, wrecked the press, and tarred and feathered a bishop. Soon a Mormon settlement was attacked and looted. As the Mormons turned in despair from legal to armed action in their own defense, civil authorities treated them as seditionists. This persecution greatly strengthened the social bond among Mormons, who were told by their prophet that he would "raise up unto my people, a man who shall lead them like Moses led the children of Israel; for ye are the children of Israel and the seed of Abraham, and ye must needs be led out of bondage, by power with a stretched out arm."[17]

Smith did call up an army of his own to march from Kirtland, Ohio, to Missouri in defense of his embattled brethren, but on his arrival he sensibly engaged in negotiations with the state government to avoid violence. Like the utopian communities of this period, the Mormon settlements provided a dramatic opportunity to secede in part from a society that had, as Brigham Young lamented, "taken a course to alienate the feelings of each other" and destroy "the little fellowship and confidence that were formerly placed in man towards his fellow man."[18] The gentiles confirmed this judgment by forcing Mormons to fight their way to the polls in state elections. Ordered to vacate their homes, the Mormons retaliated with their own looting and firing of gentile settlements, and the process of violence inevitably escalated. When the governor of Missouri ostracized the entire Mormon community and arrested Joseph Smith, leadership fell to his most loyal supporter, Brigham Young; he organized the trek of thousands of Mormons in a winter's march to seek safety in hospitable Illinois.

The Nauvoo community where Mormons held a city charter even won the praise of James Gordon Bennett's New York *Herald*. Trouble brewed again when sex reared its head in the form of polygamy. The Mormon theology of the eternal perpetuity of the seal of the marriage covenant, at a time when most married men ordinarily outlived several wives, logically implied at least a heavenly plurality of partners. The revival of Old Testament patriarchical polygamy brought this implication down to earth, just as Zion was made real in Utah. The communitarians of the mid-nineteenth century, as John Humphrey Noyes remarked, held to a common belief in "the enlargement of home—the extension of family union beyond the little man-and-wife circle to large corporations."[19] This ideal also inspired the Mormons to draw on both the Puritan doctrine of stewardship and Biblical precepts of primitive communism. The individual was obligated to consecrate his economic surplus to the common good by donating it to his bishop. In practice, for the main body of Mormons, this ideal was expressed in tithing, usually paid in goods and crops. The doctrine of polygamy expressed a similar synthesis of the Old Testament and the experience of the utopian communities. Noyes himself in the Oneida community of New York had developed the practice of "plural marriage" on the ground that in holy love sexual intercourse should not be restrained by legal limitations.

When Mormons revived the practice of patriarchical polygamy, officially announced to the world in 1852, they were also participating in a widespread cult of the family as a focus for unalienated community, a temple at whose shrine even their enemies worshiped. One of the latter, for example, in *Uncle Tom's Cabin* captured the imagination of millions by dramatizing the tragedy of the way in which the slave market broke up not only the family solidarity of slaves, as well as the communal stability of plantation life, but even that love which a black girl might have for the benevolent white master who purchased her. Except for Uncle Tom, all of Harriet Beecher Stowe's Negroes are mulattoes or quadroons, the visible sign of that white exploitation of black women inherent in the system of slavery. If Mormons were mute to her appeals, she was blind to theirs in her public attacks on polygamy as a form of slavery. Her little Eva said she preferred to live on a Southern plantation because it makes "so many more round you to love, you know." Joseph Smith with his forty-nine wives, or Brigham Young with his fifty-four children, had the same reason for preferring Mormon to gentile life.

A defense against guilt for persecuting Mormons was available in charging Joseph Smith with violation of freedom of the press when he sent his marshals to destroy a print shop run by unscrupulous apostates, who inflamed the community with wild tales of his licentiousness and complicity in acts of violence. Hounded by governors who believed these rumors, and failing to get pledges of protection from the presidential nominees of the major parties, Joseph Smith had finally turned in fury on his renegade enemies. With this evidence of his hostility to freedom, the gentiles jailed him without a hearing on the charge of treason. The defenders of freedom, just as enraged as Smith, stormed the jail and murdered him and his brother. When the Mormons headed west again, their exodus was celebrated by a hail of bullets on their departing wagons. The great Mormon temple at Nauvoo was burned by marauders, briefly used later as the site of a French utopian community, and eventually turned into mortar for a Catholic girls' school.

The West was no sanctuary so long as Mormons persisted in their peculiarity. Their own actions aggrevated the tension when they preached "blood atonement" for certain sins, particularly of apostasy. Legends of their proclivity for violence were made more credible when, fearing an invasion by federal troops, a group of Mormons at Mountain Meadows, Utah, took revenge into their own hands by joining in an Indian massacre of a party of emigrants who boasted of having helped to murder Joseph Smith. The national government would not lie down in peace with the territorial government of Brigham Young. It removed the federal courts from the jurisdiction of territorial law and indicted the prophet for "lewd and lascivious cohabitation," a charge based on a statute that the prophet himself had sponsored against adultery. The federal judge exposed the ideological issues by making it clear that "while the case at the bar is called 'The People *versus* Brigham Young,' its other and real title is 'Federal Authority *versus* Polygamic Theocracy.' . . . A system is on trial in the person of Brigham Young."[20] The United States Supreme Court invalidated the judge's system of impaneling gentile juries, but in 1890 it upheld the Edmunds-Tucker Act, which aimed to destroy both the church and the practice of polygamy. This legislative effort "to purify the American home" also abolished Utah's law for woman suffrage, which Mormons had supported, and provided that a wife or husband could testify in court against each other. When the Mormons yielded to the ban on plural marriages, Utah was allowed to join the union in 1896. Ten years later the Mormon Reed Smoot, after heated opposition, led by Protestant ministers, to seating him after his election, took his place in the United States Senate. The war between "the peculiar people" and the gentiles was over at last.

Protestantism and democracy had concurred in condemning the kind of hierarchical structures of organization that both Catholics and Mormons had built. But this extension of political democracy to religious and social life led the majority to contradict its own commitment to religious freedom and due process of law. In effect, it defined freedom in ethnic and sectarian terms, making it the mark of conformity to majority practice rather than a principle of protection for ethnic and religious variety. In fury it resorted to violence or to opportunistic exploitation of the courts. The symbiosis between democracy and religion that Tocqueville remarked was, in fact, a relationship between a certain kind of Protestantism and the American majority's will. Evangelical Protestants had appropriated the family, the public school, and the republic as their own characteristic institutions. The power of the Puritan tradition and the effectiveness of the evangelical revivalist techniques had collaborated paradoxically to produce the conditions that had spawned the challenge represented by the Mormon blend of Herbraic Puritanism, lay participation in the church, utopian perfectionism, and millennialistic expectations.

This religion was so much in the American grain that Joseph Smith could himself say a few months before his murder, "The whole of America is Zion itself from north to south." When the prophet ran for the Presidency that year he favored expansion into Oregon and Mexico, proof of his own participation in the mood of national manifest destiny. If the prophet, on the one hand, also spoke of a "theo-democracy" that in principle violated the degree of separation between church and state which the Revolution and the Constitution had made normative, on the other hand his church at a general conference in 1835 had approved a declaration of belief that condemned as unjust the attempt to "mingle religious influence with the civil government, whereby one religious society is fostered and another proscribed."[21] The issue remained ambiguous.

The lesson of Mormon experience in Missouri and Illinois was clear, however, that a people specially covenanted together for a new Jerusalem could not become an integral part of a larger state whose citizens felt that it was "God's American Israel." The unsettled territory beyond the Rockies offered a different prospect, but when the Mormons arrived in 1847, they unfurled the Stars and Stripes and within three years applied for admission to the union. It was Mormons who discovered the gold at Sutter's mill that hastened the settlement of the West and the breaking down of Mormon isolation. The "peculiar people" by accepting the law against polygamy finally confirmed their conformity to majority will. For that will, the democratic republic under Protestant auspices was itself Zion, while Catholics and Mormons were the whores of Babylon.

Tocqueville's prophecy in one sense was quite correct if his theoretical model is applied to American society in the period between the Constitutional Convention and the Civil War. A majority of Americans did not "easily give credence to divine missions" and did "jeer at modern prophets"—unless they were recognizably part of a Protestant pattern of church organization and family structure. In this sociological sense the majority did indeed find "the chief arbiter of belief within, and not beyond, the limits of their kind." Tocqueville left America too soon to witness the persecution of Catholics and Mormons; otherwise he might have had second thoughts about the relationship between religion and democracy in America. While it was true, as he said, that Americans "profess to think that a people ought to be moral, religious, and temperate in proportion as it is free," he was too sanguine in believing that "the tranquil rule of the majority" recognized the limits to its action set by the moral barriers of "humanity, justice, and reason."[22]

The majority particularly did not recognize them when religious groups themselves appeared to be a threat to the specific kind of religion that Americans had come to associate with their republic. When the issue of centralized power became linked with the family and the public school, even the "extended republic" could not protect Mormons and Catholics from interference with their religious freedom. The majority simply saw that freedom as an un-American form of tyranny. The tyranny of the majority in America spoke in the name of liberty. Tocqueville did recognize that free Negroes sometimes could not vote because the majority's prejudice against them prevented the legal protection of their rights under law. But this fear of majority tyranny came largely from his belief that under conditions of social equality man doubts himself: "Not only does he mistrust his strength, but he even doubts of his right; and he is very near acknowledging that he is in the wrong, when the greater number of his countrymen assert that he is so. The majority do not need to. force him; they convince him."[23] Neither Catholics nor Mormons could be so convinced.

The dilemma of American freedom was that its secular tolerance created the social and spiritual diversity that led men to seek community in attacking the community of others whose religious and social solidarity itself both excited and was nurtured by persecution. Protestantism helped provide a sense of purposeful community for a restless people, as Catholicism and Mormonism did for their adherents, but the very diffuseness of the Protestant movement on a large continent in a mobile society engendered a need for the sort of unity that persecution provided.[24] It was not fundamentally the political system of American democracy that ideologically conflicted with Catholicism or Mormonism; it was the extension of individualistic and egalitarian ideals to church, school, and family that raised the issues; and in this process "republican religion" played a critical role.

Deeper issues, sectionally defined, would soon split the major political parties as well as the churches, and lead the country itself into its darkest crisis. It would bring to the White House a minority President with a reverence for both democracy and the union but without a trace of religious fanaticism or bigotry, a man whom the revivalist Peter Cartwright had condemned as an infidel and a lawyer-politician who had pointed out that there was nothing in the Constitution to prohibit polygamy. When war broke out and a Mormon representative sought to discover Lincoln's policy, the President told him with characteristic humorous tolerance and shrewdness about early days as a farm boy in Illinois: "Occasionally we would come to a log which had fallen down. It was too hard to split, too wet to burn, and too heavy to move, so we plowed around it. That's what I intend to do with the Mormons. You go back and tell Brigham Young that if he will let me alone, I will let him alone." Brigham Young wired back, "Utah has not seceded, but is firm for the Constitution and laws of our once happy country."[25] If Lincoln was willing enough to plow around the Mormon problem, it was because he was tragically faced with the deeper issues of slavery and union to which neither Catholics nor Mormons bore any special relationship because they took both for granted.

The Sin of Slavery

Tocqueville knew that any American consensus on political and moral ideals, as a stable base for a democratic republic, was threatened by the inequality of the condition of the Negroes. "Slavery, now confined to a single tract of the civilized earth, attacked by Christianity as unjust and political economy as prejudicial, and now contrasted with democratic liberty and the intelligence of our age, cannot survive." He predicted that it would end either by the act of the master or by the will of the slave, "and in either case great calamities may be expected to ensue." He was equally convinced that colonization of freed blacks in Liberia was totally unrealistic as a solution, even if some two thousand Negroes had already been transported to Africa. Most ominous, above all, was a prejudice of race that appeared to be most intolerant in the states that had abolished slavery or never known it. Free Negroes could not intermarry with whites, vote freely, find justice in court, or attend theaters or schools on an equal footing. Even in hospitals, churches, and cemeteries, they were set apart as inferiors. Tocqueville's image of the New World is darkened by his awareness of this deep-rooted injustice that pointed toward revolution. "The gates of heaven are not closed against them," he mordantly observed, "but their inferiority is continued to the very confines of the other world."[1]

History contradicted Tocqueville, as it does all prognosticators in some respects, for neither the master nor the slave ended slavery. Nor did he foresee that the issue of union would precipitate the war that would destroy slavery, although he recognized "the melancholy uneasiness" of the South, which led it to strain against the tie of the union from fear of losing its influence in the national government to the growing North and West. These signs were evident in South Carolina's nullification of the tariff in 1832, which Tocqueville reported, but his two volumes antedated the agitation over slavery in all its ramifications, an issue that proved more seriously threatening to union. In 1831, the year Tocqueville began his tour, William Lloyd Garrison established the *Liberator* in Boston as an organ of abolitionist opinion. That same year the Virginia legislature began a long and heated discussion of slavery that ended by voting down emancipation and deportation as a response to Nat Turner's violent slave revolt and marked the prelude to the spreading of strict slave codes to all the plantation states, a step that drastically restricted the possibilities of manumission.

Tocqueville did not see that religion could rationalize the institution of slavery and of racial prejudice, just as it inspired much of the ardor of the crusade against them. That fervor, in an age in which slavery enjoyed growing prosperity and political influence, could not make for tranquility or stability. He believed that the South had to choose emancipation and integration on the one hand, or segregation and slavery on the other. "All intermediate measures," he confessed, "seem to me likely to terminate, and that shortly, in the most horrible of civil wars and perhaps in the extirpation of one or the other of the two races."[2] But the South would choose the second alternative—and civil war along with it.

Legalized slavery defined Negroes as property; "and yet in no country," as a recent study of slavery in Western culture points out, "was it possible to ignore the bondsmen's essential humanity, or to deny him, however inconsistently with the law, certain rights and privileges. Everywhere the more thoughtful masters had cautious hopes of augmenting those rights and privileges until, by some miracle of evolution, the obvious evils of slavery would wither away and the grateful Negro would willingly give his service without coercion. But all such dreams and hopes ran aground on the simple and solid fact, which for centuries had been obscured by philosophy and law, that a slave was not a piece of property, nor a half-human instrument, but a man held down by force."[3] In America the slave's oppression was aided by the tradition of local self-government, which had been such an important factor in the development of the American Revolution and of the federal system of the Constitution. The Convention in 1787 had, in fact, prohibited any Congressional legislation restricting the slave trade prior to 1808 and provided for the return of fugitive slaves. The principal compromise of the Convention included the agreement to count three-fifths of the slaves as persons for the purpose of taxation and representation. This solution illustrated the impossibility, even on hard grounds of political self-interest, of keeping the categories of person and of property coextensive with the categories of white and black. The fate of the Negro, however, was largely left in the hands of the states whose laws controlled his status.

Attitudes derived from Christianity, the Enlightenment, and Romanticism slowly coalesced to build up a concern for the Negro's plight as a child of God, a man with natural rights, and a person of deep sensitivity. By 1761 the Quakers, responding to the witness of John Woolman, had made importation of slaves a disciplinary offense. In the issue of slavery they found a focus for their own intense sense of obligation to others and of their own mission as contemners of unprincipled worldliness. This stand had already put them at odds with authority for their refusal to fight or pay taxes; and their own complicity with the institution of slavery in Rhode Island, a leg of the triangular trade with the West Indies in slaves and rum, made the religious dimension of slaveholding as personal sinfulness particularly evident. The social implications of slavery, furthermore, were thick enough to make it a vivid concrete symbol for Quakers of the hypocrisy of a hireling ministry, the luxury, idleness, and sensuality of worldly men, and the alienation of man from man in the larger society.[4]

Men of the American Enlightenment, like James Otis and John Adams, for their part could wonder if the refusal of the West Indies to stand with the colonies in the Revolution might not have something to do with the power of slaveholding to blind men to the British slavery imposed upon them by the Sugar Act of 1764. "It is a clear truth," wrote Otis, "that those who every day barter away other men's liberty, will soon care little for their own."[5] The citizens of Boston, no doubt, would have agreed when they instructed their representatives in 1766 to move for a prohibition on the importation and purchase of slaves. By 1851–52 Harriet Beecher Stowe could make millions who had been brought up on romantic conventions weep at the piety of the martyred Uncle Tom, who had the "soft, impressible nature of his kindly race, ever yearning toward the simple and childlike."[6] These examples reveal the major intellectual traditions on which antislavery reformers drew for inspiration in their protest during the early nineteenth century.

These intellectual backgrounds of antislavery could, however, also nurture proslavery defenses, whether Christian, rationalistic, or romantic. The Bible also had texts for slaveholders; states'-rights theorists spun an intricate system of checks and balances to improve on the Constitution so that it would better protect the interests of planters in the South; and slaveholders rejoiced in the novels of Sir Walter Scott, as if their own society were a contemporary version of the romanticized medieval past. It was not mere traditions but certain men with a particular relation to them that made the difference in the mounting of the antislavery crusade. Religion and democracy were ambiguous enough terms to cover supporters of all parties to the conflict, and anyone who seeks to identify devotees of God or of majority will with all that is good must blink the fact that Christian believers and ardent democrats were both capable of deep complicity with human slavery as an institution, particularly the churches and the Democrats.

Despite these obvious but necessary reminders, the fact remains that the major spokesmen against slavery were profoundly committed to particular religious or democratic interpretations of the dilemma, and in this sense the American agony over the crisis of slavery was a vortex that drew into its center essential elements in the tangled problem of the relationship between religion and democracy in America. Negro slavery posed fundamental moral and political questions with which present-day religious believers and political democrats are still struggling. Dealing with the issue of slavery deeply influenced the meaning of both religion and democracy as men were forced to confront the implications of their commitments; and the crisis itself, in its magnitude and violence, relentlessly judged the ideas which had helped to bring it about.

Christianity was not only the major source of social cohesion for the American Negro but also the only noneconomic connection with his masters on the plantation. Yet there were profound tensions that worked against free mingling of the races. The Dover Baptist Association in Virginia, even before slave revolts had stimulated repressive restrictions on the education of the Negro slave, reported in 1802 that uneducated blacks could not manage the business of the church and only free males should "exercise any authority in the church." While the Southern churches felt a responsibility for the religious instruction of the slaves, they also conceded that "obvious danger" might require legislative curtailments even though they believed, as the Charleston Baptist Association put it in 1835, "that no wise Legislature has anything to fear, from the Christian religion, disseminated among any class of its population." True religion, it was widely assumed, would make "good masters and good slaves."[7] Since the leading slaveholding states were dominated by the Baptist and Methodist Churches, the slaves were drawn to these evangelical denominations, particularly the former, which ensured the absence of any supervisory white bishops or elders.

The ambiguity of Christianity is vividly demonstrated by the historical fact that it was the religion of slaves, slaveholders, and abolitionists, a reconciliation to the sorrows of this world by the promise of bliss in the next, an assertion of the irreducible humanity of all races as children of God. For the Negro it was, however interpreted, the deepest element in his culture, transcending the conditioning fate of legal servitude itself. The prophets of his liberation—until the much later time of the Black Muslims—did not reject Christianity with their rejection of slavery, but instead were inspired by the traditional Biblical myths in seeking to overcome the remnants of former bondage that had been humanized as well as rationalized by the Protestant churches. The church thereafter would be the social center of Negro life and the necessary platform for all prophets of freedom.

Even for the plantation slave the role of religion was not simply consolatory. His own zest and humor, expressed in song and sermon, were testimony to how much of his humanity survived the brutalities of the labor system. Faith did not mean identification with the oppressor but transcendence of servitude through participation in a self-transforming experience. If the rhythms and animistic spirit of slave songs recall Africa, their characters had stepped out of the King James Bible, whose Old Testament history became the Negro's imagined past. For him the stories of Moses and the Exodus, Daniel and the lions, David and Goliath, Joshua and Jericho must have had a special meaning:

> When Israel was in Egypt Land,
> Let my people go,
> Oppressed so hard they could not stand,
> Let my people go.
> Go down, Moses,
> Way down in Egypt Land,
> Tell old Pharaoh
> To let my people go.

Though the convulsive evangelism of frontier Protestantism conditioned the spirituals, as it did the Negro's religious experience, those sects produced no such memorable songs, despite the similarity in material of the informal verses at the back of the revivalist's handbook. And while the spirituals were full of awe before the coming fire of Apocalypse, they treated the Fall and the Flood with a humorous, unpuritanical ease.

As Marguerite Yourcenar has observed in a brilliant commentary on her translations of spirituals into French, the world of slave poetry was surprisingly close in spirit to the paintings of Giotto and Fra Angelico. In their deeper moods the spirituals show a comprehension of the sufferings of the Lord more vivid than most of their white contemporaries could imagine, just as they confront death with greater directness. Liberation and death, profoundly intermingled, beyond any sectarian dogma, are celebrated in these folk meditations with the power of art because, as Miss Yourcenar remarks, *"nous sommes tous esclaves, nous mourrons tous."*[8]

> Deep River, my home is over Jordan:
> Deep River, I want to cross over into camp ground.

If the spirituals sang of liberation in death, they did not speak directly of abolition of slavery in this life. The familiar "Freedom Over Me" ("Befo' I'd be a slave I'll be buried in my grave"), "Kingdom Coming" ("It must be now dat de kingdom am a coming in de year of jubilee"), and "Wake Nicodemus" ("Wake me up for de grand jubilee") were, for example, written in the war years by Henry C. Work, a white abolitionist most famous for "Marching Through Georgia."[9] The pioneering antisegregationist Negro leader W. E. Burghardt Du Bois wrote in 1903 in *The Souls of Black Folk* a judgment on Negro religion that is surprisingly close in descriptive terms to Harriet Beecher Stowe's vision:

The long system of repression and degradation of the Negro tended to emphasize the elements in his character which made him a valuable chattel: courtesy became humility, moral strength degenerated into submission, and the exquisite native appreciation of the beautiful became an infinite capacity for dumb suffering. The negro, losing the joy of this world, eagerly seized upon the offered conception of the next; the avenging Spirit of the Lord enjoining patience in this world, under sorrow and tribulation until the Great Day when He should lead His dark children home,—this became his comforting dream.[10]

Yet for others, according to Frederick Douglass, who escaped from bondage, the buoyant singing of "O Canaan, sweet Canaan, I am bound for the land of Canaan," was an imprudent way of expressing hope for reaching the Canaan of the North. If so, he did not mention it in his narrative written nearly forty years earlier, long before Emancipation, when he said that during his first aborted escape plan he and his companions succeeded in keeping their feelings concealed "as much as possible." To his mind *then* the singing of slaves was like that of men "cast away on a desolate island."[11] Perhaps the truth is that the Negro slave sang of two kinds of freedom only when he could imagine achieving it.

Free Negroes could imagine both conditions without any doubt. They asserted their humanity through a separatism that revealed their religious linkage to American society and their social estrangement from it. In protest against the humiliation of enforcement of segregated church galleries in Philadelphia, Richard Allen, who had purchased his own freedom, in 1816 formed the African Methodist Episcopal Church, which by 1856 had some twenty thousand members. It sponsored its own voluntary associations—churches, colleges, credit unions, and antislavery societies. As early as 1822 the lay preacher Denmark Vesey of Charleston organized slaves and free Negroes in an aborted revolution. A haven for fugitive slaves, the AME Church contained integrationist, revolutionary, and secessionist advocates. Its major ideologist, Benjamin Tucker Tanner, a circuit-riding minister, defined the special mission of the AME Church in 1864: "The duty of the Church, General or Catholic, composed as it is of a congregation of faithful men, . . . is to evangelize the world and prepare it for the coming of its Lord and Head." Just as the Israelites were led out of Egyptian bondage by a Hebrew of the Hebrews, so also free Negroes had therefore established their own churches of "men who support from their own substance, however scanty, the ministration of the Word which they received; men who spurn to have their churches built for them, their pastors supported from the coffers of some charitable organization; men who prefer to live by the sweat of their own brows and be free."[12] This movement brought Methodism to bear upon the world and asserted its claim for Negro humanity through the cultivation of separate churches.

Two years after the organization of the AME Church the General Assembly of the Presbyterians demonstrated the moral failure of the major white churches to deal decisively with the question of slavery, which only the Quakers made a serious issue for their communicants. In 1818 a resolution came before the Presbyterian Assembly proposing to excommunicate any member who sold as a slave any other member of the church. A unanimous report on this proposition declared slavery unchristian and against natural right, urging all Christians to work for complete abolition throughout the world; at the same time, however, it asked for charity to well-intentioned slaveholders and encouraged patronization of the American Colonization Society. Slaves should be instructed in the Christian religion by their master, it lamely concluded, because faith would be a powerful means of preventing insurrection.[13]

After the slave rebellions of Denmark Vesey and Nat Turner, whites either carefully supervised, segregated, or suppressed the preaching of the gospel to the slave. There were striking exceptions, but the more literate black preachers were usually without a mass following, their talents spent on lost causes. (Lott Cary, for example, born a slave in Virginia, had been awakened by hearing the text from *John* of the interview of Nicodemus with the Lord: "Notwithstanding what I say unto you, you must be born again." Cary learned to read by studying *John,* became superintendent of a tobacco warehouse, and was granted permission to serve as exhorter in the First African Baptist Church of Richmond. Appointed a missionary to Liberia, he was made vice-agent of the colony, where he died in an explosion.)[14] For the mass of plantation Negroes spiritual life was expressed in their own songs, in which they heard the trumpets of the Lord, and the promise of liberation if only through death. The white man's church, being the instrument of the master's will, could not be the Negro's home, and with Emancipation the liberated slaves would massively reject it.

The orthodox position on slavery as taught in American colleges and seminaries was the view of William Paley's *Principles of Moral and Political Philosophy* that slavery was justifiable as punishment for a crime, as the penalty for capture in war, and as payment for debts. Conservative clergymen did welcome the end of the slave trade, but, like the Congregationalist Jedidiah Morse of Charlestown in a sermon to Negro freemen in 1808, such preachers were sure that "a slavery of vastly deeper misery" and "a freedom of infinitely richer value" were defined by the Christian categories of sin and salvation.[15] For many old Calvinists, sympathetically affiliated with Federalists and Whigs, and beneficiaries of church establishment in New England, "Puritanism, Protestantism, and True Americanism are only different terms to designate the same set of principles."[16] These nationalistic conservatives found their favorite solution to the slavery problem in the idea of African colonization.

The modified Edwardsian Samuel Hopkins, familiar with the slave trade in Newport, Rhode Island, had joined with President Ezra Stiles of Yale to sponsor the education of two slaves until the Revolutionary War interrupted their pilot project in colonization. In 1817 the American Colonization Society was organized, and Presbyterians, Methodists, Baptists, Episcopalians, Dutch Reformed, and Congregational conventions soon endorsed it. A Presbyterian minister, Ralph R. Gurley, was the moving force of the society for eighteen years. These devotees of the missionary spirit also saw in colonization an advantage for white men—an immunity against racial amalgamation whose dangers they luridly depicted as "promiscuous concubinage" and "universal profligacy." However philanthropic their motives were, they were also animated by an intense fear for the security of the state if the freed Negro population, "the most ignorant, degraded, and vicious class in the community,"[17] kept growing.

In a country as property-conscious as the United States it is not surprising that white and black antislavery reformers faced a stubbornly unyielding opposition from slaveholders. But even the strenuous insistence that slaves were men could not leap over the fact that slavery became increasingly entangled in the sectional rivalries of an expanding country, thus blurring the issue by connecting it with other interests. To complicate the problem further, the logic of the federal system entailed difficult Constitutional and legal questions that could not be resolved by any simple moral principle. The power of the ideal of self-government for local communities also strengthened the hand of those who wished to disinfect slavery of any troublesome ideological or moral dimension. Finally, there was the ominous fact that prejudice against the freed Negro was powerful in every area of the union. To put out to sea as an antislavery reformer was to head for the open ocean in a very small boat. Heckled, stoned, beaten, tarred and feathered, shot or hanged, the abolitionists aroused not only the conscience but the fury of their fellow citizens.

Abolitionists took seriously Tertullian's aphorism "the blood of the martyrs is the seed of the church." Their willingness to suffer for their convictions has aroused the skeptical suspicion of some historians in a secular age that prides itself on being familiar with the psychological dynamics of complexes. They have cast a cold eye on the strident emotions of abolitionists on the implied premise that finding neurotic or pathological elements in their personalities invalidates their ideological convictions or their heroic actions. The premise ignores the wisdom of a better psychologist, William James, who agreed with Jonathan Edwards: "The *roots* of a man's virtue are inaccessible to us. No appearances whatever are infallible proofs of our grace. Our practice is the only sure evidence, even to ourselves, that we are genuinely Christians." James was drawn to the "twice-born philosophy" the revivalists preached, because "it symbolizes, lamely enough no doubt, but sincerely, the belief that there is an element of real wrongness in this world, which is neither to be ignored nor evaded, but which must be squarely met and overcome by an appeal to the soul's heroic resources, and neutralized and cleansed away by suffering." James himself believed that since life was "neither farce nor genteel comedy" but "something we must sit at in mourning garments, hoping its bitter taste will purge us of our folly," such "twice-born" heroism was itself closer to ultimate realities.[18] To agree with James's position is not to affirm that the abolitionists were necessarily right in their solutions to the problems they faced; it is only to deny that abolitionists were necessarily alienated from reality because of their anxious concern, their stubborn dedication, or their sense of guilt.

What James called the "twice-born" philosophy was at the vital center of the abolitionist movement, and its leaders were largely drawn from the New England Yankee stock of Puritans and their descendants in western New York and the Ohio Valley. These middle-class Protestants were heirs of the covenanted dedication of the seventeenth century, the evangelical enthusiasm of the eighteenth-century Great Awakening, and the humanitarian liberalism of the American Revolution. These cultural memories were reanimated by the intense heat of the Protestant revivals of the second Great Awakening, which tempered a new religious and social disposition highly congenial to antislavery reform.

Historically, Christianity itself was thoroughly ambiguous with respect to slavery and freedom: the Christian was to be freed of the slavery of sin in order to become perfectly obedient to Christ in meek resignation and faithful service. Christianity was thus vulnerable to the charge, which Nietzsche made famous, of cultivating virtues appropriate to slaves; yet at the same time it declared that all men were created in the image of a God who promised a true freedom in the light of the gospel. For centuries this freedom was made compatible with human slavery on the ground that Christian liberty transcended the merely earthly distinctions between master and servant. Slaves, as Bishop Ignatius of Antioch put it, should "bear their slavery for the glory of God, that they may win from Him thereby a better liberty."[19]

Traditionally, Christianity had accommodated itself to slavery by viewing it as part of the punishment for man's fall from grace. But if man could by his own efforts recover from that fall and achieve a perfect obedience to Christ, the theological ground for sanctioning slavery would then crumble. In this new context holding slaves would itself appear to be a *deliberate* act of sinfulness, a form of slavery to the natural man from which the Christian's second birth was traditionally a liberation. If sinfulness itself was a form of slavery, then human slavery was a form of sinfulness. If man *could* be free of sin, then he ought to be; he should therefore have nothing to do with the sin of keeping men in bondage. On the contrary, as a Christian warrior in combat with sin, he should make war on the institution of slavery.

The abolitionists came to these conclusions because they had lived through a period of intense religious excitement that transformed the older Calvinism by stressing the power of man through his own free will to cast off sin and become perfect in obedience to the gospel. This optimistic voluntarism was common to rationalistic Unitarians, romantic Transcendentalists, and evangelical pietists, and by the 1830's all three religious groups had come to seek proof of perfection in a life of holiness made evident in social action. Charles G. Finney's revivalism was particularly aimed at producing a regenerate soul that would express itself in benevolent action.

Evangelical Christians were also inspired by a dream of the millennium that would eliminate all sinfulness. The Protestant Reformation had done much to revive interest in the apocalyptic passages of the book of *Revelation,* which foretold the coming of the New Jerusalem. "After the period of tribulations," as Ernest L. Tuveson has summarized it, "the New Jerusalem will descend from heaven, the righteous will be resurrected, a judgment will be given, and the earthly utopia—the holy city on earth—will continue for a thousand years. The period of intense happiness will be followed by a short episode of intense affliction, after which the Kingdom of God will be finally established."[20] After falling into disfavor for more than a thousand years, after the reign of Constantine had transformed a despised sect into an official religion of the Roman Empire, millennialistic themes reappeared in force during the English Puritan Revolution. In America at the time of the Great Awakening, Jonathan Edwards had himself developed a radical statement of millennialistic doctrine, and his New England followers Joseph Bellamy, Samuel Hopkins, and Timothy Dwight carried it forward beyond the Revolution.

Traditional Calvinism had emphasized the more conservative pre-millennial theory of the Second Coming, whereby the New Jerusalem would be inaugurated only after the church had suffered great trials, finally settled by the reappearance of Christ himself. Edwards had preached instead the more radical and optimistic doctrine of an earthly millennium to be achieved *before* the Second Coming. In this light, human history was much more continuous with the divine plan, and the visible and the invisible church were brought together in the glorious prospect of a downfall of "the spiritual Babylon" of Catholic Rome, the conversion of the Jews, and the enlightenment of the heathen. Then the whole earth would be as one community, "one body in Christ." Edwards prophesied that this great transformation would begin in America: "This new world is probably now discovered, that the new and most glorious state of God's church on earth might commence there: that God might in it begin a new world in a spiritual respect, when he creates the *new heavens* and *new earth*."[21] The Great Awakening was itself "a forerunner of those glorious times so often prophesied of in the Scripture," even though there would be many convulsions and conflicts before Christ's kingdom would actually be established.

Edwards's millennialism was part of a theology that was strictly Calvinist in its denial of free will and of universal salvation, but his concept of history opened a path with less severe prospects for his followers. They argued that the sweeping conversions implied in the coming of the millennium entailed the good news that most people would be saved. In this way Edwards himself provided an exit from the harsh confines of the Calvinism he expounded and paved the way for liberal theologians who repudiated his doctrines of predestined election, infinite punishment, and limited atonement. If the glorious day was imminent, then saints were called to action, and the new Arminian theologies of belief in the free will and moral striving of man were the triumphal arches through which the pilgrim soul and Christian warrior could march to glory as the trumpets sounded.

Millennialistic speculation was rife in the whole evangelical movement, and William Miller's Adventist prophecy of the Second Coming in 1843 and 1844 was only a more literal and premillennialist version of a common theme. Significantly, Miller's leading cohort, Joshua Himes of Boston, was an evangelist, a temperance lecturer, and a Garrisonian abolitionist. Like the abolitionists, the Millerites had extensive connections with their fellow Adventists in Great Britain, particular among the British followers of the American preacher Alexander Campbell, founder of the Disciples of Christ, whose principal magazine was called the *Millennial Harbinger*. Adventists mingled antislavery convictions and concern for the hardships of the poor with a puritanical contempt for statuary and painting as dangerous temptations to licentiousness, a cluster of attitudes that appealed strongly to many artisans and shopkeepers in an era of hard times.[22]

Evangelical enthusiasm for reformation became in the 1830's an Anglo-American crusade. British Baptists, Methodists, Quakers, and Presbyterians kept up a steady moral pressure on their American cohorts to come to a decisive witness against slavery. Presbyterians like George Thompson and Charles Stuart were important British workers for the American cause, actually serving as agents for American antislavery societies. An evangelical chain reaction can be traced in Finney's conversion of Stuart to evangelical Christianity and Stuart's conversion of Theodore Dwight Weld to antislavery. Transatlantic cooperation, stimulated by British emancipation in the West Indies in 1833, foundered ultimately on division in the American churches, but a millennial vision could unite evangelicals wherever deep sectional differences did not divide them.[23]

The Methodists, the Congregational and Presbyterian followers of Finney, the Unitarians, and the Transcendentalists all stressed the centrality of the individual's free moral energy, and the age of popular democracy, technological progress, and communitarian utopias was deeply committed to a progressive view of history and a faith in the perfectibility of man. Protestant evangelicalism of the modified Edwardsian tradition provided rich soil for the cultivation of the millennialistic vision. By its light, American Negro slavery appeared to be, as a militant abolitionist minister and Liberty Party candidate put it, "a formidable obstacle to the conversion of the world."[24]

The perfectionist Protestant context of abolitionism is highlighted by the fact that the Protestant rationalists of the eighteenth century, who opposed the revivalists of the Awakening, were enemies of millennial enthusiasm and allies of substantial men of property who profited from the system of slavery. For Charles Chauncy reason was a disciplinary instrument both individually and socially, and secular-minded Enlightenment leaders like John Adams and Thomas Jefferson adhered to a cyclical theory of history. The key to the rise and fall of empires they found in the recurring tendencies of temperance and industry to produce luxury, which brought vice and folly in their train, and of the lust for ambition to pervert freedom into despotism. The sober realism of *The Federalist* in its defense of the Constitution reflects a sense of history in which enlightened statesmen must build their plans upon what Madison called "a degree of depravity in mankind which requires a certain degree of circumspection and distrust" as well as upon "other qualities in human nature which justify a certain portion of esteem and confidence."[25] Only by carefully providing at the very beginning of the nation for built-in safeguards against the tendency of political systems to degenerate could Americans postpone their vulnerability to the recurring cycle of the decline and fall of empires. Jefferson anxiously foresaw the day when vacant land would disappear and men would become "piled upon one another in large cities, as in Europe," when they would "become corrupt as in Europe, and go to eating one another, as they do there"; and Madison in the Convention had been especially anxious to develop "republican remedies" against the future day when indigents with "a leveling spirit" might come to represent a majority of the population, or when landholders would be overbalanced by the growth of trade and manufacturing.[26] Eventually Adams and Jefferson would embrace an idea of progress, but it would be born as an "offspring of a union of the millennial hope with the moralism of the cyclical view of history."[27]

Enlightenment rationalism, like Christianity, had subtle resources for justifying slavery. The great John Locke saw nothing inconsistent with his own liberalism in investing in the Royal African Company or in transcribing the Fundamental Constitutions of Carolina, which provided that church membership would have no effect on the status of slaves and that freemen would be guaranteed "absolute power and authority" over them. In Locke's liberalism, as David B. Davis has shown, "the origin of slavery, like the origin of liberty and property, was entirely outside the social contract."[28] The slave had the status of a captive in war and thus fell outside the jurisdiction of the state, and insofar as he could be legally defined as property, the state was just as obligated to defend the slaveholder's "natural right" to his slaves as it was to defend the natural liberties of white men. The very popularity that the Revolution gave to the theme of the natural rights of man put a certain pressure on Americans, notably including Jefferson, to rationalize their complicity with slavery by defining the Negro as something less than a man. "I advance it, therefore, as a suspicion only," Jefferson wrote in *Notes on the State of Virginia*, "that the blacks, whether originally a distinct race, or made distinct by time and circumstances, are inferior to the whites in the endowments both of body and mind."[29] At the same time, by accepting a Lockean liberalism that stressed contractual limits on power and by participating in the rituals of adherence to a national covenant which feared bondage to Great Britain, Revolutionary idealism inspired provisions for gradual abolition in Pennsylvania and New England; and by 1804 the principle had triumphed in the North.

The fierce attack on the later "immediate abolitionists" by outraged mobs led these religious reformers to become crusaders for civil liberties as well as for regeneration. Inevitably, persecution made freedom of petition, speech, and assembly the secular cornerstones of abolitionist faith. Massachusetts men like John Quincy Adams, Theodore Parker, and Wendell Phillips, who responded with deep feeling to the heroes and rhetoric of the Revolution, saw in such evangelical abolitionists as Garrison, Weld, Elijah Lovejoy, and Charles T. Torrey contemporary martyrs to principles of freedom that the men of the Revolution had hallowed with their blood.

The heritage of the Revolution was particularly relevant in Boston. A lawyer of patrician background and connections, Wendell Phillips made his debut as an agitator in 1837 when the Unitarian leader William Ellery Channing called a meeting of five thousand people in Faneuil Hall to protest the murder in Alton, Illinois, of the New England minister and editor Elijah Lovejoy. The martyrdom of Lovejoy was on the altar of freedom of speech; his own antislavery views had only moved from colonization to gradual emancipation by the voluntary action of slaveholders. What incensed him most was the decision of a judge, appropriately named Lawless, that the actions of a mob, which had burned alive a mulatto criminal in St. Louis, were beyond the reach of the law. That the judge was a Catholic deepened the outrage in the eyes of Lovejoy, a bigoted Maine Yankee whose newspaper originally began as an anti-Catholic organ. In Faneuil Hall the attorney general of Massachusetts sneered at Negroes as animals and compared Lovejoy's murderers to the Boston Tea Party. Phillips sprang to the platform, pointed to the portraits of the Revolutionary heroes that adorned the walls, and asked why they had not broken into voice to rebuke such slander of the dead. Boston earth, consecrated by Puritans and patriots, should have yawned and swallowed up "the recreant American."[30] In that same hall the Transcendentalist-Unitarian Theodore Parker, who never forgot that his grandfather was a captain in the battle on Lexington Green, later compared

Daniel Webster's support of the Fugitive Slave Law of 1850 to the treason of Benedict Arnold. Parker later used the language of "natural rights" to justify slave rebellions and John Brown's raid.

Neither Catholics nor freethinkers were abolitionists—it was a thoroughly Protestant movement. The Church accepted slavery in principle; and the American hierarchy, although divided in opinion on the merits of sectional issues, was never split in two, as the Protestant churches were, by such differences. The Church cultivated officially a nonpolitical stand, and most of its members belonged to the Democratic Party, which was sectionally split and indifferent to the moral issue of slavery. It is a striking fact that the historian of American freethinkers in the years from 1825–1850 found among them only one notable abolitionist, a man who, however, abandoned antislavery when he gave up religion. The division in the Tappan family illustrates the point. As a rising businessman, Lewis Tappan joined the fashionable Unitarian Church in Boston; but when he moved to join his brother Arthur's import business in New York, he shifted to a pietistic Protestantism not only to accommodate his brother but also because he was persuaded that the more liberal religionists "did not in an equal degree, consider themselves as stewards, and their property as consecrated to the cause of Christianity; and that they were deficient in a devotional frame of mind."[31] His brother Benjamin, neither religious nor abolitionist, became a Jeffersonian rationalist and a Democratic Senator from Ohio, while his brother Arthur paid to free Garrison from jail and subsidized his journal, the *Liberator*.

Antislavery in the Western Reserve was linked in its origins to missionary work and the training of ministers. Theodore Weld, one of Finney's most influential converts, went west to spread the gospel of temperance and to found a center for missionary work against Catholicism. Appalled at the number of those in Cincinnati who attended no churches or only those "where *damnable* error is preached," Weld pitched his tent at Lane Theological Seminary, headed by Lyman Beecher, supported by the Tappans, and having one of Finney's associates, Asa Mahan, on the board of trustees. Weld helped choose the faculty, which included Harriet Beecher's future husband and a Negro teacher of literature. Conducting a marathon college discussion of slavery in 1834, Weld was supported by a resounding vote in favor of "immediatism" and against the colonization policy. When trustees protested this radicalism, a large contingent of students and faculty resigned and moved to Oberlin. This coeducational training ground for ministers was founded by a Finney enthusiast who was much more willing than his master to take in Negro students. Here Finney himself became a member of the faculty, paying this much tribute at least to the theological learning he had always scorned as being irrelevant to the awakened soul.

The antislavery movement was deeply enmeshed in the Congregational-Presbyterian missionary movement, which had sponsored the numerous tract and Bible societies, the temperance crusade, and the fight to save the West from the Catholics. The New School Presbyterian Absalom Peters was sure that "the voluntary, associated action of evangelical Christians" was "much better suited to the object of the world's conversion than any form of church organization" ever had been or could be. He was equally confident that "the year of his redeemed" was imminent and that modern Christianity was "organizing her legions for the last onset and for certain victory."[32] The prophesied "overturnings" had begun. "The conflict here against slavery, and all other sin," the Reverend George B. Cheever gleefully wrote Finney in 1858, "waxes hotter in consequence of the preaching of the Tract Society. We will strike up the 44th Psalm, and set forward in another campaign, depending not on man, nor man's sneaking management, but on God."[33]

The British and American opponents of the British slave trade first gave currency to the slogan "immediate abolition," and this measure became in the 1790's a proof of moral commitment and practical Christianity. Slavery gained additional force as a paradigm of sin because it dramatized the compromises of the churches themselves. The English immigrant George Bourne, who influenced Garrison, wrote in 1815 on behalf of immediate abolition in order to purify the churches. Slavery was "the *golden calf,* which has been elevated among the Tribes, and before it, the Priests and the Elders and the *nominal* sons of Israel, *eat, drink, rise up to play, worship, and sacrifice.*"[34] Truculent opposition by slaveholders to any reform, the increasing militancy of Negroes who opposed colonization or incited rebellions, and the need of evangelical religious believers to find proof of their own self-transformation in freedom from guilt converged in the 1830's on the program of "immediatism." Immediatism was synonymous with immediate repentance.[35] Jonathan Edwards, Jr., had explained in 1791, in a sermon widely distributed later by abolitionists, that the Revolution had made it clear "that all men are born equally free"; therefore the slave trade and slaveholding were even more sinful than robbery or murder because the act of violation was constantly repeated during every moment of bondage.[36] As soon as men understood this sin—which obviously would not happen all at once but gradually—they were obligated at once to cease sinning immediately.* To conquer the sin of slavery would be to win a modern triumph over the age-old slavery of sin.

* The Colonization Society also circulated Edwards's tract, but with editorial exceptions to his immediatism regarding slaveholding and his prophecy of amalgamation of the races.

The Art of Associating: The Abolitionist Sect

Tocqueville had first been inclined to take it as a joke that in America "a hundred thousand men had bound themselves publicly to abstain from spirituous liquors," but he came to believe that nothing was "more deserving of our attention than the intellectual and moral associations of America." They were the best defense against public apathy in an egalitarian society, and the progress of democratic equality would be civilized precisely as "the art of associating together" grew and improved. He would have found vivid illustration for his rule in the example of the abolitionists, and their dedication to attacking slavery and racial prejudice would have given him an example better than the temperance movement, the missionary societies, or the churches for showing concretely how the passion for religion and for liberty could be mingled together in America. Tocqueville praised this blend as a factor of moderation and stability in the new republic. He also believed, however, in contrast to aristocratic conservatives, that while a state of equality is "perhaps less elevated," it is also "more just: and its justice constitutes its greatness and its beauty."[1] But so long as Negro slavery and racial prejudice existed, he knew, such equality and such justice would be radically flawed. If it were to remedy that gross defect, however, the passion for religion and liberty could not make for tranquility. Perhaps it could somehow still have made for stability, if the majority had been willing to mingle religion and liberty in specific application to Negroes, or if the abolitionist minority had been more persuasive or less utopian, but these suppositions pose a problem too imponderable to resolve. History "solves" some problems by an agony of protracted conflict, resulting in partial advances that have continually to be rewon.

Leaders of abolitionism reflected the diversity of American religious resources available to reformers as well as a common prior experience in seeking to moralize society through voluntary associative activity. Inevitably they differed about strategy, but their tactical disputes were intrinsic to their position as a minority moral movement, increasingly disaffected from the American established world of institutions in spite of their common faith in the Declaration's postulate of unalienable rights. Whether as radicals or as reformers, their religious identity distinguished them from modern secular movements against the establishment.

In New England, William Lloyd Garrison voiced a Christian anarchist position, with a strong later infusion of anticlerical rationalism, anathema to all the churches. Arthur and Lewis Tappan, organizers of the American Anti-Slavery Society, were Christian businessmen of a pietistic Congregational persuasion, derived from the Edwardsian evangelicalism of their devout and stern mother. They were ardent supporters of the "benevolent empire" of tract, Bible, and missionary societies, until their radicalism on slavery forced them to develop their own agencies. They had much in common with the pietistic Presbyterian Theodore Weld, converted to abolitionism by the visiting Englishman Charles Stuart and by association with the American educators Charles B. Storrs, Elizur Wright, Jr., and Beriah Green at Western Reserve College.

Liberal Unitarianism, a rationalist enemy of Calvinism, also produced abolitionists when its outlook, as in the cases of Thomas T. Stone, Theodore Parker, and Thomas Wentworth Higginson, was "burned over" by the radical intuitionism of Transcendentalism. Stone, dismissed by his parish in Salem over the issue of the Fugitive Slave Law of 1850, later spoke of Roger Williams as a prophet of the idea of "soul freedom," which Stone, in a way congenial to abolitionism, interpreted to mean that "just so far as any sin, just so far freedom is lost, just so far slavery is introduced."[2] Parker's views were suffused with enough of Emerson's romantic criticism of historical Christianity to create a scandal in the New England Unitarian establishment. Higginson, who preferred Parker to his teachers at the Harvard Divinity School, joined him in protest against the Fugitive Slave Law by personally helping to ram down the door of a Boston courthouse and later participated in John Brown's conspiracy for a slave insurrection and an invasion of the federal arsenal at Harper's Ferry.

Brown himself was fierce proof that an older Congregational Calvinism, steeped in Jonathan Edwards and the Old Testament, could serve as a constant frame of reference for his own increasingly violent version of abolitionism. Like Garrison, Weld, the Tappans, Parker, and Higginson, he too came from a family of whom at least one parent was influentially and notably pious. Whether liberal, evangelical, or anarchistic in doctrine, the abolitionists were committed to actualizing their faith in social terms. However much they would differ on tactics or on creeds, they shared a common moral absolutism and activism.

Their militancy would lead them into tense and often disruptive relationships with the organized churches, which were reluctant to oppose slavery in practice. Black abolitionists were more likely to be clergymen than whites, whose churches were vulnerable to racist prejudices and regional differences in a decentralized society. Baptist and Methodist abolitionists in the 1840's had to split off from their mother churches to form their own, and so did the Free Church Synod of the Presbyterians when it discovered that neither the Old School nor the New School branch could avoid accommodating their Southern brethren on slavery. Even the Quakers, who had made nonslaveholding a condition of membership, segregated their meetings racially.[3]

The militancy of a Protestant minority on the issue of slavery was a more daring extension of a much more popular Protestant militancy on the issue of total abstinence from all alcoholic beverages. While many of the intemperate advocates of "temperance" found in this reform an outlet for their impulse to impose Puritan middle-class values of industry and frugality on workers, immigrants, and Catholics, they also provided abolitionists with a model for their moral hope of producing repentant slaveholders in the dramatic spectacle of the reformed drunkard. Even black abolitionist rallies were also temperance meetings. The whole spectrum of antislavery reform—Christian anarchist, evangelical, and conservative Republican—overlapped at one point in their leaders' sympathy for the temperance movement.

Garrison's own mother, a pious Baptist whose "second birth" had led her to be turned out of her house by her Episcopalian father, had been deserted by a drunken husband, a disaster her son did not forget or forgive. Arthur Tappan, the New York silk merchant who was the first president of the American Anti-Slavery Society, withdrew from the conservative American Colonization Society when he found that Liberia depended upon the importation of American rum. Extreme activists like Higginson and John Brown were both temperance advocates. The leading and successful advocate of the Maine Prohibition law, Neal Dow of Portland, son of a Quaker opponent of the liquor interests, would later support the moderate Free-Soil and Republican movements. Lincoln, later the leader of moderate antislavery Republicans, gave an address in 1842 that cited the movement against "the demon intemperance" as a vital ally to "the cause of political freedom," and he extravagantly compared it in relation to the American Revolution as leading to "a viler slavery manumitted, a greater tyrant deposed."*

Lincoln's imagery hinted at the ideological step that could be taken from temperance to antislavery. The emphasis on drinking as a personal sin, the attack on the iniquitous social influence of the dramseller, and the growing search for legislative means to prohibit sin would find parallels in the development of the antislavery movement. Temperance, however, was a conservative cause, fostered by those drawn to the Whig Party with strong prejudices against Masons and Irish Catholics. Abolitionists shared these prejudices but they developed a much more radical movement when they separated from the Colonization Society and challenged both church and state.

Even so, the crusade against intemperance could sometimes divide clergymen against their church, as the Unitarian minister John Pierpont discovered when his parishioners, some of whom were liquor dealers, agitated for his removal from the Hollis Street Meeting House, where he had preached against the renting out of the church's cellar as a warehouse to a rum merchant.[4] Conflict over Prohibition could also generate riots, as it did in Portland, Maine, when in 1855 a mob protested Mayor Dow's legal Puritanism and was fired on by city militia. Old School and New School Presbyterians, furthermore, divided over the issue of making temperance an official position as they would split over abolition. The moral crusade against the grogshops had a much broader and more "respectable" front than the crusade for abolition of slavery because it did not counter racist attitudes, threaten extensive property interests, or extensively divide the churches, but it was no accident of private prejudice that Harriet Beecher Stowe's Simon Legree would be portrayed as a drunkard as well as a slave beater.

* The address was given in a Presbyterian church for an organization of reformed drunkards, such as his law partner, William Herndon, who as mayor of Springfield later instituted local prohibition. Philip Van Doren Stern, ed., *The Life and Writings of Abraham Lincoln* (New York, 1940), p. 266; David Donald, *Lincoln's Herndon* (New York, 1948), pp. 65–71.

For true abolitionists emancipation was a question of salvation. A modern sociologist has usefully distinguished five ideal types of salvation theories among sects: (1) the *conversionist* emphasis on the individual's experience of a "second birth" as the saving imperative; (2) the *revolutionist* emphasis on anticipating the overturning of an evil world by supernatural action, as in the Second Coming; (3) the *introversionist* effort, as with the Mennonites, to cut oneself off from the rust and stain of the world's contagion; (4) the *reformist* stress on ameliorating the world by changing it in accordance with the dictates of conscience; and finally (5) the *utopian* effort, illustrated by many nineteenth-century communal experiments, to rebuild a world without tension and conflict by a return to sacred principles.[5] The abolitionist movement illustrated in some degree all these types, in an eclectic spirit fostered by a large, decentralized, dynamic society without an established church, but its dominant emphasis was reformist or revolutionist.

Tocqueville implicitly understood that the classic sociological antithesis (later made by Ernst Troeltsch) between radical "sect" and conservative "church" was a distinction appropriate to Europe rather than to nineteenth-century America. Tocqueville was impressed not with the variety of sects in America but with their common way of "looking upon their religion in the same light." He was responding to the normalization of religious groups that had once been in sharp tension with the established order, a process that changed sects into "denominations," accepting and accepted by the larger society as legitimate:

All the American clergy know and respect the intellectual supremacy exercised by the majority; they never sustain any but necessary conflicts with it. They take no share in the altercations of parties, but they readily adopt the general opinions of their country and their age, and they allow themselves to be borne away without opposition in the current of feeling and opinion by which everything around them is carried along. They endeavor to amend their contemporaries, but they do not quit fellowship with them. Public opinion is therefore never hostile to them; it rather supports and protects them, and their belief owes its authority at the same time to the strength which is its own and to that which it borrows from the opinions of the majority.[6]

His description is roughly true of the organized churches, and for that very reason a vigorous antislavery movement would have to challenge them. In doing so the abolitionists became a "sect," in tension not only with the larger society but also with the conventional churches. Tocqueville's praise of the majoritarian sympathies of the various denominations posed the paradox that this virtue of American religion entailed the vice of its sharing the majority's racial prejudices, which he had so keenly and unhappily noted. It is only fair to remember, however, that his journey to America ended before the emergence of the abolitionist movement or of the organized mobs, led by "gentlemen of property and standing," who sought to disrupt and suppress moral critics of the colonization program. A recent study of such rioters in Utica and Cincinnati highlights the common evangelical style of the abolitionists by finding that their tormentors (lawyers, bankers, politicians, journalists, and merchants) were far more likely than their victims to be active in formalistic or "high church" religious affiliations (such as Old School Presbyterian or Episcopal).[7] The cleavage was not in social class but in religious identifications, linked with libertarian political convictions. The American theme of republican religion thus produced a middle-class "sect" that in its aspiration to morally organize the society also suggested the Puritan establishment's will to bring religion and politics closer together, but that impulse was crucially modified by the nineteenth-century enthusiasm for voluntary societies of benevolent purpose.

The style of the abolitionist movement was intensely sectarian in several ways: its evangelical concern for an inner transformation of the self, anxious about its purity of commitment; its passion for evangelizing the heathen; its moral suspicion of the worldly surrounding culture, of hedonistic customs and pragmatic authorities; its emotional identification with the lowly and the oppressed; its lay participation in leadership roles; and finally its adventist faith in the coming Kingdom of God. In this sense the social policy of abolitionism was the strategy of a sect in fundamental tension with organized society and the churches. While the religious sects formed in the first Great Awakening were becoming normalized into "denominations" with an increasing accommodation to the mores of the larger society, the abolitionists created what in effect was a new sect whose integrity was defined by its refusal to accommodate on the issue of slavery.

This sectarian style was clearest in those, like Garrison, who most bitterly attacked the organized churches. In Adventist language he warned the American Colonization Society in 1829 of an impending apocalypse: "The terrible judgments of an incensed God will complete the catastrophe of republican America." The slave revolt of Nat Turner in Virginia two years later confirmed him in his belief that only immediate emancipation could save the country "from the vengeance of Heaven." He scorned the colonizers' acceptance of the reality of racial prejudice as a failure to recognize the unlimited power of the gospel:

I call upon the spirits of the just made perfect in heaven, upon all who have experienced the love of God in their souls here below, upon the Christian converts in India and the islands of the sea, to sustain me in the assertion that there *is* power enough in the religion of Jesus Christ to melt down the most stubborn prejudices, to overthrow the highest walls of partition, to break the strongest caste, to improve and elevate the most degraded, to unite in fellowship the most hostile, and to equalize and bless all its recipients.

As early as 1837 Garrison had defined his perfectionism in the *Liberator,* against "the general corruption of all political parties and religious sects," as a movement for "the emancipation of our whole race from the dominion of man, from the thralldom of self, from the government of brute force, from the bondage of sin—and bringing them under the dominion of God, the control of an inward spirit, the government of the law of love, and into the obedience and liberty of Christ, who is 'the same, yesterday, TO-DAY, and forever.' " Freedom for the slave, in this perspective, was not merely social reform on political and democratic grounds; it was part of the religious transformation of the soul from the bondage of selfishness and of the coercion of the social fabric. Christians were obligated to "separate from 'the kingdoms of this world,' which are all based upon THE PRINCIPLE OF VIOLENCE, and which require their officers and servants to govern and be governed by that principle."[8]

Garrison did not impose his own conclusions on the American Anti-Slavery Society; many of its members later wished rather to impose their tactics on him when they feared that his advocacy of Christian anarchism and of women's rights would jeopardize their power to influence more moderate Americans. In 1840 his supporters, including many women, were victorious, however, against his more reformist opponents, who therefore split off to form the American and Foreign Anti-Slavery Society. By then the more moderate abolitionists were anxious to engage in political action on behalf of antislavery, a cause particularly pressed by the clergymen in the movement, who were most offended by Garrison's vituperative attacks on the organized churches. Four years later Garrison was able to carry the original

American Anti-Slavery Society with him on the Christian anarchist principle of withdrawing from the political process of voting in elections until a "righteous government" had superseded the present one. He could never accept a charitable tone of moral criticism because it reflected the "absurd and dangerous dogma, that men are 'the creatures of circumstances'—not sinful, but unfortunate—not inwardly corrupt, but outwardly trammelled."[9] By this absolute moral voluntarism, Garrison marked the distance between himself and modern reformers influenced by sociological determinism.

His form of civil disobedience differed as well, for he urged only the refusal of *voluntary* allegiance or help to the government, while resignedly submitting to its "exactions." His nonresistant ethic condemned not only slaveholders but also slave insurrections and John Brown's conspiratorial actions. But by 1859, on the eve of the execution of Brown, he compromised his logic by urging "success to every slave insurrection at the South, and in every slave country," on the equivocal ground that when "carnal weapons" were thrown into the scale of freedom it was a sign of "positive moral growth" toward "the sublime platform of non-resistance; and it is God's method of dealing retribution upon the head of the tyrant."[10] When the South seceded, Garrison at first welcomed the move as an opportunity for separating the North from the dead weight of Southern sin, as if evil could be sectionalized and the North politically purified, a position hardly consistent with Christian anarchism. With the onset of the war itself he changed again to respond with reformist sympathy to Lincoln's antislavery efforts, now that it was clear that they had a chance to succeed. For some other religious anarchists (such as the Universalist minister Adin Ballou) only a utopian community could resolve the dilemmas of living in a sinful world, and a few extreme "come-outers" would be suspicious even of their own local and voluntary organizations as impediments to an antinomian freedom of soul.[11]

The abolitionists' positions were a compound of tactical shifts and various religious strategies, dictated not only by their moral ideology but by their social objective of defeating slavery and racial prejudice. Like other ideologists they found that an unpredictable history put severe strains on their logic and that a principled social policy was never as easy to follow as the certainties of their moral position seemed to suggest. Having made an explosive social issue fundamental to their cause, they could not take the sectarian path of concentrating on building individual ladders to heaven in small groups of gathered brethren. For all its perfectionism their gospel was, like that of the Puritans, always relevant to the historical world.

The majority of abolitionists, unlike the anarchists, accepted government and churches as necessary organizations in principle, but they wished to make them moral instruments of abolitionist doctrine. They were prepared to build separate churches, missionary organizations, and political parties to advance and preserve their morality, and they held more traditional views about the Sabbath and the Bible than the iconoclastic and more utopian Garrisonians, for whom abolitionism itself eventually would "by its own inherent power" overcome both church and state "as now organized."[12] The form of perfectionist morality characteristic of the more moderate abolitionists was close to that of Wesley's Methodism with its vision of the growth in holiness of the soul's development. Asa Mahan, the Congregational-Presbyterian president of Oberlin and author of *Scripture Doctrine of Christian Perfection* (1839), taught that "perfect obedience to the moral law" in the sense of the absence of all selfishness could be progressively attained. Yet man would still be subject to temptation, sinful feelings, and ignorance, as he was not in radical antinomian theories.[13] Most of these moderate perfectionists would later seek to find in the Liberty Party a fellowship of true believers.

The original consensus of abolitionists was that they would preach the "immediate repentance" of slaveholders, who would then free their bondmen, pay them wages, and educate them. The plan of this reform, as Elizur Wright, secretary of the American Anti-Slavery Society, explained, was the "gospel plan for converting the world" by setting forth "the true *doctrine* of human rights in high places and low places." Wright conceded that such missionary efforts would probably lead to a threat of secession on the part of "a great body of slaveholders," yet he had a millennial expectation that a "full tide" of public sympathy for the cause would come "at length."[14] The American Anti-Slavery Society was also a reformist sect insofar as it accepted the Constitutional right of the states to legislate on slavery within their borders; hoped to influence Congress in a Constitutional way to eliminate the slave trade, to eradicate slavery from the District of Columbia, and to keep it out of any newly formed states; and pledged itself to work for the civic and religious equal rights of Negroes *without the use of force* either by slaves or reformers.

How should one see the abolitionists in historical perspective? The revivalist sects of the first Great Awakening had also challenged the Standing Order on libertarian grounds, and to protect their voluntary churches they had tactically joined with more secular republicans to separate church from state. Yet they had implicitly accepted legal proscription of blasphemy, profanity, gambling, theatergoing, and desecration of the Sabbath, as well as legal prescription of religious teaching in the public schools. Prominent abolitionist leaders tended, however, to come from backgrounds where they had been influenced by the Congregational-Presbyterian churches of the once-established Standing Order, which had fostered alliance between church and state. In political ancestry they were much more likely to be oriented not towards the Jeffersonian Democrats but towards the Whig Party, which saw the state as a positive instrument for economic, moral, and religious objectives. In their party origins Whigs had drawn on the Protestant evangelical animus against Masonry and Catholicism, seen as insidious threats to Protestant republicanism; and abolitionists shared the Whigs' suspicion of the Democrats' talent for fostering an ethic of party loyalty on a broad secular base that included immigrants, Romanists, deists, and agnostics.[15]

They were not rationalistic or latitudinarian enough to be Jeffersonian separationists. They were too close to the Puritan tradition of using the state for religious and moral objectives to seek only their own freedom from political regulation, as Baptists had earlier done. They had too much postmillennial optimistic enthusiasm to be quietists withdrawing from secular society into the pessimistic expectation of the apocalyptic Second Coming. Most of them were not collectivistic or antinomian enough to dream of small communal utopias of the faithful. Instead they were moral activists whose history predisposed them to the stance of a reformist sect, seeking means to shape the larger society closer to their own values. But they could not do this in the spirit of a denomination that basically accepted the secular system; they could do it only in the spirit of a sect that lived in challenging tension with the larger society.

Their stand was complicated by the fact that the secular tradition itself in America was favorable in principle to what the First Amendment called the free exercise of religion and to what the Declaration of Independence called the "self-evident" truths of man's endowment by the Creator with "inalienable rights" of life, liberty, and the pursuit of happiness. They would become divided, therefore, about whether the Constitution was "an agreement with hell" or an antislavery charter for radical reform. Furthermore, as men who abhorred coercion, they would be troubled by the memory that their country's origin had been born in revolutionary violence. Even Garrisonian "disunionists" would finally subordinate their Christian anarchism to wartime political hopes for transforming American society, and before that many other abolitionists would themselves go beyond "moral suasion" to enter the sinful world of politics in third-party movements. Some supported the Liberty Party on an abolitionist program; others supported the schismatic Liberty League's attempt to offer a broader, more varied libertarian program; still others favored merging the Liberty Party with the more conservative Free-Soil Party, restricting their abolitionism in hope of gaining influence at the polls. But characteristically most of them accepted parties only if they could be political expressions of religious and moral values. In this sense they accepted formal separation of church and state as institutions without ever accepting the separation of religious from secular ideas and values. Instead of rejecting the sinful world in an "introversionist" style, they wished to transform it.

The striking fact is that, for all their suspicion of political parties and their belief in the pre-eminence of the soul over any organization, they spent much of their lives participating in conventions, organizing societies, and imaginatively and vigorously exploiting economic, legal, and lobbying tactics for influencing established authority. Despite their sectarian style, which inevitably inhibited their capacity to engage in the compromising medium of the political process, the abolitionists did win victories to offset the obvious failure of their utopian hope of converting slaveholders to repentant emancipation. They kept the public issue of slavery alive, defended free speech, and improved the position of free Negroes.

Lewis Tappan, for example, whom Weld had converted to immediatism, exercised his prodigious energies in organizing legal help for the slaves from Sierra Leone aboard the *Amistad* who in 1839 had revolted, killed the captain and cook, and dropped anchor finally off Long Island. Tappan's efforts not only aroused widespread sympathy for the black men, in danger of being turned over to Spanish authorities with the connivance of the Van Buren administration, but also secured for their cause the legal help of John Quincy Adams. His eloquence persuaded the Supreme Court to sustain a federal court's decision that under Spanish law, by treaty with Great Britain, the prisoners were illegal immigrants whose allegedly Spanish names had been forged by a Cuban company. Tappan arranged for their return to Africa, having done his best to introduce them to Christian faith. (Their leader, however, would then enter the slave trade himself.)

Negro abolitionists initiated a sustained innovative campaign for more than a decade in Boston, seeking by use of the boycott, the petition, and the legal suit to desegregate the city's public schools, and similar campaigns were mounted in Nantucket, Salem, and Rochester. These vigorous tactics were heartily supported by white Garrisonians. The Free-Soil lawyer Charles Sumner argued before the highest court in Massachusetts in 1849 for the abolition of segregated schools in Boston, and while the court reduced the "equal protection of the laws" clause in the state constitution to mean only legal protection for unequal rights in "separate but equal" schools, black and white abolitionists by 1855 had won legislative support for a statute forbidding segregation in any public schools of the state. The Garrisonians also succeeded in their campaign against the law forbidding intermarriage of whites and Negroes in Massachusetts and against the practice of segregation on three of the state's railroads.[16] Religious radicalism was fully capable of reformist efforts at legal and political change. The more moderate religious abolitionists conducted racially mixed Sunday schools, as Lewis Tappan did, operated an Underground Railroad for fugitive slaves, and financed Negro schools in Canada.

Evangelical abolitionists tended to support the political tactics of Joshua Leavitt, a former Yankee minister, temperance lecturer, author of an evangelical hymnbook, and editor of the *Emancipator*. He persuaded Theodore Weld to go to Washington as a researcher on behalf of the "Conscience Whigs" struggling against the Congressional gag rule on antislavery petitions, and by 1844 John Quincy Adams and Joshua R. Giddings had won that victory. Giddings, an elder of the Congregational Church and president of his local Bible society in the Western Reserve, had reorganized his collapsing legal career, personal finances, and political prospects by a conversion, aided by Weld, to political antislavery agitation in the House. Successively active in the Whig, Free-Soil, and Republican Parties, he kept in touch with radical abolitionists whom he sought to draw into his own party-organizing efforts. Radicals were politically canny enough to set up debates with him in order to give him a chance to define the Republican Party's stance in stronger antislavery terms than it otherwise would have taken. At the second Republican national convention, in 1860, Giddings enjoyed the deserved triumph of creating enough moral support, by walking out of the convention, to persuade the delegates on a second vote to follow his proposal of inserting the preamble of the Declaration of Independence into the Republican platform. It was a symbol of how crisis was drawing men into political commitment that the convention was moved to reconsider its rejection of the preamble by the eloquence of a delegate who had helped Thoreau build his retreat at Walden and who had once been a boarder at the utopian colony of Brook Farm.[17]

Political action posed the problem of whether abolitionists had more to lose by dilution of their own principles than they did to gain by third-party efforts. Garrison's adherents, not all of whom accepted his own anarchism, were not unrealistic in thinking that they had more to lose. Certainly the political abolitionists could not take much satisfaction in their party efforts, for they were stretched on the rack of having to collaborate with anti-Negro Free-Soilers, being satisfied with a splinter party's trivial share of the vote, or aiding the Democrats by drawing off Whig support. Lewis Tappan's experiences were typically agonizing. His efforts to induce the British to buy up Texas lands in order to provide money to compensate slaveholders for emancipating their bondmen played into the hands of the Tyler administration by stimulating fears that unless Texas was annexed the United States would be encircled by Great Britain. When his brother Benjamin, a senator from Ohio, sent him damaging information to publicize the pending American treaty with the republic of Texas, along with advice that Liberty Party men should support Democrats for the sake of Negro freedom, the Senate did respond by refusing ratification, and Van Buren was forced to take a stand against annexation. But James K. Polk, an ardent expansionist, was nominated instead by the Democrats. When the joint resolution annexing Texas carried Congress in 1845, it was Benjamin Tappan who cast the deciding vote for it in conformity with his instructions from the Ohio legislature. To heap insult on injury, he urged Lewis to follow his own opportunistic example and invest in Texas stock.[18]

Electoral politics was a frustrating experience for a religious abolitionist. In 1840 Lewis Tappan had voted with reservations for the Liberty Party candidate, James G. Birney, a former slaveholder turned abolitionist, who gloomily mistrusted a majority principle that included Masons, Catholics, and immigrants. In 1844 Tappan, unable to organize support for an alternative, had to accept the unpersuasive Birney again and see the triumph of the Democrat Polk, who benefited from the split of the Whig constituency and thus won New York's critical electoral vote. Tappan had to console himself with the surprising religious but nonpolitical fact that Polk was a Presbyterian Sabbatarian and teetotaler. Despite his opposition to the schismatic Liberty League abolitionists, who in 1848 nominated Gerrit Smith for President, Tappan could not stomach the alternative candidacy of Van Buren, backed by elements of the Liberty Party, Conscience Whigs, and radical Democratic Barnburners, joined on a minimum Free Soil platform of excluding slavery from the territories in order to keep them open to white men but closed to free Negroes. Tappan joined more than two thousand other abolitionists in voting for Smith. In 1855 Tappan himself assisted in forming another organization, the American Abolition Society. It was based on the unhistorical premise that the Constitution outlawed slavery in the states; and its first convention split over John Brown's appeal for the use of arms in Kansas. An advocate of nonviolence, Tappan nominated Smith, who now agreed with Brown, and then he reluctantly voted for the Republican John C. Frémont in the national election of 1856. Small wonder he felt far more satisfaction and success as a religious reformer in organizing the American Missionary Association and the Reform Book and Tract Society as antislavery counterparts to the more conservative organs of the "benevolence empire" inspired by the second Great Awakening.

In view of the pervasiveness of racism even among moderate antislavery men, many abolitionists increasingly despaired of any nonviolent solution to the problem of Negro slavery. Only the Garrisonians, in any case, had consistently maintained an extreme nonresistance position that rejected in principle all forms of coercion and some of them began to defect in the 1850's. A moral absolutism that converted "the Slave Power" into an infidel conspiracy of the devil was bound to further an increasing polarization that would tend to favor the resort to violence. Some abolitionists would then advocate and participate in revolutionary action. In 1854 Theodore Weld's wife, Angelina Grimké, concluded that slavery was a greater Christian crime than murder: "We are compelled to choose between two evils, and all that we can do is to take the *least,* and baptize liberty in blood, if it must be so." By 1859 one of the leading nonresistants, Henry C. Wright, could openly sponsor a resolution that obedience to God demanded forcible resistance to slaveholders and to slavehunters. Thomas W. Higginson had once argued for payment of the legal penalty as the moral price of civil disobedience to the Fugitive Slave Law of 1850, but by 1854 he was convinced that "the conflict with Slavery is not a reform, it is Revolution."[19] Higginson, the radical liberal Unitarian, and Brown, the traditional Calvinist, were ready to join each other on the bloody ground of Kansas and Harper's Ferry.

The hope of millennium would yield for many to a growing fear that it would have to come about through a prior apocalypse. History seemed to forecast the point, but those who so predicted inevitably were engaged in the dubious business of self-fulfilling prophecy. As the spiral of violence mounted, it persuaded some reformist abolitionists that only war could end slavery, while it taught the revolutionist Garrison to become more reformist in relation to the political process for the same reason. In either case Biblical Christianity had eloquent texts for rationalizing violence as well as for turning the other cheek. Tocqueville was largely right that Christianity for most Americans was a conservative influence, but the coming convulsion of American society would bring many to see what a Nat Turner or a John Brown knew in their bones: that the Bible tells some terrifying millennial stories.

XI

Day of Vengeance

Tocqueville could not easily make up his mind about America's future. In ages of equality civil wars would be unlikely because the majority party would have such great moral and physical resources against resistance movements. If there were revolutions, however, they would be brought about "by the presence of the black race on the soil of the United States; that is to say, they will owe their origin, not to the equality, but to the inequality of condition." Furthermore, he could not realistically believe "in the duration of a government" that by 1900 would have to "hold together forty different nations spread over a territory equal to one half of Europe, to avoid all rivalry, ambition, and struggles between them, and to direct their independent activity to the accomplishment of the same designs." The precipitate pace of territorial expansion greatly alarmed him, for it was bound to arouse fear, envy, and rivalry for control. He took refuge in a distinction between the union and the republic. The union would only last as long as circumstances favored it, but a republican form of government seemed to him to be "the natural state of the Americans."[1]

Republicanism suffused the society: "The father of a family applies it to his children, the master to his servants, the township to its officers, the county to its townships, the state to the counties, the Union to the states; and when extended to the nation, it becomes the doctrine of the sovereignty of the people." In the United States "even the religion of most of the citizens is republican, since it submits the truths of the other world to private judgment, as in politics the care of their temporal interests is abandoned to the good sense of the people." Whatever would happen in the interim, the time would come when one hundred and fifty million people would be living in North America

173

with "the same civilization, the same language, the same religion, the same habits, the same manners, and imbued with the same opinions, propagated under the same forms. The rest is uncertain, but this is certain; and it is a fact new to the world, a fact that the imagination strives in vain to grasp."[2] Pessimistic about the relatively short-run future, he was relatively confident about the country's long-range prospects for republican unity without monarchism or aristocracy.

Ambivalence about the future was also an American characteristic. Officially, American spokesmen were fond of boasting of their emancipation from the darkness of feudal Europe. But sober second thought often alarmed them about the possibility of decline. The "Free-Soilers" for whom Lincoln eventually spoke were unified by the belief that the republic had degenerated from an original genesis in freedom and the declension could be arrested only by "denationalizing" slavery. They envisioned the new territories as the locus of a regenerative rebirth of original principles of freedom.[3] The religious imagination, on the other hand, had available an even more dramatic myth of history in Biblical visions of apocalypse and millennium. They would seem especially appropriate when revolution or civil war was imminent. Slavery had its origins and sanctions in violence, and both its victims and their sympathizers knew that on that topic the Bible had powerful stories to tell. Appropriately, Nat Turner, Harriet Beecher Stowe, John Brown, and Abraham Lincoln would all find Biblical themes essential to their understanding of the American crisis. Turner would anticipate Brown, just as Mrs. Stowe anticipated Lincoln.

Nat Turner was born in 1800, the same year as John Brown. William Styron's *The Confessions of Nat Turner* (1967) has made the revolt both famous and controversial by his imaginative variations on the meager historical record, the report of a lawyer who saw in the event the conservative wisdom of "strictly and rigidly enforced" laws in restraint of the slaves. Styron's portrait* (as black writers have protested) creates a more isolated figure by diminishing the role of Turner's grandmother, whose religious character was a source of inspiration and affection for him; by omitting his father, who had previously escaped from slavery; and by ignoring the oral tradition that he had a black wife on another plantation.[4] Styron, in fact, invents a neu-

---

* In a prefatorial note he called his work "a meditation on history," rather than " 'an historical novel' in conventional terms," adding that he "rarely departed" from the *known* facts about Turner. The lawyer's report is the only documentary evidence about Turner, and it has (to make a grisly pun) its own ax to grind.

rotic psychosexual etiology of repression for the novel's hero, who is imagined in the bloody climax to have felt a redeeming remorse for having killed a white adolescent girl whom he had previously impotently desired. This sentiment leads him to permit the escape of another white girl who may well have alerted the planters and doomed the rebellion. The documentary Turner was less ambivalent and less compassionate, speaking to the lawyer of his intentions and deeds with "calm, deliberate composure."

Convinced by his parents that he was "intended for some great purpose," Turner displayed unusual literary and mechanical ability, as well as austere manners, devoting much of his time to fasting and prayer. Because he often believed that he communed directly with the same spirit that "spoke to the prophets in former days," he might seem to illustrate what William James called the "diabolical mysticism" of "delusional insanity," which has "the same sense of ineffable importance in the smallest events, the same texts and words coming with new meanings, the same voices and visions and leadings and missions, the same controlling by extraneous powers; only this time the emotion is pessimistic: instead of consolations we have desolations; the meanings are dreadful; and the powers are enemies to life."[5] But Turner's religion was a more literal version, adapted to his experience as a slave, of the common messianic and millennialistic revivalism of white Protestantism. The lawyer himself remarked on Turner's "natural intelligence and quickness of apprehension," however frightened he was of the captive's "fiend-like face when excited by enthusiasm." The critical point is that the grisly purpose of Turner's band ("it was quickly agreed we should commence at home on that night, and until we had armed and equipped ourselves, and gathered sufficient force, neither age nor sex was to be spared [which was invariably adhered to]") was a function both of his violent vision and of the desperate situation that any freedom-seeking blacks faced in the South.[6]

Turner's mission was first formulated in his mid-twenties. He had run away for a month and then voluntarily returned, explaining that the Spirit had appeared to him and chastised him for having his wishes "directed to the things of this world, and not to the kingdom of Heaven." The other blacks criticized this acquiescence as beneath the dignity of such an unusual person, and "about this time" he had a vision: "And I saw white spirits and black spirits engaged in battle, and the sun was darkened—the thunder rolled in the Heavens, and blood flowed in streams—and I heard a voice saying, 'Such is your luck, such you are called to see, and let it come rough or smooth, you must surely bear it.' " After this revelation of race war, he began to "receive the true knowledge of faith," was made perfect by the Holy Ghost, and baptized himself and a white man in the river. In 1828 he glimpsed the traditional apocalyptic signs of the Second Coming* and took up the yoke of Christ on his own shoulders, convinced that "the time was fast approaching when the first should be last and the last should be first."[7]

In keeping with his earlier vision, he interpreted the sound of thunder and the dark of a solar eclipse as a sign to begin the work of slaying his enemies with their own weapons on the Fourth of July. But the planning, he confessed, affected his mind to such a degree that he fell ill, until on August 21, 1831, he saw another sign in the peculiar appearance of the sky and joined his band to attack with axes his admittedly "kind master" and his family.[8] More than fifty men, women, and children were brutally murdered. The day of vengeance had arrived at Jerusalem, Virginia, in streams of blood. Having lived out in fact the apocalyptic fantasies of nineteenth-century American religion, Turner evaded capture for over eight weeks while the others were quickly apprehended, seventeen being executed at law. Carnage incited carnage, and some hundred black men were killed in savage reprisal. Dreams of battle in an apocalyptic cataclysm had ended in a nightmare of white vengeance.

One of Turner's men—eventually there were some fifty—eloquently explained his presence in the rebellion on the ground that "his life was worth no more than others, and his liberty as dear to him."[9] But the leader's formulation of his intentions in the lawyer's account is more like the grandiose effort to actualize a messianic wish to participate in the day of judgment as envisioned in a war between the dark children of light and the white children of darkness. Styron's novel, in this respect, authentically dramatizes the point that "behind all [his] talk of simple flights was a grander design involving the necessity of death, cataclysm, annihilation."**

---

* The account has him finding a bloody dew on the leaves of corn and trees, a sign of doomsday in the Apocryphal Fourth Book of Esdras. See W. W. Heist, *The Fifteen Signs Before Doomsday* (East Lansing, Michigan, 1952), p. 52.

** As Vincent Harding suggests, Styron's psychologizing makes Turner sound too much like James Baldwin. But some critics turn Nat into H. Rap Brown or Stokely Carmichael. Cf. John Henrik Clarke and Harding, in Clarke, ed., *William Styron's Nat Turner: Ten Black Writers Respond* (Boston, 1968), pp. lx, 31–32.

Harriet Beecher Stowe found an escape from what she called "the dark side of domestic life" by writing fiction. The daughter of a minister who had reduced her to tears as a child by refusing to accept her religious conversion as genuine, she married an hallucinated, melancholic Biblical scholar at Lane Theological Seminary whose given name, Calvin, suggested the harsh confines of the theology she had struggled with for so much of her life. The Beecher family had considered the fiancé of Harriet's sister irretrievably damned because he died before undergoing Presbyterian conversion. Sister Catherine had consoled herself by dedicating herself to the cause of female education, including that of sister Harriet, who was made to turn her attention to theology instead of to poetry. A marriage with seven children in fourteen years on a minister's meager salary would have been a burden to any wife, but it was made heavier for Harriet by the fact that her husband, nearly ten years older, still mourned the death of his first wife, Eliza. Calvin Stowe anxiously and gloomily wandered through a vale of tears, a man vulnerable to hallucinatory visitations that Cotton Mather might well have included in his compendium, *Wonders of the Invisible World.* If his wife knew little of Negro slavery at first hand, she knew much about repression and servitude. Her most loved child died in a cholera epidemic in Cincinnati, and she later recalled that it was at his dying bed and grave that she "learned what a poor slave a mother may feel when her child is torn away from her." Much that is in *Uncle Tom's Cabin,* she felt, "had its root in the awful scenes and bitter sorrows of that summer. The nursery and the kitchen were my principal fields of labor."[10] It was as if she herself were a Negro house servant, separated from her child.

Her earliest ventures as a writer were in the popular sentimental vein of pious domesticity that characterized such publications as the *Evangelist, Religious Souvenir, Christian Keepsake, Temperance Offering,* and *Godey's Lady's Book.* Though she had lived at Lane Theological Seminary in the center of abolitionist ferment, she did not become an outspoken advocate of the cause until the stringent Fugitive Slave Law of 1850 had aroused the conscience of thousands in the North. She had once visited a plantation in Kentucky for a few hours and had helped a fugitive slave along the Underground Railroad, but most of what she knew about Negro slavery was culled from Theodore Weld's *Slavery As It Is* (1839), a documentation of the worst horrors of the institution. Perhaps her imagination for the theme of social oppression was stirred vicariously as well by her admiration for the writing of Maria Edgeworth, whose *Castle Rackrent* dramatized the cruelty of Irish landlords. When *Uncle Tom's Cabin* first appeared in the *National Era,* a journal that mingled literature and politics to further "the great movement on behalf of human liberty," one of its editors, John Greenleaf Whittier, had already attacked the Fugitive Slave Law. The serialization of her novel in 1851–52 was a stroke of perfect timing, catapulting an obscure housewife into international fame.

"Uncle Tom's Cabin is a work of religion," she later explained; and while many of her varied accounts of its writing were themselves a kind of fiction, this statement is absolutely true.[11] The genius of the novel is its imaginative embodiment of the religious temper of her culture as it struggled with the greatest social issue of her country's history. As a work of social protest alone, however, the novel is tamely conservative in its practical conclusions. She sponsored the policy of colonization of freed Negroes in Liberia, a proposal that the leading prophets of abolitionism had long abandoned. "Let the church of the North," she urged in her Concluding Remarks appended to the story, "receive these poor sufferers in the spirit of Christ; receive them to the educating advantages of a Christian republican society and schools, until they have attained to somewhat of a moral and intellectual maturity, and then assist them in their passage to those shores, where they may put in practice the lessons they have learned in America." Her character George, a fugitive slave, heads for Liberia because "a nation has a right to argue, remonstrate, implore, and present the cause of its race,—which an individual has not." Liberation in America would be postponed until Liberia had the power in a "great congress of nations" to make its appeal. Only such power could *justify* Negro protest— certainly a very conservative argument for an abolitionist.

Her case for colonization was linked to her cult of a romantic racism that inverted the traditional distinctions by contrasting "the hot and hasty Saxon" to the morally superior blacks, who are seen as "affectionate, magnanimous, and forgiving." Nietzsche's charge that Christianity cultivated virtues appropriate to slaves was a just one in her case, for she believed that Negroes by their sufferings were closest to the Christian doctrines of love and forgiveness. Slavery was a school of Christian virtue, a position uncomfortably analogous to the proslavery apologists', who defended it as a school in civilization for savages. In neither case did the slave graduate into American citizenship. Mrs. Stowe believed that Negro integration with whites in America was morally justified by the American's "professed principles of human equality," but this policy was incompatible with her idealization of the supposedly superior moral qualities of the African race, which slavery itself had allegedly produced. The reader's sympathies are therefore divided by the story between Uncle Tom's passive acceptance of his brutal treatment, the symbol of an ultimate Christian triumph through death over evil, and by the exciting struggles of George, Eliza, and Cassy to flee the prison of slavery and escape via the Underground Railroad to Canada. In the end the Negro is offered death or Liberia for a destiny.

The social radicalism of *Uncle Tom's Cabin* is also subverted by the fact that Mrs. Stowe, as William R. Taylor has pointed out, was partially seduced by the myth of the plantation.[12] Southern writers had learned to present it as a setting for the legend of a warm paternalism in contrast to the cold wage slavery of the Northern worker at the mercy of the marketplace. The amiable planter St. Clare is the most attractive white character in the novel, a melodramatic contrast to the satanically evil Yankee, Simon Legree, and the sugary Little Eva prefers the Southern plantation with all its servants to her uncle's Vermont because "it makes so many more round you to love, you know." St. Clare's coldly respectable wife finds this sentiment "just one of her odd speeches," but St. Clare sees it, with Mrs. Stowe, as proof of her otherworldly spirituality. But his inept benevolence cannot prevent his wife from selling their slaves down the river after his death. Granted some masters were kind, still slavery was wrong as a system, and the novel makes its powerful case through St. Clare's summation: "Quashy shall do my will, and not his, all the days of his mortal life, and have such chance of getting to heaven, at last, as I find convenient. This I take to be what slavery *is*. . . . Talk of the *abuses* of slavery! Humbug! The *thing itself* is the essence of all abuse! And the only reason why the land don't sink under it, like Sodom and Gomorrah, is because it is *used* in a way infinitely better than it is." The logic of this indictment is emotionally squared with Little Eva's preference for plantation life by improbably putting the argument in the mouth of a white Southern planter. By this tactic Mrs. Stowe could manage to have it both ways—a sentimental solution that accurately reflected the tendency of the literary North to join the literary South in a weakness for the plantation ideal of community life.

The conservatism and incoherence of her social argument may have been subconsciously appealing to American readers beset by similarly unresolved anxieties, for only a very few abolitionists were publicly disturbed by her enthusiasm for colonization. "Mrs. Stowe," as Louis Filler has said, "had helped to create an emotional bond between Northerners, not an antislavery program."[13] A burdensome sense of guilt for the injustice done to Negroes could lead to an unconscious hostility to the victims whose plight provoked it—an ambivalence suggested by Mrs. Stowe's formula for Negro destiny. Even Theodore Parker, one of the most outspoken and committed of the abolitionists, remarked after John Brown's raid, which he had supported, that "the Anglo-Saxon with common sense does not like this Africanization of America; he wishes the superior race to multiply rather than the inferior."[14] The colonization argument was morally ambiguous. Many freed Negroes, who resented white domination of abolitionist societies, were themselves in the 1850's drawn in despair to colonization projects, and they also dreamed of the Christian evangelization of Africa, as earlier black emigrationists had hoped.[15] But they did not make it the only alternative for American blacks.

If Mrs. Stowe wrote in a religious idiom familiar to both blacks and whites, she also tapped a familiar vein of patronization. Other white proponents of colonization could use her case to appease the prejudice expressed in the widespread fears of miscegenation. Lydia Maria Child conciliated the prejudice for example in her *Anti-Slavery Catechism* by proclaiming that "by universal emancipation we want to *stop* amalgamation."[16] That slavery had produced amalgamation was historically true and dramatically evident in the relative whiteness of the Negroes in *Uncle Tom's Cabin*. The surest way to prevent amalgamation after emancipation, however, would be to export freed Negroes to Africa. Mrs. Stowe, to be sure, did not argue in these terms, but her solution gave readers the opportunity to come to those conclusions, even if only half-consciously. Most of the abolitionists struggled earnestly to be consistent with their principles, but in a culture as prejudiced as their own, they naturally did not entirely escape its ethnic bias. One Negro professor who married the daughter of an abolitionist minister faced so much prejudice from her family and society that he was forced to flee to England. Even one of the leading political antislavery politicians, Joshua Giddings, was embarrassingly mute when an opponent in Congress asked him if he would favor Negroes voting in Ohio. The missionary attitude of the abolitionists, given the social distance between themselves and the Negroes, inevitably had an air of condescending superiority. Mrs. Stowe's prejudice came out in reverse as a romantic exaggeration of Negro virtues, identified with her own sentimental Protestantism.

Uncle Tom's Cabin is, as she said, "a work of religion." Its social analysis is everywhere subordinated to that interest. To Harriet Beecher Stowe the New Divinity Calvinism of a preacher like Samuel Hopkins, for all its modifications of the more austere system of Jonathan Edwards, was still too harsh for human nature's daily food. Her description of it in *The Minister's Wooing* is a telling metaphor:

There is a ladder to heaven, whose base God has placed in human affections, tender instincts, symbolic feelings, sacraments of love, through which the soul rises higher and higher, refining as she goes, till she outgrows the human, and changes, as she rises, into the image of the divine. At the very top of this ladder . . . [is] the threshold of paradise. . . . This highest step, this saintly elevation, which but few selectest spirits ever on earth attain . . . this Ultima Thule of virtue had been seized upon by our sage as the *all* of religion. He knocked out every round of the ladder, but the highest, and then, pointing to its hopeless splendor, said to the world, 'Go up thither and be saved!'[17]

The revivalism of Charles G. Finney had restored the rungs in that ladder by stressing the ability and obligation of man to climb it by his own efforts through a conversion to a loving Christ expressed in benevolent action as the best witness to a God who was more of an indulgent father than he was a stern judge. For Harriet Beecher Stowe this religion was the salvation of her own oppressed soul as the daughter of a dominating preacher of hellfire, the wife of a prematurely aged scholar, and the mother of a brood whose needs chained her to a grim life of genteel poverty. Her private history intersected with the public history of her age through an emotional religion whose atmosphere dominated her novel.

Uncle Tom got religion at a Methodist camp meeting and preached a Finneyite theology: "We does for the Lord when we does for his critturs." When Misse Cassy, sunk in despair on Legree's brutal plantation, protests that God has put slaves into a situation where they cannot help but sin, Uncle Tom reprovingly replies, "I think we *can*." Tom's example converts his agnostic master to Christianity, and he puts it into immediate practice by his decision to manumit his servant. Ineffective to the end, however, St. Clare is fatally wounded four pages later. He dies holding Tom's hand, reciting a requiem, remembering his pious mother, "the personification of the New Testament," and so comes "HOME, at last!" It is a tract for the times in the religious spirit of the Tract Society. The idle habits that mark the planter's distance from Christian virtue are the familiar sins of gambling, theatergoing, and drinking, and the planter appropriately dies from a wound received in a tavern brawl. Eva's Christian death brings Miss Ophelia from New England to recognize her duty of bringing up the mischievous Topsy, in spite of a Yankee prejudice against Negroes. Eliza's husband, George, loses his "dark, misanthropic, pining, atheistic doubts, and fierce despair" when he finds in a Quaker home on the Underground Railroad "the light of the living Gospel." The dying Uncle Tom, like "One whose suffering changed an instrument of torture, degradation and shame, into a symbol of glory, honor, and immortal life," converts two of Legree's "imbruted blacks" by the radiant power of a Christlike example of "self-denying suffering love." Even Legree himself, a tractarian caricature of evil as a lecherous, profit-minded, slaveholding, hard-drinking atheist, had his own day of grace when "he was almost persuaded." His heart "inly relented,—there was a conflict,—but sin got the victory, and he set all the force of his rough nature against the conviction of his conscience."

Mrs. Stowe added sentimental force to this emotional piety by linking it at every turn of the drama with her cult of domesticity. Thus St. Clare's mother, Legree's mother, and the Quaker epitome of "motherliness," Rachel Halliday, are the good angels who hover over doubtful souls, seeking to bring them "home" to God. This cult of the family, a Victorian theme, is historically illustrative of the underlining ethical impulse of the whole humanitarian reform movement of the ante-bellum period. The communitarian John Humphrey Noyes correctly identified it as "the enlargement of home—the extension of family union beyond the little man-and-wife circle to large corporations."[18] The fundamental crime of slavery in Mrs. Stowe's eyes was its disruption of the family, whether by white exploitation of black women, dramatized by the paleness of her Negro characters, or by the slave market itself, which was indifferent to anything except the cash nexus. The climax of her book appropriately brings together the mulatto George and his wife, children, sister, and mother, all embarked for Africa. *Uncle Tom's Cabin* is a Christian hymn to the pious family as a solution to the gravest problem of American society—a simplification that says much about the source of its appeal.

Yet no account of her story is complete that ignores the power it derives from her constant invocation of that millennialistic vision which the New Divinity theologians had passed on from Edwards to the New England revivalists of her day.[19] St. Clare recalls that his mother had told him of "a millennium that was coming when Christ should reign, and all men should be free and happy." The planter concluded that "all this sighing, and groaning, and stirring among the dry bones" was evidence of "a mustering among the masses, the world over." He is profoundly affected by those heavily marked passages in Tom's Bible that the Negro and Little Eva most relish because they tell of the Second Coming and the Last Judgment. The Negroes' "lowly docility of heart" made them representatives of "the highest form of the peculiarly *Christian life,* and, perhaps, as God chasteneth whom he loveth, he hath chosen poor Africa in the furnace of affliction, to make her the highest and noblest in that kingdom which he will set up, when every other kingdom has been tried, and failed; for the first shall be last, and the last first." The time was ripe, nations were "trembling and convulsed" from carrying within them in the form of "unredressed injustice" the elements of "this last convulsion." The Protestant churches, above all, stood under judgment of that day which would burn as an oven, "and he shall appear as a swift witness against those that oppress the hireling in his wages, the widow and the fatherless, and that *turn aside the stranger in his right;* and he shall break in pieces the oppressor."

The novel vibrates with an ambiguous sense of an imminent future, as full of menace as it is of promise, the anticipation of that crisis over slavery that her own book would help to bring about. Her preface begins on the note of postmillennial optimism in a day when "the hand of benevolence is everywhere stretched out." Her Concluding Remarks quiver instead with a premillennial apocalyptic fear, warning the Northern churches that prophecy associates "in dread fellowship, the *day of vengeance* with the year of his redeemed." Already the shadow of a coming civil war darkened the roseate millennial expectations of American Protestantism. This profoundly ambiguous sense of the future links the author not only to the older Calvinism that she hated but also to the actualities of her society as its sense of crisis deepened.

Uncle Tom still has power and eloquence in its treatment of an elemental theme, though its characters are dummies for their ventriloquist. Her penchant for categorization, however, is not so much because of any deficiency in her art, or in her knowledge of Negroes, as it is a consequence of her messianic view of history, in which all persons tend to lose their individual reality in the great cosmic drama of

God's plan. Her novel speaks with almost hysterical stridency for that blatant presumption which led Angelina Grimké in 1837 to write a Negro abolitionist that Joshua Leavitt had "thrown out a new and delightful idea": the Lord had "a great work for the colored people to do" because their humiliations were "the furnace in which he was purifying you from the dross, the tin, and the reprobate silver, that you might come out like seven times refined. . . . May the Lord lift you from the dung hill and set you among princes."[20] *Uncle Tom's Cabin* was the immensely popular dramatization of this abolitionist idea. If her policy of colonization was out of touch with the movement in the 1850's, her millennialism, which supported that strategy, was at the blazing center of the furnace of abolitionism.

The escaped slave and prominent abolitionist Frederick Douglass considered *Uncle Tom's Cabin* to be "a work of marvelous depth and power." He was honored that Mrs. Stowe invited him to visit her in 1853 before she sailed for England. "I have invited you here," she said, "because I wish to confer with you as to what can be done for the free colored people of the country." She expected to raise considerable money in England and wanted to have "some monument rise" to show that her novel was no transient influence. Douglass told her that what the free Negroes needed was an industrial college of the mechanical arts for learning useful trades in iron, clay, and leather. He added that colonization was not a hope of Negroes, who had grown up with the republic. "The truth is, dear madam, we are *here,* and here we are likely to remain." At the largest convention of colored people ever held in America, Douglass announced to warm approval that Mrs. Stowe planned to support his proposal for a trade school. Meanwhile she was in England, "there meeting all the best known and best worth knowing of the higher circles," as she proudly wrote. He later defended her in his newspaper against charges that she was accumulating British gold to no good purpose. Calling again on Mrs. Stowe when she returned, he learned that she had reconsidered her plan for the industrial college. No doubt, he concluded, she had her sufficient reasons, though he did not understand them. Her change of purpose, he remarked, was "a great disappointment, and placed me in an awkward position before the colored people of this country as well as to friends abroad, to whom I had given assurances. . . ."[21]

Douglass was more impressed with John Brown, with whom, as early as 1847, he had skeptically discussed the possibilities of organizing a slave insurrection. Brown was a Samson in a cruel and bloody temple, Douglass felt, even if the raid on Harper's Ferry was clearly a rash and doomed enterprise.

The parents of John Brown joined the Congregational Church in 1800, the year that he was born, and sixteen years later he joined the same denomination. As a tanner, he enforced church attendance on his employees and his early political views were conservative, revering the Federalists and reviling the Masons. In 1832 he organized a Congregational church in New Richmond, Pennsylvania, and sometimes preached himself from the works of Jonathan Edwards. Antislavery doctrine was a family tradition. His father was on the board of trustees at Western Reserve College, where he supported the anticolonizer "immediatists." When the trustees appointed a more conservative president, Owen Brown resigned and gave his loyalty to Oberlin. His son once took Negroes into the family pew during a revival, scandalizing the congregation, which later expelled him on technical grounds of absence. A disastrously inept and unsuccessful businessman, he was also the victim of family tragedy, losing nine of his own children by 1852. The agnosticism of his older sons was a constant thorn, and his only consolation was his habit of seeing all disasters as signs of God's determination to make man feel his dependency. "God Glorified in Man's Dependence," he knew, was one of Jonathan Edwards's sermons.[22]

At Pottawatamie in the Kansas Territory, where his sons had settled, Brown found himself plunged into border warfare as proslavery and Free State factions struggled for control of the area. Six members of the latter had been killed before Brown's band, under his orders, hacked to death with broadswords five men whose crime was not in holding slaves but in holding proslavery political opinions. Famous as a hero of the border wars, Brown was a powerful persuader of abolitionists, especially since the development of events seemed to give increasing credibility to the existence of a slave-power conspiracy to dominate the territories and the political and legal system of the country. He was even able to get the National Kansas Committee, formed to get money and arms for free-state emigrants, to transfer its guns to the Massachusetts branch, subject to his influence, and to get promises for money and supplies for defense of Kansas from conservative antislavery men who wanted Kansas to be without *any* Negroes, slave or free. In advertising his aims he cultivated his legend shrewdly by either ignoring or flatly denying his connection with the Pottawatamie massacres and his record as a debt-ridden failure in the management of his business enterprises.[23]

Brown's Old Testament style was entirely honest, however, and it was enough to disarm his supporters who imagined him to be a Yankee Oliver Cromwell. Like Brown himself, some members of "the Secret Six" who financed his conspiracy to attack the federal arsenal at Harper's Ferry, preparatory to starting a massive slave insurrection in the South, stilled their doubts of his capacity by the hope that even an unsuccessful invasion might start a war that would in fact free the slaves. But it was enough for absolutists that Brown was a dedicated enemy of slavery. They did not want to know the quixotic grim details, only that he was going to deliver the slave at last through blood. Some black radicals supported him too, and thirty-four Negroes heard him outline his Provisional Government for the liberated areas at an abolitionist convention in Canada that approved it unanimously. Only one of the blacks, however, would actually participate in the raid at Harper's Ferry.

Edwards had believed that an infinite sin justified an infinite punishment, a Calvinist argument for the harsh doctrine of election which left the damned to suffer forever. Brown, according to one of his acquaintances, believed that it was "infinitely better that this generation should be swept away from the face of the earth, than that slavery shall continue to exist."[24] One of his favorite books of the Bible was *Isaiah,* where it is said:

But thus saith the Lord, Even the captives of the mighty shall be taken away, and the prey of the terrible shall be delivered: for I will contend with him that contendeth with thee, and I will save thy children.

And I will feed them that oppress thee with their own flesh; and they shall be drunken with their own blood, as with sweet wine: and all flesh shall know I the Lord am thy Saviour and thy Redeemer, the mighty One of Jacob.

Brown was vulnerable to the danger of seeing himself as God's chosen instrument of justice, a compensation for his sorrows and failures. Now he had 950 pikestaves, 200 revolvers, and 198 rifles. He also had no escape plan, if he should need it, and, worst of all, no design for alerting the blacks who were supposed to rise up with pikes against their masters. After capturing the armory at Harper's Ferry, he fatally delayed leaving before it was too late, and in the battle seventeen lives were lost, among them two slaves, ten of his own men (including two of his sons), a free black uninvolved in the conspiracy, and a mayor who had provided in his will for the emancipation of his slaves. Thus once again Armageddon came to Virginia. All but one of the conspiratorial abolitionists who had backed him fled the country, and Brown staunchly chose to face as a Christian martyr a dubious, hasty legal execution for treason against Virginia (of which he was not a citizen). Characteristically, he denied that he had ever intended either destruction of property or the provocation of insurrection, making it easier for believers in his legend. Seven conspirators were hanged, but the Senate investigating committee indicted none of his abolitionist accomplices.

Brown's moving Biblical eloquence during his trial concealed all the brutal realities of his career from the awed gaze of antislavery reformers, and their more responsible and humane minds needed an antislavery martyr more than their idealism could afford the bitter complex truth. The conservative treasurer of the Kansas Emigrant Aid Company, Amos A. Lawrence, a financial supporter of Brown's family and farm, had come to recognize his "monomania" in 1858 when Brown and an escaped convict liberated the eleven slaves and property of two Missouri planters, leaving one shot to death.[25] The event had triggered more violence in Kansas, a forecast of his final raid which, predictably, further polarized opinion about slavery and stimulated sectional mistrust by unifying the South in a paranoiac anxiety about internal security and in preparations for imminent war. For all his duplicity, however, Brown prophesied truly that "the crimes of this *guilty land* will never be purged away but with *blood*." His own messianic vision of himself as God's vengeance in a Calvinist world had brought the country a step closer toward that terrible purgation.*

Fanaticism, always a temptation to desperate and religious men, could bring war closer. But the witness of prophets was not enough to bring about abolition of slavery. That would require the moral imperatives of a war fought in the name of democratic union and the artful efforts of seasoned politicians, as well as the continued agitation and efforts of moral reformers. The temper of abolitionism would itself undergo a sea change as the emergency of war enforced a greater concern for institutional realities. The politics of the slavery issue, moreover, made it necessary for reformers to influence a President who was

---

* I do not know when religious monomania becomes delusional insanity, but it ought to be possible to criticize fanaticism without branding it pathological.

profoundly legal and political in his orientation. But if many of them showed a capacity to transcend their familiar absolutism, the President himself would come increasingly to draw for his interpretation of the great crisis on the Protestant themes that had inspired them to militant action against the crime of slavery. Once again religion and republicanism in America would influence each other creatively, far more constructively than Nat Turner, John Brown, or Harriet Beecher Stowe could have imagined.

XII

A People's Contest and the Judgments of the Lord

Tocqueville was right in expecting "great calamities" from the struggle over slavery. By 1860 his admiring summary of American republicanism in 1835 was unrecognizable:

What is understood by republican government in the United States is the slow and quiet action of society upon itself. It is a regular state of things really founded upon the enlightened will of the people. It is a conciliatory government, under which resolutions are allowed time to ripen, and in which they are deliberately discussed, and are executed only when mature. The republicans in the United States set a high value upon morality, respect religious belief, and acknowledge the existence of rights. They profess to think that a people ought to be moral, religious, and temperate in proportion as it is free. What is called the republic in the United States is the tranquil rule of the majority, which, after having had time to examine itself and to give proof of its existence, is the common source of all the powers of the state. But the power of the majority itself is not unlimited. Above it in the moral world are humanity, justice, and reason; and in the political world, vested rights. The majority recognizes these two barriers; and if it now and then oversteps them it is because, like individuals, it has passions and, like them, it is prone to do what is wrong, while it discerns what is right.[1]

The "slow and quiet action" of society had erupted into a spiral of violence that included the struggle over Kansas, the caning of a Northern Senator by a Southern Representative, and the raid by a religious fanatic on a federal arsenal. The "enlightened will of the people" was polarized into sectional hatred. The Kansas-Nebraska Act, disrupting an accepted consensus on the geographical demarcation line between free and slave territory in the area of the Louisiana Purchase, had been "allowed time to ripen" in three months of bitter debate. Morality itself was in raging dispute. For the South, slavery was a Biblically sanctioned cornerstone of a good society; for the abolitionists, the fundamental Christian sin; for the Democrats and Whigs, an irrelevancy; for the Republicans, a potential evil in the territories but acceptable elsewhere; and for most Americans, North and South, morality did not go so far as to include political and social equality for freed Negroes. Religious belief, however much "respected," was divided on sectional lines. The "tranquil rule of the majority" was a chimera: no Presidential candidate in 1860 commanded a popular majority, and the electoral victory of the Republicans precipitated a secession of seven states. While the victorious candidate did believe that the majority had to respect the limits set by "humanity, justice, and reason," as well as by "vested rights," he himself did not have the support of a majority of voters in the nonseceding states, taken as a whole.

Given this breakdown of coherence, the new President made a stubborn and eloquent effort to restore to harmony the major ingredients of the disrupted tradition and to expand its meaning for the future. His legendary role as a secular saint was realistically rooted in the doctrinal nature of the dispute, testimony to the symbiosis of religion and politics in the American republic. If Lincoln's generation could not "escape history," as he warned, it could not escape either the issues that slavery and secession posed for the civic religion of the American people.

For better and worse, Lincoln was a successful lawyer and canny politician, not an "immediate emancipation" crusader. He even argued in his debates with Senator Stephen A. Douglas against social or political equality for free Negroes. He had a stubborn preference, as late as December, 1862, for the colonization policy, which Jefferson had once advocated to avoid racial mixture; and to save the Union before it shattered, Lincoln would have accepted the legal perpetuation of slavery in the South. His famed Emancipation Proclamation of January, 1863, was made for the sake of the union as a military measure to raise Northern morale, appease radicals, and win sympathy from Europe; and it affected only areas *outside* of Northern control. He had been satisfied with the Compromise of 1850, which had provoked Mrs. Stowe to speak out; and his party represented the interests of the protective tariff, free homesteads, and land grants to railroads even more than it did containment of slavery. Modern historians have properly emphasized these conservative aspects of Lincoln's policy in order to counter the legends that have grown up about him, but they have not been able to measure him against a better statesman of his time or to deny the authenticity of his antislavery convictions.

Frederick Douglass, in an oration on the occasion of the unveiling of a freedmen's monument to Lincoln in 1876, told the white men in the audience:

First, midst, and last, you and yours were the objects of his deepest affection and his most earnest solicitude. You are the children of Abraham Lincoln. We are at best only his step-children; children by adoption, children by force of circumstances and necessity. To you it especially belongs to sound his praises. . . .

But Douglass also added that Lincoln's common prejudices "may be safely set down as one element of his wonderful success in organizing the loyal American people for the tremendous conflict before them, and bringing them safely through that conflict." By abolitionist standards Lincoln seemed "tardy, cold, dull, and indifferent; but measuring him by the sentiment of his country, a sentiment he was bound as a statesman to consult, he was swift, zealous, radical, and determined."[2] It is as fair a judgment as any on which historians are ever likely to agree.

Abolitionists themselves were divided about Lincoln's candidacy. Many rejected it as feeble temporizing; some accepted it as a half loaf better than none. Radical Abolitionists, a group centered in upstate New York and affiliated neither with Garrison nor with the Free-Soil or Republican Parties, nominated Gerrit Smith for President on a quixotic platform asserting the Constitutional right and duty of the federal government to abolish slavery in the states. Smith had been one of the Secret Six in support of Brown's raid, and after its failure he had taken refuge from the law in temporary insanity. Despite the fact that when Lincoln carried New York in 1860 a Negro suffrage amendment was defeated by a two-to-one margin, his election brought considerable satisfaction to many of the abolitionists because, as Wendell Phillips prophetically put it, "not an Abolitionist, hardly an antislavery man, Mr. Lincoln consents to represent an antislavery idea. . . . The Republican Party have undertaken a problem, the solution of which will force them to our position."[3]

Abolitionists applauded the new President's firm rejection of the Crittenden Compromise, a measure which would have *perpetually* divided the Union between slave and free areas at the 36°30′ line, the southern boundary of Missouri, extended to the Pacific, disenfranchised free Negroes, and provided for their colonization. But a basic difference between the abolitionists and Lincoln emerged when most of them urged that the South be allowed to secede in peace, thus decontaminating the North from the sins of the "erring sister." The right of revolution, they felt, applied both to the South and the slaves, who might more easily foment an insurrection in a separated South. Abolitionists were thus willing to avoid a war between whites in order to encourage one between blacks and whites. "I acknowledge the right of two million and a half of white people in the seven seceding States to organize their government as they choose," declared Wendell Phillips. "Just as freely I acknowledge the right of four million black people to organize *their* government, and to vindicate that right by arms. . . . Where is the battlefield, however ghastly, that is not white,—white as an angel's wing,—compared with the blackness of that darkness which has brooded over the Carolinas for two hundred years?"[4]

Moral high-mindedness, as James Baldwin has pointed out in our time, is often maintained at the expense of weakening our grasp of reality by a persistent tendency "to paint moral issues in glaring black and white," a trait implicated in the very separation of white men from black men in the United States.[5] Paradoxically, most abolitionists, who did more than any other group to break down racial separation in the free states, were willing to separate Northern from Southern Americans—both black and white—because of the sin of slavery. While a case can be made that civil war was too great a price to be paid for resisting Southern secession, Phillips's argument considered *any* war "white" by comparison with the "blackness" of slavery. As James M. McPherson has pointed out, "If the North had followed the advice of Garrisonians in 1861, the peculiar institution, in all probability, would not have come to an end as soon as it did."[6] The Southern Negro would have been left to the tender mercies of a Confederate government unanimous in its commitment to slavery. In this light the policy of Lincoln, for all his limitations, was more responsive to the complexities of the crisis. When the war came at Fort Sumter, most of the abolitionists changed their tune and rejoiced in the opportunity to make it a battle cry for freedom.

There is, as Lord Charnwood pointed out in his classic biography of Lincoln, a "deadly moderation" that is neither vague nor vacillating. Better than most democratic statesmen, Lincoln possessed it, once the Kansas-Nebraska Act had stimulated him into a vigorous engagement with the issue of territorial expansion of slavery. Against Douglas he pounded home the contradiction of slavery to the promise of equality in the "self-evident" assertions of the Declaration of Independence, and he exposed the speciousness of a "popular sovereignty" slogan that made democracy irrelevant to justice and ignored the national dimension of the slavery problem as it affected the new territories, for which Congress had a duty to set general standards of basic liberties.

Slavery was once considered, in both North and South, an institution on the downward path; but in the 1850's it was defended in principle, its demarcation line of the Missouri Compromise was repealed, and aggressive expansionists looked for new opportunities for its spread. The Dred Scott decision of the United States Supreme Court in 1857 had aggravated the crisis by denying the power in principle of either Congress or territorial legislatures to prohibit slavery, defined as an immutable property right. Those like Daniel Webster who pleaded the inability of slavery to "grow" because of "natural" limits of climate suitable for it were contradicted by the fact that officials in New Mexico sought and ultimately obtained a slave code in 1859. There was, for that matter, nothing to prevent slaves from being used in Western mining or Southern factories. It is true that, despite Lincoln's unyielding stand on nonextension in 1860, the Colorado, Nevada, and Dakota Territories were organized after his election without prohibition of slavery—but Buchanan was still President, the Republicans lacked a majority in Congress, and the border states still hung in the balance. In June, 1862, at the first session of the Republican Congress, slavery was abolished by statute from all the territories, a measure that kept faith with Lincoln's consistent position.[7] In January, 1865, he would use his considerable political talent for "logrolling" to muster enough votes to insure the passage of the Thirteenth Amendment, officially marking the death of slavery as a legal institution. The political skills that abolitionists notably lacked made their goal realizable through a man they distrusted.

Lincoln's election compelled him to refine traditional democratic theory. He opposed the Southern argument for secession because there could be no legitimate appeal from ballots to bullets when the election had given the Republicans a legitimate victory. Yet the rebels of '76 had affirmed the right of revolution. Lincoln himself in 1848 had defended the revolt of Texas against Mexico on the ground of "a most sacred right" of revolution, whether by a majority or a minority. His own political instincts, however, were conservative. In 1838, in his address to the Young Men's Lyceum on "The Perpetuation of Our Political Institutions," he had warned against mob violence and the ambition of a great man who might seize power. As a conservative lawyer and Whig politician, he preached "reverence for the constitution and laws" as a *"political religion."* In contrast to the abolitionists, he counseled strict observance of the laws, including bad laws, "if not too intolerable." He did not outline in this last unexplored condition any alternative tactic, such as nonviolent resistance, which became so important a part of the Negro movement in the middle of the twentieth century. His own objection to the Dred Scott decision, for example, did not comprehend resistance to the ruling.

By the time of his inauguration on March 4, 1861, when seven Southern states had announced their secession from the Union, Lincoln faced the problem of reconciling his earlier support of the right of revolution with his later commitment to the principle of preserving the Union. He had sought a single remaining symbol of the integrity of the Union by sending a relief ship to the garrison at Fort Sumter, where his hope of avoiding armed conflict was blasted. His justification for suppressing rebellion was that the right of revolution applied only to cases where a majority had deprived a minority of "any clearly written constitutional right" or when the minority acted for a "morally justifiable cause."[8] A *moral* right of revolution was not at all the same thing as a supposed *legal* right of secession: "A majority, held in restraint by constitutional checks, and limitations, and always changing easily, with deliberate changes of popular opinions and sentiments, is the only true sovereign of a free people." Secession as a theory was anarchy. Hamilton in *The Federalist* had condemned the Articles of Confederation for resting "on no better foundation than the consent of the several legislatures"—a basis that led to the "heresy" that "a *party* to a *compact* has a right to revoke that compact."[9] That heresy was now doctrinal faith in the South; when Lincoln took office only one of the seven seceding states had submitted a secessionist ordinance to popular ratification.

In 1863 the theme of national unity against internal subversion was transfigured by the memorable prose of the Gettysburg Address. On that "consecrated" ground he expanded his justification of the war by linking the principle of union to "a new nation, conceived in liberty and dedicated to the proposition that all men are created equal." It was in this light that he now interpreted the war, which was no longer merely a struggle to preserve the Union, *no matter what happened to slavery*. The conflict had become instead, as he saw it, "a people's contest" to test the ultimate validity of Constitutional democracy *and* the equality of men before the law. Late in 1863, Lincoln saw the war as the occasion for "a new birth of freedom," not merely the conservative effort to maintain a tradition. He had already issued the Emancipation Proclamation; and early in 1865 his second Inaugural Address further expanded the meaning of the war by connecting it with a God who "has his own purposes" in punishing the nation for the injustice done to the Negro through the evil of slavery. In this way Lincoln brought together in a vital synthesis the Revolutionary tradition of the Declaration of 1776, the Constitutional tradition of the Convention of 1787, and the tradition of American Christianity.

"Republican religion," as Tocqueville called it, was redefined in the crisis of the war by a man who belonged to no church and subscribed to no sect's creed, but whose rhetoric drew on Biblical sources and whose sense of history gradually developed into a belief in Providence to whom an "almost chosen people" were bound in covenant. Lincoln's case against slavery was primarily made on secular grounds, but it had some Biblical overtones as well. For him the simple but drastic evil of slavery was that it enabled *"some* men to eat their bread in the sweat of *other* men's faces." One of his notes for the debates with Senator Douglas skewered Dr. Frederick A. Ross, a Presbyterian minister who wrote *Slavery as Ordained By God* in 1857. Lincoln mocked the clergyman's complacent confidence that the Almighty, his revelation, and the Bible spoke so audibly and unambiguously on the subject— without the need for Dr. Ross to ask the slave's opinion on the subject:

So at last it comes to this, that Dr. Ross is to decide the question; and while he considers it, he sits in the shade, with gloves on his hands, and subsists on the bread that Sambo is earning in the burning sun.[10]

Lincoln's case against slavery was fundamentally built on maxims of Jeffersonian rationalism in the Declaration and his own common-sense moral objection to treating men like beasts of burden. No man was good enough, as he said, to govern another man *"without that other's consent."* This principle was "the sheet anchor of American republicanism." But the metaphorical language that Lincoln used to describe the moral evil of slavery drew also from the Biblical text "In the sweat of thy face thou shalt eat bread." Scripture viewed labor as the curse imposed upon Adam for his violation of God's prohibition.

In a fragment on free labor, probably derived from his Cincinnati speech of September, 1859, Lincoln reflected: "Originally a curse for transgression upon the whole race, when, as by slavery, it is concentrated on a part only, it becomes the double-refined curse of God upon his creatures."[11] This line of speculation, however, is more appropriate to religious acquiescence in slavery than to moral striving to eliminate it, and Lincoln's conservatism with respect to emancipation probably drew something from this Biblical strain in his thinking.

Christian denominations, freethinkers, and modern theologians have all tried to claim Lincoln as their own, but in fact he belongs to none of them. Lincoln at one point in his early life had been, as he said, "inclined to believe in . . . the 'Doctrine of Necessity'—that is, that the human mind is impelled to action, or held in rest by some power, over which the mind itself has no control. . . ." But he had (like Franklin at a similar stage) given up the "habit of arguing thus." This opinion was, in any case, "held by several of the Christian denominations." Despite the fact that he was answering the political charge of being an atheist, Lincoln defended himself only by admitting that he was not a church member, and by reassuring the voters that he had never "denied the truth of the Scriptures" and did not support open enemies of or scoffers at religion. This documented statement is a valuable counterweight against the innumerable recollections of what Lincoln is supposed to have told various people about his faith.[12]

Lincoln's rise to political responsibility coincided with his growing use of an idiom much more closely connected with Biblical faith. The usual banality of such references by American politicians is transcended in Lincoln's speeches by his deepening sense of a providentially guided historical process that brings men to judgment through a great crisis in human affairs. This conception, an extension of his earlier secular fatalism, was first invoked by his debate with Douglas in Columbus, Ohio, in 1859, when Lincoln reminded the voters that Jefferson in commenting on the slavery issue had said: "I tremble for my country when I remember that God is just!" The great Democrat had thus supposed, Lincoln argued, that those who enslaved men "braved the arm of Jehovah—that when a nation thus dared the Almighty every friend of that nation had cause to dread His wrath."[13] He had sat in the pews of Old Light Presbyterian preachers in both Springfield and Washington, and something of the old Puritan faith mingled with his own deeply personal sense of fatalism. The enormous pressures of the war and the tragedies of his own family life, particularly the death of his third son, deepened his feeling of being an instrument in a drama whose forces were ultimately beyond human control. The vision of providential guidance that increasingly dominated his great speeches not only sustained him in the anxiety of reaching his own decisions; it must also have helped mitigate the guilt that a sense of his own responsibility for the conflict would crushingly have imposed on him. These elements combined to make his Biblical rhythms reverberate with a Puritan vision of America as a covenanted community under the judgment of a stern, righteous, and inscrutable God.

The Puritans themselves had accepted slavery and made money from its trade, but Lincoln's sense of the national covenant was also informed by the secular Revolutionary-Jeffersonian theme of natural rights, applied now to the Negro insofar as he was a man working by the sweat of his brow but unjustly deprived of the fruits of his labor. For Lincoln the will of God was at first primarily concerned with the war for the Union, but increasingly he searched to discover some new meaning in it. Lincoln felt himself to be part of a drama whose script he did not himself write, but he was not yet sure of his own role in it or of the full meaning of the story. Among his papers is a document reflecting this mood, probably written after the Second Battle of Bull Run:

The will of God prevails. In great contests each party claims to act in accordance with the will of God. Both *may* be and one *must* be wrong. God cannot be *for* and *against* the same thing at the same time. In the present civil war it is quite possible that God's purpose is something different from the purpose of either party—and yet the human instrumentalities, working just as they do, are of the best adaptation to effect His purpose. I am almost ready to say this is probably true—that God wills this contest, and wills that it shall not end yet. By his mere quiet power, on the minds of the now contestants, He could have *saved* or *destroyed* the Union without a human contest. Yet the contest began. And, having begun, He could give the final victory to either side any day. Yet the contest proceeds.[14]

The uncertainty of Providence became less inscrutable as Lincoln himself made good an earlier "vow before God" to issue an emancipation proclamation *if* he could link it to a Northern victory in battle.[15] That decision was inspired by contingent military and political factors, which he had carefully assessed before acting, but once done the deed reflected back upon him to foster his appreciation of the magnitude and meaning of the crisis that had engulfed his countrymen. The closer he moved to seeing that the issue of union was subordinate to the larger question of human freedom, the more he spoke in a religious idiom that connected the war with a providential meaning in terms of the emancipation of slaves. In so doing he created his own Scripture for an American civic religion.

That meaning emerged most eloquently in his Second Inaugural Address. He expected it to wear better than anything else he had written, although he feared that it would not be immediately popular because "men are not flattered by being shown that there has been a difference of purpose between the Almighty and them." If there was "humiliation" in it, he explained, it fell "most directly" on himself. This humility before a God of judgment made him the least pharisaical of Presidents who quote Scripture.

In this Puritan sense of history Lincoln made contact with a religious theme of *Uncle Tom's Cabin*—the war was the woe visited on the nation for the offense of slavery. Like Mrs. Stowe, he was not inclined to find Southerners especially culpable. She, in fact, had put the blame for slavery mainly on the moral spinelessness of the Northern churches and the easy conscience of the mass of people in the Northern states: "The people of the free states have defended, encouraged, and participated; and are more guilty for it, before God, than the South, in that they have *not* the apology of education or custom." In 1862 Mrs. Julia Ward Howe's "Battle Hymn of the Republic" more militantly and self-righteously used the millennial theme to encourage the Northern armies, cast in the role of defenders of "a fiery gospel, writ in burnished rows of steel," and destined to "crush the serpent with his heel" in a righteous war through which His truth was "marching on" toward "the glory of the coming of the Lord." Lincoln's Second Inaugural incorporated the abolitionists' linkage of slavery with human sinfulness, but it invoked a God who had his own ends and a judgment that spared no one. No section or group could identify itself with his purposes or pass righteous judgment on another. It was a rare moment of disinterested meditation rather than of political exploitation of conventional rhetoric, an expression of national guilt and humility without any pulpit unction.

Only a man who with profound seriousness took the Union to be a national covenant could have risen to the eloquence of his great speeches. Lincoln, as his wife said, "was a religious man. But it was a kind of poetry in his nature, and he never was a technical Christian."[16]

That poetry, however, was also conviction, and the combination gives the Second Inaugural its grave power:

It may seem strange that any men should dare to ask a just God's assistance in wringing their bread from the sweat of other men's faces; but let us judge not that we be not judged. The prayers of both could not be answered; that of neither has been answered fully. The Almighty has his own purposes. "Woe unto the world because of offenses! for it must needs be that offenses come; but woe to that man by whom the offense cometh!" If we shall suppose that American Slavery is one of those offenses which, in the providence of God, must needs come, but which, having continued through His appointed time, He now wills to remove, and He gives to both North and South this terrible war, as the woe due to those by whom the offense came, shall we discern therein any departure from those divine attributes which the believers in a Living God always ascribe to Him? Fondly do we hope—fervently do we pray—that this mighty scourge of war may speedily pass away. Yet, if God wills that it continue, until all the wealth piled by the bondman's two hundred and fifty years of unrequited toil shall be sunk, and until every drop of blood drawn with the lash, shall be paid by another drawn with the sword, as was said three thousand years ago, so still it must be said "the judgments of the Lord are true and righteous altogether!"

Lincoln's "poetry" was given substance by the course of the war. His attempt to restore the coherence of democracy, constitutionalism, and republican morality could succeed only if slavery could be eliminated, the South defeated, and the Union restored. This much Northern victory had ensured under Lincoln's wise strategy. But education, land, and the ballot for free Negroes had yet to be faced. Lincoln had urged in his last public address that the educated Negro and the Negro soldier be given the vote immediately. At that time Negroes could vote on equal terms with whites in only five states. Lincoln's own suggested Reconstruction policy, however, while it stressed education for the Negroes would have left the disposition of Negro rights to the mercies of the reconstructed states and therefore to the economic needs of a landed oligarchy. Only the continuing pressure of abolitionist agitation for Negro equality could make the war and its aftermath point toward the redemption of the hopes that Lincoln's administration had raised.

Abolitionists, divided over Lincoln in 1864, were split as well over the merits of immediate suffrage for the freed Negroes in the South. The paternalism of their religious doctrine of benevolence sometimes conflicted with their commitment to justice and equality, just as their previous emphasis on the degradation of the Negro through slavery was in tension with their need to prove false the widespread belief in the permanent inferiority of the Negro race. They were even at loggerheads about the merits of continuing their organization after the legal end of slavery. And they had at first an entirely mistaken confidence in Andrew Johnson, whose hatred of rebel planters was entirely compatible with a dislike of Negroes and an indifference to their fate. Despite these limitations, the abolitionists in pressing for equal pay for Negro troops, for Negro education, for land reform, and for the ballot were the vanguard of the Negro's freedom.

In this struggle Christianity reinforced democracy through the role of the evangelicals in the Freedmen's Aid Bureau and the American Missionary Association, which cooperated with the secular freedmen's aid societies in educating the Negro. This alliance shattered on the issue of evangelical teaching in such work, but by 1879 graduates of Negro schools established by the AMA were teaching 150,000 pupils in the South, laying the basis for the later rise of Negro preachers and leaders. Wendell Phillips himself enjoyed the signal honor of helping to break the legislative deadlock over the Fifteenth Amendment by his persuasive prudent appeal for a guarantee less sweepingly phrased than the one suggested by the Senate. By May, 1869, the American Anti-Slavery Society resolved at its annual meeting that the Amendment for Negro suffrage had provided "the capstone and completion of our movement; the fulfillment of our pledge to the Negro race."[17] The abolitionists knew, however, that their transformation from despised martyrs into triumphant and honored prophets was not the end of the Negro's humiliations.

This insight was entirely consistent with the original movement for immediate emancipation, which had aimed at a social regeneration inspired by a religious perspective which both reflected and transcended the secular culture itself. In this respect democracy had profited from a religious vantage point which, though convinced that it was in league with the larger forces of history, dreamed of a covenanted society which no society on earth could ever quite realize until the millennium itself had arrived. That perspective had often displayed notably bad judgment on political issues and political candidates; it had indicted more than it had persuaded the conscience of most Americans; it had never captured the organized churches; and it had found its major opportunity in a victorious war that it had hoped to avoid. But it had been a persistent pressure to spell out the democratic meanings that President Lincoln had formulated in his speeches. Unfortunately, the end of military Reconstruction and the legal emasculation of the new Amendments by the Supreme Court deprived the abolitionist movement of its fulfillment in the "capstone" of the Fifteenth Amendment. If it failed, it was part of the larger failure of the whole country to make permanent the gains of the war.

The abolitionist mind inherited the Puritan drive to make the state a holy commonwealth. It was unaware of its own inner ambivalence about the secular state, and it therefore oscillated between a despairing anarchistic withdrawal from the rust and stain of the world's contagion and a passionate attempt to bend society to its own moral will. Insofar as it rested its case against slavery on an extension of the egalitarian principles of the Declaration, abolitionism posed no sectarian issues, but its Biblical judgment against the institution was thoroughly Protestantized and vulnerable to entanglement with nativist passions against Catholics, just as with the temperance crusade which Protestants had mounted, as if Catholic Irishmen were not part of the republic. Lincoln understood much better than the abolitionists that there was a difference between his moral preferences and his responsibilities as a political leader in a Constitutional context, just as he had also a much greater feeling for the political arts of wirepulling and logrolling.

The crisis of war to some extent changed the abolitionists themselves, though most of them remained radically individualistic in their values and analysis. Abolitionists accepted *compensated* emancipation for the District of Columbia in 1862, just as Wendell Phillips broke the deadlock over the Fifteenth Amendment by a strategic prudence. Moral perfectionism persisted in the lack of interest that Garrison and Phillips had in the early work of the freedmen's societies during the war, when some ten thousand slaves had been liberated by the federal capture of the Sea Islands off the South Carolina coast. Some abolitionists, however, did see their opportunity to work out their faith. James Miller McKim, who seceded from his Presbyterian ministry and his office in the Pennsylvania Anti-Slavery Society, joined Lewis Tappan, the American Missionary Association, and capitalist advocates of free labor from New England on the Sea Islands. There they built churches and schools, trained Negroes to work the land on their own, and co-operated with the government in the "Port Royal Experiment." "For the battering-ram we must substitute the hod and trowel," McKim explained to skeptical abolitionists; "taking care, however, not to 'daub with untempered mortar.' "[18] The Port Royal experiment set an example for Reconstruction by proving that freed Negroes could live in orderly communities of freedom. By 1865 Garrison himself would abandon the American Anti-Slavery Society for freedmen's-aid work.

After the war, republican religion would have to be redefined if religion and democracy were to nurture each other or sustain a fruitful tension. The abolitionists had exalted the innate potency of the individual soul and exaggerated the sufficiency of a regenerated altruism. These themes were inadequate to the social problems of making the slave's emancipation more than a formal legal victory. The educational effort of the evangelicals was testimony to their own refusal to abandon the Negro after emancipation, but on economic planning for rehabilitation of the former slaves the abolitionists never came to any coherent, consistent agreement.[19] Postmillennial perfectionism was not morally pertinent to preventing the tragedy of Reconstruction because it was too individualistic, moralistic, and optimistic in its understanding of the world, for all its depth of dedication and moral courage.

Ideologists of the triumphant North tended to define the moral terms of victory in a theory of historical progress that evaded the undemocratic aspects of the outcome emerging from the failure of Reconstruction. John William De Forest, for example, in *Miss Ravenel's Conversion from Secession to Loyalty,* finished in 1865 and appearing two years later, voiced the confidence republicans enjoyed before Reconstruction. His Dr. Ravenel, a renegade Southerner who, like the author himself, had worked with freed Negroes, located the war within a grand theodicy of history:

"These Europeans judge us aright; we have done a stupendous thing. They are outside of the struggle and can survey its proportions with the eyes with which our descendants will see it. I think I can discover a little of its grandeur. It is the fifth act in the grand drama of human liberty. First, the Christian Revelation. Second, the Protestant Reformation. Third, the War of American Independence. Fourth, the French Revolution. Fifth, the struggle for the freedom of all men, without distinction of race and color; this democratic struggle which confirms the masses in an equality with the few. We have taught a greater lesson than all of us think or understand."[20]

But De Forest's novel also contained the ambiguities that undercut this confidence in the historical process. The novel's only "common man" is presented as a cowardly, conniving, ignorant prizefighter turned corrupt politician, whose fortunes are promoted during the war because he is politically popular and therefore useful to his state's governor. After the war he becomes a petty politician and businessman whose influence "in a ward meeting or in a squad of speculators on 'Change'" has "ten times the influence" that would be accorded the novel's hero, a New England Puritanized gentleman-lawyer. De Forest's vision of progress was of an "industrious democracy" that had killed off "the evil spirit of no-work," symbolized by the planting aristocracy. After the war, however, the gospel of work that his spokesmen preached as a democratic form of "practical Christianity" would become the ideology of an aggressively expanding monopolistic capitalism that cared very little for democratic processes. In ten years De Forest himself would be writing novels of political corruption in the Gilded Age. At the same time another Northern writer who had worked with the Freedmen's Bureau would publish a novel about the subversion of Reconstruction by the Ku Klux Klan. Albion W. Tourgée's hero in *A Fool's Errand* was forced to conclude that Reconstruction was a "failure so far as it attempted to unify the nation, to make one people in fact of what had been one only in name before the convulsion of the civil war. It was a failure, too, so far as it attempted to fix and secure the position and rights of the colored race."[21]

Herman Melville, in the supplement to his book of Civil War poetry, *Battle Pieces,* concluded: "Let us pray that the terrible historic tragedy of our time may not have been enacted without instructing our whole beloved country through terror and pity; and may fulfillment verify in the end those expectations which kindle the bards of Progress and Humanity." There was terror enough, and some pity as well, but the two did not classically combine in the national aesthetic catharsis for which Melville hoped. Neither Lincoln's God of history, De Forest's Grand Drama, nor Melville's bards of Progress and Humanity could adequately symbolize a process that led from the eloquence of the President's tragic vision of the war to the final failure of Radical Reconstruction. If the war was the woe for the offense of slavery, what name should be given to the betrayal of the promises of the Thirteenth, Fourteenth, and Fifteenth Amendments by judicial emasculation? Lincoln had redefined the national traditions of democracy, Constitutionalism, and republican religion so as to exclude both slavery and secession. Having compromised with slavery for more than two hundred years, the churches in America had little difficulty joining other citizens to acquiesce in compromises with the freed Negro's rights within a decade of their legal establishment. Northern Methodists had strongly supported Radical Republican Reconstruction, but by 1884 the General Conference felt that unity required racially separate churches and schools.[22]

Lincoln believed that in the old days God and his angels had made themselves known to men in dreams, as in so many of the Bible stories. He himself had dreamed of his own death at the hand of an assassin. Seeing himself as an instrument of God's historical purposes, he must have felt unconsciously that for such a role tradition had prescribed a martyr's death. And it came when his mission was over. His own hopes for the liberated slaves were modest, limited by his own deference to white prejudice, to states' rights, and to the ideal of sectional unity. For all his yearning for colonization as a solution, however, he had justified the war by the hope of "a new birth of freedom," language that echoed the "twice-born" theme of evangelical Protestantism and pointed toward the inclusion of the Negro in the national covenant. By 1877, when the federal troops were withdrawn from the South as part of a bargain made for economic advantage, that new birth was stillborn.

The covenanted white people, absorbed in gain, were in no mood for jeremiads or messiahs. The Negro, segregated in the churches, as he was by 1900 in other areas of public life, was left with the solace of ethnic fraternity, the yearning for equality, or the consolation of other-worldly hopes. Radicals could not ultimately carry the country with them, given an unrepentant South; a President whose sympathies were strongly identified with poor whites and their prejudices; a Supreme Court hostile to Congress and racially biased; a thriving business community eager to get on with expansion and production for profit; and a voluntary, sectionally divided system of churches, reflecting the easy consciences of its members with regard to black Americans. The civic religion, most memorably expressed in the judgment on American Negro slavery, threatened to become only a white tribal cult.

XIII

The Power of Worldliness

In the 1950's sociological commentators on American religion tended to converge on the theme that a belief in believing, a piety toward religion in general, was emerging as a communal characteristic. They deplored a lack of prophetic judgment in the new religiosity, and they feared that secularization as a process of conformity to the world was the mark of a loss of specific theological content. Religion merely provided sanctification, as Will Herberg put it, "for goals and values otherwise established." Secularism was not a demonstrative hostility to religion; it expressed itself rather through people "sincerely devoted to religion."[1] Yet this theme was first developed well over a hundred years earlier by Tocqueville. He wryly noted that he found it difficult to tell from the sermons of ministers in America "whether the principal object of religion is to procure eternal felicity in the other world or prosperity in this."[2]

Yet, unlike the commentators of the later period, he did not begrudge the Americans their tendency to "place in this world" the interest that made them follow religion. He was more generous because he felt that in ethical terms the principle of self-interest, "rightly understood," meant that Americans justified their virtue by showing "with complacency how an enlightened regard for themselves constantly prompts them to assist one another and inclines them willingly to sacrifice a portion of their time and property to the welfare of the state."[3] It was not that their virtue was merely egoism under a more flattering name; it was rather that they felt themselves required to justify their concern for the community by a utilitarian ethic. Civic zeal was rationalized by appeals to prudence.

The belief in believing, furthermore, found original and intellectual form at the beginning of the twentieth century in William James's great work *The Varieties of Religious Experience*. He subscribed not to traditional doctrines but to the therapeutic function of "overbeliefs" in the lives of religious people and to the psychological truth of the Methodist type of emphasis upon the crisis of conversion in the divided self. The "subliminal self" was a link to "a wider world of meaning." He opposed more intellectualized and blander versions of liberal theology that had lost the sense of "radical evil" in the nature of things by acceptance of a melioristic evolutionary popular science. James also spoke in intimate awareness of his father's religious development, as well as of his own deep psychosomatic turmoil in attempting both to follow and to challenge his father's constraining wish that his son might become a scientist rather than an unsuccessful theologian.[4] In part he wanted to redeem in his own way his father's lifelong absorption with a strange blend of Calvinist-Swedenborgian-Fourierism by going against the grain of an age responsive to an aggressive scientific materialism. Moreover, while as a psychologist James seemed to privatize religion in disengaging it from social expression, he actually believed that charity in some saints was "a genuinely creative social force, tending to make real a degree of virtue which it alone is ready to assume as possible." It freed men to imagine "dreams of social justice."[5] Trained in science and medicine, James was himself more agnostic than Christian, but his reformulation of the issue of religious belief was both a rebuke to "secularizing" tendencies and an illustration of them. His book found a wide popular audience.

The sociologists of the 1950's also belatedly identified an earlier process in which the churches became vehicles for the ethnic identities of their members in a time of massive immigration. In this context, being a Catholic or a Jew was a way of preserving some pre-American values in a general Americanizing process. By 1900 the population had grown from about thirty-one and a half million in 1860 to nearly seventy-six million. The number of Methodist, Congregational, and Presbyterian churches had roughly kept up in rate of growth with the population, and the Episcopal churches had slightly exceeded it. Jewish, Catholic, Baptist, Disciples of Christ, and Lutheran churches had, however, far surpassed it. Only the Dutch and German Reformed, the Unitarian, the Universalist, and the Quaker churches had lagged behind the growth in the population. By 1900 the ratio of the number of churches to the total population (405 habitants for every church) was almost the same as it had been in the colonial America of 1650.[6]

But such statistics tell too simple a story. The majority of the country were not church members, and the place of religion in the secularized world of 1900 had a very different meaning from that prevalent in the seventeenth century, when religious categories were fundamental for political, social, and intellectual life. A church (like the Quaker) that lagged behind the rate of growth of the population, furthermore, might have more deeply committed members than a church (like the Episcopal) that had exceeded it. The number of churches was itself connected with the fact that massive immigration made the churches especially significant not so much in religious as in sociological terms—providing close community ties for strangers in a new land. Linked to ethnic identities, the churches could thrive on the fact that religion was portable. Yet even the churches were profoundly influenced by the culture in which they flourished; and like the immigrants themselves, they bent to accommodate themselves to a world in which other forces were powerfully active. Tocqueville had recognized the process, and in the last quarter of the century it accentuated the power of worldliness he had observed.

In this period Max Weber's point about the Puritan legacy to capitalism had its counterexample in a capitalist ethos that reformulated religion to serve its interests. In the time of the Gilded Age ministers preached a moralized gospel of work that celebrated the business hero of the self-made man, while the economically successful reciprocated by ostentatious support of their local churches. This mutual embrace served both parties well in their common pursuit of prosperity and prestige. Sober stewardship and entrepreneurial enthusiasm were blended in a philanthropic program of funding schools, colleges, and universities on the ground that they would provide ladders of opportunity whereby others could someday learn to prosecute their individual enterprises with the tenacity and success of the moguls.

The most vulgar statement of this Protestant calling for capitalists, given thousands of times all around the country, was Russell H. Conwell's speech "Acres of Diamonds" with its insistence on the duty of making money "because of the power there is in money." Conwell naturally recommended honorable Christian means, but he assured his hearers that these would surely "sweep us quickly toward the goal of riches," a debasement of the Protestant ethic that would have scandalized the Puritans. As in many Horatio Alger stories, the villain of Conwell's piece was the foppish rich man's son, denied the great American experience of making his fortune. Greatness lay not with public officials but with private men who could give the people better streets, homes, schools, and churches through the power of their money. Everyone could find acres of diamonds in his own backyard if only he applied himself to his local opportunities for getting rich.

Conwell's outlook intermingled, in a way characteristic of his age, an unabashed new worldliness with an inherited idealism. He was brought up the son of a poor farmer in the Berkshire Hills of western Massachusetts, where his father, who had known John Brown and Frederick Douglass, had worked for the Underground Railroad. Conwell earned money at school by selling a biography of Brown with an accompanying sales pitch on the martyr's life. Wounded in the Civil War, Conwell moved on into newspaper work, invested in real estate, practiced law, dispensing free legal advice to the poor, organized a businessmen's civic associaion, and ran a huge Methodist Bible class, which did settlement work in Boston's North End slums. At the age of thirty-seven he seemed to have thrown up his career to become a minister in a small dilapidated church in Lexington. But a story that ended there would not have impressed the Gilded Age. Conwell had married a wealthy woman, and he was a promoter by instinct. He soon raised the money to restore the church to flourishing life. He went onward to Philadelphia; his popularity in the pulpit and his fund-raising talent enabled him to erect a Baptist temple seating more than three thousand people and equipped with kitchens, boilers, dynamos, telephones, and audiphones. Organization was his watchword, and the "institutional church" was built, he boasted, by using as deacons and trustees "men whom the banks would trust."[7]

Conwell had found in religion a field for the American organizational talent that was building industrial and financial trusts throughout the country. It led him to sponsor as well a hospital and a night school—later Temple University—"to teach people to be more useful to their employers and thus be of more help to themselves and those dependent on them." It was this experience that backed the preaching of shrewdness in the "Acres of Diamonds" speech, inspiring a group of businessmen to found a brick and tile company, an ex-convict to go into Congress, or another prophet to make up his own lecture on "Nuggets of Gold." Not surprisingly, Conwell wrote campaign biographies of Grant, Hayes, Garfield, and Blaine, his platitudinous theme the rise of men from obscurity to success. A sermon outline of Conwell's, retrospectively describing his extemporaneous preaching, betrays the naïve level of his style of thought:

If we believe in a man's character, we desire to be like him. Napoleon, Washington. Parent. Christ. If we desire to be like Him, we will naturally act like Him. Dime novels. Circus. Play. Jesse James. Grant's cigars. Artemus Ward. Moody. Loyola. Charles V. Christ.[8]

Protestantism in America was vulnerable to being defeated by its success, submerged in the materialistic aspirations that dominated the culture of post-Civil War life. It could become a sanctification of the life style of the business leaders, admired both for their success and for the philanthropy which that made possible. Tocqueville observed respectfully that in America religion was "warmed by the fires of patriotism," but he would have been shocked to see it so heated by the lust for material success. He might even have joined William James in his complaint of a "certain trashiness of fibre" produced by "the worship of material luxury and wealth which constitutes so large a portion of the 'spirit' of our age." Perhaps, James speculated, some needed "moral equivalent" of the heroic strenuous code of the soldier could be found in the old religious idea of "voluntarily accepted poverty":

We have grown afraid, literally afraid, to be poor. We despise any one who elects to be poor in order to simplify and save his inner life. If he does not join the general scramble and pant with the money-making street, we deem him spiritless and lacking in ambition. We have lost the power even of imagining what the ancient idealization of poverty could have meant: the liberation from material attachments, the unbribed soul, the manlier indifference, the paying our way by what we are or do and not by what we have, the right to fling away our life at any moment irresponsibly,—the more athletic trim, in short, the moral fighting shape.[9]

James's criticism, although justified, did not come to terms, any more than Conwell did, with the facts of involuntary poverty. Stewardship by the well-to-do churchgoers was not in itself an adequate Protestant response to the problem. Josiah Strong pointed out in *Our Country* (1886), written for the American Home Missionary Society and selling 175,000 copies before his death in 1916, that the average annual increase in wealth of Protestant church members of the Evangelical Alliance during the decade 1880–90 was forty times greater than the sum of both home and foreign missionary offerings.[10] Strong himself, a product of Lyman Beecher's Lane Theological Seminary, was nevertheless persuaded that the evils of the time—monopolies, lawlessness, alcoholism, poverty—could be met by evangelization, the conversion of lost souls, if only Christians met their obligations as stewards by supporting home missionary work. Like the pre-Civil War evangelists, he saw the cloven hoof in Mormons and Catholics, but new heresies now threatened in the form of anarchism and socialism. Like most rural-minded Protestants, Strong saw the cities as potential carriers of contagion to the heartland of America. Fortunately, in his vision, Anglo-Saxon Americans were aggressive expansionists, and if faithful to their trust, they were destined to make America "God's right arm in his battle with the world's ignorance and oppression and sin."[11] While Strong looked favorably on cooperatives as a possible solution to growing class conflict and later supported "direct democracy" techniques of the initiative, the recall, and the referendum, his evangelical faith in the power of religious conversion, in Protestant teaching in schools and colleges, and in nationalistic expansionism dominated his tract. With its blend of muscular rhetoric and social statistics, its documentary and hortatory intentions, *Our Country* was a country cousin to *Uncle Tom's Cabin*. But while Mrs. Stowe imagined a millennialist Africa for Christian blacks, Strong envisioned an imperial "Anglo-Saxon" destiny.

Tocqueville had noted a unifying "republican religion" in the early nineteenth century, but in theological terms liberal religion did not in fact flourish widely until after the Civil War. Many of the leading liberal Protestants had studied in Germany, where scholars like Albrecht Ritschl, Adolf von Harnack, and Rudolf Lotze had introduced them to historical criticism of the Bible, an experience bound to subvert confidence in literalism or in static conceptions of doctrine. The impact of Darwinian biology, furthermore, gave enormous prestige in all fields to the idea of process. Defending himself successfully against charges of heresy brought in Chicago by the Presbyterian Church, Professor David Swing quite justifiably accused his accusers: "Not one of you, my brethren, has preached the dark theology of Jonathan Edwards in your whole life. Nothing could induce you to preach it, and yet it is written down in your creed in dreadful plainness. Confess with me, that our beloved church has slipped away from the religion of despair, and has come unto Mount Sion, into the atmosphere of Jesus, and He was in life and death, full of love and forgiveness."[12] Even before the war a Congregationalist graduate of the orthodox Andover Theological Seminary had emphasized the historical development of Christianity as the "spontaneous and *inevitable* evolution out of a germ" originally implanted by God, but he had stoutly maintained (even more than St. Augustine or Jonathan Edwards) a division between profane human history and sacred church history, though both were subject to evolution, an idea of "genetic development" that historians could find in the scientific discussion of vitalism in biology.[13] This separation would be challenged by liberal theologians on evolutionary grounds. By 1886, amidst heresy trials, Andover Seminary was successfully invaded from within by the new theological liberalism.

Its historical spirit was manifest in a discourse given by a church historian at Lane Theological Seminary in 1892. He too believed that there were divine revelatory "germs" planted back of human history in Christ and his truths, but out of these germs had come the substance, as well as the form, of theology. The mind historically trained could now estimate more justly the play of other forces in the growth of the church. Exploiting the language of Darwinism, he celebrated historical thinking:

To study an organism in its antecedents and in its genesis, to trace the course of its growth, to examine it in the varied relations which it has sustained to its environment at successive stages of its career, to search for the forces within and without which have served to make it what it is; to do it all, not with the desire of supporting one's own theory or of undermining the theory of another, but in order to understand the organism more thoroughly . . . this is the historic method, and this is the way we study the church today. This is the way the modern scholar studies all the factors of Christianity in all their varied phases.[14]

This historicism led to the corollary of continuous revision of doctrine in the light of the present age. By the early years of the next century "modernism" would achieve status in Protestantism as a self-conscious effort to *adapt* religion to its surrounding culture by emphasizing social activity and cooperation with an immanent God, rather than the definition of theology or tradition. The modernist, instead of challenging contemporary secular thought, proposed to find relevant patterns in its achievements, confident that democracy and the sciences could supply the guiding ideas that theological tradition no longer provided.

This process of development in American religion, whether Protestant, Catholic, or Jewish, was particularly vulnerable, for all its good intentions, to debasement into a strategy of mere acquiescence in dominant ongoing movements. The vulgarization of the Protestant ethic and the erosion of theological integrity in the Gilded Age were, in part, desperate efforts of the churches to keep alive by identifying themselves with the powerful momentum of secular forces in American life. They had always found their strength in a close connection with the culture that supported them; and rather than assume the burden of standing in judgment upon it, they were easily tempted to become assimilated to it by embracing a popular and complacent secularism, disguised as Christianity. In this situation it would be hard to see what had been lost in the process, because a religion that sacrifices its integrity to its cultural relevance is less obviously a failure than a religion that sacrifices its cultural relevance to the psychological security of maintaining intellectually archaic doctrine.

The popular novel by the 1880's began to reflect the crisis of belief in sympathetic portrayals of agnostic repudiation of old-fashioned Calvinism. In *John Ward, Preacher* (1888) Margaret Deland presented a minister's wife who refused to bend her mind to the harsh implications of Edwardsian theology even if it meant separation from her husband. Many public libraries banned the novel, but twelve years later the public did not fall into line behind the religious press's condemnation of James Lane Allen's *The Reign of Law,* the story of the conversion of a Bible-college student to Darwinian science. Allen merely translated conventional religious values into a cult of popular science, however, finding in it charity, radiant hope, and the knowledge of God.[15]

Hawthorne in *The Scarlet Letter* and *The Marble Faun* had dramatized in Hester and Miriam independent-minded, heretical, sensual women. Henry Adams's *Esther* (1884) created another Biblically named heroine of nonbelief, but of a more neurotic cast. She is at odds with her flesh, unhappily unemployed as an upper-class woman, and overidentified with her agnostic father, whose death leaves her desolated, like the author's own suicidal wife. The Old Testament Book of Esther makes no mention of God, and Adams's Esther sees eternity, infinity, and omnipotence in nature, exemplified in Niagara Falls. She is congenial to the idea of the scientist who defines immortality as "having one true thought," but she loves the domineering minister who unsuccessfully demands that she have the Christian faith proper to a minister's wife. In the end she flees to Europe with a girl friend, like the unhappy heroine of Adams's other novel, *Democracy* (1880), who lost her nerves and her democratic faith in her entanglement with a dominating, corrupt Senator, an example of the degeneration of the republic from the private honor and public simplicity that Adams idealized in George Washington's eighteenth-century character.[16]

Disbelief is not necessarily more honest than belief, and the Victorian struggle with modernism made it vulnerable to a specious religious liberalism. The possibilities of this theme were dramatized with great skill in Harold Frederic's popular novel *The Damnation of Theron Ware* (1896). Set in the 1880's, like Adams's drama, the novel examines the religious and social situation of an upstate New York town, familiar to the author from his newspaper days in Utica and Albany. Ware and his young wife are compelled to accept a Methodist pastorate in the small town of Octavius, where the congregation condemns his wife's taste in clothes, pays him a pittance, and wants him to preach "the burnin' lake o' fire an' brimstone," along with the edifying legends of the deathbed repentances of Voltaire and Paine. Ware bends by sacrificing his wife's decorated bonnet to the "puritan" prejudices of his congregation and meanwhile plans to write a book on Abraham in order to make money. At this point his real initiation begins, and it appears at first to be a gradual illumination.

Accidentally drawn into the life of a Catholic priest and his rich lady friend, the provincial Ware discovers to his surprise and fascination that they are much more "advanced" than he is: in fact, they find amusing his own ignorance of scholarship, art, and the world. Disoriented by worldly sophistication among Romanists, Ware preaches neither consistent old- nor new-school doctrine in his church, and he slides into a bland aesthetic religious skepticism, influenced by Renan, while losing all sense of solidarity with his congregation. In private he finds himself excited by the scientific rationalist skepticism of John W. Draper, W. H. Lecky, and Robert Ingersoll. Impressed with his own growing enlightenment, Ware speculates that the necessary progress of science will result in a "universal skepticism" with the church surviving only for its social functions, illustrated in the frolic of a Catholic beer-drinking picnic. Ware's Protestant prejudices make him suspicious of his patroness's relations with the priest, and they dismiss him as a Yankee outsider and presumptuous bore whose only charm lay in his former innocence. The priest has told him that "the truth is always relative," just as Ware himself had come to believe in matters of faith. But the remark is also sociologically applicable to Ware's position as a provincial Protestant who has lost his convictions without losing his prejudices. At the end of the story he has his eye on the West and a future career as a politician who can sway the crowd with his rhetoric, a posture that as a preacher he had already exploited so damagingly to himself and his wife.

The novel exposes a general dislocation in the relation of believers to their church and society. Ware's conformist and pecuniary-minded congregation is mean, but a frivolous aestheticism, a cynical philistine scientism, or a glib agnosticism in clerical garb offer no worthy alternatives. Normatively, the novel looks backward and salutes the "zeal and moral worth" of the old circuit-riding Methodists whose aging representatives briefly appear at the conference in the opening chapter of the tale. Ware may have fallen but he began as a minister without a true sense of vocation, too extravagant for his salary and toying with the idea of becoming a lawyer.[17] A much more profound analysis than any made nearly three decades later by Sinclair Lewis in *Elmer Gantry,* Frederic's novel is a well-lit window on the plight of Protestantism in a bewildering secular world where art, science, and liberal religion have their own distortions and the dreaded "Romanists" have the largest church in town.

The power of American culture to shape religion to its own ends was evident to some degree even with respect to the more doctrinally rigid and European-oriented Roman Catholic Church. Four statesmen of the American Church—Cardinal James Gibbons of Baltimore, Archbishop John Ireland of St. Paul, Bishop John J. Keane of Washington, D.C., and Bishop John Lancaster Spalding of Peoria—played important roles in adapting the Church to modern American life. Confident that in Pope Leo XIII they had a sympathetic ally, these liberal Catholics stressed secular learning and formal education, hoped to break up the ghetto by colonization in the West, and took a tolerant view of the Christian truths embodied in American sects. Their liberalism led them to encourage Catholic participation in the Parliament of Religions at the Chicago Columbian Exposition of 1893 and to praise American religious liberty and separation of church and state for, as Cardinal Gibbons put it, "binding together priests and people" in a union better than that of church and state.

They had little sympathy for the conservatives in the Church who emphasized ethnic loyalties, castigated the public school, and branded social reformers, like Henry George, or workingmen's organizations, like the Knights of Labor, as subversive threats to property, order, and the faith. The Catholic liberals were themselves Republicans, temperance advocates, and only mild supporters of unions, but they were able to persuade Rome of the imprudence of condemning the Knights of Labor or putting *Progress and Poverty* on the Index. Responding to these pleas, the Pope rescinded the excommunication of Father Edward McGlynn, who had supported George and cooperated with the Knights of Labor in defiance of orders from his archbishop. On the parochial-school issue liberal Catholics accepted a compromise whereby they could for a nominal fee rent out parochial schools to the public-school board with the secular curriculum being taught to Catholics by Catholic teachers paid by the school board, while religious instruction was given after hours. Implicit in this proposal was the principle of accepting the permeation of the state's schools by the religion of the majority, however Protestant it might be. This compromise, which fitted no neat categories of "separation," was tolerated only reluctantly by conservative Catholics.

Like their Protestant colleagues, the liberal Catholics minimized the contemplative virtues and preached the virtues of industry, practicality, philanthropic zeal, and the inner action of the Holy Spirit. But in 1895 the liberals found that they had no ally in Rome. Pope Leo's encyclical to the American Church emphasized the "error" of taking American separation of church and state as an ideal, or even as "universally lawful or expedient." In a letter to Cardinal Gibbons in 1899, the Pope cited "Americanism" as a heretical overemphasis on the active virtues and on new methods of winning converts that entailed compromises of doctrine and cooperation with heretics. The liberals prudently accepted the rebuke on the assumption that it was aimed not at them but at the French liberal Catholics who had misinterpreted the American example. But the fact was that Archbishop Ireland had written an introduction to the French translation of a biography of Father Isaac Hecker that had led to the controversial excitement over "Americanism," and he was forced to withdraw it from sale. The liberal American prelates had deliberately worked to make the American Church a part of the age, believing with the convert Father Hecker that American political institutions were in advance of those of Europe with respect to "helping a man to save his soul."[18]

In retrospect, it is arguable that this claim was the unacknowledged nub of the "error" from the point of view of Rome and conservative American Catholics in the hierarchy. From the vantage point of the liberals it was an assertion that had the desirable effect of undercutting the nativist propaganda, particularly strong in the rural Midwest, instigated in the 1880's by the American Protective Association and casting American Catholics in the role of alien subverters of the American way of life. Liberal Catholics had to labor also under the weight of the unpopular condemnations of modernism made by Pius IX in

1864 and Pius X in 1907. These sweeping indictments of all individ-ualistic, evolutionary, or symbolic interpretations of religious truth and experience attacked theological tendencies that many Americans found increasingly attractive. Father Forbes in *The Damnation of Theron Ware* would have found more congenial company in certain French and Italian Catholic intellectual circles than he would have among Catholic Americans in a subculture noted for its indifference to intellectual life. But Theron Ware's attraction to modernism was common enough among Protestants. The American Church was caught in a cultural predicament generated by disestablishment. Al-though the Pope carefully explained in his rebuke of "Americanism" that he did not mean to criticize American government, laws, or cus-toms, he had in 1895 already rejected the liberals' ideal of separation.

The full story of the controversy warrants the conclusion that Rome was rebuking the *way* in which certain officers of the Church in Amer-ica held to their faith and that way was informed by the effort to re-late the Church more closely to prevailing American dispositions. Archbishop Ireland's introduction to Walter Elliott's *The Life of Fa-ther Hecker* (1891), which had sparked the "Americanism" contro-versy on both sides of the Atlantic, praised his subject as "the flower of our American priesthood" and a model for others. Asserting that "life is action, and so long as there is action there is life," Ireland extolled American interest in the concrete and in the natural virtues, rather than in the monastic life, while, in a neo-Emersonian flight of rhetorical extravagance, he announced that "the need of repression has passed away" so that "each Christian soldier may take to the field, obeying the breathings of the Spirit of truth and piety within him, feeling that what he may do he should do."[19] In their Republicanism, temperance advocacy, concern for Americanization of the immigrant, and idealization of American disestablishment, the liberal Catholics were in fact much more closely related to their Protestant fellow citizens than to the medieval spirit of papal decrees. The criticisms of Americans made by Pope Leo XIII were themselves proof of the ab-surdity of the nativist American Protective Association's warnings against an un-American Catholic medievalism, supposedly infecting the body politic.

Whatever dangers to Catholic doctrine the efforts of the liberal Catholic statesmen may have entailed in certain rhetorical excesses, they had done much to show how absurd was the nativist charge that being American and Catholic was like squaring the circle. Any religion must walk a tightrope in trying to preserve intellectual and spiritual integrity as well as cultural relevance to its society; the liberal spokesmen in the American Church deserved more credit for their agile efforts than Rome was willing to grant. By comparison with Josiah Strong, Russell Conwell, or Henry Ward Beecher, popular Protestant spokesmen, the liberal Catholics made far fewer concessions to the vulgarized temper of the age. This was one of the advantages of a Church with a centralized theological authority and a more docile membership of immigrants, only partially assimilated to American life. For American Catholics it would be primarily the problem of relevance, intellectual and social, not the question of doctrinal integrity, that would demand their attention for a long time. For Protestants, eager to assimilate modernist tendencies in secular thought, the threat of dissolution of doctrine would be much greater. But for both Catholics and Protestants, facing disruptive social and economic conflicts in the larger society, the problem of relevance would be severe so long as a gospel of work and private philanthropy was clearly inadequate.

A tempting escape from recognition of this tension with the world lay at hand in the promise of the new American religions of "mind cure." These religious therapies tended to make health itself an ultimate end, needing neither charity, reform, nor education because the soul in touch with Supreme Mind by positive thinking could overcome the hard facts of disease, strife, poverty, and death. Donald Meyer, in his study of *The Positive Thinkers,* has pointed to the historical reasons for "a religious medicine of feminine genesis" that logically led in the 1870's to Mary Baker Eddy's Christian Science. These reasons included a genuine sensitivity to the limitations of medical materialism in a pre-Freudian age, as well as to the pathos of middle-class women in industrial society. But if mind cure's psychological presupposition of "a female-oriented unconscious" was an implicit protest against the "tunnel-vision of a straining male world of ego," rampant in American society, its theology was marked by its rejected origins:

In its post-ascetic visions of Supply its desires remained submissive. In its dependency, it projected upon that on which it was dependent the same closed self-sufficiency it dared not claim for itself. And in its triumph over sickness it gained a health that had no ends. For survival, the weak propitiate; in the case of mind cure, that which it propitiated was its superconsciousness, and this meant just one thing—its sense of American society as a completed and self-sufficient world.[20]

Tocqueville prophesied that "if ever the faculties of the great majority of mankind were exclusively bent upon the pursuit of material objects, it might be anticipated that an amazing reaction would take place in the souls of some men. They would drift at large in the world of spirits, for fear of remaining shackled by the close bondage of the body." Furthermore, he pointed out, when men feel themselves weak and insignificant, a pantheistic system that envisages all things as parts of an immense Being, itself alone eternal, will have "secret charms" because it destroys the finite individuality of men, fostering their pride "while it soothes the indolence of their minds."[21] In this sense mind cure, with its rejection of matter as "an error of mortal mind," paradoxically demonstrated the power of worldliness in late nineteenth-century America.

William James treated mind cure with tolerant sympathy, not only because he knew that his own long bout with "neurasthenia," as he called it, escaped the categories of "medical materialism" but also because he knew that, in comparison with Europeans, his fellow citizens' faces showed "a wild-eyed look" either of "too desperate eagerness and anxiety or of too intense responsiveness and good-will."[22] The various mind-curing sects might usefully counter the gospel of work with "the gospel of relaxation" and "not caring." His hopes, however, were too sanguine. After 1900 a spate of popular books would flood the market to teach people how to manipulate themselves into automatons of success. The Protestant ethic, shorn of all ethical or theological meaning, was debased into an instrument for the submission of the self to the world in the disguise of masculine self-assertiveness. These perennial pamphlets for self-propulsion did not depend on any Tocquevillean qualifications of self-interest "rightly understood"; they made individual prosperity in this world the sum of human felicity, precisely the result he most feared would follow from "virtuous materialism."

"Virtuous materialism" was the trap lying in wait for all the modernist movements in religion, including that of Judaism. Antitraditional American Jewish leaders wished to edit Mosaic law to suit the conditions of American life, but they had no common political position. Before the Civil War the Bohemian immigrant Isaac Meyer Wise was as antiabolitionist and as pro-Democrat as the German immigrant David Einhorn was antislavery and pro-union. It was in fact the traditionalist Jewish leaders who made in 1862 the effective effort to persuade Lincoln and the Congress to rescind the prejudicial measure that provided for only Christian military chaplaincies, an important event in the country's incipient consciousness of an emerging pluralism. A representative leader of middle-class and educated German immigrants, Rabbi Wise founded the Union of American Hebrew Congregations (1873), Hebrew Union College (1875), and the Central Conference of American Rabbis (1889) to propagate Reform Judaism with a modernized prayer book and ritual. By the 1880's some two hundred of the major Jewish congregations had been made over in the new style, leaving only a handful of important traditional Orthodox synagogues. In 1885 the Pittsburgh Conference summed up Reform principles: a respect for "modern discoveries of scientific researches in the domains of nature and history," a rejection of all Mosaic laws "such as are not adapted to the views and habits of modern civilization," a repudiation of the belief in bodily resurrection and in hell or paradise as "abodes for everlasting punishment or reward," a commitment to the cause of social justice, and a new consciousness of themselves as "no longer a nation but a religious community."[23]

Ironically, this Judaic rapprochement with liberal Protestantism, a convergence that blurred the identity of both faiths, was made in the same period in which Protestant Americans began to exclude Jews from clubs, hotels, and private schools. In his synagogue the Reform Jew of this era was scarcely distinguishable from his Protestant counterpart—sermons in English, no hats or shawls, mixed choirs and mixed seating for men and women. A middle-class church for a middle-class people was common to both Jew and gentile. But the growing elaboration of "Anglo-Saxon" racial theories in America, designed to rationalize segregation of the Negro, benevolent neutrality toward British imperialism, and immigration-restriction legislation, also helped justify social discrimination against the Jews. Just because it would have been impossible to make an issue of Reform Judaism as a foreign ideology with un-American practices, blatant social snobbery was more nakedly evident in the system of exclusion against Jews.

The Reform impulse had a double root. Not only the pressure of the American environment, but the prestige of German-Jewish rationalist scholarship, supported the success of the new movement. In Germany the improvement of the social and economic position of the Jew seemed obviously congruent with the modernizing effort to minimize the notion of the Jews as a separate people. In America, where ethnic pluralism was becoming increasingly characteristic of community life, this separation of the faith from its people seems in retrospect particularly paradoxical. Yet so long as the American nation was itself "a chosen people," as Puritans, Jeffersonians, and Lincoln Republicans had maintained, then any other claims to chosenness were bound to seem competitive. Furthermore, Jews traditionally did not define themselves religiously through dogmas as Christians did, but through a way of life instead. If the practices themselves, except for circumcision, had come to seem incongruous to many American Jews, there was little else they could hold to in theological terms to compensate for the disappearance of rites that they felt were archaic.

The usual history of a religious group that breaks in a reformist spirit from its institutional tradition is characterized by sociologists as the development of a "sect," in tension with its surrounding society, in contrast to a "church" that accepts it. But America had already blurred this distinction in the history of the Puritans, who became the established church in New England. The American Jews illustrated another variation by splitting off from the tradition of Orthodoxy in order to have *less* tension with the larger society.[24] But the Jews, like both Protestants and Catholics in the American world of the late nineteenth century, experienced a common process of accommodation to the secular, rationalistic, and middle-class ethos of a modernizing industrial and urban society with democratic traditions. In this sense Jewish history was not an anomaly, and it produced its own version of this process in Abraham Cahan's *The Rise of David Levinsky* (1917).

Cahan himself represented the new immigration of Jews from Eastern Europe, a great influx that was markedly different from the earlier German middle-class emigrants. Its grimmer circumstances of ghetto life had made for a more tenacious traditional piety, a stronger sense of peoplehood among different nationalities, or a more radical passion for secular social justice. The small group of American Jews who had in 1885 formed the Jewish Theological Seminary Association in New York as a protest against the sacrifice of tradition by the Reform movement would find its opportunity for influence in the flood of the new immigration. Cahan himself was a Russian Jew with a passion for Russian literary culture and for socialism. Emigrating to America in 1882 as a political exile, he mastered both English and Yiddish, edited the *Jewish Daily Forward* in the language of its readers, and worked as an organizer in Jewish labor unions. By the turn of the century his literary work had earned the praise of William Dean Howells, and *The Rise of David Levinsky* was, in one sense, a Russian-Yiddish study in "realism" to match the American's *The Rise of Silas Lapham.*

Howell's Yankee hero finally forsakes the material advantages that complicity with sharp practices could have brought him and abandons Beacon Street for his native Vermont. More faithful to representative social actuality of its period, Cahan's novel portrays the slow economic rise in the garment industry of the lower East Side of a Jewish immigrant from Russia. Levinsky begins as a rabbinical student in the Russian ghetto, steeped in the Talmud but distracted by guilty sexual desires. Stricken by his mother's death, he is rescued from sinking into desperate poverty by an educated and prosperous Russian girl who is close to gentile culture. Subsidizing his exodus, she resolves to achieve her vision of him as an educated man. On American shores the process of his adaptation to the economic and social conditions of his new world completes his alienation from Orthodoxy. Levinsky begins to see Americanization as the "tangible form of becoming a man of culture," because he regards even the most learned and refined Europeans as "greenhorns." Yet at the same time he retains an ambivalent feeling that American education is a "cheap machine-made product." The outward signs of his conventional earlier identity as a rabbinical student, his earlocks and beard, disappear in his struggle for economic advancement and for sexual satisfaction in the teeming world of the East Side. The hope of going to City College, occasional lectures on Ethical Culture, the Darwinism of Herbert Spencer's *Sociology,* and the dream of a close family life come to take the place of his training in rabbinical studies. Evading union regulations, thereby winning the support of big manufacturers, and copying his rivals' designs, Levinsky becomes increasingly prosperous, able to donate to the Antomir Synagogue, which is a sentimental link for him to the world of his mother, who had been killed by anti-Semites. If he studies poetry it is as a strategy to get to the poet's daughter. But he is as out of place in her Hebrew-speaking milieu of advanced literature, socialism, and Zionism as he is among pious traditionalists. Both ends of the Eastern European spectrum of Jewish life are equally distant from his new life.

Levinsky fashions for himself a new identity as a highly successful leader in the women's ready-made cloak and suit business, but his doggedly honest account of his rise is also a recurrent lament for his lost ambition, his disappointments in love, his aching, nostalgically distorted feeling that the Talmudic student that he was in Russia had more in common with his "inner identity" than the self that he has made in America. His autobiography is the only way he can express his wistful vision of himself as a person "born for a life of intellectual interest." But his own story also shows that even as a schoolboy he had a vengeful dream of becoming rich and influential so as to punish his tormentors and that after his mother's death he had lost his interest in the Talmud and was looking for "some violent change, for piquant sensations." It is in this mood that the image of America seized his imagination. His divorced Russian-speaking patroness had made it clear to him that she found his piety and his Jewish look equally ridiculous. She prophetically expects America to make "another man" of him. Shaved and outfitted in his first American clothes, Levinsky mentally parades his "modern" look before her. In America his reading of the Talmud at the Antomir Synagogue is only a palliative for homesickness and a refuge from the strains of his struggles as a push-cart operater. Levinsky feels that his rigid native religion cannot be bent to the spirit of his new surroundings without breaking. But what makes the most critical difference in his development is the shame reflected in his decision to shave: he cannot bear to be called a "green one." His teacher in a public evening school, an American-born Reform Jew of German descent, devoted to the English Bible, to Dickens's novels, and the Democratic Party, is his instructor in accommodation to the New World, a midwife to the immigrant's representative experience of a second birth.

Cahan himself, though equally alienated from Orthodoxy, had a quite different development in the New World, preserving his ties to Russian literature, to socialism, and to the Yiddish culture of the East Side Jews. The artfulness of his novel is not so much its authentic documentation in detail of a closely observed world but its cumulative exposure of the psychology of a Jew whose successful adaptation to American life of the late nineteenth century leaves him with a residual melancholy sense that his past and his present "do not comport well." While liberal modern culture had demoralized Theron Ware through a self-deceived "illumination" incompatible with his professional role, David Levinsky is not destroyed but successfully made over in a businessman's role that only fitfully troubles him in retrospect. His wistful feelings are derived from the ideals that his mother and his benefactor had fostered in his youthful imagination. Despite his adaptation, however, Levinsky knows that he cannot marry a gentile woman to whom he is attracted, and he is still enough of a Jew to know that he is not really an educated man, that he has not served the cause of social justice, and that his connection with a fashionable synagogue is only external. Theron Ware never knows what has really happened to him; Levinsky earns our sympathy for his plain prosaic honesty in accounting for his success. If he has missed much in achieving it, he knows, as his creator does, that it has been a representative experience in a country testifying to the power of worldliness.

That power has been able to exert its force over him so thoroughly because a process of change had already begun in him before he crossed the sea. In Levinsky's life Cahan dramatized the portentous fact that Judaism in America, like Catholicism, would be intimately connected with the problem of ethnic identity, thus complicating the problem of religious belief in America to the benefit of sociologists if not to believers. Tocqueville had observed a peculiar mingling in America of patriotism and religion. If he had returned at the turn of the century, he would have had to add a missing chapter on immigration. Even in 1835 he had briefly noted with his usual keenness that economic success in America often forces the European emigrant "to unlearn the lessons of his early education." Cahan's novel refines that observation by making it clear that for many of those who find the motive and the means to emigrate, the unlearning has already begun before the crossing.[25]

The Social Gospel and the Aristocracy
of Manufactures

Between the publication of his two volumes on American democracy Tocqueville visited England. In Manchester he saw the factories that provoked his fears of a dangerous future, and they found muted expression later in his chapter on "How an Aristocracy May Be Created by Manufactures." The division of labor in developing the science of manufactures lowered the class of workmen and raised the class of masters. But the new class of masters was not fixed like the old class of aristocrats: it had no common traditions or hopes, and its aim was not to govern the workers but to use them. "Between the workman and the master there are frequent relations, but no real association." The new aristocracy was becoming "one of the harshest that ever existed in the world"; but at the same time it was "one of the most confined and least dangerous."[1] Still, he predicted, if ever a permanent inequality of conditions penetrated into the modern world, it would enter by this gate.

It was the "taste for physical gratifications" that led men to engage in commerce and manufacturing, a taste nurtured by equality of conditions, as in America. Such a taste could dangerously absorb men in "a kind of virtuous materialism" that would enervate the soul and prevent men from combining together to accomplish great actions. But these were primarily dangers of the future, particularly for democracy in Europe, the main object of Tocqueville's concern. While the passion for physical gratification *could* lead men to conclude that "the turmoil of freedom disturbs their welfare before they discover how freedom itself serves to promote it," the Americans, in his view, had "fortunately escaped" this peril. The American passion for worldly welfare was "vehement," but it was not "indiscriminate"; and reason, if it did not restrain it, still directed its course. The Americans had such a passion for both "their own welfare and for their freedom that it may be supposed that these passions are united and mingled in some part of their character."[2]

This favorable judgment on the American case in the 1830's would have seemed much too complacent fifty years later. By then the problems of poverty, monopolistic industrial and financial power, and the corruption of government were steadily accumulating vivid evidence for documenting the anxious fears that Tocqueville had hinted at in his earlier warning to the friends of democracy.

Tocqueville himself placed the problems of modern politics in a Christian perspective; he was convinced that the liberal revolutions of the eighteenth and nineteenth centuries represented the introduction of Christian charity into politics. Though he admitted that Christian morality was traditionally weak with respect to the public virtues of the citizen, he insisted, against the views of his friend Comte Joseph Arthur de Gobineau, that the new principles of modern politics were in fact only the new consequences in a new situation of the old principles of Christianity.[3] "The organization and the establishment of democracy in Christendom," Tocqueville wrote in his account of America, "is the great political problem of our times. The Americans, unquestionably, have not resolved this problem, but they furnish useful data to those who undertake to resolve it."[4] At the same time he was a vigorous critic of socialism because he rejected its materialistic emphasis and its regulatory paternalism. As the harsh problems of industrial society mounted, however, reformers responsive to Christian ideals would increasingly be moved toward affiliation with those secular humanitarians whose programs demanded greater use of state action or toward socialism itself, translated into Christian terms. If Tocqueville tended to underestimate the extent to which liberal reformers of earlier times, particularly in France, had deliberately challenged Christian ideals and traditions, he might later have pointed out the extent to which many of the modern "socialistic" reforms he rejected would be supported, particularly in America and Great Britain, by those who drew heavily on Christian traditions for their idealism.

The problem of distinguishing and relating secular and religious ideas in American reform movements of the late nineteenth and early twentieth centuries is a profoundly puzzling one. To some extent secular vocations in political economy, sociology, or settlement work became substitute religions for those who could no longer hold on to traditional religious doctrines. To some extent as well another process was often at work by which religious vocations were themselves transformed by experience with the profane life of the cities and the secular doctrines of the worldly philosophers. Some advocates of Christian socialism appear to be more socialist than Christian, while some advocates of fundamental reform appear to be more Christian than socialist. Between them lie the group of reformers whose blending of secular and religious traditions defies all neat categories of distinction. Just as in the formative period of the republic when a symbiotic relationship developed between pietists and republicans, so now Protestants, Catholics, and Jews, in their different ways, developed a social gospel, largely in spite of their hostile conservative majorities, to overlap the reforming activities of men who did not primarily define themselves in religious terms. But the modern situation was complicated by the worldly transformation that religious traditions as such had undergone in their development within American culture. A modernist movement in religion with respect to doctrine and temper had narrowed the difference between the religious and the secular traditions on which reformers might draw. The symbiotic relationship had become more one of interpenetration. A religion friendly to republicanism and a republicanism friendly to religion also required new definitions of both terms in the bewildering glare of modern conditions.

The republicanism of early America had never been indifferent to economic and social classes. In fact, *The Federalist* was notable for its emphasis on "the various and unequal distribution of property" as "the most common and durable source of factions." Madison had identified "a landed interest, a manufacturing interest, a mercantile interest, a moneyed interest," among others, and he held "the regulation of these various and interfering interests" to be "the principal task of modern legislation."[5] The development of the social gospel in religion, insofar as it recognized economic conflict as a proper subject for governmental action, was in no way an advance over the secular tradition, which in the eighteenth century had a more clear-sighted view of the concrete divisions of society. But Madison, like Jefferson, was concerned to protect the interests of landholders against the day when they would be overbalanced by the growth of trade and manufactures. In that context he feared the future power of an indigent class with "a leveling spirit" and argued in the Constitutional Convention for protection through the republican principle of a Senate elected for a long term.[6]

By the late nineteenth century, however, the development of capitalism had made the Senate a bastion of defense for the very interests of trade and manufactures whose overbalanced growth he had feared. The farmers themselves through their Alliances and the Populist Party would then seek redress of their grievances through programs that conservatives would condemn for being animated by leveling principles. At the same time the factory workers would seek more equal bargaining power through the formation of unions, and many reformers were forced to recognize that traditional political democracy had been subverted and was not itself, even if uncorrupted, sufficient to master the new problems of industrial society.

For the churches the crisis of modern capitalism was ambiguous. They had gone very far in promoting a gospel of work that served to rationalize capitalism, and in the Protestant movement the dominant middle-class congregations dramatized the isolation of the churches from the working class. Inevitably, a social gospel critical of capitalist conditions would be engaged in battle *within* the church. The effect of the new preaching on society at large would be considerably inhibited by the need to transform the religious community itself. Furthermore, it would be necessary even for the boldest exponents of a new social gospel to confront the fact that, particularly in Europe, the radical socialist tradition had profoundly secular roots and an antireligious animus. Their missionary efforts would thus be further displaced by the need to convert the socialists themselves.

These limitations were severe enough, but they were supplemented by the difficulty that secular socialists themselves were faced with the competing power of the republican tradition in America, which made its own persuasive and time-honored claim on the ideals of liberty, equality, fraternity, internationalism, technological progress, and materialistic abundance. This plea might appear obviously fraudulent to socialists, but it would not seem so to many ordinary citizens for whom the New World itself was the secular church of a political religion. Socialists had their own frustrating missionary problems, because the social-gospel advocates could draw upon the American predisposition toward a confirmed hospitality to religious rhetoric and religious traditions.

In view of these peculiar boundaries of the problem, it is not surprising that those who found the most political profit in the American case were nonsocialist moderate reformers, like Theodore Roosevelt and Woodrow Wilson, who could speak in a moralistic idiom that

drew on Christianity, democracy, and patriotism in a way that
Tocqueville would have understood with his usual appreciative irony.
In this sense, despite all the complications that the modern world had
brought to American political and religious life, Tocqueville's theme of
the power of republican religion was still pertinent. But that relationship which Tocqueville had praised was, even in the mid-nineteenth
century, more ambiguous than he had realized. It had always been
vulnerable to the parochial limitations of Protestant zeal in a country
that included increasing numbers of men and women of other religious
persuasions and traditions. By any objective test the chief success of
a Protestant reforming politics after the Civil War was the fulfillment
of the earlier temperance movement in national legislation of Prohibition, and it unified a majority on a repressive program that could
not be enforced and did not deal with the serious problems of the
nation. The churches, furthermore, would play a chauvinistic role in
the First World War, which for all its democratic rhetoric ended in
a passion for the suppression of civil liberties at home. When the
Northern churches supported the Lincoln Republicans, they were at
least pertinent to the great issues of republican union and equality that
the slavery crisis had generated; when the nation's churches supported
the First World War and Prohibition, they had no fundamental or
lasting relation to the democratic values that Tocqueville had seen in
American republican religion. They only dramatized the limitations
of Protestant vision in a pluralistic society or the common vulnerability
of the churches to the self-righteous nationalism of war.

The extent to which social reform was envisaged in religious terms
in the late nineteenth century can be measured from the unusually
widespread popularity of several books. *Progress and Poverty, Looking
Backward,* and *Caesar's Column* were the *Uncle Tom's Cabin* of their
age. Henry George, Edward Bellamy, and Ignatius Donnelly led independent social movements, but they held overlapping positions and
spoke for a common hope that society could be transformed in the
light of Christian ideals.

Henry George, the Moses of the land tax as the way to restore equal
rights by confiscating rent for social purposes, often lectured on the
actual Moses. In his mayoralty campaign of 1886 in New York City
he won more votes than Theodore Roosevelt and gained the support
of more than forty priests and sixty Protestant clergymen as the candidate of the Central Labor Union. His Anti-Poverty Societies graced

their meetings with sermons and hymns, and George successfully defended the Christianity of his views in an open letter to the Pope, who responded indirectly by reinstating one of George's disciples, a priest who had been excommunicated. Two utopian colonies were established on Georgeite principles in the American South in the late 1890's, and one of them, which published the *Social Gospel,* was called the Christian Commonwealth Colony.[7]

When Edward Bellamy lost his Baptist faith, he still retained the postmillennial vision of an era "when war and strife should cease." His "nationalism," as dramatized in *Looking Backward* (1888), envisioned a coming utopia without pecuniary competition as "God's kingdom of fraternal equality," and he believed that the revolutionary change was not only implicit in the increasing large-scale organization of society but would also represent, in revivalistic terms, "a melting and flowing forth of men's hearts toward one another, a rush of contrite, repentant tenderness" in a "literal fulfillment" of Christ's religion.[8] *Looking Backward,* like George's work, figured largely in the intellectual lives of many prominent ministers of the social gospel. Like George's supporters, Bellamy's tended to support the Populist Party.

Donnelly, another self-taught prophet with a penchant for utopian writing, had held political office as Republican lieutenant governor, Congressman, and state senator from Minnesota. An organizer, lecturer, and executive for the Farmers' Alliance, he edited a Populist newspaper and wrote the preamble and much of the platform for the People's Party in 1892. *Caesar's Column* (1890) was set in the future, like Bellamy's earlier story, but instead of envisaging a postmillennial theme of progress it darkly forecast the nightmare of a bloody revolution, launched by debased proletarians against a decadent oligarchy and ending in the destruction of civilization. Only a colony was left in Africa to put Populist principles in practice: a dominant House elected by workers and farmers from their own ranks, paper money, no lending at interest, individual land sale and settlement, an eight-hour day, a minimum wage, and the making of corruption a treasonable crime.

Donnelly's narrator, appropriately called Gabriel, invokes the social-gospel image of Christ: "He who drove the money-changers out of the temple and denounced the aristocrats of his country as whited sepulchres, and preached a communism of goods, would not view to-day with patience or equanimity the dreadful sufferings of mankind. We have inherited Christianity without Christ; we have the painted shell of a religion, and that which rattles around within it is not the burning soul of the Great Iconoclast, but a cold and shriveled and meaningless tradition." True religion should "take possession of the *governments* of the world and enforce *justice!*"⁹ But the religion of 1988, as the narrator discovers, is worldly, sensual, and acquiescent in evil. The despair that animates Donnelly's farrago of popular science, sentimental romance, and gothic horror is the fear that it was too late for republican reform or for a decent revolution, but not for an apocalypse.

Much like *Uncle Tom's Cabin,* only with industrial slavery substituted for Negro slavery, his story also envisaged Africa as the place where a Christian republic could be founded. Mrs. Stowe would have understood him perfectly when Gabriel points back to the Civil War as an exemplar of the bitter truth that "God wipes out injustice with suffering; wrong with blood; sin with death. You can no more get beyond the reach of His hand than you can escape from the planet."¹⁰ His analysis of social evil was also ultimately a moral one—greed, vanity, and cunning had displaced faith in the fatherhood of God and the brotherhood of man. His novel was a jeremiad, as he explained in his preface, to warn his readers (as Mrs. Stowe had) of the coming "day of vengeance" if they did not act so as to redeem themselves.

But Donnelly's doubts were much gloomier, and the millennium was reduced, in his "paranoid" style, to a small outpost in Uganda, fortified against the mad disorder of America and Europe alike by Populist virtue. His own failing political career no doubt helped fuel Donnelly's literary energy, but his categories of interpretation were drawn from a Protestant tradition of millennial speculation, mixed with the conspiratorial fantasies rife in American political demonology with its images of insidious Jacobins, Papists, Masons, Mormons, Lords of the Loom and Lash, and giant trusts. Donnelly had politically defended despised minorities, but his fictional imagery was often drawn from scapegoating prejudices against Asiatic immigration, Jewish moneylenders, and the "Negroid" features of his rebel Caesar, a South Carolinian of Italian descent who leads the brutal mob of the Brotherhood of Destruction. The conventions of gothic horror and conspiratorial melodrama turned much of his novel into a kind of political pornography, but his vision of a rebellion against civilization exploited fears that also imaginatively attracted Mark Twain. His *A Connecticut Yankee in King Arthur's Court* ended in apocalyptic violence, leaving the power-seeking crusader for democracy, technology, and religious disestablishment in losing battle with the force of tradition and the established Church, as well as in doubt about whether Arthurian England or late nineteenth-century America is home.

The development of monopolistic capitalism, with the widespread corruption of the political and legal process, posed a problem for reformers in the 1890's much like that which Negro slavery had posed in the 1850's, and some of the same dilemmas had to be faced again —how could religion be made politically relevant, how could the sin of selfishness be converted to virtue, was history on the side of reform, revolution, or apocalypse? As in the ante-bellum period, there were those who concluded that only small utopias could resolve the problem of living in a sinful world, and there were those instead who became Christian anarchists, reformers, or Christian Socialists. Earlier strains of American evangelicalism—revivalism, temperance reform, and anti-Catholicism—also reappeared in the later social gospel.

Just as ante-bellum reformers had realized that slavery was a social system as well as an individual sin, so also the social gospelers, inheriting an evangelical emphasis on the need for individual conversion, were compelled to go beyond it to assess the institutional pattern that had grown up around them and to search for social remedies. The alternative was to rest with the traditional Protestant emphasis on individual conversion and philanthropy or merely to supplement this nonpolitical stand with Prohibition as a legislative aim. This conversionist response to social injustice was reflected in the popular tractarian novel of the Congregational minister Charles M. Sheldon, *In His Steps* (1896). Unlike Mrs. Stowe, he could not find in exodus from America a facile solution and so was all the more dependent on individual conversion experiences, which affected only a small minority of believers living in the cities of his story.*

On a very much higher but still popular level of art William Dean Howells had also dramatized the need for a social gospel in *A Hazard of New Fortunes* (1890). It pointed toward a characteristically muted affirmation of Tolstoy's Christian pacifism. The journalist-hero Basil March gradually discovers his own complicity with the larger social and economic injustices of big-city life and responds vicariously

---

* So far as social reform *is* urged, the destruction of the saloon is the major theme. See Paul S. Boyer, *"In His Steps:* A Reappraisal," *American Quarterly,* 23 (Spring, 1971), 65. The continuities between the social gospel and prewar views of evangelicals are highlighted in Timothy L. Smith, *Revivalism and Social Reform: American Protestantism on the Eve of the Civil War* (New York, 1965), Chap. 10. But he ignores the conservative anxieties Boyer finds in Sheldon's unconfident view of the future.

through his sympathy for the well-to-do Margaret Vance, "a Sister of Charity among the poor and the dying," and the settlement worker Conrad Dryfoos, unhappy son of a capitalist. Conrad's death in the streetcar strike as an innocent bystander intent on preventing violence becomes for March an emblem of the necessary principle of a Christ-like suffering for the sins of others.

These martyrs, however, are not shown in terms that are unequivocally admirable. Margaret's upper-class Episcopalian sympathy for the workers' grievances is genuine, but her wish to stop the fighting is basically a defeatist conviction that someone should tell them "how perfectly hopeless it was" to resist the companies or drive off the scabs. The miserable Conrad, distractedly wandering in the streets, feels a longing primarily for her sake to do something "to save those mistaken men from themselves," and he is shot by a random bullet before he ever articulates his impulse to stop a policeman from clubbing down the embittered old socialist Lindau. March himself is willing to give up his editorial job if the owner should fire Lindau for being a socialist, but he thinks this old unionist soldier is wrong to support the strikers against the law and to "renounce the American means as hopeless." All the novel's resolutions are finally personal: Conrad's only moment of happiness is in the trust Margaret has shown to him just before his death; Margaret stills her own qualms about her role in Conrad's death by becoming a nun with a serenity that seems to reflect "the peace that passeth understanding." March is left with the conventionally pious hope that "we can put our evil from us with penitence; and somehow, somewhere, the order of loving kindness, which our passion or our wilfulness has disturbed, will be restored."

Howells himself was moved by Tolstoy's Christian anarchism; he had cooperated with the first "Nationalist Club" in Boston; and he was briefly associated in 1890 with the Church of the Carpenter mission organized by the Christian socialist W. D. P. Bliss. Yet he could not follow Tolstoy's example, accept the creeds of the church, or believe in the practicality of Bellamy's hopes. He expected instead that labor's troubles would eventually compel party politicians to put a socialistic plank in their platforms. From his own problem of commitment he knew to a large extent the hesitancies of his journalist-protagonist.[11] In *A Hazard of New Fortunes* (1891) Basil March listens to those "who dealt with Christianity as a system of economics as well as a religion," but he jokes to his wife that he intends to follow all the prophets he has heard, a different one every Sunday, and so "they got their laugh out of it at last, but with some sadness at heart, and with a dim consciousness that they had got their laugh out of too many things in life." This wry, self-critical tone dominates the novel until the melodramatic climax. While March finds an alien fanatical streak in the characters of both Margaret and Conrad, he has no answers except to praise their martyrdoms. He has changed enough not to share his wife's lament for the "literary peace, the intellectual refinement" of the Boston literary life they had left behind in coming to New York; its security now seems to him like "death-in-life." But no social solution to the country's ills is foreseen by this narrative with its focus on individual acts of charity.

As a novelist Howells was at his best in demonstrating his secular belief that personal change is never dramatic because (in March's words) "we are each several characters, and sometimes this character has the lead in us, and sometimes that." His imagination was not well suited to making either Conrad's or Margaret's religious significance credible or their attitudes persuasive; they remain weak symbols of a Christian anarchism that only a heroic Tolstoy or a Garrison could vivify. March's espousal of their religious meaning in the last scenes of the novel provides no social alternative to a resigned acceptance of the workers' inevitable defeat; instead it seems to reflect indirectly Howells's own stoical coming to terms with the private tragedy of the death of his daughter during the composition of the story. In this light his prefatorial remark (written twenty years later) that at the time when he wrote the novel "the solution of the riddle of the painful earth through the dreams of Henry George, through the dreams of Edward Bellamy, through the dreams of all the generous visionaries of the past, seemed not impossibly far off," is belied by the resigned tone of the novel's conclusion. In his focus on a guilty sense of complicity with an unjust society, on a cautious desire to get into touch with threatening but more vital aspects of modern life, and on a wistful yearning for an ethic of Christian nonviolence and sacrificial suffering, observed from a sympathetic distance, Howells must have faithfully articulated the uneasy middle-class conscience of liberal Christians.

Howells by 1892 was disaffected from the Republicans and saw hope only in the Populist People's Party. In 1896 he voted for William Jennings Bryan, nominated by the Democrats with Populist support, because the Republicans were no longer the party of antislavery idealism. The Democrats were traditionally the party of Jeffersonian laissez-faire principle, which in practice meant not only less emphasis on the federal government's responsibilities but also more tolerance for immigrants, who could find freedom from the regulatory imposition of Protestant middle-class moral values on their own mores. The Republicans had emphasized national power in terms both of prohibition of slavery in the territories and of the protective tariff for industry. Bryan's role as a Populist candidate was largely symbolic because while he eloquently preached that mankind should not be crucified on the cross of gold, he tended to nail the Populists on the narrow plank of free silver. Even so, his own religious heritage, compounded of Baptist, Methodist, and Presbyterian strains, and his moralistic advocacy of temperance made him congenial to Protestant evangelicals who had supported the antislavery Republicans, as well as to agrarians who shared their religious prejudices, as Donnelly's example illustrates. The Populists themselves, while endorsing Bryan, ran for Vice-President Thomas E. Watson of Georgia, a virulent anti-Catholic. Bryan had given the Democratic Party an unprecedented evangelical character, and as a consequence in the Midwest the support of traditional Democrats declined in 1896, while the support of evangelical religious groups, native and immigrant,* rose to a level higher than that which they had usually given to Democratic candidates. Bryan's rhetoric stressed agrarian values and class conflict, but the Populists had worked to draw off many Prohibition Party men to the Democratic standard in an effort to create a party that would represent the forces of morality—understood in identifiable traditional Protestant terms.

The early workers' movements were themselves often led by men with a Christianized vision of reform. George E. McNeill of the recently established American Federation of Labor wrote in the *Labor Leader* in 1890:

The influence of the teachings of the Carpenter's Son still tends to counteract the influence of Mammon. In this movement of the laborers toward equity, we will find a new revelation of the Old Gospel, when the Golden Rule of Christ shall measure the relations of men in all their duties toward their fellows. . . . Then the new Pentecost will come, when every man shall have according to his needs.[12]

* These would include evangelically oriented Norwegian and Swedish Lutherans, Protestant Irish, Cornish and Welsh Methodist, and Dutch Reformed. See Paul Kleppner, *The Cross of Culture: A Social Analysis of Midwestern Politics, 1850–1900* (New York: The Free Press, 1970), p. 88. The particularly noteworthy defectors to the Republicans in 1896 included Catholics and high-church German Lutherans.

In Boston, several clergymen had established a Christian Labor Union in 1872, one of them later playing an important role in the passage of a bill setting up a state bureau of labor statistics and another helping to organize the Knights of Labor. While the leader of the Knights, Terence V. Powderly, distrusted the churches, he was himself a Christian believer and his union (like many of the craft unions) advocated the temperance movement, the favorite reform of the evangelicals. Frances E. Willard, president of the Women's Christian Temperance Union, was herself initiated into the order of the Knights in 1887; more than ten years before, she had drafted the WCTU platform endorsing labor's demands for a living wage and an eight-hour day. Unions and progressive evangelicals could cooperate for both secular and religious reasons not only on temperance but also on a petition to Congress in 1889 for a national Sunday Rest Law. Charles Stelzle, who had spent eight years as a machinist before he began to preach to working-class churches, was a prominent member of the American Federation of Labor and was published regularly in hundreds of labor papers as a Christian spokesman for the Department of Church and Labor of the Presbyterian Church. Forced from his position by conservatives in 1913, he left as his monument the only enduring labor church, the Labor Temple, established three years earlier for settlement work and adult education on the East Side of New York.[13]

After Bryan's defeat in 1896 a new note would enter into the reformers' campaigns, reflecting the professionalization of middle-class life and the new secular fascination with scientific method and administrative techniques. Men who called themselves progressives after the turn of the century would not need to rely on religious traditions and vocabularies but could seek sustenance in the development of social science. Many of those who became influential for the interpretation of American political life—Herbert Croly, Lincoln Steffens, Walter Lippman, Walter Weyl, Charles A. Beard—were deeply secular minds, critical of moralistic discourse in reformers for all their own strong passion for reform. Yet an earlier style of social science incorporated religious tradition, as with Richard T. Ely, a founding father of the American Economic Association in 1885. It aimed to unite younger scholars in a break with conventional laissez-faire orthodoxy and a hospitality to the new ideas of evolution and relativity of judgment, fostered by their own education in German universities. But Ely, who spent seven years with the American Institute of Christian Sociology in the Chautauqua adult-education movement before becoming a controversial professor at the University of Wisconsin, spoke in familiar language of the need for "a profound revival of religion . . . a great religious awakening which shall shake things, going down into the depths of men's lives and modifying their character. This religious reform must infuse a religious spirit into every department of political life."[14] For Ely social science taught men *how* to love their neighbor, and he was a popular speaker in churches, proud that his books on economics were widely used by Methodist divinity students.

Ely had felt the influence of the Presbyterian Calvinism of his father in upstate New York; and the liberal minister Washington Gladden, who made his name in the Middle West, had also grown up in the "burned-over district" area of New York under the tutelage of his Presbyterian uncle. What Germany had been for Ely the factory town of North Adams, Massachusetts, was for Gladden, and his career was built on the effort to make his mild philanthropic Congregationalism, which feared art, ecstacy, and dogmatism in religion, relevant to social reform in Columbus, Ohio. A popularizer of "the higher criticism" of the Bible, Gladden had a vision of history that was optimistically linear and continuous without breaks or cataclysms, one long, slow preparation for the coming Kingdom, hailed in the very name of the social-gospel journal he helped edit. He was an executive of the American Missionary Association, which established Negro universities and lower schools, and he slowly came to advocate the familiar progressive measures—collective bargaining, compulsory arbitration, municipal ownership of public utilities, the short ballot, the initiative and referendum on a local level, the direct primary, and woman suffrage. In elections he supported Theodore Roosevelt and Wilson, complacently accepting the growth of an American empire and converting to Wilson's missionary diplomacy and intervention in the war, while taking special comfort in the war's contribution to Prohibition.[15] His career in its decency, its bland theology, its moderate reformism, and its vulnerability to widespread paternalist assumptions about "Anglo-Saxon" superiority was representative of much of the liberal sentiment in the Protestant churches for which he was recognized as an eloquent spokesman.

The left wing of the social-gospel movement was torn between communitarianism, pacifism, and political socialism, but it could have housed them all under the rubric of Christian Socialism, or the vision of the Cooperative Commonwealth. Three Christian Socialists played a particularly significant role: William Dwight Porter Bliss, an Epis-copalian; George D. Herron, a Congregationalist; and Walter Rausch-enbusch, a Baptist. Among them they represented the roles of the organizer, the prophet, and the theoretician, and they illustrated the difficulties Christian Socialists had in making themselves felt as a political force.

Bliss was ubiquitous and eclectic, a dynamo of reform energy who supported at various times the Knights of Labor, Bellamy's "National-ism," the Populists, the Massachusetts Labor Party, and ultimately the Socialist Party. He also gave his talents to the Church Association for the Advancement of the Interests of Labor, the American Fabian League, the mission of the Church of the Carpenter in Boston, a popular front of Progressive reformers known as the Social Reform Union, and finally the Christian Socialist Fellowship, which endorsed the Socialist Party. Appropriately, he was the author of the *Encyclo-pedia of Social Reform* (1897), and he shepherded through the presses the *Dawn,* the British-inspired *American Fabian,* and Sunday-school lessons in the social gospel, *The Gospel of the Kingdom,* pre-pared for Josiah Strong's American Institute of Social Service.

This diffusion of commitment was always guided by a Christianized democratic socialism, but Bliss's politics were split by the impulse to sponsor "a great Chautauqua movement in Social Reform," in which he could join forces on brief occasion with a wide spectrum of reformers, including labor leaders, reform politicians, journalists, preachers, and socialists, and the wish to sponsor a specific party and program. Even after endorsing the Socialist Party, Bliss did not expect the churches to deal in programs and parties: "I do not ask that the Church declare for a Socialist programme or for a Socialist party. That is a small affair. It is not the function of the Church to adopt programmes or endorse parties. I simply ask that the Church dare to preach and to live her own Gospel, and be true to her own Christ."[16] Yet the secretary of the Christian Socialist Fellowship, which Bliss joined, could say in 1910 that the "new earth" prophesied in Scripture *was* the coming kingdom of socialism: "The time is near. Repent, the Kingdom of Heaven is at hand. Come out for Christian Socialism. It is God's call."[17] Like the abolitionists and before them the pietist Whigs, the Christian Socialists saw history in evangelistic millen-nial terms, however willing they were to translate the familiar message into Fabian tactics and programs. The thousand who met, for ex-ample, at their fourth annual conference in effect lent their strength to the right wing of the Socialist Party, congenial to its condemnation in 1912 of crime, sabotage, and violence as socialist tactics. At the same time Bliss did not abandon his hopes for a more broadly based movement of labor leaders, liberal social-gospel preachers, settlement-house workers, and Progressives, joined together in support of direct democracy, woman suffrage, conservation, and local option for Prohibition, organized in order to win the churches and other religious organizations. Perhaps it would be easier gradually to convert Christians to socialism than to convert socialists to Christianity.[18] In either case the structure of the situation defined severe limits to the horizon of any revolutionary dawn in which Bliss might reasonably expect to be alive.

The problem was not his strategy but his perception of the nature of the case. He distrusted what he called the "narrow class-conscious delusion" of some socialists who, as in the Socialist Labor Party, had cultivated a doctrinaire alienation from effectiveness, and it took the proved growth of the more moderate Socialist Party after 1901 to earn his endorsement. Even so, he seems to have been more anxious to convert the churches to a socialist form of religion than he was to convert them to a socialist form of politics. This double concern for theology and practice made it difficult for Bliss to steer a single course, because he could not simply equate socialism with Christianity. Furthermore, the *Christian Socialist,* organ of the Fellowship, came out strongly for Wilson's view of the war, and by 1918 the editor could resentfully call the Socialist Party "a bigoted, bitter, unscientific, foolish, anti-religious sect."[19] The relationship between Christian Socialists and the Socialist Party was vulnerable to differences in their respective traditions. American Christian reformers could call on a tradition of clerical engagement with the country's wars that ran back to the Revolution, and the linkage of reform and war under Lincoln must have seemed about to repeat itself in Wilson's moralistic and even messianic version of the conflict. This ill-tempered desertion of the Socialist Party during the war provides a more justified basis for blaming the Christian Socialists than does Bliss's earlier diffidence about the Social Democratic Party, which has led a historian of socialism to complain unfairly that Bliss's reluctance to support "a promising and essentially revisionist socialist political party, indicated a lack of political courage characteristic of the whole middle-class socialist movement."[20]

Courage was not George Herron's problem. A platform spellbinder of evangelical Congregational background, he attacked the organized churches in a revivalist spirit similar to that of the pietists in the Great Awakening who had lamented the unconverted state of the established clergy's souls. "Believe in the Lord Jesus Christ and thou shalt be saved, is God's answer to all modern questions," he intoned. For him, the Sermon on the Mount was science, political economy, and law; the state only needed to become converted to the gospel. Herron revived the perfectionism of the abolitionist evangelicals with a postmillennial faith in the coming earthly realization of the Kingdom, which seemed to loom on the horizon in the shape of the Populist Party as a modern type of the Protestant Reformation. From his chair of applied Christianity at Iowa College (Grinnell), Herron introduced his students to the writings of Josiah Strong, Richard T. Ely, and Washington Gladden, as well as those of Mazzini, Ruskin, and Hegel. Herron was a star of the lecture halls, and his addresses were inspired by a millennial vision of a new church and state that would end the present separation of church and state and supplant coercion with the reign of love. The Christian conscience was the enemy of the churches, he felt, and he looked to the Social Democratic Party as a political form of religion that would lead ultimately to the gospel liberty of love.[21]

Herron's socialism was paradoxically grounded in a radical pietism that moved toward an antinomian belief that each individual incarnated God. But society itself could become converted through socialism, which was seen as a political Second Coming, institutionalizing the ethic of sacrifice. By acclamation he was made temporary chairman of the Social Democratic Party at its unity convention from which emerged, with his reconciling help, the Socialist Party of America. The subscription list of his journal the *Kingdom,* first taken over by the *Social Gospel,* was after 1901 taken over by the *Internationalist Socialist Review.*[22] Herron's contribution to organizational politics fizzled like a falling rocket. The year of his chairmanship, 1901, was also the year of his divorce and his remarriage to the youthful daughter of his academic patron, and the scandalmongering of the newspapers drove him not only from his church but out of the country to sunny, unshockable Italy. It is hard to imagine that Herron's perfectionism, reminiscent of Garrisonian pre-Civil War reformers, could have survived a permanent intellectual marriage with the secular socialism of Eugene V. Debs, but Herron's brief role in the party is indicative of the mixed background of its tradition in America, which later produced Norman Thomas, a former minister, as its perennial candidate for President.

Christian Socialists who linked themselves to the Socialist Party organized in 1906 as the Christian Socialist Fellowship. They had a double mission—to persuade the churches to support the Socialist Party and to persuade the socialists not to reject religion—but in practice their evangelism was directed at the denominations. The fellowship's organ, the *Christian Socialist,* considered Walter Rauschenbusch the best exponent of their position, though he himself was not a member of either the fellowship or the party. Neither organizer nor orator, Rauschenbusch made the most notable effort to build a bridge connecting modern Biblical scholarship, a theology of the social gospel, and social analysis of contemporary problems. Though Tocqueville opposed socialism because he feared centralized power, he might well have been led by the new conditions of the industrial world to see in Rauschenbusch an exemplar of a modern form of "republican religion" in America.

With six generations of Lutheran German pastors behind him, Rauschenbusch took up a Baptist pastorate for eleven years near Hell's Kitchen in New York's West Side before taking a professorial post at Rochester Theological Seminary. A student of German scholarship and the English Fabians, he was also sympathetically familiar with the writings of George and Bellamy. In 1889 he had founded *For the Right,* a Christian Socialist monthly for workingmen. Nearly two decades later he published *Christianity and the Social Crisis* (1907), linking political democracy and Christian morality through the common ideal of equality, which he found threatened by the development of economic inequality under plutocratic conditions. Neither the courts nor public opinion, traditional democratic resources, were adequate to control the corruptions produced by modern commercial life. Rauschenbusch expounded the Bible so as to emphasize the social teachings of the prophets and the revolutionary character of Jesus as a Hebrew prophet, preparing men for a righteous social order as well as for individual salvation.

Rauschenbusch drew his Biblical portrait in the light of his own responsiveness to contemporary historical and sociological scholarship: "Jesus had the scientific insight which comes to most men only by training, but to the elect few by divine gift. He grasped the substance of that law of organic development in nature and history which our

own day at last has begun to elaborate systematically. . . . He was
seeking to displace the crude and misleading catastrophic conceptions
by a saner theory about the coming of the kingdom. This conception
of growth demanded not only a finer insight, but a higher faith."[23]
Thus Rauschenbusch made Jesus a postmillennialist, polemicizing in
his parables against the premillenial apocalyptic visions of primitive
Christianity. It was not necessary to await the Second Coming that
would make the kingdom of social perfection possible.

Early Christianity had not merely cultivated charity and love. In
Rauschenbusch's view it had also been a democratic social force of
unrest and reform. But that impulse later was lost through ecclesias-
ticism, ceremonialism, ascetic individualism, and theological dogmatism. The great opportunity that confronted his generation derived
from the waning in modern times of these historical causes of the dis-
tortion of Jesus's good news. Human emancipation stemmed from the
Renaissance, the English Puritan Revolution, the French Revolution,
and the growth of modern social science. Already crucial aspects of the
Christian social gospel were to some extent immanent in certain
American institutions: the family, the school, and the democratic
churches. Yet social and economic inequality was corrupting the
country, and the future of the churches themselves was threatened by
an alienated working class. Rauschenbusch took hope from the radical,
evangelical, and Calvinist American tradition because it historically
had a "strong bent towards politics." Churchmen should see that by
identifying themselves with labor the churches could rise with the
workingman's movement, just as Puritanism had lifted and been lifted
by the middle class.[24]

Rauschenbusch realistically warned that there was no return to a
preindustrial era, no general solution in communitarian colonies, and
no wisdom in ecclesiastical efforts to form "Christian parties" or to
control the reform movement rather than to ally with it. Americans,
furthermore, needed to be on guard against their moral optimism and
confidence that truth would triumph by itself. "Concrete material
interests" had to enter into "a working alliance with Truth" so that
enough force could be rallied "to break down the frowning walls of
error." The wageworker was that force, and its "ultimate and logical
outcome" was socialism. To that end, professional men, some businessmen, and clergy could contribute an ameliorating influence for evolutionary progress, but moralists should not forget that in this "war of

conflicting interests" workers would necessarily use political leverage, group selfishness, and angry coercion.[25]

Yet Rauschenbusch still betrayed in his own analysis some of the typically moralistic assumptions of earlier Protestant evangelicalism. "In the last resort," he wrote, "the only hope is in the moral forces which can be summoned to the rescue." In this vein his solution to the social problem was revivalistic, foreseeing "a new tide of religious faith and moral enthusiasm" based on self-sacrifice, through which "the intrenchments of vested wrong will melt away" and "a regenerate nation will look with the eyes of youth across the fields of the future." Like the revivalists, he was distressed that alcoholic drinks were appearing in "respectable and educated homes" and urged "a new temperance crusade with all the resources of advanced physiological and sociological science." Marxist socialists would not call him "comrade" on this barricade, nor would they find him joining them for women's rights.* As much as Harriet Beecher Stowe, he idealized the family as "the foundation of morality, the chief educational institution, and the source of nearly all the real contentment among men. To create a maximum number of happy families might well be considered the end of all statesmanship." It disturbed him that some women, instead of learning housekeeping, preferred the practice of a profession, and he was appalled to think that contraceptives were debasing "womanly purity" and making "sin easy and safe."[26] Secular socialists were the most determined advocates of woman suffrage, but the issue does not appear in Rauschenbusch's book.

His extensive idealization of the home as the incarnation of his social ethic, an idea common to the ante-bellum reformers as well, is matched by his lack of attention to the specific economic or theoretical issues of socialist thought. Rauschenbusch's argument for socialism is, in one sense, merely a moral conclusion following from his desire to extend the model of the family to the whole society, as if love, rather than justice, were an appropriate organizing standard for a complex, bureaucratic, urban industrial society, a sentimental assumption that none of the Founding Fathers would ever have made. In the midst of the tragedy of the First World War he could assert in *A Theology for the Social Gospel* (1917) that "the social gospel is based on the belief that love is the only true working principle of human society."[27]

* Prominent female socialists were often from Christian reform backgrounds. See James Weinstein, *The Decline of Socialism in America 1912–1925* (New York, 1967), p. 55.

Rauschenbusch wished to identify Christianity with social justice and not merely with charitable love, but his idealization of the family led him to blur this distinction. Justice was only love in a wider social context than philanthropy.

This difficulty was common to Christian Socialists and common, at bottom, to Christians, whose traditions taught that surrender of life and its interests was in some sense the highest good. This sacrificial theme was inevitably at odds with the necessary emphasis in the labor movement on a firm assertion of rights and claims. Rauschenbusch, more than most Christian Socialists, felt the pressure of this problem in *Christianity and the Social Crisis* even if he did not resolve it. More than most also, he qualified his sense of the millennial promise of the present: "History laughs at the optimistic illusion that 'nothing can stand in the way of human progress.' It would be safer to assert that progress is always for a time only, and then succumbs to the inevitable decay."[28] His own postmillennial emphasis on development, rather than catastrophe, was shaken by the First World War not so much in ideological terms as in his private feeling: "Since 1914 the world is full of hate, and I cannot expect to be happy again in my lifetime."[29]

Rauschenbusch spoke out of a firmly held Christian tradition but he was heard by many outside his fold. The muckraking journalist Lincoln Steffens, who wore a gold cross on his watchchain, had once called on Rauschenbusch for advice on a project to study the historical Jesus. Steffens was a popular symbol of the unshockable inside dopester of the corruption of the cities and would eventually pride himself on his emancipation from liberal moralizing as a "scientific" admirer of dictators. "I want to tell Christians what their Christ said they should do," Steffens wrote in 1909; "I shan't pretend to accept it all myself, but I will show how that would solve the problem."[30] Appropriately, in 1918 Rochester Theological Seminary asked Steffens to memorialize Rauschenbusch. This connection between the professor of church history and the muckraker was not an anomaly. One of the founders of the Bureau of Municipal Research in New York, concerned with the scientific management of the budget and other government functions for welfare purposes, also wrote in social-gospel terms *The Church and Society,* published in the same year as Rauschenbusch's *Christianizing the Social Order* (1912).[31]

By 1912 some thirty denominations were represented in the four-year-old Federal Council of Churches of Christ in America, which in its advisory capacity officially defined the social gospel so as to include the abolition of child labor, social insurance against injury, unemployment, occupational disease, and mortality for workers, a six-day week, shorter hours, a minimum living wage, and protection against the liquor traffic. It also defended the right to organize, for both business and labor, if exercised in the context of conciliation and arbitration. God, sin, judgment, and redemption, it finally affirmed, applied both to individuals and social life.[32]

In political terms the spirit of the Federal Council by 1916 was reflected in its most politically influential member, Woodrow Wilson. Grandson on his mother's side and son on his father's side of Presbyterian ministers, he was a ruling elder of the church in Princeton. Wilson moved from his traditional Protestant individualism to the recognition of the social gospel's insistence that men could be saved only as part of the redemption of the world. In 1916 he forsook his laissez-faire prejudices by supporting a federal child-labor law, and in his campaign that year for re-election to the Presidency he asserted that "Christianity was just as much intended to save society as to save the individual, and there is a sense in which it is more important that it should save society."[33]

Three years later Father John A. Ryan, who had been inspired in his youth by Donnelly's Populism and Ely's social-gospel economics, would draft a social prospectus for four bishops who were the executive agency of the National Catholic War Council. He had successfully sponsored minimum-wage legislation in Minnesota, and his 1919 agenda for social action on Catholic principles comprised broad legal protection for the welfare of workers, regulation of monopoly and utility rates, cooperatives, and progressive taxation of incomes, excessive profits, and inheritances. This progressive program, however, had no future until the New Deal, and Father Ryan himself had defended the restrictive wartime legislation that jailed radicals, socialists, aliens, conscientious objectors, pacifists, and any reformers whose speech could be loosely construed by the Attorney General or the courts as interfering with the conduct of the war or threatening revolution. But by 1921 he was himself an active member of the Joint Amnesty Committee working for the release of a hundred political prisoners and protesting the expulsion of five duly elected members of the Socialist Party from New York's legislature. As he pointed out to a conservative Catholic leader in the Union League Club, the speaker of the Assembly who led the movement to expel the socialists had in the session of 1919 prevented the enactment of a minimum-wage law and an eight-hour law for women workers and of a law to insure wage earners against sickness.[34]

Chauvinism and the Red scare, stimulated by the war, would tend to isolate religion from democracy and the social gospel, blasting the hopes of an era of reform. Liberal social gospelers like Gladden, Ely, and Ryan had supported Wilson and the war; a majority of the Socialist Party had opposed it. The war not only bitterly divided reformers in their struggle to tame the beasts loose in the urban, industrial jungle; it spawned its own monsters. Furthermore, the reforms that it furthered—woman suffrage and Prohibition—had little to do with ameliorating the harshness and inequalities of industrial life.

XV

The Great Crusade for Prohibition, Woman Suffrage, and the War

Our modern distaste for "Puritanism" has ill fitted us to understand the popularity and severity of repression in the war years at the very moment when two Progressive reforms triumphed. Prohibition, woman suffrage, and the war have much to do with Tocqueville's vision of American religion, while recent historical investigation of them helps us to put limits on the scope of some of his observations and to highlight the relevance of others in ways that would both have confirmed his judgment and surprised it.

Between 1914 and 1917 seven Western states adopted Prohibition and all of them also granted the vote to women. The support for these reforms in the Midwest and West also drew heavily on those who favored a literacy test for immigration, vetoed as undemocratic by President Wilson. Similarly, the opposition to woman suffrage in these areas came from those who were also opposed to Prohibition and the literacy test. Through the war these three measures became nationally victorious in legislation or Constitutional Amendments as electoral support for them mounted rapidly in the East and South. "The world war, no doubt, hastened this change," Alan P. Grimes has suggested, "for the austerity and nativism implicit in Puritanism were reemphasized under the protective cloak of patriotism."[1] It is clear that the reform of Prohibition, whatever its realistic merits in relation to the political influence of the liquor lobby, also incorporated the ethnic-religious impulses of middle-class Protestants to transform the mores of Catholics and immigrants. Even suffragettes, though they received support from trade unionists and socialists, were capable of arguing that "those who fear the foreign vote and the colored vote should remember that there are more native-born women in the United States than foreign-born men and women; more white women than colored men and women."[2] In the House votes on Prohibition (1914), woman suffrage (1915), and the literacy test (1914), only the group of Eastern, Midwestern, and Western Progressives heavily supported all three measures, vivid testimony to the linkage of these proposals to the age of reform.[3]

In 1920 the Interchurch Report of the great 1919 steel strike was still critical of business's role in breaking the strike and did much to generate sentiment in the Federal Council of Churches, the National Catholic Welfare Council, and the National Council of Rabbis for abolition of the twelve-hour working day, despite the wave of anti-labor company unionism.[4] But the fact remains that notable progress in legislating the social gospel belonged to the crusaders against liquor, who increasingly escalated their restrictions. By 1917 two-thirds of the states had passed antiliquor laws of some kind, and the holdouts were areas where, whether in the East, Midwest, or West, under half the population was composed of old-stock Americans or church members.[5] Prohibition was an example of an achieved reform peculiar to "republican religion" in America. It was seen not only as a corollary of the Protestant economic virtues of industry, frugality, and thrift but also as the ally of a virtuous happy electorate in a free society. Though it was Protestants in the Anti-Saloon League who organized the political movement for Prohibition, the general crusade for temperance was the one reform that could connect the pre-Civil War abolitionists, the Knights of Labor, the Populists, the Progressives, the Federal Council of Churches, liberal Catholics, and suffragettes.

The Anti-Saloon League itself was a striking example of grass-roots organization, based on individual churches and led by concentrated executive power at the top level of federated state leagues, that systematically and effectively endorsed specific candidates in political elections.[6] It was in this sense a perfect example of Tocqueville's theme of the power of associative activity in the American democracy. It was also proof, though it might have dismayed him, of his ancillary theme that one function of religion in the republic was to make for an austerity of manners. But that austerity, as secured by statute and amendment, had one egregious flaw ignored by the advocates of Prohibition. The legislation was increasingly irrelevant to, and therefore unenforceable in, a society shifting its center of balance to cities, where non-Protestant immigrants congregated, and to a mass-produced prosperity that favored a consumption-oriented hedonism subversive of the Puritan ethic. Moreover, by its astounding legislative success the Prohibition movement had reduced an era of reform to a temporary and parochial issue that left out much of the point and purpose of the social gospel's reformulation of "republican religion" for an urban industrial world. The abolitionists had succeeded during the Civil War despite their failure before it; the temperance crusaders had largely succeeded even before American entrance into the European War. The war and its aftermath extended their success at the price of paving the way for an era of "normalcy" in national politics that vulgarized religion, fostered conservative fundamentalism, turned intellectuals against the churches, and celebrated a cult of the "aristocracy of manufactures" that Tocqueville feared.

Yet he knew that Americans were "at the same time a puritanical people and a commercial nation," even if he was wrong in thinking that by emphasizing stable marriage these traits would forbid American women to step beyond the "narrow circle of domestic interests and duties."[7] Indeed, it was precisely what Tocqueville called "the purity of her morals" and regard for the "order and prosperity of the household" that had led men in the American West first to favor political inclusion of women on the ground that they would act as a conservative force for the spread and maintenance of public civilities. And it was the suffragettes themselves who argued that women would bring into politics "the great proportion of temperance, morality, religion and conscientiousness" and so redeem the promise of the ideal of "the grandeur of a republic" threatened in their view by crime, illiteracy, the gambling house, the brothel, and the saloon.[8] In this sense the securing of the ballot to American woman, though it did little to change American politics, constituted an acting out by the majority of Tocqueville's own view of American women as religious "protectors of morals" and "an orderly life."[9]

Like Prohibition, woman suffrage was an attempt to raise the quality of American life in an age whose popular fictional images of the future and organized reform from Populism to socialism had significantly drawn upon the traditions of American Christianity and "republican religion." The postmillennial enthusiasm that had engendered such hopes and fears was as old as Jonathan Edwards, as recent as Harriet Beecher Stowe. Its early twentieth-century echo was resonant in Woodrow Wilson's hope of "making the world safe for democracy" and the missionary diplomacy by which he unsuccessfully tried to commit the United States to a League of Nations as "a community of power" to end the scourge of war.

The Church Peace Union, organized in 1914 and endowed by Andrew Carnegie, supported Wilson's original position of neutrality and opposed any increase in armaments. But once Wilson had entered the war its president, Bishop David H. Greer, who had once recommended excommunication for anyone who took up the sword, thanked God that England and America were "shoulder to shoulder in the great crusade against tyranny and aggression." The about-face was executed *en masse,* and in *Preachers Present Arms* Ray H. Abrams extensively documented the extraordinary extent to which the clergy embraced the passions of war. As the Episcopalian *Churchman* put it in retrospect: "We hated as our Governments bade us hate. We spread lies about our enemies as those lies were meted out to us in official propaganda. We taught unforgiveness even as our rulers and diplomats inspired us to do."[10] Only those religions that had remained sects, rather than becoming acculturated denominations, preserved their pacifist witness, except for a few preachers, mostly Unitarian. Out of an estimated 360 religiously motivated conscientious objectors court-martialed and sentenced, the largest group were from the small sect of Mennonites; none of the major faiths produced any significant number of objectors. Twenty-seven of the fifty-nine antiwar clergymen of the regular denominations thus sentenced were forced out of their positions by outraged congregations; more than fifty clergymen in the whole spectrum of faiths were arrested for alleged violation of the espionage and sedition laws. Spokesmen of the major denominations condemned their dissenting brethren without mercy or shame, despite the fact that distributing a pamphlet on Christian pacifism to a mere handful of persons was treated as grounds for a fifteen-year sentence for obstructing recruiting.[11]

Tocqueville had noted that "religious zeal is perpetually warmed in the United States by the fires of patriotism."[12] He was thinking of settlement in the new Western states in order to spread Christian republicanism. In 1917, however, the churches warmed the zeal of patriotism with the fires of religion. Abrams's study reflects its publication date (1933) in emphasizing the role of religion in rationalizing the "vested interests" of capitalism, but many of those devoted to the social gospel had put themselves in a critical position with respect to capitalistic practices and attitudes.* A recent study of the leaders of liberal Protestantism in the prewar era found that only four of twenty-seven were "uncritically favorable to business," while seven of eighteen leaders still living in 1917 were "strong supporters" of American participation in the war and half were reluctant followers of Wilson's position.[13]

Tocqueville accurately observed that American clergymen "allow themselves to be borne away without opposition in the current of feeling and opinion by which everything around them is carried along."[14] The conformism of the clergy also drew on the anxieties of a community recently subject to massive tides of immigration. In this context the meaning of belonging was often put in question by suspicions of the alleged danger of the divided allegiances of those who had homelands in European countries, and leaders like Theodore Roosevelt and Wilson had stirred these doubts and resentments by their ideologizing of "one hundred per cent Americanism" in opposition to "hyphenated" citizenship. The melting pot threatened to boil over with a loud hiss when feelings about England and Germany were entangled with American foreign policy; and Catholics and Jews who, for both ethnic and religious reasons, had reason to fear the persecuting tendencies of Protestants were particularly anxious to demonstrate their loyalty in a time of war by uncritical support of government policy. German Lutherans had cultural sympathies for their former homeland, bringing them under the suspicious surveillance of the Department of Justice, but they firmly supported the war in practice because their conservative Lutheran tradition emphasized the subordination of the citizen to the state through obedience in all temporal matters.[15] Where many other Protestants tended to idealize the secular in sacred terms, the Lutherans sharply accented the distinction between believer and citizen, salvation and political action. Liberal and conservative religious traditions alike thus led their adherents to support the war.

The uncritical chauvinistic nature of this support would eventually lead churchmen in peacetime to renounce the war in the same revivalistic spirit that had marked their commitment to it, conversion following conversion with the same indulgence of righteous indignation

* George D. Herron, an ardent socialist, worked for Wilson abroad and called him "a colossal Christian apostle, shepherding the world into the Kingdom of God." See Mitchell P. Briggs, "George D. Herron and the European Settlement," *Stanford University Pubs. in History, Economics, and Political Science, 3,* no. 2 (1932), 19.

and lack of intelligent discrimination. The whole episode of clerical collaboration with the worst features of militarized politics would have deeply disturbed Tocqueville, for whom collaboration between church and state was a matter of an alliance between "the spirit of religion" and "the spirit of liberty." No doubt churchmen convinced themselves, as so many did, that the aims of the war did involve large ideals of liberty, in contrast to German policies, but in terms of what concretely was happening at home the overt commitment of the Federal Council of Churches, for example, to freedom of speech and conscience was sabotaged by its moral failure to implement that ideal in the midst of popular passions for repression of dissent.

Wilson's administration was more liberal than Congress in specifying the possibility of noncombatant service even for nonreligious conscientious objectors, but the military's administration of this policy, often by brutal bullying methods, forced the great majority of objectors to accept some kind of military duty. Politically motivated objectors were treated as if they were traitors and subjected to courts-martial with extreme penalties. Even traditionally pacifist small sects, such as the Mennonites, were sometimes subjected to physical harassment or to severe prison terms for refusing to don military uniforms. Only the Quakers and the secular American Civil Liberties Union, as some historians have pointed out, "sought to preserve in America those things for which the newspapers said the nation was fighting in Europe."[16]

The debacle of civil liberties was ensured by the demand in the government and among community leaders of opinion for more stringent legislation to curtail all vocal opposition to the war as an alternative to mob action. The model for a federal sedition law was a Montana statute that had recently been enacted against the radical Industrial Workers of the World organization, stiffly penalizing any "abusive language" about the government, its symbols, or the military. Even the attempt in the Senate to limit the law by an amendment defending the right to speak the truth with good motives for justifiable ends was opposed by the Attorney General's office on the ground that under this qualification religious pacifists particularly might engage in antiwar propaganda. The unlimited statute, making a crime of seditious libel, passed the House in the spring of 1918 with only one negative vote. The common assumption in the country, which the President made explicit, was the belief that the right of free speech ceased once war had been declared.[17] The Red scare, instigated by strikes and a rash of bombings in 1919–20, continued the passion for repression into the early postwar years, delaying response to demands for amnesty for political prisoners. Wilson insisted that they would have to demonstrate their repentance, like good Calvinists. Proponents of the "great crusade" had treated Wilson's war policy as an issue of faith, and the test of the American soul was its willingness to convert or repent. The nation itself was seen as a covenanted community of true believers eager to prove their faith in public and alert to crush out heresy, as if in a relapse into seventeenth-century Puritanism.

Lincoln had memorably brought to bear on the Civil War a civic religion of Christian themes, relevant to the tragedy of the conflict and tempered by his own undogmatic, unsectarian, and compassionate religious sensibility. In Wilson's crusade, however, the civic religion displayed its worst potentialities for self-righteousness and intolerance. Not only did Wilson lack Lincoln's temperament, but the war itself, directed against a foreign enemy, was much more vulnerable to self-righteous nationalism. As a traditional pride in isolation from European strife confronted intervention, messianic fervor was bolstered by an anxious conformism that was haunted by the ethnic tensions of American life, the troubles of the new industrial order, and the growth of non-Protestant believers.

There had been no prior widespread, deep-rooted popular opinion supporting the Allies or American intervention. The crusade for the war, immediately based on preserving neutral rights at sea, was not realistically related to substantial issues of morality, democratic ideology, or institutional survival, as the Civil War had been. Certainly German submarine warfare had shocked Americans, but it was not equivalent to the horrors slavery had represented. The war fever seemed rather to express a passion for communal certainty that betrayed an inner lack of it in a sudden shift from neutrality to engagement. The hysterical clamor for unity served as a defense also against the anxiety generated by a fearful awareness of economic, social, and cultural differences arising in an increasingly industrial and ethnically pluralistic country. Clerical chauvinism, like rhetoric in literature, was, in Yeats's phrase, the will doing the work of the imagination.

Old landmarks were losing their familiar contours in fact; in rhetoric, therefore, they had to be affirmed all the more strenuously if men were unwilling to jeopardize their peace of mind by drawing new maps. Furthermore, nationalism itself was one of the major consequences of secularization everywhere, and nationalism in wartime offers itself as a surrogate for religion, a displacement of ultimate values and ritual celebrations on to secular life. Nationalism as an ideology for crisis is always attracted to the theme of the chosen people's mission, and in America that theme was readily available in the country's past with its tradition of joining religion and republicanism, an honorable one on many occasions but vulnerable to dishonorable exploitation through self-interest, fear, or bewilderment. For its own previous relative historical immunity from European wars the United States paid the price under Wilson of having to idealize its loss all the more strenuously because in realistic terms of economic or strategic stakes the case for war was so hard to make. It was easy only for those economic determinists who were sure that bankers and munition makers were behind it all, but these ideologues were against the war.

Five years after the war the government at last publicly accepted pleas on behalf of amnesty for political prisoners. Clearly, the war had split asunder what Tocqueville had seen as joined together: the spirit of liberty and the spirit of religion. This linkage had characterized the Revolution, the struggle for disestablishment, the movement for abolition of slavery, and the campaign for woman suffrage. But it was vulnerable in a context of international war when the political need for unity highlighted the actual ethnic and religious pluralism of the country, engendering fears of division. The civic religion had a Protestant bias, and nativism was at least as old as the 1850's and as recent as the anti-Catholic venom of the American Protective Association in the 1890's or the Ku Klux Klan's revival in 1915. Furthermore, efforts to restrict immigration had been part of the prewar reform movement itself. Radical perspectives, whether anarchist, socialist, communist, or syndicalist, had put traditional institutions and ideas on the defensive; and those most identified with the balance of forces favoring management had since the late nineteenth century tried to collapse the idea of liberty into the Supreme Court's dogma of liberty of contract, in which the mores of monopoly capitalism were rationalized in libertarian rhetoric derived from the Declaration of Independence. "Liberty" was redefined as corporate escape from regulation, and for many "democracy" merely stood for the infallible and implacable power of "Anglo-Saxon" majority opinion.

Tocqueville was aware that under modern conditions middle-class men, defensive of their property interests in a society that "naturally urges men to embark on commercial and industrial pursuits," might in coming generations "arrive at such a state as to regard every new theory as a peril, every innovation as an irksome toil, every social improvement as a stepping-stone to revolution, and so refuse to move altogether for fear of being moved too far." On his own visit to America he had been struck by "the difficulty of shaking the majority in an opinion once conceived or of drawing it off from a leader once adopted. Neither speaking nor writing can accomplish it; nothing but experience will avail, and even experience must be repeated." The erosion of civil liberties for minority opinions in modern democracies was one of his most serious worries for the future, only "slightly perceptible in political society" in 1831, but already evident in the decline of "manly candor and masculine independence of opinion" in many American candidates.[18]

These observations were especially pertinent more than three-quarters of a century after Tocqueville's visit. The war years brought out the salience of one of his more ominous themes, the tyranny of the majority. If he had underestimated the dangers in the power of American religion to lend sanction to the despotism of public opinion, nevertheless in his warnings for the future he had provided an epigraph for the war years: "All those who seek to destroy the liberties of a democratic nation ought to know that war is the surest and the shortest means to accomplish it."[19] By 1917 Tocqueville's bleak observations on the future state of democratic societies in general, rather than on America in particular, were becoming much more relevant than they had been in the 1830's, when his comments on America were fundamentally hopeful. The unsettling question proposed by the war years was the extent to which the relevance of the confident historian in his work would be displaced by the relevance of the fearful prophet. Prohibition and the war would enforce on the historical consciousness a re-evalution of his theme of the structural significance of "republican religion" in American history. Not its power but its civilizing value would be put in doubt unless it could come to terms with a new nation in which cities, immigrants, Jews, and Catholics would play an increasingly important role.

XVI

A Catholic Native Son in a "Puritan Civilization"

Religion may serve a politics of conscience directed against other forms of belief and thus serve a politics of sectarian bigotry. In America this possibility has been grounded in the fears, resentments, and aversions aroused on all sides of the ethnic fences in a country characterized by massive influxes of immigration. Recent historians, armed with sophisticated quantitative methods of studying election returns in relation to the ethnocultural identity of various groups in American life, have consistently highlighted the political significance of questions that often link religious and ethnic attitudes, such as drinking habits, parochial-school aid, Sabbatarianism, foreign-language instruction in the public schools, and even foreign policy where it connects with a religious ideology. Such ethnocultural issues can be found in the republic even in Tocqueville's day and they also had entered into the crisis over slavery. In 1859 Massachusetts Republicans passed an anti-Catholic amendment limiting the voting rights of naturalized citizens, causing Lincoln to disassociate himself from such "Know-Nothing" tactics, which threatened to lose him support among immigrants, though Germans and Irish might be divided on Protestant-Catholic lines over his party.[1] These quantitative studies have discovered religion as a political factor while often qualifying it by stressing the greater relevance of immigrant life in America. Often both elements seem to work symbiotically in a way that defies separation.

A major political issue crucially involving religious ideology appears to have been the failure of a Catholic candidate to win the Presidency for the Democrats in 1928, a defeat he felt was rooted in Protestant fears of Rome.* But quantitative study has cast doubt on this common presumption. Alfred E. Smith was also a critic of Prohibition, a big-city politician, an Irish American, and a liberal governor of New York. It is not self-evident which of these qualities was more important to his weakness or his strength as a candidate. Clearly the Catholic issue has been a recurring one in American political life, and the American Protective Association succeeded the Know-Nothings in promoting anti-Romanism. A Presbyterian minister coined the phrase "Rum, Romanism, and Rebellion" in 1884 to characterize the Democratic Party, and the Republican candidate, James G. Blaine, himself the son of a Catholic mother, believed that the backfiring slogan had cost him the crucial state of New York.[2] The 1924 Democratic convention, sorely divided on the issue of condemning the recently revived anti-Catholic Ku Klux Klan, was pushed to 103 ballotings to settle on a candidate. Anti-Catholic ideology, a traditional legacy of Protestant republicanism, had powerful reinforcement from prejudice against immigrants, nostalgia for rural America, and moral disapproval of political bosses and their machines.

The 1928 campaign did bring the Catholic issue into public debate, both overtly and covertly, but its impact was not only negative. Al Smith's strength as a candidate, measured by his ability to lead his party's Congressional ticket, was very strong, and the Tammany-bred man from the Fulton Fish Market on the lower East Side, with a taste for the theater and a solidly impressive record as a four-term governor of a major state, polled a larger proportion of the popular vote than the Democratic candidate had done in the two previous elections. Smith won only eight states, but two of these, Massachusetts and Rhode Island, had previously been Republican ever since Lincoln, except for 1912 when Theodore Roosevelt's Progressive Party split the Republican vote. By Smith's day these two states were among the first three both in proportion of Catholic church members and percentage of white persons of foreign stock (that is, first- and second-generation immigrants). Smith also lost six Southern or Southwestern states that had traditionally been Democratic ever since 1896, except for close Republican victories in Tennessee and Oklahoma in 1920, and these six states were among the lowest in percentages of Catholics and persons of foreign white stock.

* Dissident Democrats had nominated a Catholic Presidential candidate in 1872, but he did not campaign.

A recent highly sophisticated statistical analysis of the election concludes that it is "doubtful that in 1928 a 'dry,' Protestant Democrat from Hyde Park could have trimmed Hoover's popular margin any more than the 'wet,' Catholic Democrat from New York City did. One might argue that Smith's membership in the Democratic Party was a greater liability to him than his membership in the Roman Catholic church."[3] Ruth C. Silva's measurement of Smith's gain in 1928 over John W. Davis in 1924, compared to Hoover's gain over Coolidge in the same elections, finds that neither church membership nor attitudes toward Prohibition (at least as measured by votes for its repeal) account for any considerable part of the variance in the states of the index of Smith's comparative gain. Only the presence or absence of white first- and second-generation immigrants turns out to be of statistical importance when correlated with a state's voting behavior.

By 1907 the great majority of immigrants, unlike earlier immigration, came from Southern and Eastern Europe and were predominantly Catholic or Jewish. In 1921 and 1924 Congress passed discriminatory legislation to restrict the quotas from these areas. By 1930 first- and second-generation immigrants made up 36.2 per cent of the total white population, and 34 per cent of church members were Catholic.[4] Protestant immigrants had to weigh their anti-Catholic feeling against their feeling for the Democratic Party as the organization traditionally hospitable to immigrants and against their awareness of the prejudicial nativism in recent immigration legislation, as well as in much of the criticism of Al Smith.

During the campaign of 1928 negative attitudes toward liquor, Tammany Hall, Catholicism, and immigrants were closely mixed together in the charged images that Smith's opponents formed of him. His meaning for them was symbolic. He was, in fact, a third-generation immigrant; having earlier immigrant lineage was probably a minority trait by 1928; he was not by then the mere creature of Tammany Hall; and his Catholicism in no way controlled his appointments or his legislative programs. His candid pledge to work for repeal of Prohibition was congenial to both his coreligionists and Tammany Hall, but German-American Lutherans also were opponents of Prohibition.

The most sober challenge to his candidacy was made in the *Atlantic Monthly* by Charles C. Marshall, a lawyer and Episcopalian. He correctly noted that papal encyclicals recognized the American situation of separation as only a relative good appropriate to special circumstances, not an ideally desirable one, and asserted the Church's belief that in principle the state should not hold all religions in equal favor. For the rest, Marshall's legalistic argument was, in lawyer's idiom, "a parade of imaginary horribles" deduced from these abstractions, arousing the fear that somehow Catholic doctrine *could* become, in American practice, inconsistent with "the peace and safety of the State" and American Constitutional law. Counseled to reply, Smith simply and pragmatically answered the charge of an implicit conflict between his religious loyalty and his patriotism by saying: "Everything that has actually happened to me during my long public career leads me to know that no such thing as that is true." If there were such a conflict, he added, "I, of all men, could not have escaped it, because I have not been a silent man, but a battler for social and political reform."[5]

Until the Church itself revised its traditional thinking on church and state, American Catholics would be vulnerable to Smith's embarrassment. Chapter and verse were quoted at him in an effort to show that the more conscientious a Catholic he was, "the more unqualified should be his acceptance" of conceptions which, however contrary to American principles, were in fact irrelevant to his actual life as an American Catholic citizen. Marshall claimed that the Roman Church asserts the right to decide what should be rendered unto Caesar, and therefore Smith's loyalty to American civil power was necessarily secondary. But, as Walter Lippmann pointed out, the governor's position in affirming the ultimacy of his conscience was characteristically modern and American in making the Church "a distinct and closely compartmented section of an otherwise secular life."[6] In his reply to Marshall, Smith affirmed ideals of unqualified freedom of conscience and equality of churches and beliefs before the law that even Jefferson would have approved, with the single exception of Smith's approval of parochial as well as public education, in accord with American Constitutional law.* He came before the electorate realistically as a liberal, efficient, and seasoned governor of New York, a genial common man who had made good in authentic American terms, just as Hoover in his way had also done.

* *Pierce* v. *Society of Sisters* (265 U.S. 510) in 1925 affirmed the right of two private schools to enjoy freedom from unreasonable interference by the state of Oregon with the liberty of parents and guardians to direct the upbringing and education of children under their control or with the property interests of the schools. The decision invalidated a Klan-backed law aimed against parochial schools. See Kenneth B. O'Brien, Jr., "Education, Americanization, and the Supreme Court: The 1920s," *American Quarterly, 13* (Summer, 1961), 161–71.

The campaign of 1928 was also marked by rancorous prejudice against Smith's religion, which was an inextricable element of his mythical role as a symbol of everything imagined to be a threat to what the journalist William Allen White called "Puritan civilization." Bishop Adna W. Leonard of the Methodist Church, president of New York's Anti-Saloon League, called for "Anglo-Saxon unity against foreigners, particularly the Latins." The United States, in his view, was a Protestant nation and "Anglo-Saxons" were "keepers of the Constitution, of the flag and of American citizenship."[7] In this context the Catholic issue as a political question was inseparable from an American Protestantism that was to a large extent nativist. Such criticism presupposed a point of view that arrogantly identified itself with the state as a sectarian possession. In this light, Protestant fears about Catholic infidelity to separation ironically attributed to the traditional enemy its own transgression of separation by a de facto Protestant establishment, uneasily aware of its anomalous position in an increasingly urban world.

This suspicion was accelerated in the 1920's by the growth of fundamentalism as a reaction to liberal Protestantism. Literalist belief in the inerrancy of the Bible, the virgin birth, miracles, the atonement, and the Second Coming led to the drive for anti-evolution statutes in nearly all Southern states and secured them in five, engendering the notorious "monkey trial" in Tennessee of John T. Scopes and more consequential campaigns to censor the recruitment of teachers and the use of textbooks. Baptists, Methodists, and Presbyterians in the South had been separated from their Northern brethren ever since the crisis over slavery, and the first two of these groups were particularly susceptible to fundamentalist movements. They played a leading role in boldly and openly organizing to defeat Smith at the polls. For them Prohibition was the one cause that could diminish internal theological friction in their own organizations by providing a common front against its enemies.[8] In this region Smith was a victim of the social gospel's success in making religion politically relevant. The Republican Assistant Attorney General also urged Methodist groups to vote against Smith as a "wet," even though Hoover himself repudiated the stirring up of any religious issues.

It is probable that these efforts were effective in helping break down the party loyalty of Virginia, North Carolina, Tennessee, Florida, Texas, and Oklahoma in 1928. This Southern campaign cannot explain, however, the fact that the margin of Smith's gain over Davis,

compared to Hoover's gain over Coolidge, was very high in North
Dakota and Minnesota, putting them very high on a ranking of his
comparative gain for all the states. These Midwestern states also
ranked much higher among the states in percentage of first- and second-generation immigrants than they did in percentage of Catholic
church members.[9] Studies on a more microscopic level, however, show
that in Minnesota six counties of predominantly Catholic church members, four of them usually voting Republican, went for Smith, while
seven out of ten counties of predominantly Lutheran church members,
usually voting Democratic, gave him a smaller percentage of the county
vote than he earned in the state as a whole. In North Dakota, Smith's
share of the vote in the twelve counties that strongly favored the agrarian radicalism of the Non-Partisan League, which was usually supported by many Protestant Scandinavian immigrants, was ten percentage points lower than the 55 per cent he earned in the eleven
counties where parochial Russo-German Catholics made up 30 to 70
per cent of the population. These local Midwestern results point to a
vote for and against Smith in some areas that would seem to have
more to do with his religion than with his political record.[10]

Even so, on the whole it was in the South that Smith lost what a
Democrat could otherwise expect to win, and it was in the South
that being a Catholic "wet" urban liberal of immigrant stock was most
intensely, openly, and commonly considered to be a liability. Yet if
Smith had won all of Hoover's votes in the six states that broke Southern tradition by voting Republican, Hoover would still have had decisive electoral and popular majorities in the nation. The election was
lost and won elsewhere than in the region where the most ardent
nativist campaign was made against Smith. Certainly in the new states
that he won for the Democrats his symbolic traits were an asset that a
Protestant Yankee Democrat would not have had. In New York, for
example, Smith won only nine counties, but a comparison with
Franklin D. Roosevelt's strength as a gubernatorial candidate in that
same year points to the positive value of Smith's Catholic identity in
the four counties where he did better than Roosevelt. The mean of the
percentage-point gap between the two men's share of the vote in all
the state's counties is positive (pro-Smith) only in the three counties
with the lowest number of Protestants and the two counties with the
highest number of Catholics.[11]

In terms of the big-city vote Smith's record set a new pattern of
importance to the future. In 1920 and 1924 the Republicans had won

pluralities in the twelve largest cities. Smith inaugurated the modern tradition of Democratic victories in these areas.[12] In this respect his candidacy prefigured the pattern of Franklin Roosevelt's ascendancy, and like him Smith was a progressive governor of New York with a record of energetic commitment to such liberal measures as workmen's compensation insurance, shorter hours for women and children, factory safety measures, and regulation of utilities. Memorably, Smith also had the courage and principle as governor to veto the repressive Lusk Committee measures, curtailing free speech, that emerged from a legislature responsive to the Red scare.

The shadow of Smith also has a darker hue, however, that is often forgotten. By 1936, bitterly disappointed by the decline of his political fortunes as Roosevelt's rose, he could address the Liberty League of rich reactionaries in demagogic terms that associated the New Deal with vaguely imagined importations of foreign "isms" from Soviet Russia. This charge was more than a personal fret of a Democrat turned Republican and more than the alarm of a fiscal conservative, because, as Oscar Handlin has pointed out, the election of 1928 left, particularly among Irish Americans, "a sense of irritating inferiority, sometimes finding an outlet in the reassurance of super-patriotism, sometimes finding expression in resentment of the 'conspirators' in Washington who had seized control of the nation, only to betray it."[13] Feelings of ethnic resentment, which the campaign and Smith's defeat stimulated, fed later into influential isolationist voting against Roosevelt's interventionist foreign policy and by the 1950's into support for the sort of repressive Red-baiting measures that Smith had once vetoed. Both the Happy Warrior of 1928 and the unhappy warrior of 1936 were prophetic of the future of American politics.

Tocqueville had expected Catholicism to grow in America because he thought its doctrines were more congenial to equality than to independence, which Protestantism favored. But it was immigration, not ideology, that nourished American Catholicism, and this politically ambiguous base provided soil for rural conservatism, for big-city machines, for Smith's and Roosevelt's welfare liberalism, and also for smoldering ethnic resentments that could sometimes support xenophobic chauvinism and conspiracy-mongering demagogues. Tocqueville's prophecy was in this respect too deductive, but his point about the Protestant penchant for independence was a valuable one because the ideal of individualism classically defined the American Protestant's hostility to an ecclesiastical hierarchy, an authoritative traditionalism, and papal dogmatism in faith and morals. On a more sociological level it was also individualism that Catholics rejected in their ethnic loyalty to kin, tribe, and party in the Yankee's world, and ideologically their corporate tradition had never been hospitable to the more antinomian or millennial enthusiasm of Protestant reform, for all the other adaptations to the culture that churchmen like Gibbons, Ireland, and Keane had preached. It was a radical Protestant individualism that had been most concerned about Negro equality of rights and a Protestant postmillennial optimism that had most cherished the experiment, "noble in purpose," as Hoover had called it, of Prohibition.

Smith did prove that Tocqueville was right in noting (as secular liberals often ignore) that most Catholics, however, have taken satisfaction in the American separation of church and state and have viewed their religion much in the same light as Protestants have with respect to encouraging believers not only to look to the other world but "to court prosperity in this."[14] Already in the years that Tocqueville's work appeared, anti-Catholicism was developing as a violent virus; and the world of big cities, bosses, immigrant enclaves, and parochial schools eventually would make many old Americans increasingly and contemptuously distant from the newer citizens. Mutual estrangement would become more evident than Tocqueville's image of the republic as a busy, active, restless community surprisingly stable on fundamental matters of opinion, principle, and values. Though he rightly emphasized the widespread American fear of revolutionary social and political change, he came to America too early to reckon on the suspicions and animosities, ethnic and religious, that would make the sense of being an American not a secure and common possession but a painful, precarious anxiety, vulnerable to religious and political exploitation.

Yet the simple and old-fashioned truth remains that in his rise to the role of Democratic candidate Al Smith did exemplify in his own career the political compatibility of different religions in America, a point that had impressed Tocqueville. Smith pointed out that his cabinet was composed of two Catholics, thirteen Protestants, and one Jew. His most valued assistant was Belle Moskowitz, and New York's Jews warmly responded to his urban liberalism with their votes, displaying an identification with the Democrats that would become characteristic.[15] The largest single item of increased appropriations in his administration was for the support of common schools. It is no wonder that he should have been greatly surprised and hurt by the concern shown by some Protestant groups about the congeniality of his religion to the demands of the office of the Presidency. Before his politics were soured by his disappointment, he was an attractive example of how Catholic devoutness and democratic liberalism could easily go together, as Tocqueville believed. His defeat, whatever it meant in the minds of his opponents, could not rob him of the wider meaning of his earlier political success.

The victory of Herbert Hoover, a Quaker, did not mean that Protestantism had won in 1928, or that there was an unwritten law that kept Catholics from becoming President, though not from becoming legislators, governors, or even Supreme Court justices. It did mean that in many minds Smith's symbolic status as an immigrant, a Tammany Hall politician, a "wet," and a Catholic blotted out perception of the truth of his own belief that his political life exemplified the separation of church from state in American terms. A little more than a decade after Smith's defeat the Gallup Poll reported that 38 per cent of a national sample would refuse to support a Catholic for President, despite the fact that the Constitution specifically affirms that "no religious Test shall ever be required as a qualification to any Office or public Trust under the United States."[16] To that extent at least, a significant minority in the republic was far from believing with Tocqueville that "in the United States no religious doctrine displays the slightest hostility to democratic and republican institutions."[17] Future events would show that on some libertarian issues many American Catholics would, in fact, tend to a conservative intolerance to match the dogmatism of their nativist enemies, but their Presidential aspirants, from Smith to the Kennedys, Eugene McCarthy, and Muskie, would be liberals, in no way verifying the nativist stereotype.

We do not know what percentage of the people in 1928 would have answered as the 38 per cent of the sample did in 1940. We do know that most of the nearly 41 per cent who voted for Smith must have rejected any religious test for the Presidency. The ultimate irony of his defeat lay in his fundamentally secular grasp of the political world. His political career did not represent a doctrinal Catholic influence on politics, as antislavery, Prohibition, and women's rights had represented a Protestant influence. It illustrated instead a practical humanitarian liberalism that transcended religious traditions and reflected more of his experience as an urban Irish American than anything he might have learned in parochial school. His worst enemies were much more inclined to shape the world to a sectarian morality.

Tocqueville did not foresee the possibility of a nativist Protestantism that would subvert republican principle or of a clergy that would actively participate in political campaigning, nor did he envisage that in growing through immigration Catholicism would become entangled with conservative ethnic fears and hopes having political relevance to both religions. That much the campaign of 1928 might have taught him, but it might also have persuaded him that Hoover's theme of "rugged individualism" was proof of the enduring political significance of the Protestant value of independence. The election, however, was in retrospect greater testimony to the tendency of continued prosperity, artificial as it was, to favor the Republican Party, for a major depression would soon ensure the victory of a Protestant Democrat from Hyde Park who made "rugged individualism" a shibboleth of business propaganda against the New Deal.

XVII

Crisis Theology from the Crash to the Bomb

The social gospel had triumphed in wartime with a Prohibition movement that did not come to grips with the major economic and social problems of industrial society, or express the full range of social Christianity's search for a reformed America. In the New Deal, however, the liberal social gospel indirectly found its fulfillment, even though it was not a prime mover of any of its achievements. A symbolic example is Father John A. Ryan, pupil of Ignatius Donnelly and Richard Ely as well as of liberal Catholics. Ryan had played the leading part in outlining the Bishops' Program for Social Reconstruction (1919), which included proposals for a minimum wage, social insurance, limitation of child labor, labor's right to organize, public housing, progressive taxation on inheritance, income, and excess profits, and regulation of utility rates and of monopolies—a forecast of much of the New Deal itself. But he played the role in the 1930's of "the New Deal's ambassador to Catholics." In 1936, for example, he spoke for the Democratic National Committee in a radio defense of President Roosevelt against Father Charles E. Coughlin, who had thrown his weight, along with the Reverend Gerald L. K. Smith, behind the populistic anti-Semitic Union Party. It had merged Minnesota Farmer-Labor Party planks with profascist propaganda and nationalistic conservatism—a version of radical rightism that appealed to many German-American and Irish-American Catholics in the Middle West, though to less than 2 per cent of the national vote.[1]

In 1932 the issues of Catholicism and Prohibition, raised by Al Smith, were still active enough to persuade the liberal *Christian Century* to vote Republican, but as the depression deepened, the churches moved left. Of the three major faiths the Jews were the most consistent Roosevelt supporters, particularly after 1936, because they saw him as anti-Hitler as well as the sponsor of the New Deal.[2] A poll of 20,000 clergymen in 1934 showed that 51 per cent sought a "drastically reformed capitalism," 28 per cent preferred socialism, and less than 5 per cent chose capitalism. A larger number of the clergy (67 per cent) also wanted the churches to stand firm for pacifism.[3] Liberal Protestants especially were identified with the popular missionary diplomacy that took satisfaction in the Kellog-Briand Pact of 1928 as a form of taking the pledge against war, much as Protestants had taken the pledge against demon rum. The memory of clerical chauvinism in 1917 was profoundly guilt-ridden, and the logic of sin entailed repentance as its remedy.

The New Deal, however, was a profoundly secular movement of reform. By 1941 one of its supporters could even call attention to its minimization of ideology and moral principle as a reduction of politics to a conflict between "past-adapted and future-adapted animals."[4] In regulating capitalism, underwriting and patronizing organized business, farmers, and labor, and instituting new social services, the New Dealers had substituted institutional changes for "the moralities." These pieties were abandoned to the conservatives, who had nothing to propose except the archaic ideas of "derelict and tired liberals" of a nineteenth-century stripe. The social gospelers of the churches, nevertheless, supported the domestic reforms of the New Deal in a different spirit of traditional belief in moral progress and humanitarian sympathy for the disadvantaged. "Roosevelt and the New Deal were the political expression of our stand," noted the director of the Congregational Council for Social Action.[5] Increasingly the Protestant churches accepted the idea that money for social services should come not from religious but from secular sources. Whereas in 1903 a third of benevolent institutions were church-connected, by 1940 in thirty-four urban areas more than 90 per cent of relief, health, and welfare funds came from public agencies.[6] The major share of the very small increase in church membership from 1926 to 1936 (2.3 per cent) went to conservative groups, like Christian Scientists, Mormons, and fundamentalists, rather than to the social-gospel churches.[7] The religious "depression" of the 1920's in this respect continued into the economic depression of the 1930's.

As the Roosevelt administration slowly took steps toward limited intervention in the struggle against Hitler's domination of Europe, many of the social gospelers reacted with bitter disappointment. The *Christian*

Century, strongest voice of liberal Protestantism, opposed conscription, the destroyer-bases agreement with Great Britain, and the Lend-Lease program, taking what dubious comfort it could from the morally puritanical measures against vice of France's Vichy government. The editor was convinced that "our goodness, our moralism, is in large measure the expression of our relative detachment." This confession of the importance to liberal Protestantism of diplomatic isolation from the rust of Europe's corrosive history suggests that its moralists could preserve their own sense of relevance to politics only in parochial terms. "The social gospel might work at home," as Donald B. Meyer has remarked; "in the giant chaos of the world it could not even be imagined."[8] Some liberal church groups, however, like the Congregational Council for Social Action, after Munich supported collective security in foreign affairs.

Radical Christians split into three camps: fellow travelers, traditional pacifists, and the group around Reinhold Niebuhr and *Radical Religion,* which was in the process of developing a "socialist Christian" criticism of the other camps. For some religious radicals, involvement with the larger world of history was made feasible, ironically, by a sentimental identification with the Soviet Union, the vanguard of secularism. For such men, fellow-traveling was a surrogate religion. Harry F. Ward, a leader in the Methodist Federation for Social Service and chairman of the American League Against War and Fascism, hailed "a central purpose" for life in the Soviet Five-Year Plans. William B. Spofford, Jr., director of the Episcopal Church's League for Industrial Democracy, envisioned in Soviet policies "a star in the east" that "wise men will follow as far as its beams cast light and do so without fear merely because its color happens to be red," while Stephen H. Fritchman, director of American Unitarian Youth, similarly proclaimed that "the millennial hope of the ages is now in process of realization on a grand scale—in Soviet Russia." Jerome Davis, in succession a YMCA worker, Yale Divinity School professor, and head of the American Federation of Teachers, wrote a book, *Behind Soviet Power* (1946), idealizing Stalin, the purge trials, and even the secret police. It was once mailed by the Methodist Board of Missions to 22,000 ministers. Communist youth groups were particularly successful in manipulating church-affiliated groups as window dressing for the American Youth Congress, thus profiting from a climate of opinion in which the popular front against fascism and the wartime alliance with the Soviet Union gave moral prestige to the party line.[9]

For radicals who were dedicated pacifists, the illusions of fellow traveling were no comfort. The small group around Kirby Page, editor of *World Tomorrow,* and in the Fellowship of Reconciliation were often early critics of Soviet policies and popular-front tactics. But their discernment was purchased at a price. Without the use of coercion how could decent men stop fascist imperialism? The lack of convincing answers inevitably posed a problem for Christians who did not make a religious substitute out of an idealized Russia or believe that nonresistance was politically relevant to this problem.

The most remarkable heir of the social gospel in this situation was Reinhold Niebuhr (1892–1971), an American of German background from Missouri and a pastor in the Evangelical Reformed Church. Theologian, political theorist, journalist, and social reformer, Niebuhr articulated in an original way a democratic religion that was both affiliated with and critical of American tradition. Like Jonathan Edwards, he defended Reformation doctrines with an arsenal of philosophical weapons influenced by modern thought; like Walter Rauschenbusch, he aimed to make Christianity relevant to a politics of democratic socialism; like William James, he trenchantly challenged rationalistic absolutism and the "sky-blue" optimism of the "once-born" souls who lacked a sense of the "radical evil" inherent in the nature of things. Niebuhr's prodigious productivity was a brave and bold effort to meet a perennial problem of the churches: to preserve the integrity of traditional religious teachings without becoming irrelevant to modern secular culture and political life.

Niebuhr acknowledged that in Jeffersonian days "sectarian Christianity was able to put religious passion behind the social goals of secular liberalism and actually gain a victory over the enemy." But this success, which Tocqueville had appreciated, had generated the problem of modern Protestantism: it had too easy a confidence that it had made the world Christian. It lost its tension with the world, Niebuhr felt, at the worst possible time, when American society was being "transmuted into the sorry realities of industrial capitalism." The Prohibition movement reflected "a rather pathetic effort" to preserve that tension, but its political success was also a measure of the extent to which religion had become secularized in America.[10] What Protestantism needed most, in his view, was the capacity to see that "the most stubborn evil in human affairs" appears in connection with "large social aggregates" powerful enough "to dominate and destroy life beyond themselves."[11] For Niebuhr this insight required a reconstruction of both theological and political thinking in the United States.

By 1932 "the theology of crisis" in Germany, worked out in various ways by Karl Barth, Emil Brunner, and Paul Tillich, had become familiar to American vanguard elements in the seminaries.[12] In a similar strategy Niebuhr revived ideas of original sin and divine judgment, separated them from fundamentalism, and linked them to socialist politics. He had experienced the harshness of industrial life in a Detroit parish for thirteen years, where he viewed events from the perspective of Christian Socialism. "If you set the message of a gospel of love against a society enmeshed in hatreds and bigotries and engulfed in greed," he wrote in 1922, "you have a real but not necessarily a futile conflict on your hands." Six years later, as he was preparing to move to the faculty of Union Theological Seminary, he was still committed to making the principle of love "effective as far as possible," but he was aware that in his own creed the principle was qualified by "considerations of moderation," what might be called "Greek caution" but which "an unfriendly critic might call opportunistic," because otherwise the Christian ethic "degenerates into asceticism and becomes useless for any direction of the affairs of a larger society." He was not ready to claim for his strategy "the full authority of the gospel" because he found the principle of love unqualified in the Bible, yet he could not see its success outside the family and the church. Already he had also expressed his characteristic mediation between the ideas of religion as either fantasy, on the one hand, or historical fact on the other, by affirming his view that instead it arrives at truth through a "poetic symbol" that gives "a clue to the total meaning of things."[13] His intellectual career was a long and complex elaboration of these two reflections on the limitations of love and on the symbolic status of dogma.

Two years before the crash of the stock market Niebuhr wrote a book with the familiar Christian Socialist thesis that the major problem of modern society was to bring "great social and political groups under the domain of conscience and moral law." Vital religion asserted the essential trustworthiness of man in the sublime "foolishness of faith" in brotherhood. He attacked any effort to give absolute prestige to compromises between the "pure idealism of Jesus" and a prudential morality of calculation. The religion most adequate to the moral needs of the day would be an ascetic one, and the means of this moralization of the world were primarily religion and education. Looking ahead, he found the "greatest hope" in missionary work in the Orient and a layman's movement of "spiritualized technicians" who would scorn greed and seek "a perfect ethical freedom," making "no compromises with life's immediate necessities."[14] Niebuhr later would become an eminent spokesman for realism in political life, but it was a realism haunted by an ultimate perfectionism that could never settle for what he came to consider to be humanly necessary. The terms of his problem—to be realistic without cynicism, idealistic without illusions—were shared by many thoughtful modern men, but he tried to resolve it with a restless dialectic that was attracted by the insights of the children of darkness and the ideals of the children of light. He wanted both of them to testify at the bar of history on behalf of the same client, a case any logician or moralist might blanch to take.

Niebuhr's perspective drew on an older pre-Romantic Protestant sense that the Christian gospel of love was at war with "the immediate impulses of human nature from the very beginning," and in Marxism he found warrant for believing that self-interestedness was more nakedly expressed in modern civilization than in any other. The function of the church was to remind its believers of the pervasiveness of selfish sin in the light of "a rigorous analysis of society." Only then could "spiritual vigor and social intelligence" work together to make the gospel effective. In 1931 he combined the two elements in the insight that since men could not see other men's interests as clearly as their own, it was necessary for an individual to give his fellow man the opportunity "to match power with power." If this idea of sin engendered the idea of justice as equalizing the terms of conflict, what was the role of love? He still thought it could be relevant if it were made more serious by being extended beyond the familiar boundaries of family and philanthropy "to the important relationships of life or it will die with our dying civilization."[15]

In the year before the New Deal he published a book that subordinated Christian love to justice in the political order, in the name of realism, while at the same time projecting his ultimate hopes for reform in terms of a secularized religion of socialist millennialism, which he did not literally accept any more than he literally accepted the Biblical stories. Events had accentuated his despair of the moral forces of persuasion and his convictions about the failures of capitalism. Now he felt that not only was mere preachment inadequate; the principle of love was itself inadequate to the problems of society. *Moral Man and Immoral Society* (1932) is generally taken to be

Niebuhr's most forceful statement of the inevitable disjunction between a religious ethic of love and a political policy of opposing power against power so as to bring about the justice of equal opportunity. Society, in this view, can be made more just only by adding to persuasion coercive techniques, ranging from strikes to revolution, that are in conflict with the Christian ideal of nonresistance, a principle appropriate only for the internal relations of families or small groups of believers. Actually, the book expresses an ambivalence about wholly accepting such a dualism or completely resolving it in a new synthesis. Niebuhr's dialectic differs most clearly from others by being both a dialectic of either/or and a dialectic of both/and. Characteristically it embraces paradoxes, rather than fending them off, and his dualisms are partly definitive of choices to be made and partly definitive of choices that ultimately cannot be made. In this sense the reader is sometimes driven to feel that no one has made more capital out of both having and eating his cake or out of both not having and not eating it as well. Niebuhr's defense would be that the realities of experience are paradoxical and require just such complex evasion of clear-cut choices.

Niebuhr challenged the faith of Protestant moralists and dedicated pacifists that preaching the law of love could by itself produce social justice, but he also wanted to bridge religion and politics by pointing to some religious resources for achieving justice. "Wherever religion concerns itself with the problems of society," he noted, "it always gives birth to some kind of millennial hope, from the perspective of which present social realities are convicted of inadequacy, and courage is maintained to continue in the effort to redeem society of injustice." Niebuhr himself participated in this tradition, which embraces the Calvinist Whigs of 1776, the revivalists of the two Awakenings, the abolitionists, the social gospelers, and the Christian Socialists. The contemporary form of that hope, he felt in 1932, was "the modern communist's dream of a completely equalitarian society," a secularized but still "essentially religious" version of Christian eschatology.[16]

But what distinguished Niebuhr's version from liberal theology was his responsiveness to the premillennial catastrophism of the Bible, a rebuke to American postmillennial optimism about the possibilities of a "gradual and inevitable evolutionary process." Furthermore, Niebuhr, unlike his pietistic forebears, emphasized the sense of justice as being "a product of the mind and not of the heart," not of "the sentiment of benevolence," which had dominated the revivalist tradition ever since Jonathan Edwards. He believed with Troeltsch that "religious idealism never arrives at equalitarian political ideals without the aid of rationalistic political thought," a proper acknowledgment of the crucial relevance of the secular Enlightenment for formulating the goal of equality of opportunity as a standard of justice.[17] In this fundamental sense Niebuhr incorporated both religious and secular elements in his political ideology, as the tradition of American republican religion had always done.

Though Niebuhr spoke with Marxist accents about the importance of class conflict in modern life, he was highly critical of any optimism about revolution. Even in 1932 he thought that Western civilization would not be ripe for proletarian revolution for many decades and perhaps never, unless there was another large-scale war. He did not think the farmer could be counted upon as a political ally of the industrial worker, and he doubted that any single political force could reorganize modern society. He also was reluctantly inclined to concede that "it may be equally natural that nationalistic impulses should gain the ascendancy over class loyalties." What he admired in revolutionary Marxism was not its specific historical analysis but its eschatological hope. He was clearsightedly aware that this fervor spawned dangerous and fanatical illusions, risking "the welfare of millions" and the possibility of transmuting coercion into "unbearable tyrannies and cruelties," nevertheless, he concluded that Communists were "the most effective agents" of redemption because only the illusion of perfect justice could provide the energy for its approximation.[18] Thus Niebuhr's early strategy for exposing the illusions of pietistic perfectionism contained within it the irony of accepting for tactical reasons a catastrophic Marxian perfectionism, which he knew risked worse evils than the depression that led him to endorse it.

Tactics also led him to favor Gandhi's theme of active nonviolent resistance in contrast to Christian passive nonresistance. In a prophetic analysis he urged the boycott as a strategy particularly relevant to the emancipation of Negro Americans. To this extent religion *could* make a basic contribution to political life, and the spirit of "moral goodwill" in forming a reconciling temper was itself necessary if justice, built by checking power with power, was not to be lacking in "the beauty of human life."[19] *Moral Man and Immoral Society* thus wavers between "a frank dualism" of politics and morality on the one hand and an effort to bring them together at certain points on the other. Niebuhr wanted to strengthen moral and rational forces with nonrational ones, rather than to force a choice between them—except at the spectrum's extremes of Christian love and socialist revolution.

By 1937 Niebuhr still believed that Marxism was superior to both rationalistic humanism and the cynical romanticism of fascism, but neither one, he stressed, could do justice to the Christian emphasis on sin and repentance. Christians were right to hold that ultimately only the law of love was normative, not the habits of a sinful world, and only love could perfect justice.[20] To this extent he was himself perfectionist but more inclined now to use religious rather than Marxist language. While liberal theologians could point to the New Deal as an exemplar of their own confidence in human nature and progress, Niebuhr drew support immediately for his more pessimistic doctrine from his deep skepticism of New Deal reform and his awareness of European fascism, ultimately from his emphasis on the darker side of the self. Public history gives way to the aggressive individual will as his favorite focus of evil in his sermons collected in 1937 under the title *Beyond Tragedy*.[21]

Through the thirties he became increasingly critical of left-wing illusions about the Soviet Union because no place could realistically be viewed as a moral center of pure disinterestedness. The purge trials were of a piece with the cynicism of the Nazi-Soviet Pact. At the same time Hitler's conquest of Europe provoked in Niebuhr a much more appreciative assessment of Anglo-American political culture, especially in Great Britain. In 1940 he explicitly defined the aims of the Fellowship of Socialist Christians as attempting to strive for social justice "without illusions, without fanaticism and without the despair which is the inevitable consequence of disappointed hopes and dissipated illusions." That winter he conceded for the first time that Roosevelt's achievement in reconstructing the Democratic Party into "an instrument of essentially progressive legislation" was "a political feat of a high order."[22] History had "discounted social catastrophism as a political philosophy," but he still believed in the New Testament view of history as a process "moving toward a climax in which both Christ and anti-Christ are revealed."[23] His premillennialism now was theological, not political as well.

In the late 1930's Niebuhr found himself engaged in polemics against other religious radicals who, once persuaded with him that social justice demanded a struggle incompatible with Christian non-resistance, now expressed themselves as religious pacifists in the international arena. "Thus Christian faith is buffeted about by every wind of doctrine arising from the historical cave of the winds," he complained, "and is formed and reformed in the light of every historical exigency."[24] He accepted as a desirable symbol of Christian love the pacifist as "ascetic saint" and the pacifist as pragmatist who merely felt that no essential issues of justice were involved in a specific conflict. What he challenged was the attempt to use the idiom of the former on behalf of the latter.[25]

Niebuhr's turning against international pacifism was also instructed by events. In 1927, as a pacifist, he had hoped for a "more intimate fellowship with Europe" by the revision of American policies regarding the war debts, tariffs, and immigration restriction. So long as they did not share our advantages, other nations could not be trusted to be trusting, for love required sacrifice to be credible. When he left the Fellowship of Reconciliation in 1934 because he took a pragmatic view of force, he was still sure that war was suicidal but that nonhatred, rather than nonviolence, was the important symbol of Christian faith.[26] Fascism in Europe induced him to reappraise war.

The liberal Protestant churches tended to identify the gospel with the political slogan "Keep America Out of the War." This posture deeply offended Niebuhr's political and especially his moral feelings. He knew that it played into the hands of the Roosevelt administration's fear of alienating the Democratic Party's powerful urban machines with their conservative Catholic prejudices against the Spanish republicans, embattled with fascist-supported Franco forces. Even the *Catholic Worker,* he noted, while critical of Franco, supported the embargo against aid to the Loyalists out of pacifist scruples. Niebuhr also detected behind the neutralists and isolationists a self-righteousness that inhibited a charitable concern for the refugees from fascism, most notably expressed by the Jews,* and substituted instead an "abstract and negative perfection of peace in a warring world" for the concrete meaning of love as pity, sympathy, and responsibility "for the weal and woe of others."[27]

The standard of love in this sense of responsible concern now came to have a political meaning for him, as it had in 1927, in spite of his efforts in *Moral Man and Immoral Society* to limit its definition to self-sacrificing good will as the code of small-group behavior. In 1932

* The National Refugee Service, largest of such organizations, derived its funds from Jewish sources. Scholars, émigrés, and socialists were also active in emergency operations for exiles. See Laura Fermi, *Illustrious Immigrants: The Intellectual Migration from Europe 1930–41* (Chicago, 1968), p. 81.

he had contrasted Christian love with the "careful calculation" needed for political morality, but writing after German victories in Holland, Belgium, and France, he condemned American moralists for failing to understand that "people and nations which face an imminent threat of enslavement do not make nice calculations of alternative consequences." Such calculations were irrelevant when slavery or survival was the issue. While it was a political fact that national and ideal interests had to merge to prompt action in a crisis, it was "morally dubious and politically ambiguous in its import." The vital interests of a nation, he pointed out, might be "ultimately imperilled without being immediately imperilled. To wait until ultimate perils become immediate means to wait too long." Neutrality, furthermore, left to other nations the brunt of defending a civilization that transcended the mere existence of those nations. The policy of the *Christian Century* was therefore both bad morals and bad politics.[28]

Christian perfectionism threatened in this light to become indistinguishable from "a bourgeois love of ease." It did not fail from aiming too high so much as it failed from being too self-satisfied and too unimaginative to comprehend the "heights to which malignant power may rise." Against this "unholy Pharisaism" he preferred the American secular Whigs with their concept of checks and balances, which had entered into the Constitution—proof that sometimes secular thinkers might be better Calvinists than the ostensible heirs of Reformation policies. Niebuhr was also drawn in sympathy to Britain because he felt that Scottish Calvinism and Anglicanism had taught Britons, despite their imperialism, how to combine moral purpose and political realism. American imperialists would alternate instead between disavowing the task for the sake of their souls or following the course of "manifest destiny" with cynical self-interest. He must also have felt some envy for a country where the Socialist Christian League could include three members of the House of Lords and sixteen members of the Commons.[29]

In 1940 Niebuhr resigned from the isolationist Socialist Party and moved closer to the New Deal on both the foreign and domestic fronts. In the fall of the previous year, though he was still a socialist in goals, he had concluded that Roosevelt was the only hope of "maintaining the real gains which have been made in the past years of the depression."[30] In 1941 he launched *Christianity and Crisis* as a weapon against neutralism in the churches. His proximate secular judgments would increasingly find favor among New Deal liberals, while it would become more and more difficult to see how his ultimate standards of judgment could be operative during the war. Niebuhr believed that not reason but the law of love was always valid as a "potential perfection" in a man, but the remoteness of this standard from the demanding actualities of the historical moment meant that it could function in time of war only as a prohibition against hatred of the enemy. Just as he had been prepared in 1934, when he resigned from the Fellowship of Reconciliation on domestic issues to traffic with "the devil of vengeance" in the interest of the future justice of revolutionary socialism, so now he was prepared to traffic with the devil of war for the sake of defending in the present "the relative virtue of a decent scheme of justice" against "the real peril of tyranny."[31] The pragmatic relation of means and ends was the same; the difference lay in the shift from an envisaged future to a present actuality. The relative success of the New Deal in dealing with the depression, the chilling example of Stalin's totalitarianism, and the noninterventionist policy of the Socialist Party had given Niebuhr a place to stand in the present much closer to the Roosevelt administration than where he had stood in 1932.

During the war Niebuhr urged consideration of humane policies regarding Jews, Negroes, and the future of international security, but in retrospect the most significant issue for dramatizing his own historical philosophy was the waging of the war itself. In 1944 the Allies escalated their bombing to include saturation raids on civilian populations in both Europe and Japan, tactics that had scandalized most Allied spokesmen when they were first used by the fascists in Spain. Niebuhr believed that the Allies were becoming increasingly dependent upon their physical superiority in material resources precisely because they were failing to define any significant positive goals for the future. But he was not prepared to risk drawing "absolute distinctions between what is, and what is not, permissible in a total war," because its "melancholy necessities" grew inevitably out of a technical society that converts what is possible into what is necessary. Once the instruments of total war are introduced, he asserted, then they "will guarantee defeat for the side that fails to use them, whether from want of resolution, or failure of organization, or moral scruple." When the bombing of the Ruhr Valley had taken place earlier, he had cited the event as proof of the necessary antecedent and concomitant guilt involved in even the most righteous political cause. The only "moral freedom" men had amidst these "cruel necessities of history" was to "do these things without rancor or self-righteousness."[32]

The Federal Council of Churches, in its Commission on the Relation of the Church to the War in the Light of the Christian Faith, condemned strategic bombing in 1944, but it was divided by those who would in extremity also accept such tactics if they were deemed essential to success in a just war. Only after the two atomic bombs had been dropped without warning on Japanese cities did the Council unambiguously also condemn the earlier incendiary bombing, which on one night alone produced nearly as many Japanese casualties.[33] Niebuhr himself favored the atomic strategy of a warning and a demonstration in a minimally populated area, but although he criticized Allied statesmen for their "lack of imagination" about the moral advantages of such a policy, he wondered if they were not "driven by historic forces more powerful than any human decision."[34] The speculation shows that Niebuhr carried over from his earlier Marxism a historical determinism that was impressed by grim fatalities in history that knew nothing of reason or morals, and the Calvinist idea of Providence contained its own fatalism. This kind of historical sense made little room for moral decision, elbowed out by the burly presence of historical "necessity." But to sacrifice scruples to necessity, which may be unavoidable in emergencies, is tragic if the "necessity" is only a fallacy. In this case, systematic later study of strategic bombing in Europe showed that the city raids aimed at the morale of the industrial worker had little effect on war production, and the same raids in Japan had not been very much more effective.[35] The argument from military necessity was vastly overrated. The acceptance of cities as targets in 1944 blunted and brutalized later thinking about the use of the atomic bombs, unnecessarily narrowing the options.

Niebuhr's theology insisted on the inherent guiltiness of historical action; therefore avoiding guilt could never be an effective argument against an action. The difficulty of this position, in contrast to that of some Catholics who had earlier formulated traditional moral objections to bombings of civilians,[36] was that he purchased his hold on the morality of waging war in terms of contrition and repentance, factors that could operate only after the event. If history is defined as sin, furthermore, then there is little incentive to formulate moral distinctions within it. Niebuhr's rejection of the pacifist condemnation of force as such, a rejection that in principle freed him to distinguish morally among the various uses of force, was sponsored by his belief that all politics beyond moral suasion was coercive and subject only to pragmatic criticism in terms of means in relation to ends. Even on this basis, however, a limited objective for the war, rather than "unconditional surrender," would entail limited means. What was crucial was the freedom of men to be creators, as well as creatures, of the historical process, and in Niebuhr's Marxist-Calvinist vision fate was more vivid than freedom.

Niebuhr admitted that he took the Reformation doctrine of justification by faith very seriously; for this reason only God's mercy, he felt, could redeem men from "the contradictions of human history."[37] What God might provide, men could not supply when realists engaged in a war they accepted as inevitably total because of modern technology. Niebuhr's feelings were entirely humane about the moral consequences of total war; what was lacking was a sufficient check in his own thought against the shrinkage of the idea of moral freedom to the expression of contrition and repentance. He himself had pointed to a similar defect in 1928 when he justly complained that reformers had the habit of "confessing the sins of their group from which they imagine themselves emancipated." Thus did white radicals beat their breasts about their racism, yielding to the seductive temptation "to be humble and proud at the same time." The trouble with this indulgence, Niebuhr noted, was that it got in the way of "dealing objectively" with social facts and problems. "To repent of group sins," he observed, "has moral meaning only if the person who makes the confession has had some responsibility for the actions of the group."[38] Niebuhr joined the Federal Council of Churches in its report of 1946 condemning the bombings of Japan, but the responsibility for initiating the earlier fire raids, which had made cities targets, belonged to General Curtis LeMay, who was not inclined to repentance. Not the guilty but the sensitive were likely to practice contrition, and it could not retroactively influence political action, however much it might please God. As it turned out, traditional pacifists, some Catholic moralists, and the formerly isolationist *Christian Century* were virtually alone in condemning the crucial escalation to bombing civilians by conventional weapons.[39] The majority of secular and clerical public voices were not prepared to disavow any means that might bring victory, and public opinion did not share Niebuhr's morally preferred strategy for the atom bomb.

The British Council of Churches, in its report on atomic power in

1946, was also unable to resolve the atomic dilemma: a threat of reprisal with atomic weapons might, in some circumstances, reduce the danger of aggressive war, while at the same time representing an outrageous affront to Christian ideals. It concluded candidly that it had "no solution of the dilemma to offer."[40] Niebuhr himself, with equal candor, said in 1961 that he knew of "no principle, Christian or otherwise," that would resolve the dilemmas of nuclear deterrence.[41] His theology of history, with its emphasis on war as the revelation of perennial sinfulness, found inevitabilities more impressive than the moral drama of decisions taken, consciously or by default.

The terrifying risks of the nuclear arms race would eventually sponsor widespread apocalyptic fears, and in 1961 Niebuhr himself felt that modern history had moved into the eschatological dimension in which all judgments are "under the shadow of the final judgment." His moral was Biblical: "May the Lord have mercy on our souls."[42] From a catastrophist socialist millennialism he had moved gradually to a democratic meliorism, but apocalyptic fears had counterbalanced hopes, whether millennial or modest, at both ends of the spectrum he had traveled.

Niebuhr's fame was in part the "denominationalizing" of his own prophetic religion. It also disproved his wartime belief that Great Britain had a unique history in deriving social reform from Christianity rather than against it. Just as Tocqueville had emphasized the stabilizing features of American political life in connection with its religious tradition, so did Niebuhr make the same point about Great Britain, believing it to have "the most secure and least catastrophic future of any nation."[43] This prophecy was correct enough, but Niebuhr looked to Britain as an example of a less secularized political culture when in fact from 1900 to 1950 weekly Anglican church attendance had dropped from 11.5 per cent to 3.5 per cent of the population, while Nonconformist attendance had declined from 9.5 per cent to 3 per cent and Catholic attendance had also gone down from 3.5 per cent to 2.75 per cent. "English religion is much less well integrated into the patterns of social and economic life than is American," a British social philosopher has recently observed.[44] It is also to the point that Niebuhr has no English counterpart of comparable importance. By 1957 he had come around to Tocqueville's view that for historical reasons America was both "more religious and more secular than any other nation."[45] This reappraisal was linked to the widespread revival of interest in religion during the 1950's, a mood very different from the debunking style of the 1920's when Sinclair Lewis's *Elmer Gantry* had symbolized the low prestige of the clergy. Niebuhr himself had done much to restore the vocation of the preacher as intellectual.

Niebuhr's dialectic was agile and his reading extraordinarily wide, but he did not cure the disease of oversimplification in the social gospel. He saw with clarity the deficiencies of the pietist's obsession with a morality of intention, of Biblical literalism, and of an individualistic effort to make a direct application of personal values to social life, if only because, as he candidly admitted, he was often "most critical of that in other men to which he is most tempted himself."[46] He preached a more complex view in which men had to make discriminate political judgments with empirical knowledge of the facts and in which they had to take historical responsibility for imperfect social causes. But men in his view also had to accept the inevitable linkage of freedom and sinful pride, of responsibility and guilt, standing under the adverse judgment of a hidden God. In this sense Niebuhr's outlook was consistent with the long Protestant-Puritan tradition of identifying self-interest, individual and collective, with evil. The Catholic theologian John Courtney Murray has pointed out that this "neo-orthodox" style of reasoning always eventuates in ironic dilemmas, paradoxes, and morally ambiguous situations because its facts are always filtered first through its own categories. Complicated political tasks, like complicated surgery, he protests, are difficult but not inevitably ambiguous: "The work may be done deftly or clumsily, intelligently or stupidly, with variant degrees of success or failure; but why call it in either case 'ambiguous'?" Niebuhr's attack on simplistic utopianism had its own simplistic consequence of monotonously imprisoning the moral life of man in "the single moral dimension of ambiguity."[47]

For Niebuhr, "pure religious idealism does not concern itself with the social problem."[48] If this is true, then only secular morality is relevant to politics, but he resisted the conclusion for the sake of making an impossible ideal somehow a judgment on all human efforts. His dualistic statement of the relation between religion and political life was made on behalf of an attitude of moral involvement in political affairs, but its very formulation usually identified political power with corruption and pure idealism with the nonhistorical. This definition of the problem, despite his intentions, inevitably encourages either moralistic withdrawal from politics for the sake of higher values or cynical withdrawal from morality for the sake of power politics. Such a dualism was involved in the American penchant either for finding smug moral virtue in political isolationism from the system of European politics or, if forced to engage in international political life, for embracing the use of power with cynical abandonment. In *The Children of Light and the Children of Darkness* (1944) Niebuhr himself attacked crude American wartime criticisms of British policies because America itself had little moral consciousness of its own tendencies to disavow the responsibilities of power out of a fear of its corruptions, or to display "an adolescent pride of power and a cynical disregard of its responsibilities."[49] Yet his own way of stating the problem of political morality in such dualistic terms tended to authorize the very attitudes that he lamented.

Niebuhr's battle with perfectionist Protestants, or with liberals who exaggerated the power of abstract reason to control nonrational forces or who failed to devise strategies to tame them by using them, was on some issues a good fight. Yet he often spoke as if his enemies were definitive of the whole cultural situation instead of representing only an element in it. Perfectionism was not at all characterisic of the most influential political men in American history: the founders of the Constitution, Lincoln, the second Roosevelt. Nor was it a dominant characteristic of notable American political philosophers like John Adams, James Madison, Thomas Jefferson, John C. Calhoun, Walter Lippmann, Herbert Croly, or Charles Beard. It was a vital aspect rather of the Transcendentalists, abolitionists, Christian Socialists, liberal Protestants, pacifists, and academic enthusiasts for World Government. The force of much of Niebuhr's polemic is blunted by its obsession with the intramural problems of Protestant culture. In the 1960's millennial and apocalyptic left-wing politics did become very fashionable again among eager trend followers on the campuses and in the mass media, but recent studies show that adolescents, whether in America, England, or Germany, are distinctly antiutopian "realists" with a somewhat dismaying and surprising intensity, convinced with Niebuhr of the assertive selfishness of human nature.[50]

Niebuhr himself conceded that the Founding Fathers were notably sober about human nature and about power. But if James Madison had also esteemed checks and balances, he had recognized, with eighteenth-century *mesure* rather than with Calvinist guilt, "a degree of depravity in mankind which requires a certain degree of circumspection and distrust," just as he had also believed that there are other qualities in human nature "which justify a certain portion of esteem and confidence." For Madison, moreover, republican government presupposes the existence of reliable qualities "in a higher degree than any other form."[51] Like Madison, the theologian affirmed man's capacity for justice as well as injustice, and he even occasionally alluded to the need to respect "natural social impulses," leading at some levels to a "natural harmony," yet strategically and polemically Niebuhr invested most of his public energy in attacking what he considered to be the dangerously excessive confidence of modern liberal culture.[52] It was a tactic that seems remarkably unaware of the extent to which radical pessimism about the human situation is a commonplace in twentieth-century literature and would come to be characteristic of secular existentialist philosophy after the war. He addressed himself to the severe political limitations of conservative pietism, pacifist nonresistance, liberal theology, and fellow traveling as if they were definitive of the whole American mind.

To represent secular thought, Niebuhr usually took John Dewey as his example, finding him, with justification, guilty of overconfidence in the political and moral usefulness of social science, while unjustifiably ignoring the extent to which Dewey's own version of pragmatism similarly stressed the relativity of perspective inherent in the making and understanding of history, just as it paralleled Niebuhr's path in finding the New Deal too opportunistic.[53] The preacher was, in fact, remarkably resonant on many themes with the other great pragmatist, William James. The author of *The Varieties of Religious Experience* also believed that "radical evil" is part of the "normal process of life." The facts of evil aggressiveness might "after all be the best key to life's significance, and possibly the only openers of our eyes to deepest levels of truth." Just as Niebuhr identified the highest Christian virtue with an ascetic sainthood, so did James think that asceticism stands for "nothing less than for the essence of the twice-born philosophy," and he appealed to it against the "general optimism and healthy-mindedness of liberal Protestant circles." James, who had read Kierkegaard, could even speak of the "indestructible vital meaning" of "the folly of the cross, so inexplicable by the intellect"—language that almost sounds like Niebuhr's own. James noted in his own vivid, more humorous idiom: "Naturalistic optimism is mere syllabub and flattery and sponge-cake in comparison." Rather like Niebuhr also, the agnostic James considered the saintly qualities "indispensable to the world's welfare," as heralds, harbingers, and leavens of a better social order, while conceding that saints would be completely adapted only to a "millennial society."[54] In human terms the excellence of sainthood was relative, not absolute.

James was much more concerned than Niebuhr, however, to find "the moral equivalent for war," which the philosopher improbably proposed in 1902 as a "voluntarily accepted poverty."[55] James was faced with the gospel of wealth and the bellicosity of imperialists in the era of the Spanish-American War rather than with the great depression and Hitler's conquests. Niebuhr's constant complaint about the superficial optimism of modern liberal culture ignored, nevertheless, the luminous example of this very American and influential philosopher. In 1961, in response to papers honoring his work, Niebuhr would call himself a pragmatist, guided by Western ideas of justice, but he never pointed to the fact that James, entirely on secular grounds, characteristically had observed that "the bigger the unit you deal with, the hollower, the more brutal, the more mendacious is the life displayed"—a one-sentence compression, in effect, of Niebuhr's social doctrine of sin.[56] What both thinkers tended to lack, in fact, was a strong feeling for the status of social life and organization, not as strategy or as sin, but as the expression of autonomous human needs.

Niebuhr's outlook was a brave and bold attempt, nevertheless, to solve the problem of preserving both the integrity and the social relevance of Christian doctrine. Yet to the extent that he gave the church mainly a mission for repentance, while other agencies did the work of the world, he illustrated rather than prevented the modern secularization of life. Even more damaging to his intentions, his preachment of "realism" was vulnerable to the risk of failing to convert secular utopians, who could dismiss his Biblical ideas, while succeeding only too well in reinforcing unimaginative resort to force as the substance of American foreign policy. Events in the Cold War years would underline this irony, but at his best in the 1930's Niebuhr exposed with candor and insight not only the obvious moral complacencies and political stupidity of conservative apologists for unregulated capitalism and continental isolationism but also the more subtle pretensions of alleged wise men of the tribe who did not reckon with the hard choices of history or with the blindness, rational and moral, that can afflict men of good will. Above all, he knew what the trouble was with "all the comrades and semi-comrades": "They have found a Christ in history. . . . They have found the devil in history. . . . Communism was Christ. Russia was the Kingdom of God. Hitler was the devil. The pluto-democracies were the Laodicean believers who were suspected of lukewarm faith and were challenged continually to choose between Christ and Belial, between Stalin and Hitler."[57] Against this surrogate religion he called men to remember a Christ and a Kingdom at the edge of history and not within it.

In the eyes of a distinguished political scientist, Niebuhr was the only creative political philosopher in America since Calhoun. For his part, however, Niebuhr modestly thought in his late years that all a Christian political thinker could do was "seek to prevent premature solutions of essentially insoluble problems, hoping that time will make some solutions possible tomorrow which are not possible today."[58] If that contribution seems severely limited by its essential negativity, the negative task of stopping Hitler without nurturing illusions about Stalin was worth a good deal more than what passed for wisdom in most of the spokesmen for the churches in the days when Niebuhr was working out his characteristic position. In 1929 Niebuhr presaged his future course by saying he did not think the statesman Abraham Lincoln was morally inferior to the prophet William Lloyd Garrison, and in 1961 Niebuhr was acclaimed for having rediscovered the autonomy of "Political Man."[59] But Niebuhr's legacy was a double one. After the war his writings provided texts for statesmen who sought a rationale for anti-Communist containment policies.[60] But his earlier strategy of nonviolent resistance for dealing with the American racial problem also came alive in the movement for civil rights, when the Supreme Court had provided an occasion in 1954 for democratic religion to make a contribution to social justice. In this way the moralist in Niebuhr, who had been dominated by the historical realist after 1941, preserved his relevance to American politics.

XVIII

The Winding Wall of Separation and
the New Pluralism

Legal disestablishment of the churches in the nineteenth century functioned in the context of a Protestant cultural establishment that was challenged in the mid-twentieth century by those who had stood outside that tradition. Jehovah's Witnesses, Catholics, Jews, and agnostics fought their case to the Supreme Court, where so many political problems eventually arrive in American history; and the justices hacked out a tortuous course in trying to reconcile a legacy of separatism that was both liberal and evangelical with the modern pluralistic realities of an expanding Catholic influence, a waning Protestant hegemony, and a more aggressive secular liberalism. The Court's engagement with these problems forced it to formulate its own conflicted sense of what republican religion and religious republicanism had meant and should continue to mean in new circumstances.

The First Amendment had settled the issue of disestablishment in its own day by allowing either disestablishment or establishment on the state level and raising a standard of legal separation between church and state only on the national level. With the passage of the Fourteenth Amendment certain liberties were in principle though not yet in fact, protected against infringement by the states because of the Radical Republican crusade to complete the emancipation of the Negro. In the next century the Supreme Court began to find some of the earlier freedoms in the Bill of Rights currently alive in the Fourteenth Amendment as valid defenses against actions by the states. But it was not until late in this process that the Court spoke directly to the issue of freedom of religion. While it is still speaking, it is, to use a religious metaphor, so much at odds with itself and often with history that its glosses on the Constitution sometimes may appear to sound more like *glossalalia* than like convincing argument. Yet the Court cannot be blamed for the difficulty of reconciling eighteenth-century agreements and compromises with twentieth-century pluralistic conflict over basic assumptions. Apart from the snags in its reasoning, the Court's record in finding some navigable path between favoritism to religion and hostility to it has not been a mean one, and there has been no weighty legal or philosophical wisdom beyond the Court rising with impressive authority and clarity above the acrid smog of the controversy that has swirled around the issues the Court has had to face.

The first and most striking fact with which to begin this complicated modern chapter in the story of religion and democracy is a matter of a date. Not until 1925 did the Court decide that, in principle, some liberty contained in the capacious First Amendment could be invoked by a defendant against a state. It was not until 1940 that it held, in principle and in fact, that such an appeal could successfully be made to the clause protecting "the free exercise of religion," and it was not until eight years later that it invalidated a state action as a law "respecting an establishment of religion." Not till then did Madison's original defeated provision to make the religious clauses of the First Amendment applicable to the states come into its own.

Six years before the landmark decision of 1940, some sons of Methodist ministers, responding to the pacifist position recently taken by the General Conference of the Methodist Episcopal Church, had sought exemption from the compulsory Reserve Officer Training Corps program at the University of California. The Court conceded that the due-process clause of the Fourteenth Amendment included the right to entertain and teach religious pacifism, but it held that draft exemption for conscientious status was merely a matter of Congressional policy, not of Constitutional right. Under the Morrill Act, granting public lands to the states for the support of public education, the teaching of military tactics was indicated; and the regents of the University of California, the Court agreed, could set their own conditions for fulfilling the requirement, even if it forced the Methodist students to go elsewhere for a more expensive education. This rejection of any Constitutional concern for the case of the complaining believers was supported by the liberal justices, Benjamin N. Cardozo, Louis D. Brandeis, and Harlan F. Stone, on the ground that the right of private judgment could not be elevated that high above the powers of the government. The Court simply took for granted the right of Congress to make draft exemption in practice turn exclusively on holding certain sectarian beliefs and affiliations, traditionally identified with only a few pacifist sects.[1]

In 1940 Jehovah's Witnesses confronted the Court with a claim for religious freedom that it felt obligated to support. The Witnesses, an expanding modern example of an apocalyptically oriented sect of the lowly, awaiting the last days and rejecting idolatrous secular gestures such as flag saluting, defied the Enlightenment's vision of history as a progress in secularization. The Court's doctrines in the area of religious freedom would be hammered out first under the pressure of this persecuted sect's claim for justice. In New Haven three Witnesses were arrested for canvassing without a license, and one of them was also charged with disturbing the peace by playing records that disseminated anti-Catholic propaganda in a Catholic neighborhood. The Court in *Cantwell* v. *Connecticut* explicitly affirmed the relevance of the First Amendment's religious clauses to the Fourteenth Amendment and found it a violation of religious liberty through prior restraint for an officer of the state to determine that a particular cause was (or was not) a religious one and therefore entitled (or not) to a soliciting license. His judgment alone could thus make a cause a crime. Cantwell, furthermore, had not created any "clear and present danger" of riot, the test devised earlier by Justices Holmes and Brandeis for determining when speech could be Constitutionally limited by state action. He had asked and obtained permission from his hearers to play the record, and he had quietly left the scene when he discovered how angry his audience had become.[2] The Court majority in this decision grasped an important social truth: the Witnesses were a despised minority, just as the Baptists had been in the days when Madison had sympathized with their plight and joined political forces with them.

This feature of the story was vividly highlighted by the contention aroused over the Witnesses' refusal on religious grounds to salute the national flag in public-school rituals. In *Minersville School District* v. *Gobitis* (1940), Mr. Justice Felix Frankfurter, speaking for the Court, held that the young Jehovah's Witness children had no Constitutional right to refuse participation in the public school's flag-saluting exercise because the government could take whatever measures it thought wise to foster "the binding tie of cohesive sentiment" without thereby becoming vulnerable to the charge of directing legislation against the "doctrinal loyalties of particular sects." Frankfurter held no brief for the ritual used to inculcate loyalty, but he did not think the Court should adjudicate "pedagogical and psychological dogma." He wished to prevent the Court from saying in effect that "there is no basis for a legislative judgment that such an exemption might introduce elements of difficulty into the school discipline, might cast doubts in the minds of the other children which would themselves weaken the effect of the exercise."[3] Frankfurter not only respected national loyalty in a time of world war; he was fearful of reviving in another area the Court's historic tendency to inhibit reform legislation by its own dogmas about liberty.

The weakness of his closely reasoned opinion, however, was that it minimized the extent to which the rite involved belief and not merely sentiment. The Pennsylvania school board had made the flag salute compulsory (rather than a custom) only after the Gobitis children had stopped saluting it, thereby leading to their expulsion. Two weeks before the *Gobitis* decision, the Court in the *Cantwell* case had for the first time made religious freedom explicitly part of the Fourteenth Amendment. Chief Justice Stone still accepted the judgment that required religious pacifists to take ROTC courses as a condition of attending a university, but he would not compel these children to make "public affirmations which violate their religious conscience." The action demanded in this case was itself a form of belief. Because of the First Amendment it was up to the state to find other ways to teach patriotism than by compelling belief. It was not enough for the Court to exercise its self-restraint in Frankfurter's way so long as remedial processes of majority rule were available. It was the Court's duty to make searching inquiry into legislative judgment when the religious rights of "this small and helpless minority" were at stake. The Constitution is more than the affirmation of the importance of democratic processes; it is also, he insisted, the affirmation of "freedom of mind and spirit," an ideal binding upon the government itself.[4] Stone's dissent foreshadowed the Constitutional future.

Local authorities often took it upon themselves after the Court's decision to define the children of Jehovah's Witnesses and their parents as delinquents. Some states tried to condition licensing privileges for itinerant evangelical canvassing upon conformity to the flag-salute ritual, and in small towns in Maine, West Virginia, Nebraska, Texas, and Oklahoma, violence flared up against the Witnesses.[5] Three years after this bitter harvest of the *Gobitis* case, aided by the appointment of two new justices to the Court, the supreme tribunal reversed itself in *Board of Education* v. *Barnette,* giving its opinion with symbolic appropriateness on Flag Day. Speaking for the majority, Mr. Justice Robert H. Jackson reaffirmed the preferred-position status of First Amendment freedoms and also defined them as barriers against coercing consent. The religious aspect of the case was not crucial. No students, in this view, could be compelled to salute the flag.* Jackson thus went beyond Stone, but like him he also saw the ritual as a rite coercing belief, not just as a measure regulating educational policy, as Frankfurter saw it.[6]

Frankfurter still held to his position in a dissent that emphasized his fear that "sectarian scruples" were being elevated above general civil authority in a way that Jefferson would have found unjustified because he knew that religious minorities could "disrupt society."[7] In historical fact, however, much as Jefferson did scorn sectarian dogmas, his Act for Establishing Religious Freedom also enunciated the principle that the time for government to interfere was when "principles break out into overt acts against peace and good order."[8] It would be difficult to imagine, for all his patriotism, that he would have seen in scruples against saluting the flag in school an overt threat to civil peace, which the Court in 1878 had seen in the Mormon practice of polygamy, a crime Virginia itself had outlawed with the death penalty two years after the passage of Jefferson's act.[9] Frankfurter wondered why respecting parental objections to flag saluting would not entail justifying William Jennings Bryan's notorious efforts to prevent a schoolteacher in Dayton, Tennessee, from teaching evolution to children whose parents found Darwinism morally offensive to their fundamentalist religion.[10] But the majority on the Court saw that saluting was a rite, not an idea or hypothesis involved in scientific theory. Not every conscientious claim would tip the scales against the state's interest.

In the year of its great reversal the Court in *Murdock v. Pennsylvania* found a Pennsylvania municipal statute, which laid a flat licensing fee on canvassing or soliciting in a residential area, to be in effect a prior restraint on the religious freedom of itinerant evangelists. Mere hucksters and peddlers could be so regulated, but First Amendment freedoms occupied "a preferred position" and no one could be taxed as a condition for exercising them, even though itinerants

---

* It is doubtful, however, that his supporters on the Court went this far. They seemed more inclined to think that religious motivation gave a favorable hue to rejection of the ritual. Similarly, the Court in 1972 upheld the claim of an Amish parent in refusing to allow his child to attend school beyond the eighth grade (though Wisconsin law requires school attendance until age sixteen), citing the First Amendment's clause on the free exercise of religion. *Wisconsin v. Yoder.*

charged a small fee for the disseminated material. Mr. Justice William O. Douglas, reversing an earlier opinion on a similar issue, affirmed that the hand distribution of tracts was as much a part of evangelism as a revival meeting.[11] In another case, without citing the religious clauses as such, Mr. Justice Hugo L. Black also sustained Witnesses on free-speech grounds against an ordinance aimed at preventing the ringing of doorbells of householders in a community where many worked a swing shift, sleeping in the daytime. Even so, an itinerant could not become a trespasser without prior warning by the householder to keep out. Like Armageddon itself, the message of the Witnesses was to come to the householder by entering into the windows "like a thief in the night," and they had organized campaigns to saturate neighborhoods with regiments of persistent evangelists.[12]

The dissenters to these decisions were concerned to keep the Court from ignoring the rights of other believers or of nonbelievers. "Instead of all bearing equally the burdens of government," complained Mr. Justice Stanley F. Reed, "this Court now fastens upon the communities the entire cost of policing the sales of religious literature." An ordinance that penalized distributors of tracts as such, rather than overtly aiming at protection of the householder's privacy or safety, might indeed be invalid, but to the dissenters the Court's majority appeared to be sanctioning aggressive methods that it would not tolerate in secular defendants. Freedom's limits should not be breached, Mr. Justice Jackson protested, "under the cloak of religious evangelism."[13] City authorities, Jackson pointed out, had specifically justified the ordinance against doorbell ringing by the needs of an industrial community to be protected in its hard-earned rest from the danger of professed peddlers who might really be thieves in disguise. Yet, as Justice Black pointed out, political canvassers practice methods similar to those used by the Witnesses, or by the government in its war-bond drive.

The Court's inner division reflected two different legitimate concerns. Those who were anxious to defend civil liberties in a world where Communists and fascists had explicitly repudiated them were understandably drawn to emphasize the rights of Witnesses, particularly after the persecution that had followed the *Gobitis* decision. The dissenters, on the other hand, feared a recrudescence of the Court's earlier dogmatic blindness in refusing to acknowledge the facts of life in industrial America, a dogmatism that had led it to impose in economic matters its own concept of "liberty of contract" against every

attempt of state legislatures to deal in a regulatory way with the pressing problems of workers' wages, hours, and unionization. These justices wanted more attention paid to the judgment of legislators that
the methods of evangelism pursued by Witnesses were intrusions on
the legitimate interests of other citizens.

In giving the First Amendment a preferred position against state
claims the majority on the Court was responding to the traditional
logic of liberal democracy with its stress on moral limits to majority
action. American constitutionalism always had recognized the possibility of majority tyranny. In the past the Court had shown far more
zeal, however, in making this point with respect to the economic interests of corporations than with respect to the civil liberties of persons.
The Court in the New Deal era constructively changed that bias, but it
also ran the risk of incurring a charge of favoring religious motivation.
In the future, complaints by agnostics and atheists for equal treatment
would tend to point up the paradox in the Court's advocacy of religiously motivated claims while seeking a position of neutrality that it
wanted to find in the clause against laws respecting an establishment.
Exempting Witnesses from the burdens of all nondiscriminatory, non-
punitive taxation would amount to indirect subsidization, and some
justices were worried that in this way the free exercise clause would
come into conflict with the anti-establishment clause.

Frankfurter was alarmed that the Court had threatened Jeffersonianism by decisions tending to make the consciences of a minority
"more sacred and more enshrined in the Constitution than the consciences of a majority."[14] All conscientious claims against laws might
soon come to have a privileged status. But the Court majority never
went so far; indeed, it did not sustain a canvassing child Witness
against a statute prohibiting child labor, and it even allowed the Illinois bar to exclude a conscientious objector from its ranks because of
the state constitution's requirement of militia service in time of war.[15]
Frankfurter did foresee, however, the coming of painful issues about
Bible reading and aid to parochial schools, once the Court began to
scrutinize legislative judgment in school policy. Conscientious claims
were made on all sides of these questions: a parent might even demand equality of treatment because religious scruples forbade him to
send his child to a public school. It presented "awful possibilities to try
to encase the solution of these problems within the rigid prohibitions
of unconstitutionality." In a few years, nevertheless, the Court would
entertain these "awful possibilities" as it came to terms with the

scruples of Catholics, Jews, and agnostics, and its wavering course helped to document Frankfurter's fear that the Court would fall into the vice of merely reflecting "the pressures of the day."[16]

On a clear day in Constitutional interpretation you can see the eighteenth century. But you seldom can see it plain, for two views of history have backed up different judgments of the Supreme Court in interpreting the Constitutional clause against laws respecting an establishment of religion. Mr. Justice Wiley B. Rutledge, for example, took it for granted that Madison had triumphed not only in Virginia but also in Philadelphia: "All the great instruments of the Virginia struggle for religious liberty thus became warp and woof of our constitutional tradition, not simply by the course of history, but by the common unifying force of Madison's life, thought and sponsorship."[17] This argument for a very broad interpretation of disestablishment did not pause to consider the fact that the First Amendment religious clauses had emerged as a compromise between House and Senate proposals, not as a carbon copy of Jefferson's act in Virginia.

Mr. Justice Reed spoke for the alternative historical view of the Amendment in pointing out that Madison during the debates had explained that "he apprehended the meaning of the words to be, that Congress should not establish a religion, and enforce the legal observation of it by law, nor compel men to worship God in any manner contrary to their conscience." In this reading, Congress aimed only to prevent the setting up of a national state church, not to ban all relations between the churches and governments.[18] Reed, however, did not pause to consider the fact that the Senate had not been able to get House approval on a wording that would have limited the prohibition to a ban on Congressionally established articles of faith or mode of worship. This impasse had led to the conference committee's final wording of the amendment, and no notes exist for what went on in that last meeting of minds. The fairest conclusion would be that the result aimed at a settlement somewhere between Rutledge's and Reed's views of what had happened during the debates, but accepting on the state level a very wide variation in the standard of religious liberty, including tax-supported churches.

American practice, in any event, was a denial of dogmatic separation. Churches won tax exemption, public money was used to support chaplaincies, and Presidents appointed religious memorial days and gave religiously oriented addresses. Before 1940 the Supreme Court had upheld a contract between the District of Columbia and a Congressionally chartered hospital run by Catholic sisters; it had sustained public payments, under a treaty, to support Catholic Indian schools; and it had justified the payment of public funds for nonsectarian textbooks used by parochial-school pupils in Louisiana.[19] Despite their rhetoric of absolute separation between church and state, not even Roger Williams, Isaac Backus, Jefferson, or Madison had practiced it. Ministers led services in the Rotunda of the University of Virginia in Jefferson's day, Virginia (like Rhode Island in Williams's time) passed a Sunday law in 1792, and Madison himself voted to pay army chaplains out of public funds. All these matters of history challenge any effort to turn Jefferson's metaphor about "a wall of separation" into a legal rule or a description of institutional realities.* Moreover, though the Fourteenth Amendment provided an expanding maxim of liberty and equality for measuring state actions, it did not contemplate or speak about "establishment" as a threat needing new legal defenses.

In the nineteenth century President Grant proposed an amendment against granting any public funds or taxes for the aid, "directly or indirectly," of religious groups, but there was no two-thirds majority for it in Congress. During the debate no Senator suggested that use of state funds on behalf of denominational schools was already prohibited by the First Amendment or the Fourteenth, but Congress may well have lacked the needed majority because many felt that the states already had strong guarantees against such subsidies,[20] and in time such Constitutional prohibitions against state subsidy of religious schools became widespread, not without signs of Protestant suspicion of Catholics. The Judiciary Committee that reported out James G. Blaine's version of Grant's idea forbade any public funds for private religious schools in the same paragraph that it accepted Bible reading in the public schools. Congress did, however, require that new states adopt guarantees for public education, and it restricted the use of public-land townships, set apart for education, to nonsectarian public schools.[21] This evidence justifies the conclusion that Congress and the states were strongly opposed to granting money directly to parochial schools but were willing to accept a Protestant influence in the public

* Sidney Mead points out that Madison's metaphor of a "line of separation between the rights of religion and the Civil authority" is realistically more fluid than Jefferson's "wall." "Neither Church nor State: Reflections on James Madison's 'Line of Separation,'" *Journal of Church and State, 10* (Autumn, 1968), p.349.

schools. It is understandable that Catholics would have strong doubts about the neutrality of this position and therefore feel penalized in paying both for public-school taxes and maintaining their own parochial schools by voluntary contributions.

In *Everson* v. *Board of Education* (1947) the Court upheld payments for bus transportation to the parents of parochial students in New Jersey. Mr. Justice Black was sure there had not been "the slightest breach" in Jefferson's "high and impregnable" wall.[22] The legislature had merely found a new public purpose in the reimbursement of parental cost of commercial bus transportation to three public high schools and four Catholic parochial schools. Black felt that it would be a denial of legal neutrality and of the free exercise of religion to exclude anyone for religious reasons from receiving the benefits of welfare legislation aimed at public safety, though he also believed that no direct grant of aid to parochial schools could be legally justified. Mr. Justice Jackson in his dissent pointed out that the school-board measure was not stated in general terms, as the authorizing statute had been, but was instead discriminatory in singling out only Catholic beneficiaries of the provision for parochial-school parents. In this sense the arrangement was quite different from measures for police or fire protection, which were generally available without reference to religious identification. Mr. Justice Rutledge spoke for others who felt that Madisonian principles, as formulated in Virginia, applied to the issue, so that even if the resolution had been nondiscriminatory it would still have been unconstitutional. No public purpose could be religious.

The confusion in this case was prophetic. The majority defended both the metaphor of the "wall" *and* the reimbursement of parochial-school parents. The minority attacked the measure because it was discriminatory *and* because it did not matter whether it was or not. At least six state courts gave lip service to the Court's opinion while declaring similar laws invalid.[23] What was lacking was a historical interpretation that did not lean on the abstraction of absolute separation but did stand guard against discrimination, a point Black had set aside because petitioners themselves had not raised it. Otherwise, however, the case for making the parents of all students the beneficiaries of a policy justifiable as a welfare measure under the rubric of public safety was itself a persuasive one and in line with earlier decisions.

The case of *McCollum* v. *Board of Education* (1948), responding to the claims of a rationalistic agnostic, marked the first time in more than a hundred and fifty years since the passage of the First Amendment that the Court found an example of what it considered to be a prohibited law respecting an establishment of religion. Justice Black for the Court found that the religious use of school buildings and the supervision by public-school teachers of religious teachers, brought in under the "released-time" program, represented the sort of "close cooperation" forbidden by the Amendment.[24] Justice Reed in his dissent protested against the recurring use of the metaphor of the wall as a rule of law, and in *Zorach* v. *Clauson* (1952) he seems to have convinced Justice Douglas. Speaking for the Court, Douglas supported "released-time" classes held outside the schoolroom because "cooperation" between state and church represented "the best of our traditions." Otherwise the absurd conclusion would follow, he said, that many public rituals invoking God would flout the First Amendment. "A fastidious atheist or agnostic," he observed, might even object to the appeal to God that opens every session of the Supreme Court.[25]

It was those justices who had fretted about exaggerating the liberties of canvassing Witnesses who were now worried about minimizing the liberties of nonparticipators in the "released-time" cases. Justices Frankfurter and Jackson were deeply concerned that the Court had not been fastidious enough in looking for the elements of coercive pressure exerted on nonparticipators in a program taking place during school hours, whether held in or out of regular classrooms. Jackson was even moved to suspect that the decision would be interesting to students of psychology as an example of the Court's expediency in having drawn back from its decision in *McCollum* because of the pressure of the criticism that the Court had received from organized religious groups.[26] The volume of complaint was growing louder through the 1950's. Late in 1952 both the National Council of Churches, representing believers from thirty Protestant bodies, and the Roman Catholic bishops at their annual meeting stressed the importance of religion in the American tradition and asserted the need for an expansion of religion in educational life in order to avoid the alleged threat of secularism. They did not want a state religion, but they did want a religious state.[27] Jewish organizations, along with most Baptists and Unitarians, consistently opposed the "released-time" programs as well as prayers and Bible reading in the public schools; and some political organizations, like Protestants and Other Americans United for the Separation of Church and State and the American Civil Liberties Union, were actively engaged in working against such measures. The Court, as so often happens, was at the eye of a storm of angry pressure groups.*

During the 1950's the country experienced a quasi-religious revival. Spurred by a foreign policy of containment against Communist power, weekly churchgoing rose to its highest point of 49 per cent in 1958, and Congressmen, responding to the defensive and declamatory mood, put conventional religious references to God in the Pledge of Allegiance and on all currency. A new stamp was issued bearing the national motto "In God We Trust." Dr. Norman Vincent Peale, Bishop Fulton J. Sheen, and Billy Graham were popular preachers on the mass media, while Hollywood spewed forth a flood of Biblical spectaculars. President Eisenhower spoke his own prayer at his inauguration and joined a church, and even cabinet meetings were opened by invoking the divine blessing. The float in the inaugural parade honoring God denoted a church with enlarged photographs of scenes of worship. "The faith is not in God but in faith," as William Lee Miller observed; "we worship our own worshiping."[28] In political terms the new cult of religion was conservative, nationalistic, and self-congratulatory.

This mixture of religion, commerce, patriotism, chauvinism, and partisan politics inevitably made the Supreme Court vulnerable to passionate criticism as it took up the burden of responding to new challenges against the nineteenth-century compromises between the tradition of separation and the dominance of Protestant culture-religion. The Court trod erratically and defensively along a brambly path in the intensely controversial area of education. As it developed its view of the religious clauses in the Bill of Rights, it provoked Mr. Justice Jackson to quip that the "wall of separation" in Jefferson's metaphor threatened to become in judicial opinions "as winding as the famous serpentine wall designed by Mr. Jefferson for the University he founded."[29] He illustrated the point of the jest himself in the *McCollum* case, however, by associating himself with Frankfurter's

---

* A public-opinion poll in June–July, 1952, showed that 79 per cent of Catholics supported aid to parochial schools, in the form of bus transportation and textbooks, while only 41 per cent of Protestants did. Jews and others were almost equally divided over the policy. In all four groups those who favored released-time religious education outnumbered those who did not. The Supreme Court, in short, challenged public opinion much more in the *McCollum* case than it did in the *Everson* case. See John L. Thomas, *Religion and the American People* (Westminster, Md., 1963), pp. 144, 150.

dissent and at the same time concurring with the majority's finding in an opinion devoted mainly to criticism of its reasoning. The peculiar mixture of religion and republicanism, of evangelical and rationalist traditions in American history was driving the Court up against a wall of frustration as it tried to define the "wall of separation" in a society no longer overwhelmingly Protestant.

The idea of religious pluralism surfaced in the late 1950's as spokesmen for various traditions tried to take seriously the fact of radical differences in ultimate philosophical perspectives. "Dialogue" became a watchword in seminars and panels. Outside, however, the embattled groups were much less civil. Catholics often sought to limit other people's opportunities by censorship campaigns or by defenses of statutes against birth control originally passed by Protestants; some Protestants and secularists drew a menacing caricature of Catholicism in America to warn against an allegedly monolithic expanding system of intolerant power; and some Jews provoked bitter community tensions by challenging vestigial remains of a Christian influence in the public schools. Whatever the merit of the justifications for the actions, the spirit of the antagonism was fearful and suspicious.

Even at the most civil and intelligent levels of debate, pluralism seemed to be relativized: its sophisticated spokesmen drew the political consequences from pluralism that one might expect from knowing their religious identifications. In theory, pluralism eschewed any specific religious phrasing of its form, yet there was a Catholic pluralism, a Protestant pluralism, and a Jewish or secular pluralism. At a seminar on Religion in a Free Society held by the Fund for the Republic in 1958, for example, John Courtney Murray, S.J., concluded that "distributive justice" entails a Catholic share in government allocation of school funds; Niebuhr's pluralism included an acceptance of minimal religious observances in the public school and some few fringe benefits in relief of Catholic demands for financial aid to parochial schools; and Leo Pfeffer was sure that the Constitution and "a free society" prohibited all government aid to religiously controlled organizations.[30]

The religiously minded pluralists were especially concerned about the "amiable syncretism" developing in America that diluted the historic gospels into a valuing of religion in general, or elevated a liberalism related to Locke, Jefferson, and John Dewey into a religion of democracy and a celebration of the public school as an incarnation of the ultimate verities of the Constitution. "Rightly understood and valued," as Mrs. Agnes Meyer had put it, "secularism will accelerate its Christian democratic mission to make us all brothers of one another."[31] Religion was the handmaiden of republicanism. In Martin E. Marty's Protestant view, this crystallizing secular tradition was becoming the fourth religion in what a Jewish sociologist, Will Herberg, had called "the Triple Melting Pot" of the three major faiths. Marty, like the other pluralists Murray, Niebuhr, and Herberg, saw this civic religion most vividly emergent in the battle for the schools, and like them he called for "pragmatic, terms-understood cooperation and in a decrease of tension which can come only as each conspiracy re-evaluates its potential contribution to the pluralistic life in what Albert Camus calls *la civilisation du dialogue.*"[32]

Much of the case for pluralism was made by Catholic theorists. It was often, as Daniel Callahan has remarked, "defensive in its thrust: the answering of attacks, the allaying of suspicions and, internally, the theological struggle to convince other Catholics (in Rome and at home) that the American system was one favorable to Catholicism."[33] Politically, the Presidential victory in 1960 of John F. Kennedy seemed to represent the most visible sign of the success of this pluralism. The candidate himself had explicitly identified his own views on the school issue with those of the Supreme Court, upholding tax benefits only in the already accepted areas of buses, lunches, health services and secular textbooks. Even so, the Southern Baptist Convention, the Assemblies of God Church, the American Baptist Association, the Augustana Lutheran Church, the Conservative Baptist Association, the General Association of Regular Baptists, and the National Association of Evangelicals opposed the possibility of a Catholic President. Dr. G. Bromley Oxnam, a leading Methodist; Dr. Eugene Carson Blake, a leading Presbyterian and head of the National Council of Churches; Dr. James A. Pike, Episcopal Bishop of California; and the popular Dr. Norman Vincent Peale all expressed doubts about Kennedy's fidelity to the First Amendment—without any complaint about Protestant influence in the public schools.[34]

The Kennedy forces were convinced that the religious issue, on balance, would favor rather than hinder their candidate, and after the election they could point to the fact that by comparison with Stevenson in 1956 Kennedy had won over a large bloc of Catholic votes and lost no more Protestant votes. Yet Kennedy lagged behind his ticket in the South and Midwest, where Protestants are strongly represented, and the 1956 election was an aberrant Republican landslide when measured against a long-range pattern of voting. On the basis of a hypothetical model of what a Democratic candidate could "normally" be expected to win in 1960, four political scientists have concluded that Kennedy lost more than he gained because of his religious identification. They found in their sample that 90 per cent of the small number of Democrats who had shifted from support of Stevenson to support of Nixon were Protestant, while 60 per cent of the much larger number of Democrats who had shifted from support of Eisenhower to support of Kennedy were Catholic. The defection of Democratic Protestants to Nixon rose according to the regularity of their church attendance and was much greater than their defection to Eisenhower in the previous two elections.[35] Fear of a Catholic President was therefore very much alive in the voting as well as in the campaign. Even if it was not sufficient to deny Kennedy a very close victory, it probably played more of a role than it did in Al Smith's case because the potent immigrant image was not present to complicate the mixture of elements in aversion to Kennedy.

Liberal suspicion of Catholicism was easily justified in terms of European historical realities, but Catholicism in America deserved to be judged on the basis of its own record. (The difference would be evident, for example, in 1964 at the Third Session of the Vatican Council, where the American bishops were scandalized by the maneuvering that led to the postponement of even a mildly phrased Declaration of Religious Liberty, a statement that they had unanimously supported.)[36] Political suspicion of Kennedy's Catholicism was not rooted in the facts. Catholics made their way to the Supreme Court, the Congress, and state governorships without demonstrating the realism of Protestant fears. On the record, city councils and state legislators were much more amenable than national political leaders to accommodating their policies to Catholic needs and doctrines. Like Al Smith, Kennedy believed in "a President whose views on religion are his own private affair," not imposed as a condition for holding office, and he stressed his independence of the Church in public matters. Responding to a grilling by three hundred ministers in Houston, Kennedy conceded that separation between church and state, as comprehended in the First Amendment, was a legitimate issue to raise about a candidate's religion, but on that score he was in agreement with the majority decisions of the Supreme Court.[37] The liberal *New Republic* noted that though the National Catholic Welfare Conference opposed federal aid to education for public schoolteachers' salaries, eight prominent Catholic Senators, including Kennedy, supported passage of the bill.[38]

The stand of barring the door of the White House to a Catholic candidate is ultimately explained, as Arthur Hertzberg pointed out, by the tendency to identify the Presidency with the inner temple of Americanism and to equate that ethos with individualistic Protestantism: "Such Protestantism, in the deepest sense, is the American 'establishment' as Protestants envisage it, and the Presidency is as much its head as the Queen of England is the head and highest exemplar of the Church of England."[39] Thoughtful Jews could see this symbolism more clearly than anyone else. As a group, Jews are more liberal than Catholics on political issues, but they sympathized as voters with Kennedy's point that his critics were imposing an unofficial and unconstitutional religious test for the office.[40]

Kennedy's election proved that a Catholic could be elected to the Presidency, as Daniel Callahan observed, "if he went to Harvard, was a Democrat, had a rich father, a beautiful wife, a finely tuned political machine and some plain good luck."[41] But the event also signified a liberalizing of the coming of age of American Catholics. In the 1950's many had taken satisfaction in identifying themselves with Senator Joseph McCarthy* because his stance as the crusading American foe of Communism, however spurious and shabby in fact, seemed to confirm them ethnically as solid Americans. "In the era of security clearances," as Daniel P. Moynihan wryly remarked, "to be an Irish Catholic became *prima facie* evidence of loyalty. Harvard men were to be checked; Fordham men would do the checking."[42] Kennedy represented a culture hero more on the lines of Al Smith in domestic policy, but his election did not inaugurate a consistent pluralism. Its limits were soon made evident by the intensity of Catholic indignation over the Court's prayer and Bible-reading decisions. Their response showed, liberal Catholics complained, that for many Catholics acceptance of separation between church and state in America was enthusiastic "so long as it does not jeopardize a favored place for religious values in our cultural, political and juridical life."[43] Like so many Protestants, as Callahan noted, they could not understand the satisfaction of the Jew in making the public order freer of Christian symbolism, a sign of his own more equal treatment in American life.

* Gallup polls showed that in January, 1954, 58 per cent of Catholics supported McCarthy and only one bishop publicly took a stand against him. But 49 per cent of Protestants were also favorable to him. See Vincent P. DeSantis, "American Catholics and McCarthyism," *Catholic Historical Review*, 51 (1965), pp. 1–30.

Similarly, some Jewish liberals in 1966 chided Jews for clinging to a traditional legal separationism that in a time of acute need for federal aid to education, or to church-related antipoverty programs, tended to put them in strange company with the laissez-faire dogmatists who had once complained that the government could not take money from them to support education for their neighbor's children. Milton Himmelfarb argued that Jews needed to accept the pluralist principle of promoting other "loci of interest, affection, and influence besides the state" and to recognize that:

All the evidence in America points to education, more than anything else, influencing adherence to democracy and egalitarianism. All the evidence points to Catholic parochial education having the same influence. (And all the evidence points to Catholic anti-Semitism as no greater than Protestant, and possibly less.) Something that nurtures a humane, liberal democracy is rather more important to Jews than 24-karat separationism.[44]

This trenchant plea, however, left the difference between separation and dogmatic separationism unclear by making so much of the compatibility of civil liberty and nonseparation in the English example, which has no written Bill of Rights to complicate the life of judges.

"Good fences make good neighbors" Frankfurter once proposed as a metaphor for church-state relations, but when the fence was built, bad neighbors were quick to make their presence known.[45] The new fence upset earlier compromises between legal separation and the majority's expression of its preference for deference to religion in the schools. The majority on the Court provoked a torrent of angry criticism from most Catholic and some Protestant groups when it moved to strike down prayers and Bible readings from public-school opening ceremonies. These practices, in one form or another, had flourished in a majority of the states. No state had outlawed such exercises by statute, and twelve states had required it in laws almost all passed since 1913. President Kennedy and Governor Nelson A. Rockefeller of New York distinguished themselves among political leaders by refusing to join the chorus of bitter complaint against the Court.[46]

Republican religion in its linkage of Christianity and patriotism was badly prepared to consider the liberty that might be affected by such programs in the eyes of liberals, Jews, or agnostics who sensed in such exercises a "derogation of unbelievers," as Mr. Justice Black had put it in the *Zorach* case.[47] The pressure of the ideal of equality, which the

Court had recognized in psychological terms by striking down statutes supporting racially segregated schools, was emerging also in the religious cases. Atheistic petitioners in a Maryland case, for example, had urged before the state Supreme Court that even voluntary religious exercises tended to render their own beliefs "sinister, alien and suspect," and they protested that self-exile from the ceremonies denied them equal protection of the laws because of the bad effect of their invidious separation from other pupils.[48] This egalitarian concern had earlier also colored the anxieties of several justices in the "released-time" cases. They saw the public school as "a symbol of our secular unity."[49] Division *within* the school was now evident in terms not only of older disputes about the sectarian nature of the King James Bible but also of the new presence of agnostics and atheists, offended by traditional religious belief itself. The Court's willingness to assess the problem of prayers and Bible reading was heartening to Jews, who were now active in bringing suits. The Central Conference of American Rabbis had opposed Christianizing the public schools as early as 1904, but fearing the costs of opposition it had supported "released-time" in 1917, until in 1940 it had concluded that such compromises created "an opening wedge for the violation of the American principle of church-state separation."[50]

The freedom not to be Christian was, indeed, part of Madison's and Jefferson's fight for separation, although it is very doubtful that their tolerance had much resonance in the Congress that debated the First Amendment while allowing a multiple form of Protestant establishment to exist in New England. As late as 1958 a Gallup Poll found that 75 per cent would not vote for a Presidential candidate who was an atheist, while only 25 per cent would not vote for one who was a Catholic.[51] Like racial equality, however, religious freedom is an expanding ideal that discovers new applications in new settings, and the Court in seeking them out was faithful to its traditional role of speaking for the modern implications of organizing ideals that have entered into the original compact. Striving to speak for a public wisdom that rises above the mere sociological facts, it needed to keep vital connection with the informing legacy of traditional principles, current social reality, and the capacity of citizens to redefine principles in a changing world. The difficulty was to perform that demanding task without falsifying the historical record or muddying the flow of Constitutional doctrine.

In 1951 the New York State Board of Regents had recommended

that students recite a nonsectarian prayer, acknowledging dependence upon God and begging the Lord's blessing in one sentence, done in company with the pledge of allegiance to the flag. It was an expression of republican religion in miniature as an attempt to "pass on America's Moral and Spiritual Heritage" in defense against "attacks by an atheistic way of life upon our world."[52] The prayer policy was only a recommendation, its content had been worked out in consultation with representatives of various faiths, and its observance was voluntary. It seemed to avoid the charge of sectarianism, more easily raised by Bible reading, and the charge of coercion, which some justices had seen in the released-time programs. Therefore petitioners, a group of parents aided by the state branch of the American Civil Liberties Union, attacked it on the ground that it violated the ban against laws respecting an establishment; and Mr. Justice Black, speaking for the Court in *Engel* v. *Vitale* (1962), agreed with them.

The majority opinion relied on Madison's view, congenial also to Roger Williams and Isaac Backus, that religion is "too personal, too sacred, too holy, to permit its 'unhallowed perversion' by a civil magistrate."[53] This thought, Black alleged, lay behind the First Amendment, a position that concedes even more to the evangelicals than to the rationalists, who were at least as worried about the effect of religious establishments on republican politics as they were about the effect of governments on conscience. But pietists had been leaders in the fight for a Bill of Rights, persuading Madison himself, for example, that such a supplement to the Constitution was necessary. Recognizing that the extent of government encroachment upon religion by the Regents seemed "relatively insignificant" compared to practices commonplace in the eighteenth century, Black in his peroration quoted Madison on the danger of accepting entering wedges where liberty was at stake.[54]

But if liberty *was* truly threatened, some show of coercion would have been proper. Black insisted that the establishment clause does not depend upon any showing of compulsion and is violated when an "official religion" is established "whether those laws operate directly to coerce nonobserving individuals or not."[55] It is hard to imagine, however, that any official religion could be effected without coercing some believers, particularly if psychological evidence of pressure for social conformity is allowed to enter the scales. History speaks to the point. In 1910, when Catholic parents had protested against the reading of the King James Bible, the singing of hymns, and the recital of the

Lord's Prayer in public school, the Illinois courts had held that even though they were excused from compliance, the exclusion of a pupil in this respect "separates him from his fellows, puts him in a class by himself, deprives him of his equality with the other pupils, subjects him to a religious stigma and places him at a disadvantage in the school, which the law never contemplated."[56] There is no reason why the same logic would not apply in 1962 to Unitarians, agnostics, or atheists who found the Regents' prosy prayer offensive, though it might be argued that the more appropriate Constitutional clause would be that respecting "the equal protection of the laws" in the Fourteenth Amendment.

Coercive stigmata were in evidence in the succeeding cases when the Court, in a scatter of differing opinions, also declared Bible reading in the public schools of Pennsylvania and Maryland to be banned by the First Amendment's clause against laws respecting an establishment. The Schempps of Abington Township, Pennsylvania, for example, brought suit on behalf of their children against Bible reading and prayer in the public schools. The eldest son in this Unitarian family had been compelled to stand during the prayer, shunted to the guidance counselor's office for the rest of the year, and told to attend the devotions during the following year. The circuit judges found the ceremony an indoctrination, aided by the subtle forces of "social suasion" and forbidden by both clauses of the Amendment.[57]

Mr. Justice Tom C. Clark for the Supreme Court, in rejecting the practice of Bible reading in this case and in a similar one raised by an atheist in Maryland, relied instead upon the notion that a valid law under the establishment clause had to have "a secular legislative purpose" and "a primary effect that neither advances nor inhibits religion."[58] He borrowed his concept of neutrality from Judge Alphonso Taft of the Superior Court of Cincinnati, who had eventually been upheld by the state's supreme court in his dissent of 1870 on behalf of the right of a city school board to end the practice of Bible reading and hymn singing in the public schools. Ohio's constitution forbade any legal preference to any sect, prohibited tax funds for parochial schools, and also made religion "essential to good government" and thus required the legislature to pass laws to protect all denominations and to encourage schools. It was clear to Judge Taft, a Unitarian, that the school board was right to find that the use of the King James Bible and Protestant hymns, an offense to Catholics and also Jews, created a legal preference that was Constitutionally forbidden. The dissent was suitable to Mr. Justice Clark's case some ninety years later because Taft was sensitive not only to the objections of Catholics and Jews but also emphasized in his *obiter dicta* the fact that, despite current opinion, it was "not a constitutional idea" that a rationalist or atheist has "less conscience than the believer in any one of the accepted forms of faith." In his opinion the state's "mantle of protection and encouragement" charitably covered rationalists as well as Protestants, Catholics, and Jews and without "peculiar favor" to any of them. Nor would it make the petitioners' case any better if several sects agreed "in a certain degree and kind of religious instruction and worship," as a large majority of the community: "So long as there are any who do not believe in or approve of their mode of religious worship or instruction, they can not insist that it is not sectarian, or that any non-believing tax-payer shall be compelled to submit to it in the common schools."[59]

Clark's intention was to stabilize the Court's wandering course in a summation that would hold past, present, and future together within a conceptual order, but in fact five other justices felt obligated to give their own differing reasons, and the concurring opinions stressed ideas of "accommodation" and lack of "involvement" as explanations of what "neutrality" really meant.[60] A legal historian has pointed to the Court's unpredictable path:

To insist that the suggested equalities must be respected—that the non-religious heretic must be given the same dispensations from displeasing law as those that are made available to religious non-conformists—fulfills two significant impulses of today's Court. It continues the movement toward equality and it furthers the Jeffersonian objective of denying special favors to religion. That happy convergence of two dogmatisms has not, however, always led the Court to reach the result which the one or the other would seem to require.

In holding that a Seventh-Day Adventist, whose faith does not permit her to work on Saturday, cannot be denied unemployment compensation if employment without Saturday work is not available, or that a juror may refuse to serve for religious reasons, the Court gave special sanction to religious nonconformity, but this sensitivity to religious conscience is difficult to reconcile, as Mark DeWolfe Howe has pointed out, "with the principles of cold neutrality so recently enunciated in the cases on prayer and Bible-reading."[61] Sometimes, as he suggests, the Court seems to respond to the evangelicals' high estimate of religious motivation, sometimes to the Jeffersonian distrust of the influence of organized religion on society.

If this ambivalence seismographically registers a double line of influence in the actual making of the eighteenth-century legal tradition of religious freedom, it does not meet the charge, raised by some Catholic theorists, that in repairing so often to the metaphor of the wall, the Court tends to make normative an individualistic theory of church-state relationships especially favorable to Baptists and deists. In this light, genuine neutrality would require a legal formulation that did not so paradoxically run the risk of establishing a sectarian position in the very act of defending disestablishment. The purpose of the ban against laws respecting an establishment, from this point of view, is not to reflect a religious or secular metaphysics of church-state relations but to articulate a political and practical rule that would be suitable for a pluralistic society. Such a rule, as the Reverend John Courtney Murray argued, would have to "abandon the poetry of those who would make a religion out of freedom of religion and a dogma out of separation of church and state. We have to talk prose, the prose of the Constitution itself, which is an ordinary legal prose having nothing to do with doctrinaire theories."[62]

Prose is not so easy to speak as it might appear. Murray concluded from his understanding of the Amendment that there is every reason for applying in the area of education "the fully developed principle of accommodation of the public service to the genuine spiritual needs of our religious people." He himself admitted that it "will not be easy" on this basis to draw the line between accommodation "in aid of religion in education" and "unconstitutional aid to religion itself."[63] Apart from the long tradition in the states of sharply separating public and parochial schooling for tax purposes, it is hard to see how the Court, for all its serpentine wandering on the wall, could better its record by boldly making "the spiritual needs of a religious people" the direct object of governmental service. Politically, such a step would further harden rather than melt the prejudices of religiously varied traditions, even though it might license a program of federal aid to education, now blocked by dispute over the limits of separation.

Mr. Justice Douglas had proclaimed Americans to be "a religious people," but he fell into his own sort of poetry in saying that our institutions "presuppose a Supreme Being."[64] The sober legal prose of the Constitution never mentions God or any of His philosophical aliases. For that matter Justice Douglas himself, perhaps scandalized by the hearty approval given to his opinion in *Zorach* by Catholics pressing for aid to parochial schools, concluded ten years later, in a notable lurch of changed direction, that *all* the usual examples of financial aid to religion, apparently including even the slogan "In God We Trust" on the coins, are unconstitutional. Douglas now cited Mr. Justice Rutledge's philosophy of Madisonian separation and plumped for "neutrality," rather than "cooperation," in order to avoid "divisive" influences among "a religious people."[65] Anyone looking for a compass in his version of the historical situation finds a needle drawn to both poles.

History itself, however, pointed in more than one direction. Most states did develop constitutional provisions against financial aid to parochial schools, but the federal government had financially aided religious groups in setting up and running schools for liberated blacks in the Reconstruction period, and some of these schools, particularly those of the Methodist Freedmen's Aid Society, were also churches. An official government report of the missionary effort to educate the freedmen conceded that "the educational was always subordinate and tributary to the need of the religious uplift and moral reformation of these people."[66] Ironies abounded in a situation in which modern Catholics urged an equal right to participate in educational subsidies while at the same time abandoning their old protests against public-school religious exercises in favor of a nonsectarian solution worked out first by Horace Mann, a Unitarian, and challenged in the modern period by aggrieved Unitarians. Secularists and Protestants, for their part, who saw in every measure that might also benefit Catholics a fatal breach of a sacred wall were themselves defensively clinging to an archaic past in which Catholics had played only a small and suspect role. Given these anomalies and prejudices, the Court had its work cut out for it, even if it could have better based its findings in history and in logic than it often did.

The Court was not alone in its agonized struggle to find a dominant consensus that would stabilize the issue. By 1965 even traditional Jewish agreement on separation was split by the support of Orthodox Jews for federal aid to secular aspects of religious schools, a position increasingly favored also by the American Jewish Committee. The opposition of the National Catholic Welfare Conference and American bishops to any bill of federal aid for only public institutions stymied legislation until in 1965 the Johnson administration was able to secure broad support, including that of the Protestant National Council of

Churches, for the Elementary and Secondary Education Act and the Higher Education Act. These measures loosely incorporated a more or less conscious acceptance of the "child benefit" solution that pluralists had supported. They aimed at improving the educational lot of the specially disadvantaged, including parochial-school children with regard to certain remedial and welfare services, and at the level of higher education provided federal scholarships to needy and deserving students whether in public or nonprofit colleges.[67] To this extent a majority consensus, in practice, was achieved in Congress.

The serpentine wall of separation seemed fated to wind on in the middle ground between two flawed polar views of what the First Amendment historically meant. In 1971, having upheld tax exemption for church property used for religious worship, the Court sustained federal construction grants for parochial-school buildings used for secular purposes in the area of higher education, but it rejected state reimbursement of parochial-school teachers' salaries for secular subjects, trying to find in the degree of involvement that was entailed a criterion for distinguishing between valid and invalid programs. The majority opinion candidly confessed that the Court could "only dimly perceive the boundaries of permissible government activity" in the sensitive area of education, and it found the "wall" to be "a blurred, indistinct and variable barrier depending on all the circumstances of a particular relationship."[68]

It was all too dim and blurred for the minority. Just as they had seen no Constitutional differences in the released-time cases, so here they saw an equal danger of meddling surveillance entailed in both programs of subsidy, if sacred and secular purposes were to be clearly divided in parochial schools. No such policing had been required in the aid given to parents regarding buses. Dissenters also pointed out, in a previous case, that for New York to give parochial schools the initiative in suggesting which secular textbooks were to be used was not equivalent to providing the same service to all pupils, as had been the case in Louisiana when the Court first had upheld a textbook provision of aid.[69] These nice differences were significant if "the circumstances of a particular relationship" were taken into account, but the majority had its own less strict version of what circumstances were important, and its reading hinged more on the degree of surveillance required than on the presence or absence of it. Only a rash historian would predict what degree of involvement the Court in future would find intolerable. The Court was well launched on the dubious career, as Mr. Justice Frankfurter had feared, of sustaining whatever five judges thought was reasonable in the area of aid to schools. Consensus about the meaning of separation between church and state was no longer alive, least of all on the Court itself.

There was much more of a consensus, however, on the "civic religion." Opposition to the prayer decision was bitter enough to produce evasion of the law, sometimes encouraged by politicians in Congress who read prayers into the *Congressional Record* for use by dissident school officials, and a movement was launched to restore school prayers by amending the Constitution. The absurdities of the backlash produced by this judicial opinion were demonstrated in New Jersey when a mayor, who hung "One Nation Under God" pennants on four municipal flagpoles in response to the urgings of two Catholic organizations, was accused by a member of the Americans for Democratic Action and the American Civil Liberties Union (with their support) of violating the laws regulating the display of the flag.[70] The mixture of religion and patriotism that Tocqueville had noted in America was a powerful one, and righteous sticklers over small signs of deference, whether they were believers or nonbelievers, could uncover the intensities of feeling involved by challenges devoid of charitable tact or a sense of proportion on both sides.

Large numbers of Americans could not see any difference between practicing patriotism and practicing nondenominational religion in the public school, because the two were entangled for them in a civic religion that had long been alive in the customs of the people and sometimes could be eloquently moving, as it was in the great addresses of Lincoln. In November, 1971, with a Republican Baptist supporting it and a Democratic Catholic priest rejecting it, contrary to the usual pattern, an Amendment proposal for voluntary prayer and meditation in the schools was defeated in the House by a margin of twenty-eight votes.[71] To this slim extent the Court had earned reluctant consent for its decision by the inability of an older consensus to find a large enough majority in Congress. The Court in this area, however, added more burdens to the meaning of the establishment clause by basing judgments on its opaque phrasing rather than on the more visible effect the "civic religion" had on the equal treatment of non-Christians, agnostics, and atheists. It was not only hard to see the eighteenth century clearly in judicial versions of history; it was difficult as well to grasp firmly the twentieth-century facts.

In Tocqueville's eyes, republican religion was expressed by a Catholic priest he had met on a voyage across Lake Michigan: "I repeat, the less religion and its ministers are mixed with civil government, the less part will they take in political dissensions, and the more power religious ideas will gain."[72] That position, which Jefferson, Madison, and Baptists would also have heartily supported in principle, was no longer self-evident to many contemporary Americans. A critic of Tocqueville's thesis might point to England as an example of a liberal democracy, despite the presence of a state church, with civic tolerance and social stability. These achievements were, however, the product of a history without great ethnic diversity and with massive contemporary disaffection from the churches. It was Tocqueville's point, furthermore, not that state churches frustrated democracy but that they frustrated the growth of religion itself: "In Europe, Christianity has been intimately united to the powers of the earth. Those powers are now in decay, and it is, as it were, buried under their ruins. The living body of religion has been bound down to the dead corpse of superannuated polity; cut but the bonds that restrain it, and it will rise once more."[73]

History supports Tocqueville's observation with modern statistics. Weekly attendance at all churches in England declined from about 40 per cent of the adult population in 1851 to 10 per cent in 1964, while in America the comparable figure for 1964 had declined only four percentage points from the peak of 49 per cent in the previous decade.[74] In England religious exercises are common in all schools and denominational schools receive state funds, practices that are generally accepted without even being considered part of the special relation between the Church of England and the state. A dissenting voice to the recent Report of the Bishops' Commission on Church and State (1970) doubted, however, that the Church of England idiom in English life represents any realistic pastoral opportunity, being rather a folk religion, "a comfortable mix of ancestral attitudes (everything from astrological superstition to yesterday's liberalism), inconsistent both with each other and with the historic gospel." In this context of the third generation of "urban indifference," a man who involves himself with the church and practices his faith does so "not with but against the conventions of society and increasingly against the grain of his cultural inheritance." The church-state relationship as a relationship between centralized authorities formed links that would have to be "modified, broken, before the Church can in any way begin to release, or to feel within its structures the energies of its 'ordinary' congregations."[75] Tocqueville would have recognized the point as one of his own.

The American political struggle for parochial-school funds may aid the process of secularization itself as religious schools meet standards set by the government. Even theology itself in the 1960's became enthusiastically secularized, stimulated by the doctrines of Dietrich Bonhoeffer, Paul Tillich, Dr. John Robinson, and Harvey G. Cox. In this process the redefined Christian positions lost so much of their specific traditional content that it was possible for critics to point out that there is nothing these theologians affirmed which a convinced secularist need deny, except the strange language in which they said it.[76] At the same time, religious groups were turning toward the secular in order to bring moral pressure to bear on social and political causes, but this process also expressed a disenchantment with secular authority and a search for higher standards. Any reading of the development as a linear process of secularization would be too simple and premature. The civil-rights movement engendered challenges to the churches as the abolitionist movement had done in the nineteenth century, but it too drew on religious ideology and commitments in the new struggle over the place of the Negro in American society.

The Court itself responded to the secularization of conscience in 1961 by invalidating Maryland's archaic requirement of a belief in God for all state officeholders, including notaries public.[77] The ban on laws respecting an establishment was the legal refuge for agnostics and atheists as well as for believing Jews. Only in some cases, involving Jehovah's Witnesses and Adventists, did the Court seem to value religious more than secular immunities under the First Amendment's "free exercise" clause.[78] The Court put a burden on the state to justify the exercise of its ordinary police powers, if they conflicted with religious scruples, in upholding an Adventist's right to unemployment benefits, despite her refusal to take Saturday work. It acted not because the law suppressed the believer's right to believe, or to act on belief, but because it made the exercise of that right more difficult. Yet this preference for religious motivation was later qualified by a ruling in a case on conscientious objection to military service that the internal demands of conscience are just as compelling as the externally derived commandments of God traditionally have been in the eyes of the law, despite Congress's stipulation in 1948 that it meant to exempt only those whose training and belief was in a religion of "a Supreme Being." The Court interpreted this theistic qualification out of existence by accepting for itself a broad view of religion, citing in support fashionable secularizing theologies, that virtually equates it with moral seriousness. Yet it has drawn back from following this logic when it points clearly to accepting selective conscientious objection to particular wars.[79] However muddied in logic, the drift of the Court's judgments was to respond to new demands for recognition of the secular conscience as part of its "neutral" role, even though in upholding Sunday laws it dramatized the fact that modern societies are never purely neutral but are inclined in some direction by previous religious forces, which have become largely secularized.

In the new pluralism, not yet internalized by many citizens, modern America differs from the time when Tocqueville was impressed with the widespread unquestioned status of Christianity. Tocqueville knew that while Christians in America mainly accepted democratic and republican institutions, at least as those existed in the 1830's, they often did differ about governmental policies. But the conflicting intense responses of Protestant, Catholic, and Jewish groups to the issues of birth control, abortion, aid to parochial schools, and public-school religious exercises did not illustrate in practice his assertion that American sects "all agree in respect to the duties which are due from man to man."[80] Tocqueville hoped to find tranquility and stability for a restless acquisitive society in the powerful presence of disestablished religion in America; but as the Supreme Court began to deal with the legal meaning of the religious clauses in the First Amendment, neither quality was very appropriate to describe the actual situation because the consensual meaning of the tradition of nonestablishment was itself in question.

Despite all the acrimony of debate, however, the emergence of Jehovah's Witnesses, Catholics, Jews, and agnostics into the domain of the modern Court's Constitutional concerns was marked by much less violence and disruption of democratic procedures than was the case with the effect of its efforts to undertake judgments respecting the deeper deprivations and injustices suffered by American blacks. In this comparative sense, Tocqueville was right to emphasize that the true danger of fundamental divisiveness and instability in the republic stemmed from conflicts over race and not religion. He also foresaw that the tendency of American society was "to become more and more democratic" under the pressure of the ideal of equality in a restless society.[81] The emerging but contested new pluralism with respect to religion and the public order demonstrated his prophetic power. Whether pluralism could find a rationale that was more than the tug and haul of pressure groups was still moot. Without it, however, the question of legitimacy, the Court's special province, would have only shaky answers.

The difficulty for the prestige of the Court was that its struggle to find a pluralistic view of separation and free exercise was contemporary with its bold attempt to reverse the tradition of discrimination and segregation in racial matters. The vision of a modern consensus on the relations between religion and the public order was just becoming clearer when the conflicts over the place of the Negro in American society became more intense and disruptive than at any time since the years before the Civil War. The insecurities of that tension would tend to foster social nostalgias for an older America that had not been forced to confront a radically pluralistic world.

XIX

Modern Prophets in Babylon

Tocqueville admired a religion that was politically liberal and morally conservative, and the eighteenth-century pietists and the nineteenth-century abolitionists fitted this model. The late nineteenth-century liberal or socialist social gospel still had similar characteristics, but increasingly in the middle of the twentieth century the guardians of traditional morality saw themselves as embattled defenders of conservative theology and politics as well. At their shrillest they saw republican religion in xenophobic and fundamentalist terms, and they were politically attracted to the far right of the Republican Party, expressing a movement with roots in a hostile response to the welfare liberalism and alliance diplomacy of the New Deal and its Democratic heirs.

The liberal social gospel of the pre-World War I years had been flawed by its conspicuous neglect of the issue of the Negro's position in American society. It was a revisionist critic of the social gospel, Reinhold Niebuhr, who had most articulately called attention in 1932 to the need for applying a moral and political strategy on behalf of Negro rights. In the late 1950's Martin Luther King, Jr., a Baptist preacher who had studied Rauschenbusch and Niebuhr, reinvigorated the social gospel with dramatic effect. At the same time, while the liberal social gospel in white churches was bitterly opposed by a fundamentalist conservatism, in the Northern cities alienated ghetto blacks found in the Muslim religion a conservative morality, an anti-Christian theology, and a sectarian withdrawal from politics. Right-wing white Protestants clung to a mythicized vision of an American past; the Black Muslims dreamed of a mythical future where King's goals of liberty, justice, and equality would be realized in a separate black territory on American soil. The alignment that Tocqueville favored between liberal politics and conservative morality was no longer applicable to the new conflicts in American society.

Fundamentalist opponents of the social gospel often complained about politicizing religion, but they were deeply engaged in the same process. They set flinty faces against ecumenism, liberal theology, liberal politics, socialism, foreign aid, the United Nations, and the civil-rights movement. In the Protestant underworld, ultra right-wing leaders politically exploited religious literalism and parochialism. The American Council of Christian Churches, led by Carl McIntire, a defrocked fundamentalist Presbyterian, mingled anti-Communist, anti-Semitic, anti-Catholic, and anti-Negro themes with antimodernism in theology. Protofascist demagogues, such as Gerald B. Winrod, Joseph P. Kamp, and Gerald L. K. Smith, formed a Christian Nationalist Party that marched for the candidacy of General Douglas MacArthur at the Republican convention in 1952 and peddled anti-Semitic propaganda, denigrating Eisenhower as the symbol of the "internationalist" tendencies they abhorred.[1]

In the Truman and Eisenhower years the official Cold War policy of containment of Soviet power was easily inflated by right-wing advocates into a crusade against a caricatured Communist ideology and an obsessive fascination with the specter of internal subversion at home. This movement of the half-educated gave itself Christian airs in the itinerant evangelism of the Reverends James Fifield, Fred C. Schwarz, and Billy James Hargis. Such efforts were not confined to the lunatic fringe but increasingly infiltrated high schools, especially in the South and West, and also military training centers, often with the support of high-ranking officers, who were responsive to Defense Department policies for mobilizing opinion. Atypically, neither Fifield nor Robert Welch, founder of the John Birch Society, was a fundamentalist, and the latter admired "the Baptist John Birch, the Catholic Hilaire Belloc, and the agnostic Thomas Jefferson" because they all opposed "the degenerative disease of collectivism."[2] Christianity and liberty had contracted an American alliance, in Tocqueville's theory, but in fact during the Cold War years the idea of liberty in these reactionary quarters was shorn of its historical connections with ideals of equality or justice and identified with an archaic nationalistic capitalism. For a spokesman like McIntire even Secretary of State John Foster Dulles, despite his outbursts of similar missionary-style rhetoric against "neutralism" and "international Communism," was seen as a radical. McIntire's

Council welcomed Congressional investigation of alleged Communist clergymen as a strategy of warfare against the ecumenical and social-gospel elements he had always fought within American Protestantism.[3]

At the respectable conservative center of the political spectrum the popular evangelist Billy Graham preached a Biblical premillennialist pessimism about the world, making social reform irrelevant to the imminent "last days." Ignoring his apocalyptic Biblical theology, the public and the politicians blandly assimilated him for his traditional Protestant belief that "America is truly the last bulwark of Christian civilization."[4] Graham's remarkable success as a television star and friend of men in power was not a matter of cynicism but of the assimilative power of a culture that had long lost any widespread sense of theological tradition but wished to buttress political conservatism with a vague nostalgia for "the old-time religion."

Political fundamentalism grew in the 1950's and 1960's not only because of the fears and suspicions exploited by right-wing Republican obsession with internal subversion but also because of the more visible emergence of the non-Anglo-Saxon minorities, who had benefited from the liberal administrations favored by social-gospel ministers. Threatened by a sense of displacement from a previously enjoyed dominance, many old-line Protestants, especially in the South and West, were shocked to find themselves no longer in "a Protestant nation with a prevailing Anglo-Saxon tradition" but rather in "a pluralistic nation with a Protestant tradition."[5] The concept of the new pluralism, which theorists had developed to dissolve anti-Catholic prejudices, had to be expanded to include the highly vocal and belligerent minority of Protestant fundamentalists. The embittered scene would have bewildered Tocqueville and undermined his own confidence in identifying American religion with only benign effects.

Tocqueville neglected in his own time the role of crusading minorities inspired by religious beliefs, who would find themselves in tense opposition to the "established" culture because of their efforts to bring to bear on political life the reforming possibilities of a social gospel that was keenly sensitive to American failures to incarnate ideals of liberty and equality in new contexts of injustice. Ever since 1954, when the Supreme Court outlawed legally enforced racial segregation in the public schools, the modern movement that best illustrated this historical function of democratic religion was the struggle for fulfillment of Negro rights. The best-known spokesmen for the Negro in this period

—Martin Luther King, Jr., James Farmer, James Baldwin, Malcolm X—were sons of clergymen; King and Malcolm X were themselves ministers. The Court was responsive to a secular tradition of democratic rights before the law, for which the NAACP was the oldest and most effective and consistent advocate, but religious ideology was profoundly involved in the thinking of the leaders who had the most charismatic influence on popular movements.

The American Negro had always found in the church a focus for his group life. In slavery it had been his means of institutionalizing an associative life independent of his white masters, and the Biblical stories had offered moving parables of liberation, both historical and mythical, activist and consolatory, with which he could identify his own condition and destiny. Ultimately the Christian legacy was ambiguous. King found it a resource for struggle and emancipation; Malcolm X saw it as part of the white man's emasculation of the black man. Both had sufficient reasons to support their stand. The contrasts in their social origins and careers, as well as in their ideologies, were profound; but history, by ending their lives in the horror of assassination, finally framed them together as tragic heroes, portrayed on a vast canvas that linked them emotionally in American consciousness to the traumatic political murder of Lincoln and the Kennedys.

The strategy of nonviolent resistance, which Niebuhr had proposed for Negro emancipation in 1932, came into life in 1955 at Montgomery, Alabama, "the Cradle of the Confederacy," when Mrs. Rosa Parks, a Negro seamstress, refused to give up her seat on a crowded bus to a white man. She was arrested and charged with violation of segregation laws. She had once been a secretary of the local NAACP, and it was the president of the local branch of that organization who first suggested the response of the boycott. In his moving story of the Montgomery movement, King noted that he had not originated or inspired the protest but only "responded to the call of the people for a spokesman." The movement itself consolidated his philosophy and turned it into "a commitment to a way of life," resolving in practical terms his earlier intellectual problems in formulating a theory of nonviolence.[6]

Moving through Morehouse College, Crozer Theological Seminary, and Boston University from 1944 to 1954, King sympathetically encountered the ideas of Thoreau, Rauschenbusch, Niebuhr, Gandhi, Hegel, and philosophical personalism. Eclectically, he assimilated them partially to his own perspective. Inspired by Rauschenbusch's concern for relating social and economic life to the gospel, King learned from Niebuhr to criticize Rauschenbusch's optimism about human nature and history, though he usually shared it in his public speeches. He also accepted Niebuhr's criticism of pacifism to the extent of agreeing with him that the pacifist would "have a greater appeal if he did not claim to be free from the moral dilemmas that the Christian nonpacifist confronts." But King felt that Niebuhr mistakenly confined pacifism to "passive nonresistance to evil expressing naïve trust in the power of love," while Gandhi saw that true pacifism was "nonviolent resistance to evil" in which courageous acceptance of the opponent's violence may arouse his shame and "bring about a transformation and change of heart." Gandhi was an exemplar of a reformer lifting "the love ethic of Jesus" to the status of "a powerful and effective social force on a large scale," and King came to feel that nonviolent resistance was "the only morally and practically sound method open to oppressed people in their struggle for freedom."[7]

King's account of Niebuhr, however, blurs the fact that *Moral Man and Immoral Society* carefully distinguished nonviolent resistance from nonresistance, and it specifically acknowledged that "the spirit of moral goodwill" in dealing with an opponent had "tremendous" social and moral effects in Gandhi's campaigns, which were also characterized by realistic political compromises with standards of "pure nonresistance." Furthermore, Niebuhr found Gandhi's methods especially appropriate to the emancipation of the Negro minority in America because nonresistance and violent rebellion were both hopeless strategies. Niebuhr also doubted that the secular imagination alone could develop a Gandhi-style strategy for America, and King eloquently proved his point. Niebuhr recognized the utility of civil disobedience, boycotts, and strikes, but since they could also result in coercive and destructive consequences "not totally dissimilar from those of violence," he did not want to give them the moral prestige of a Biblically sanctioned ethic of love that spurned all coercion.[8] King implicitly acknowledged the relevance of Niebuhr's analysis by his own awareness that White Citizens Councils in the South had often used boycotts as economic reprisals against blacks and liberal whites who protested segregationist defiance of the law. For this reason, in Montgomery King had emphasized Thoreau's principle of noncooperation with an evil system, rather than a strategic purpose of running the bus company out of business in order to bring it to terms.[9]

In fact, nonviolent resistance worked admirably as a discipline for King's supporters, but it did not shame their opponents, who resorted to misrepresentation, legal harassment, and bombings. The boycott was also supplemented by legal suit for redress of grievances, and the federal courts finally declared the city's segregation policies unconstitutional. Moreover, King himself admitted that most of Montgomery's Negroes did not believe in nonviolence "as a philosophy of life" but rather as "a technique."[10] King made that technique luminously actual, however, with eloquent dignity and in courageous disregard of his safety, because it had become for him a step toward his Christian vision of a reconciled, racially integrated, socially just community.[11] Traditional pacifists, like the Reverend Glenn Smiley and Bayard Rustin of the Fellowship of Reconciliation (which King had never joined), probably did much to consolidate his own theoretical position when they helped him to plan and prepare the black community for the experience of integrated busing after the legal victory had been won.

Among the rank and file, secular idealism was more activist than religious. The student-initiated sit-ins and the Freedom Rides carried further the use of civil-disobedience techniques against the pattern of enforced segregation that the federal courts were systematically declaring unconstitutional. A study of 176 selected white civil-rights activists from four different organizations showed, however, that in 1964 less than 1 per cent saw religion as a means of bringing about full equality, and only 32 per cent considered themselves to be "very religious," though not orthodox.[12] Among blacks in general a similar story could be told for the same date. A very large majority of blacks polled believed that King, of all black leaders, had done most to help Negroes, but black opposition to discrimination and segregation rose with the decline of the sense of importance of religion and was highest among those least conventionally religious in belief and in attendance at church. Even in the South only 35 per cent of the activists in the Congress of Racial Equality, which sponsored the Freedom Rides campaign, were morally, not merely pragmatically, committed to nonviolence.[13]

At his greatest public moments, as in his memorable address at the grand March on Washington in 1963, organized by Bayard Rustin, King splendidly orchestrated the exultant emotions of his hearers, the libertarian and egalitarian rhetoric of Jefferson and Lincoln, the imagery of the Bible, the folk music of the American Negro, and the public-speaking techniques of the Southern Baptist preacher. Like Lincoln, he wove democratic and Christian themes together to interpret for the nation the growing American racial crisis. King's ground note was always optative, but his effects were not at all merely rhetorical. He constantly pressured the administrations of Kennedy and Johnson to pass legislation that would prove the reality of their verbal commitments; and his demonstrations, far from merely evaporating in enthusiasm or masochistically suffering the wounds of barbarous police actions, brought major legislative responses in civil-rights bills on public accommodations, voting rights, and housing.

The high point of his success was also, however, the moment of fission within the liberation movement: the March from Selma to Montgomery, Alabama. Set upon by police tear gas, cattle prods, and clubs, some blacks hurled back rocks. Refusing to violate a federal injunction or to risk more violence, King upset his militant critics in the Student Nonviolent Coordinating Committee and CORE by privately accepting an agreement on the federal government's terms to turn back the second march after crossing a bridge in Selma. He knew that President Johnson was about to announce a voting-rights bill in an address to Congress, in which the Texan remarkably identified himself with the civil-rights movement by using the title of its theme song, "We Shall Overcome." Two days later a federally authorized and protected march to Montgomery, with the participation of celebrities and clergy from all major faiths, was led by a one-legged white on crutches, a black and a white flag-bearer, and a bandaged black fife player, piping "Yankee Doodle." In Montgomery, where the civil-rights movement had begun a decade earlier, King preached to some thirty thousand listeners the social and religious message of "the glory of the coming of the Lord."[14] It was a moment of incarnated hope that represented a modern climax in the tradition of republican religion, and it is already historically distant in a time no longer capable of such symbolism, linking a historical civic religion to the ideal of racial equality in liberty.

Already, however, in the eyes of King's critics within other militant Negro organizations, he had been too cautious, or too accommodating to the Johnson administration. Furthermore, in 1966 Stokely Carmichael would raise the slogan of "black power" during a Mississippi campaign, and King's philosophy would seem increasingly irrelevant or harmful to the new breed of black militants. At the same time King's move to a morally consistent and perceptive public attack on the administration's Vietnam war divided his own followers and alarmed his more conservative allies. In the North the technique of a large-scale demonstration, others reasoned, might only serve to mobilize white resistance prematurely. White Northern "backlash" against the Negro movement had grown with the fears and anxieties produced by the despairing and destructive ghetto riots, ever since the explosion in Watts during the summer following the Selma-Montgomery march. The logic of exposing moral evil and appealing to guilt in whites was increasingly ineffective in matters where economic interests, rather than Constitutional rights, were at stake. King's last campaigns were centered on the issue of poverty, but it was an issue on which the optimistic meliorism of the social gospel, which he had inherited from Rauschenbusch, had proved inadequate before.

King's moralism, like Gandhi's, was linked to a political awareness and judgment, however, for which few gave him credit. When President Johnson decided not to seek re-election, King himself realized that the resolution of the war and the reappraisal of domestic poverty were "suddenly freed of their taboos. A Democratic victory in 1968 —whether by Humphrey, Kennedy, or McCarthy—would almost certainly result in a national rededication to the issues Martin was courageously expounding." Just as he had called for a moratorium on demonstrations during the elections of 1964 in order not to give any ammunition to Senator Goldwater, so now to guard against any disorders that might aid Richard Nixon, he had decided to postpone the Poor People's Campaign, which his successor ineffectively carried out after King was murdered by an escaped white convict and made "free at last" in Memphis.[15] If Lincoln was basically a political man with a religious sensibility, King was basically a religious man with a political sensitivity. Both harbored a brooding prescience of their own violent deaths, a prevision that seemed macabre at the time and a sign of tragic insight later. King in retrospect is a moving exemplar of American democratic religion, but the point was not widely appreciated in his time. In 1967, even before he had taken his position against the Vietnam war, only 29 per cent of a national sampling of whites agreed that he was "an outstanding example of making Christianity relevant and meaningful for our day."[16] In this failure of perception a majority of his white contemporaries were also like Lincoln's. Only assassination could canonize both men and draw another kind of veil over historical reality.

The emergence of black-power militancy had alarmed King by its contempt for collaboration with whites and for nonviolent doctrine. But he saw the validity of the new emphasis on black pride, black history, and the need for black leverage in economics and politics. His last book, *Where Do We Go From Here: Chaos or Community?*, reflected his assimilation of these themes, as well as the new stress on economic issues in the Northern cities. Already he had the bitter experience, however, of having been jeered in a Chicago mass meeting by young blacks. His book did not abandon his former faith, but it did have a stronger emphasis on the realism of his tactics and on the pragmatic weaknesses of his opponents' exaggeration of the capacities of separatism. King now found Niebuhr prophetic for having pointed in 1932 to the usefulness of the boycott; and whereas he had once minimized the coercive aspects of the boycott in Montgomery, he now stressed its practical effectiveness in Birmingham.[17] He was proud of his organization's developing strategy of Operation Breadbasket, using boycotts, tenant unions, and rent strikes on economic issues. Devastating riots in several cities in 1967, a few months after the publication of his book, seemed to dramatize, however, a bitter end to the era of nonviolent demonstrations. Increasingly, King's repute among younger blacks was eclipsed by their admiration for Malcolm X, slain by Muslims during a meeting of his own organization two years before. The new hero was himself a minister, as dedicated as King, but he was the product of a religion native to big Northern cities and to those thoroughly disenchanted with Christianity.

American Negro Christianity in the store-front churches of the cities was often pietistic and Calvinistic in temper, but without the commitment to secular reform characteristic of earlier expressions of a religion that was also based on what Edwards had called "a sense of the heart." More often, the civic leadership of the Negro communities came from the churches of higher social prestige, Episcopalian, Presbyterian, or Congregational. The more emotional forms of faith, as with many white believers in the South, stressed personal sins and the rewards of the afterlife, rather than a politically relevant social gospel. Increasingly in the twentieth century, secular institutions supplemented or supplanted the social functions once virtually monopolized by the churches. The style of lower-class black Christianity both reflected and sustained a low level of expectation regarding the possibilities of social amelioration.[18]

The Black Muslims occupied a position that both overlapped and challenged the conventional piety of store-front churches. Like them, it stressed personal virtues of a self-improving kind; like them, it did not preach participation in social reform. But unlike them, it insisted on the social injustice of the black man's position in American society, and it rejected the consolatory Christian hope of an immortal life. Its political hopes and remedies were worldly but were vaguely specified as a nationalism obscurely projected into an eschatological future.

The Mormons had also been separatist to the point of seeking insulation from persecution by the gentiles and autonomy for their own social and economic life in Utah, but they had participated in national beliefs about America as the promised land, and Joseph Smith had once announced his candidacy for the Presidency. They were also successful in evangelizing people in Britain and Scandinavia. To some extent the Mormons also shared in the cultural prejudice of limiting the opportunities of American Negroes. Their prophet had deciphered an Egyptian papyrus so as to use it as authority for denying Negroes the opportunity to become priests, or full church members. The Muslims remained a special case of a persisting sect, formed on racial lines, with the consolatory dream of a native sovereign soil, located not, as with Jews, in another country but within American territory. It is important not for its size but for its measure of despair in the Northern cities and for its leader, who eventually became a spokesman for an influential secular black separatism, which retained some of the crucial characteristics of the religion he had once preached.

Pollsters found, late in 1964, that an overwhelming majority of sampled Afro-Americans thought that King, of all black leaders, was doing the most for the Negro. This finding was true even for New York City.[19] Yet by early 1965, when Minister Malcolm X of the Black Muslims was murdered in Harlem, King's most eloquent ideological opponent had increasingly come to dominate discussions of the movement for black liberation. *The Autobiography of Malcolm X,* which has gone into more than twenty paperback printings since 1966, has been one of the most widely read books on college campuses. In black and white intellectual circles the dominant opinion steadily formed that Malcolm X had relegated King to an archaic, ineffective role. The voice of the ghetto, of true black dignity, of uncompromising radicalism, of black nationalism, of Pan-Africanism, of "the Third World," of internationalist humanist socialism, of the future itself—all could be heard instead, it was said, in the speeches of this extraordinary Muslim orator.[20] Yet in his last year Malcolm X had turned against the leadership of the Black Muslims, as it had turned against him, and he was struggling to keep alive a small group of disorganized followers under the banner of the wistful title of the Organization of Afro-American Unity. He had led no demonstrations, urged no legislation, and made no alliances with other leaders.

The murder of King did much to persuade younger blacks that those Muslims who sympathized with the belief that riots helped the Negro were right.[21] As the major cities convulsed in ghetto riots, while the Johnson administration escalated a war in Asia without credible justification or public candor, the integrity and coherence of American society itself seemed brutally put in question. Pessimistic premillennial apocalyptic views seemed more appropriate than the postmillennial optimism of Martin Luther King, Jr., who could chant to his followers, after the march to Montgomery, a vision of future success in their struggle for justice: "How long? Not long, because the arm of the moral universe is long but it bends toward justice."[22]

Malcolm X also saw the world in religious terms, and like King he was fond of saying, "You will reap what you sow." But for him the moral drama was chiliastic. The leader of the Muslims, Elijah Muhammad, had foreseen Armageddon in the United States. America was Egypt and Babylon before the bar. "God Himself is now the administrator of justice," Malcolm X asserted in 1963, "and God Himself is to be her divine executor!" The "race of devils" in America could "repent and atone" for its guilt and escape "divine disaster" only by accepting the message of the Muslims that the subsidized return of twenty-two million ex-slaves to their "own land" would alone permanently solve the problem of American injustice. The solution, Malcolm X believed, was given to the Honorable Elijah Muhammad by God, and it was the same solution "that God gave to Moses when the Hebrews in the Bible were in a predicament similar to the predicament of the so-called Negroes here in America today, which is nothing other than a modern house of bondage, or a modern Egypt or a modern Babylon."[23] He could preach this salvation with impressive conviction because as Malcolm Little he had come from the depths, a ghetto hustler and convict, to experience his own redeeming conversion to the Muslim religion. He was the John Bunyan of the disinherited alienated portion of the black community, his autobiography its *Pilgrim's Progress*. He had met the giant of despair in the slough of despond and had a visionary encounter in jail with the black Messiah. Not for nothing was his mother a Seventh-Day Adventist, a believer in the coming end of the world. In his own terms her son held to a similar faith, joined with his father's commitment early in the century to Marcus Garvey's Black Nationalism.

Muslimism was the religion of those who rejected Christianity as a major enemy because they saw it as part of the enslavement of black people to a corrupting white world. They had their own Messiah, who had come to Detroit in the flesh in the 1930's as W. D. Fard, son of a black man and a white woman. Before the fall into Hell on earth only black men had inhabited the world. Then Adam, or Yacub, had created the white "blue-eyed devils" who would rule for six thousand years. Before the year 2000, American Negroes would redeem the world in a triumphant realization of the Black Nation, after the coming of Armageddon and Judgment.[24] It was a non-Christian counterpart of Harriet Beecher Stowe's vision without her postmillennial optimism.

This visionary eschatological religion of the oppressed, structurally similar to many Biblical themes, fitted with Malcolm X's own realistic perceptions of his social condition. It had given him a cynically sharp eye for the hypocrisies and brutalities of American racism, which had violently doomed his father and conventionally dismissed his own youthful aspirations to be a lawyer. His skill in debate and argument found release instead in public witness to the Muslim's religion. A master of sarcastic humor, rapid-fire polemic, and vernacular imagery, he proudly excoriated American society from the vantage point of "the victims of your democratic system."

In political terms this stand rejected both the means of nonviolent resistance and the end of integration because, like early Christian sects, Muslims were in fundamental tension with the dominant culture. They did not intend to join it, reform it, or control it, but to separate themselves out of it in order to redeem a part of it. In immediate terms their social contribution lay in successful moral rehabilitation of many in the black hustler's world. Religious radicalism of this sort is often animated by puritanical values and fundamentalist beliefs, and in these respects the Muslims conformed to type, having their own "Protestant ethic." But whereas sects like the Mennonites believed in the afterlife and pacifism, the Muslims rejected the other world as a transhistorical heaven and emphasized the right of self-defense. Like the early Mormons, tithing their members, encouraging business enterprise, and considering stimulants, fornication, and crime sinful, they dreamed of a territory of their own within the United States.

The growth of the Muslims pointed to the small difference civil rights could make in the ghetto. Malcolm X's scorn for "these old religious Uncle Toms" who "keep you from fighting back" by teaching blacks "to suffer peacefully" made its appeal to young blacks who had seen (if only on television) barbarous attacks on Negroes in Albany, Birmingham, Selma, and Chicago. Malcolm X's polemical talent performed the trick of making nonviolent resistance seem to be mere fearful cringing for the sake of trivial objectives: "a desegrated public toilet; you can sit down next to white folks—on the toilet." He carried over from his pre-Muslim days the rule that "the worse thing in the hustler's world was to be a dupe," and it spurred him to bitter deflation of the idealism of civil-rights activists.[25]

Malcolm X's recurrent rhetorical theme was the hypocrisy of whites, Christians, and the established powers. This attack was his substitute for the activism of the demonstrators. Privately, he came to feel regrets because the Muslims had not "amended, or relaxed, our general non-engagement policy." In his autobiography he asserted that "wherever black people committed themselves, in the Little Rocks and the Birminghams and other places, militantly disciplined Muslims should also be there—for all the world to see, and respect, and discuss." It was increasingly said in the streets, he acknowledged, that "those Muslims *talk* tough, but they never *do* anything, unless somebody bothers Muslims."[26] Urged by the students at Tuskegee Institute in Alabama, he went to Selma and told Mrs. King he meant to help her husband by scaring whites into accepting the Baptist preacher-leader as the lesser evil.[27] Before he left for the Middle East and Africa on his hajj to Mecca he spoke for the strategy of using the United Nations to bring to bear on the United States pressure from African powers, a tactic formulated by Harriet Beecher Stowe's nationalist-minded hero, who goes to Liberia with a similar hope in *Uncle Tom's Cabin*.

The political emergence of Malcolm X went hand in hand with his break with Elijah Muhammad. The Messenger of Allah had been caught out in adulterous relations with his secretaries, scandalizing his loyal follower, who always abhorred hypocrisy. Furthermore, the minister had broken the leader's discipline of political silence by pointing to President Kennedy's assassination as a divine vengeance on white Americans. Making his own declaration of independence from the organization in March, 1964, Malcolm X came out at Harvard for the black man's vote as "the only valid approach toward revolutionizing American policy." Nine months later on the same campus he pledged himself to work with civil rights organizations on voter registration.[28]

At the same time, however, these specific immediate goals were linked to a long-range hope that American Negroes would find their way "back to our homeland" as an "independent nation." This separatist dream, oscillating between visions of Africa and demands for American territory, was for American blacks a recurrent one, and Malcolm X in following it was carrying on the tradition of his murdered father and his former leader. In developing an incipient Third World orientation he was also restating the Muslim view that "black" meant "nonwhite" and therefore included other colored peoples of various shades in Asia and the Middle East.

In his autobiography Malcolm X presents his trip to the Moslem World (where he had been before) as if it were a stunning novel encounter with a believable religion that included white men. After his return, he did underline a new theme, for all the dramatic exaggeration of his account. "Thoughtful white people *know* they are inferior to black people," he had said in 1963, bolstering his racist theory with biology on the ground that white genes are recessive and black genes are dominant. After his return from the Middle East and Africa, however, he spoke at Harvard on "the brotherhood of all men," while still reminding his hearers that in his view both brotherhood and bloodshed had to be seen as "a two-way street."[29] In Moslem worship he had found a lack of racial exclusiveness, and he began to emphasize African cultural roots, rather than genes, as definitive of American blackness.

After his break with the Black Muslims, Malcolm X became increasingly political-minded, but his politics was a mixture of the elusive separate-territory dream of Garvey and Elijah Muhammad, the international tactic of finding African allies in the United Nations, the appeal to the abstraction of a nonwhite Third World, revolutionary rhetoric, and an emphasis also on the black vote in America. More and more idolized by militant young blacks, he unified these disparate views only by his constant moral critique of the injustices and hypocrisies of American treatment of the Negro, a dazzling polemic made in terms of rhetoric that blended bitter truth and hyperbole in a way his white audiences could never quite disentangle. His campus followers found a surrogate for his separatist militancy in the disruptive demonstrations and occupation of buildings in 1969, especially when they were entangled with demands for black educational programs emphasizing the cultural African legacy and the political theme of Black Nationalism, while insisting on an ethnically separatist organization of faculty and students.[30]

His transition from the religious evangelist of a God who "has come to close out the entire old world" to the militant secular radical was not such a difficult leap. The conservative program of the Muslims was inspired by a religion that expected an imminent supernatural transformation of the world in which the last would be the first and the first last, turning the established state of things upside down in the millennial triumph of black freedom and equality. Because Muslims rejected an afterlife, they had already a religion of this world. Minister Malcolm became Malcolm X the political man by a displacement of his former creed and a reformulation of his Muslim apocalyptic ideas in secular terms: the imminent Armageddon was "a clash between the oppressed and those that do the oppressing."[31]

Whether as Black Muslim or as Moslem radical, Malcolm X spoke for American black victims with authentic and eloquent indignation. His identification of the American Negro exclusively with victimization, however, drove him to the unhistorical conclusion that he is "a person who has no history; and by having no history, he had no culture."[32] Slavery had destroyed the slave's name, language, and identity. He sought to develop group pride by pointing to ancient African, Sumerian, Indian, and Egyptian civilizations for morale-building proof of the superiority of dark-skinned people, who had developed high culture and civilization before the Europeans.

In his own life, however, there was a source of pride much closer home. He had moved from the status of convict to one of the most sought-after speakers on college campuses; sentenced in Cambridge, Massachusetts, as a common thief in 1946, he had returned in 1961 as a guest speaker at the Harvard Law School. "This is the best example," he told an interviewer, "of Mr. Muhammad's ability to take nothing and make something, to take nobody and make somebody."[33] Self-educated in prison, he had remarkably spurred the growth of the Muslims by his energies, living out a version of the archetypal success story. Like Benjamin Franklin's, his autobiography commemorated the rise of a man who began in obscure poverty and ended by talking with kings. Made a guest of the state by Prince Faisal of Saudi Arabia, Malcolm X felt overwhelmed with honor: "Who would believe the blessings that have been heaped upon an *American Negro?*"[34] But the tragedy of Malcolm X was that when he lost his identification with the Black Muslim organization, he became at the same time a hunted man who did not expect to live long enough to read his autobiography in its finished form. His international fame could not provide him with a solid constituency at home nor protect him from his Muslim enemies.

In their last months Malcolm X and King moved toward each other in some degree as they grappled with the racial crisis, but their differences remained stubborn ones. King could assimilate the slogans of "black is beautiful" and "black power," while Malcolm X could favor black voting registration and appreciate a nonracial Moslem religion, but King's Christianity and nonviolent morality never attracted Malcolm X. King's logic and rhetoric made his followers "insiders" who represented the denied truths of venerable American covenants. Malcolm X spoke for the "outsiders" who sought an independent destiny. Even if, hypothetically, they both could have agreed to see "nonviolent resistance" as one of several possible strategies, their differences in perspective would still be much deeper than arguments over tactics. Even the anguish of the condition of the ghettos could not unite black leaders, though among the rank and file the cleavages were less sharply defined, for many supporters of separatism still favored public-school integration, and some people might praise riots and radical rhetoric without ever intending to act out their language.[35] Given the constant glare of the TV cameras, greedy for sensational images and events, black spokesmen were easily tempted to outbid each other in militant postures and forms of guerrilla theater, which gullible whites, either in dread or enthusiasm, solemnly took to be the voice of history itself.

While the hope that King and Malcolm X would have collaborated is tenuous, the wish draws on a legitimate sense that both men had— in varying measure—a piece of the complex truth about American race relations. Tocqueville's pessimism about the American future was mainly based on his belief that whites and blacks would find it harder to live "upon an equal footing" in the United States than elsewhere. He saw no solution to the problem, nor did he ever integrate this judgment with his fundamentally optimistic sense of the stability of the American republic. He brought to bear a logic too abstract in its formulations. For him there were only two chances for the future: "the Negroes and the whites must either wholly part or wholly mingle."[36] In historical practice the more probable chance, difficult as it has proved to be, is neither wholly one thing nor the other: seeking to equalize rights and opportunities, while respecting valuable cultural and social differences. In his day religious pluralism was narrow in scope, and its political consequences were much less divisive than the gap between the Protestant right and Martin Luther King, Jr., or Malcolm X, because slavery had not yet become an ideological and moral issue. More than a century later, King and Malcolm X in their careers dramatized the two poles of Tocqueville's envisaged future for the race problem, but both men also demonstrated by their frustrations the social limits of their religious ideologies.

XX

The New Secularism and the New Pluralism

Tocqueville believed that Christianity itself was congruent with the process of secularization because it "speaks only of the general relations of men to God and to each other, beyond which it inculcates and imposes no point of faith."[1] In modern times, he believed, religious belief and rituals would have to be simplified, and asceticism would have to bow to a decent respect for material prosperity and the opinions of a dominant majority. The style of American Christianity seemed to him to point the proper way. Only within these limits could it perform its valuable function of curbing the indulgence of an "inordinate love of material gratification" and the modern tendency of men to become isolated from each other. Christianity, in rendering much to Caesar, thus allowed science, law, and politics to develop autonomous energies. While the American clergy praised civil freedom and patriotism, it kept out of direct participation in politics.[2] These self-limitations favored its indirect influence. In these terms Tocqueville developed an original theory of secularized religion, a phenomenon that in the late 1950's came to fascinate sociologists and theologians in America.

The sociological study that in effect most strongly supported his own commentary on the character of religion in America, however, did not include him in its bibliography or index. Will Herberg in *Protestant-Catholic-Jew* (1955) argued that America was steadily moving into a cultural situation in which membership in the Protestant, Catholic, or Jewish socioreligious groups was increasingly seen as the legitimate mode of being an American. His corollary was that not differences among these groups, but instead a common obeisance to the democratic American "way of life" as the religion of religions, marked this development. In Herberg's perspective, greatly influenced by Niebuhr's neo-orthodoxy, the critical, prophetic function of Biblical faith, aware of a transcendent dimension of judgment, was muffled in a self-congratulatory, complacent style of belief and worship, identified by Herberg with secularization.

Gerhard Lenski's *The Religious Factor* (1961) followed Herberg in emphasizing the importance of socioreligious subcommunities, and of the "secularizing" style at work in American Protestantism in particular, but he felt that the political controversies linked to race and religion which had characterized the election of 1960 might well be prophetic of future heightened tensions between socioreligious groups. Lenski, whose work was based on polls made in Detroit, was worried about the growth of the Catholic subcommunity to parity with a declining white Protestant group in large urban areas because the trend seemed destined to encourage parochial and authoritarian attitudes. He feared that "pluralism" might become "a polite euphemism for a 'compartmentalized society' " that would heighten intergroup political conflict.[3]

In view of Tocqueville's thesis, the themes of Herberg's book were not matters of historical novelty except insofar as the ethnic factor had been added to the Frenchman's account. Lenski's accent on group differences, moreover, exaggerated the role of religious ideology as an explanation when social heritage and status position more clearly and convincingly, in relation to his evidence, functioned to differentiate the groups he analyzed. Lenski constantly had to distinguish Jews and Negro Protestants as exceptions to his ideologically based explanations. Herberg and Lenski were reconcilable, however, in terms of the thesis of the search for social identity as a common impulse animating the formation of the major subcommunities. In this respect they both overlapped Tocqueville's argument that the social function of religion was to overcome the isolation experienced in modern society, lacking in the articulated stratifications of traditional life. They merged also with his emphasis on the way in which American religion came to terms with aspirations for material improvement. It is possible to conclude from Lenski's data, as one of his sharpest critics has pointed out, that the conflicting social norms of religious groups actually pertain not to ultimate values but rather to different strategies and *"means* of climbing the economic and social ladder."[4] Seen in this light, both Herberg and Lenski tended to lend support indirectly for the persisting relevance of Tocqueville's insights.

Neither Herberg nor Lenski, however, did justice to the sociore-ligious changes that were taking place. Both had to concede that Negro Protestants and Black Muslims were anomalies in their theories. The first group shared many subculture attitudes that were more like Catholic ethnics' than like Protestants', while the second had no share at all in either Christianity or the civic religion. One black Christian professor argued in 1964, furthermore, that the racially separated in-dependent Negro denominations actually constituted a fifth religion, not to be identified with Protestant, Catholic, Jewish, or even secularist outlooks. It was a folk religion produced by slavery, segregation, and discrimination. Originally inspired by secular aspirations for freedom and equality, it has also engendered out of frustration a consolatory dream of otherworldly happiness. Developing popular and entertaining preachers, ethnic politicians (like Adam Clayton Powell, Jr., of the Abyssinian Baptist Church in Harlem), and social workers, this "dis-inherited Protestantism" in its isolation was fixated theologically in the emotional evangelical style of the nineteenth-century frontier.[5] More-over, the *aggiornamento* in the Catholic Church, inaugurated by Pope John XXIII, undermined familiar sociological stereotypes about Catholic conservatism and stability of doctrine.

At the end of the 1960's a sociologist of religion, Jeffrey K. Hadden, reflected the new consciousness of fission rather than fusion in the title of his study of religious public opinion: *The Gathering Storm in the Churches*. His polls showed, for example, that twice as many Jews as Christians in 1967 saw Martin Luther King, Jr., as "an outstanding example of making Christianity relevant and meaningful for our day."[6] During the Vietnam war, moreover, a majority of the general public, nearly a third of the laity at a meeting of the National Council of Churches in 1966, only 16 per cent of its parish clergy, and merely 9 per cent of the Council's staff believed that the United States should "increase the strength of its attacks on North Vietnam."[7] The denomi-nations themselves broke down into at least four groups of fundamen-talist, conservative, neo-orthodox, and liberal blocs, defined in terms of theological outlook. No massive consensus on traditional Christian belief emerged among the laity in any denomination except the South-ern Baptists and small Pentecostal sects, which were more united than the Catholics.*

---

* If we compare Protestant and Catholic belief in the divinity of Christ, for example, between 1952 and 1965, it drops from 92 per cent to 86 per cent for Catholics and from 82 per cent to 69 per cent for Protestants. Cf. Hadden, p. 63,

Polling also revealed that among Protestant clergy, fundamentalists and conservatives were dominantly Republican (65 per cent), while only a minority (37.5 per cent) of neo-orthodox and liberal ministers preferred the Republican Party. Conservative theological beliefs among clergymen also strongly correlated with rigid adherence to the "free enterprise" economic system and the support of Senator Barry Goldwater for President in 1964, regardless of ordinary party preference.[8] In this respect Tocqueville was still right in saying that "by the side of every religion is to be found a political opinion, which is connected with it by affinity," but while this affiliation marked the liberal-conservative split among clergymen, the pollsters were not at all sure that such a connection could be found within the confused laity.* In any case, Protestant and Catholic laity were evenly divided internally on whether clergy should speak out on social issues, though a majority in both faiths and also among Jews opposed clerical participation in demonstrations.[9] In general, laity held much more conservative social attitudes than clergy on civil rights.

Sociologists of the religious revival of the 1950's had been critical of the complacent conservative secularism they detected in the style of American belief and worship. By the mid-1960's, however, secularization was embraced by vanguard theologians themselves, who welcomed it in a context of radical reform. The theological best-seller of 1965 was Harvey G. Cox's *The Secular City*. Writing for inner-city ministers, urban laity, and college students, Cox ingeniously interpreted Biblical stories and themes so as to rationalize a modern style of life, identified with an urban, pragmatic, relativistic, mobile, organized worldliness. He celebrated precisely the "sins" against which fundamentalists of his own Baptist denomination had always fulminated. In part an effort to Americanize Dietrich Bonhoeffer's moving attempt to redefine theology within the context of his Christian martyrdom as an anti-Nazi resistance fighter, *The Secular City* was also a revised version of the social-gospel tradition of relating the Kingdom of God to a process of social change, interpreted as if it were guided by immanent normative goals.

At the level of sociology Cox's image of the city as an abode of

with John L. Thomas, *Religion and the American People* (Westminster, Md., 1963), p. 56.

* Although Baptists, for example, disproportionately supported George Wallace's third-party movement in 1968, it is probably because of the greater support he had from transplanted Southerners than from those reared elsewhere. Seymour M. Lipset and Earl Raab, *The Politics of Unreason* (New York, 1970), pp. 387–92.

individual freedom was seriously flawed by its underestimation of the frustrations that led a black section of Los Angeles to erupt in violence the very year his book was published, and he also underestimated the persistence and function in the city of conventional elements of ethnic socioreligious group life. Cox's popularity was, however, a striking modern example of Tocqueville's point about the concern of American preachers for being sympathetically relevant to the secular values of their world, and *The Secular City* also illustrated his theme of republican religion in Cox's wish to make speaking to God translatable into participating in political action when it is motivated by feelings of mutual concern. Cox's argument could not explain, however, why a self-sufficient secularity needed revisionist Biblical interpretations any more than it needed old-fashioned fundamentalist readings, and it cheerfully ran the risk of being dismissible as only another trend-spotting effort to keep theology alive by putting a spiritual gloss on the very forces that were making it seem irrelevant.[10]

In practice, however, Cox's temper was increasingly reflected in the activist urban clergy, who became involved in welfare unions, tenant councils, rent strikes, and school boycotts, often allied with black leaders and secular organizers of the poor. In 1967, at a conference on religion in America published in *Daedalus,* he could himself identify a "New Breed" of churchmen, allegedly standing in the succession of Williams, Penn, the Free-Soilers, abolitionists, feminists, and social gospelers. The list is historically blurred, but it was true that with the New Breed the Kingdom of God, which for Niebuhr's supporters was beyond the bounds of historical realization, had become "once again something for which to work."[11]

The new situation held some ironies within it. Traditionally, Jews have been more sympathetic than Protestants or Catholics to secularization, finding their own freedom in the development of wide separation between church and state and in the growth of religious tolerance. It was Jews, however, at the *Daedalus* conference who were critical of the recent Christian enthusiasm for secularization. They were more aware of the persisting Christian influences in American life, and they were more sensitive as well, remembering the death camps, to the guilt and despair that believers and nonbelievers alike had reason for experiencing in the secular world.[12] The image of the secular person celebrated by the vanguard theologians was strangely bereft of any feeling for tragedy, as if secularity was inevitably complacent and optimistic, a prejudice long shattered in philosophy and literature. The extent to which the New Breed, as Cox believed, really had "learned its lessons from Reinhold Niebuhr" remained to be seen.

Another irony of the situation in the late 1960's was that while many of the socially activist clergy were enthusiastically responding to black separatism by treating sympathy for it as a test of radical sincerity, the Catholic Church, undergoing an unprecedented internal transformation, in which doctrine, authority, rituals, and practice were all subjected to intensive re-examination, was breaking out of its traditional separatist position. At the highest level the Second Vatican Council encouraged doctrinal emphasis on a turn to the world in the spirit of responsibility for its reformation in terms of community and justice. In this light the closed community is seen as "less holy, as un-Christ-like." Discarding much of the medieval legacy, the new Catholics had their own version of Cox's celebration of the secular city: "The hope of creating a better future in an evolving world takes the place of faith as the central theological virtue in this period of transition. Original sin becomes man's apathy in moving toward making a just and loving world."[13] The *National Catholic Reporter,* institutionalizing the new critical spirit of the laity, discussed in its pages secular issues of civil rights, urban renewal, and problems of peace and poverty.

This spirit of change among Catholics was in direct conflict with the separatist style of traditional American Catholicism. The new pluralism of the 1950's had created a sympathetic intellectual climate for understanding that older identity in contrast to the harsh secularistic criticisms of the Church made by Paul Blanshard; in the late 1960's, however, vanguard Catholics made many of the same criticisms of Catholic anti-intellectualism, authoritarianism, and lack of social consciousness. They pointed out that Catholic-school pupils were no more observant of conventional Catholic practices than public-school students, and they deplored the tendency of the parochial system to insulate Catholics from the larger world. In 1960 the National Catholic Conference for Interracial Justice was organized, and it promoted Catholic clerical participation in the marches on Washington and Selma at which King spoke so movingly. But by 1968 lay Catholic opposition to the active role of priests and nuns in political and social matters was rising in a backlash against urban riots, while the Black Catholic Clergy Caucus was angrily condemning the Church as a racist institution.[14]

The Catholic Left surprisingly emerged as the vanguard of the anti-Vietnam war movement. Drawing eclectically on the social activism of the worker-priests in the French resistance movement, the voluntary poverty and pacifism of Dorothy Day's *Catholic Worker* group in America (organized in 1933), the Marxist insights of the Socialist Party, and the civil-disobedience tactics of the civil-rights campaign, Catholic radicals also dreamed of reviving the mood of the persecuted underground Church of early Christianity. Two priests, Philip and Daniel Berrigan, attracted national attention in 1967 and 1968 by engaging in two acts of civil disobedience, defacing with blood and destroying with homemade napalm large quantities of draft records in two cities. "Since politics weren't working anyway," Father Daniel Berrigan explained, "one had to find an act beyond politics: a religious act, a liturgical act, an act of witness. If only a small number of men could offer this kind of witness, it would purify the world." This search for risky and dramatic acts of witness, in which large numbers of people could not be expected to participate, was inspired by a Biblical apocalyptic sense of history. It shared with some ultraradical and often violent student groups a despairing view of American society as being hopelessly corrupt. "Our act was aimed," Daniel Berrigan said, "as our statement tried to make clear, at every major presumption underlying American life today. Our act was in the strictest sense a conspiracy; that is to say, we had agreed together to attack the working assumptions of American life."[15]

Majority Catholic opinion was conventionally chauvinistic and uncritically conservative. Few American Catholics had ever been conscientious objectors, and in 1967 only seven bishops publicly protested the bombing of Vietnam. The Catholic Left, in bad odor with the hierarchy, lived out a revolt aimed not only against the government but at their own Church. "Goaded by the silence of his Church's hierarchy and of its hawkish flocks," as Francine du Plessix Gray has observed in a sympathetic study of the Catholic Left, "the Catholic radical can become a desperado." But he could also find support in the fact that the Pope had condemned the Vietnam war, while the Vatican Council had called for governmental recognition of the rights of conscientious objectors. The trial of "the Catonsville Nine" in Baltimore, before an audience of participants in the peace movement, brought together a united front of secular, Protestant, Jewish, and Catholic protesters who made their headquarters in a Jesuit church: "Rabbi Heschel, Bishop Pike, Harvey Cox, Rennie Davis, Howard Zinn, Noam Chomsky, I. F. Stone mingled in the basement of Saint Ignatius with hundreds of Jesuits, with parish curates and seminarians from twenty states, with nuns in habit, nuns in high heels and teased hair, nuns writing their Master's theses on the development of Daniel Berrigan's theology."[16] The brutalizing, seemingly interminable war, propping up a repressive regime in Saigon, generated an ecumenical protest that had been earlier produced by the civil-rights movement.

Some Catholic radicals, however, were led by their bravado beyond the classic patterns either of individual witness or of large-scale civil disobedience. After the Catonsville trial Father Daniel Berrigan and two other defendants played a game of hare and hounds with the FBI, evading capture for several months. Berrigan's teasing, mocking wit and talent for publicity were much in evidence, and his actions delighted his campus constituency at Cornell University (where he had been a chaplain) when he made a brief appearance at a regional New Left rally and escaped from the police by hiding inside a giant puppet of an apostle. The classic tradition of personal witness in challenging unjust laws, however, was reduced in this way to the ploy of evading the law by an entertaining caper. King was always able to expose the moral illegitimacy of segregation statutes with the help of the Supreme Court itself. Berrigan could not play the same role with respect to the draft laws, nor would the courts pronounce judgment on the war, authorized in effect by the Tonkin Gulf Congressional resolution.

Berrigan's campus constituency, moreover, tended to be an indiscriminate mixture of "counterculture" trippers and disruptive Students for a Democratic Society members, not of religious pacifists like himself. In the summer of 1969, he noted, protesters on his own campus found him "old hat" and were moving in a new direction: "seizure of a building, hit and run, anger, inner division, threat of sabotage."[17] Yet, in an interview with an SDS sympathizer, Berrigan celebrated the organization, made no criticism of coercive tactics, and leveled his polemic at the faculty for allegedly representing "the total violence of the rotting intellect, pleading in its demise for something called civilized discourse and dialogue."[18] This sophistical redefinition could only provide glib rationalizations for violence-prone protesters who lacked his own disciplined training and religious sensibility. Apocalyptically, he looked ahead grimly to coming voices of "public violence and chaos" rather than of civil disobedience, because he believed that the courts were becoming part of the system of repression he opposed, but the charge was hardly justified by the behavior of the amiable judge who sympathized with his stand at Catonsville and gave the defendants scope to express their social views against the government.

Philip Berrigan, who had joined the Society of Saint Joseph in 1950 out of deep sympathy with its mission for ameliorating the lot of American Negroes, had taken the lead in subjecting himself to the risks of prison with energetic and cheerful courage, but it was also darkly colored by a bleaker impulse, expressed in his grim conviction that the gospel and history compelled a man of faith and duty inevitably toward "crucifixion—whether imprisonment or death."[19] This will to martyrdom was proudly contemptuous of less melodramatic, daring, or despairing actions, and the Berrigans were conspiciously absent in 1968 when Clergy and Laymen Concerned About Vietnam, which they had once led, converged on Washington to hear Martin Luther King, Jr., among others, protest the war. The fierce moral absolutism of the Berrigans was certainly the stuff from which the churches' martyrs are made, but for the same reason it could not become the focus of a collective movement of ordinary people.

The "identity crisis" of the Catholic Church was a special case of a widespread frustration with familiar institutions. A historian of American pietism has celebrated this development as another Great Awakening of pervasive scope. "The search for a new vocabulary, for ultimate values, for transcendent meaning and self-identity has entered all realms of life," he pointed out. "The sacred and the secular merge into each other; something profound in our culture is being transformed." In this view the skeptics of the religious revival of the 1950's became Old Lights, rationalistically and defensively opposing the antirational and popular New Lights, who came into their own a decade later. This formulation of the case does justice to some political and cultural celebrations of feeling and action which Puritans would have called antinomian, but the historical analogy translates into Protestant categories too many changes that transcend them. Furthermore, it too easily turns "Old Lights" and "New Lights" into a tendentious contrast. McLoughlin hailed the times for their "hope, excitement, and exhilaration."[20] But the evidence was very strong by 1969 that the light was also dimmed by intolerance, disintegrative impulses, mindless political sloganeering, and faddish hyperbolic criticism. The spirit of fashionable dissent in the churches, eager to cram rock-and-roll, encounter groups, and confrontation politics into "the Jesus bag," had its own corruptions of the spirit.

Tocqueville's image of a unifying ethos of republican religion was a casualty of history. He had linked it to a liberal politics, but that linkage, manifest in the civil-rights movement, was alien to a despairing left-wing radicalism and to an angry right-wing reaction in a Goldwater or a George Wallace. Yet Tocqueville himself pointed out that "in no country in the world is the love of property more active and more anxious than in the United States; nowhere does the majority display less inclination for those principles which threaten to alter, in whatever manner, the laws of property." What he most feared therefore was that because of the power of majority opinion in modern democracies, in the future every reform would be looked upon as a step toward revolution and men would fearfully become sunk in a comfortable conservation, unable to make "a strong and sudden effort to a higher purpose."[21] By the logic of his own analysis American religion, in its sympathetic relation to popular opinion, should have tended, however, to accentuate this very danger.* Tocqueville never recognized this implicit conflict in his theory. Similarly, he produced another paradox by his admiration both for vigorous intellectual freedom and a wide moral and philosophical consensus that could tame the majority's will. Religion favored the latter at the price of diminishing the former. The limits of this consensus would be tested by Mormons and Catholics shortly after Tocqueville's journey, and the issue of slavery would split the churches on regional lines. His fears about the tyranny of the majority were to some extent historically grounded in the very factor of popular religion that he identified instead with influences favoring liberal democracy.

These paradoxes trouble Tocqueville's coherence as a theorist, but the unreconciled elements usefully point in practice to an actual ambiguity in the historical function of American religion, which has played conservative, liberal, and radical roles in varying degrees and at different times, depending upon the circumstances. Its functions in a post-Puritan disestablished world were subject to the tendency of merely becoming the mores of one of many subcommunities, organized around family values. A contemporary sociologist has described the modern results: "Religion manifests itself as public rhetoric and private virtue. In other words, insofar as religion is common it lacks 'reality,' and insofar as it is 'real' it lacks commonality."[22] If this description of the case were entirely true, no book about the historical meaning of

---

* Given the need for denominations to be relevant to the general welfare through what unites them and the pressure to pay tribute to democracy as a civic religion, "the way is left open for the uncritical adoption of whatever standards do actually prevail in the society." Sidney Mead, *The Lively Experiment* (New York, 1963), p. 141.

republican religion could be written. This sociological model only points to a limit: secularization, aided by religion itself, tends to make religion "a dependent variable" with respect to the forces moving the world. The larger world then finds its meaning in other types of belief. Yet insofar as American republicanism developed a style of disestablishment in a common Protestantism, this "privatization" of religion, specified in the sociological model, was thus checked by counter forces. Tocqueville's emphasis on a common American religious style indirectly reflected that historical fact. Even when the voter's choice of party is mainly a matter of economic or status position, modern sociology recognizes that the mediation of that position partly through religious affiliation "affects the quality of the secular political response."[23]

Modern disestablishment has made pluralism more genuine, and even the civic religion has been broadened. The Catholic funeral ceremonies for the Kennedys invoked some of the themes, connecting religion and political ideals, traditionally associated with Lincoln.[24] Inevitably, to some degree pluralism has also promoted secularism by enforcing a search for neutral principles by which to interpret the religious clauses of the First Amendment. But the secularism that has pressed for wider separation between the churches and public policy is not necessarily tolerant or judicious, and it can act with as much dogmatic passion as it traditionally has attributed to its foes. In New York State, for example, the American Civil Liberties Union and Americans for Democratic Action combined with conservative Republicans in 1967 to defeat the new constitution that would have substituted the broader language of the First Amendment for the old constitution's explicit denial of indirect aids (except for transportation) to parochial schools. Both sides to the conflict refused to allow a separate vote on the church-state proposal. Despite the fact that the state Court of Appeals was not inclined to read the old provision very strictly and that both parties had previously pledged themselves to greater help for church schools, the new constitution was defeated with the help of fiscally conservative Catholics in Brooklyn and Queens. "Only the poor," as a student of the issue has remarked, "went for the new constitution."[25]

Most major creative achievements in modern science, art, and historiography have come from deeply secular imaginations, but secularism has been made problematic by the emergence of "the demonic" in secular movements themselves. The horrors of Hitler, Stalin, and nuclear war, the vicious circle of racism and ghetto poverty in the human creation of the city, the moral obtuseness and ultimate irrationality of the technocratic rationalism that entered into the American conduct of the Vietnam war, all have made secularism more humble, compared to earlier more confident and messianic versions of rationalist criticisms of religion. None of these developments makes an intelligent and morally sensitive secularism impossible or undesirable. They do help to make understandable, however, the persistence of religious radicals and millennarian religious movements in a secularized world. To some extent contemporary religious radicals seem merely to have borrowed familiar leaves from the notebooks of secular radicals in order to keep in touch with their volatile constituencies, and competition among the churches for believers does introduce a principle of consumer preference in a shrinking market. But the Protestantism of King or the Catholicism of the Berrigans, for example, cuts deeper into their personal histories than any such sociological unmasking can explain.

Tocqueville's larger point, whatever his historical exaggerations and omissions, was that friends of majority rule, civil liberties, equal rights, and disestablishment should not be enemies of religious belief, and he looked to the United States for proof of his case that religion needed to be nurtured as "the most precious bequest of aristocratic ages." But he himself stressed the idea that in many respects the lot of Americans was "singular" and "quite exceptional." He knew also that Europe could not simply imitate the laws and customs of America; they provided "examples rather than lessons to the world."[26] How generalizable was the American example of republican religion? He did not say, but his hopes, clearly, were for finding European equivalents of its specified role. Yet history did not oblige him with other examples; Tocqueville the prophet therefore had to bow to Tocqueville the historian, who could point to the past rather than the future.

He did not want to be a Cassandra because for him the future was compatible, depending on how wisely men acted, either with liberty or despotism. The contemporary situation is much like his description of his own time. Were men condemned to live, he asked, in "a world like the present, where all things are not in their proper relationships, where virtue is without genius, and genius without honor; where the love of order is confused with a taste for oppression, and the holy cult of freedom with a contempt of law; where the light thrown by conscience on human actions is dim, and where nothing seems to be any longer forbidden or allowed, honorable or shameful, false or true?"

His work expressed the confidence that God had destined "a calmer and a more certain future to the communities of Europe."[27] In the 1960's no American could justifiably claim that calm and certainty. The prophet of the future's dangers seemed much more relevant than the theorist who had looked in America for "a new science of politics for a new world."

As historical sociologist, however, he had underlined a dimension of American experience that his modern readers often ignored by pointing to the political significance of the special character of American disestablishment. It made liberals and radicals favorable to religious rather than atheistic ideologies, gave legal shelter to Puritan attitudes, nurtured an evangelical mood of reform and millennial hopes, and concealed the real problems of pluralism by an implicit de facto Protestant establishment that has been slowly and reluctantly abandoned.

The French visitor to American shores was not free of that seductive tendency found in other continental thinkers to celebrate too much or damn too harshly the strange ways of the "Anglo-Saxons" across the ocean, but he had a rare jugular instinct for the historically important. Republican religion did much to lay the historical groundwork for the tradition of religious liberty and limited separation of church and state, as it did to nurture creative minorities like the abolitionists, social gospelers, and civil-rights protesters. While it worked to demean and harass Negroes, Mormons, Catholics, Jews, and agnostics, especially where Protestant views of the family or the school were at stake, it also provided Afro-Americans with institutions of their own and bred nearly all black public leaders. Through Lincoln it articulated the ideological meaning of the Civil War. In Wilson it mingled missionary nationalism with a vision of internationalism, and in the eloquence of Martin Luther King, Jr., it found a voice for the revitalization of a civic religion in the context of demands for the renewal of the premises and promises of the ancient covenants. Shorn of parochial and obsolete encrustations, republican religion also came to serve the Supreme Court in its lurching efforts to define a pluralism for modern America wider and deeper than anything the Founding Fathers had known.

Tocqueville feared the growth of paternalistic bureaucracy, class division, and racial strife, and he was also properly worried about the potential for concentrated power in the American executive. But he was more confident than not about the American future, in contrast to Europe's, because among other safeguards Americans had a tradition of republican religion. Yet in practice it was too weak when liberal or too conservative when strong to prevent the evils of the future that he had identified. It did favor the vitality of popular participation in religious organizations, in contrast to a developing indifference in the European setting. And on some issues, such as disestablishment, anti-slavery, Prohibition, and civil rights, religious men did become crucial leaders of reform. Tocqueville's historical sociology of American religion was too optimistic in its evaluations, but he knew even in 1831 that racial inequality, not religious diversity, was the most dangerous threat to republican union. For all the pain of the friction and the loss of intellectual bite in overcoming it, the accommodations of major American religions to a Protestant culture were for the most part rather like Tocqueville's model, even though pluralism had to grow wider in scope and deeper in meaning to include more authentically Catholics, Jews, and nonbelievers.

Tocqueville, far from being conservative, wished to "increase the rights of democracy" precisely when conservatives complained that "the laws are weak and the people are turbulent" and "passions are excited." And he did not expect the consequences to be bland. Liberty was always established only with difficulty "in the midst of storms" and could only be "perfected by civil discord."[28] He looked to republican religion for a way of keeping that necessary discord from collapsing into mere fragmentation or uncivil anarchy. His remedy, always a historically limited one, does not now shine with the promise that he saw in it. Keeping discord civil, however, is no luxury, and its precariousness in American life requires Americans to distinguish for themselves, as he did for Europeans, between a "salutary fear" that "keeps watch and ward for freedom" and a "faint and idle terror" that only "depresses and enervates the heart." They may well also ask themselves where they can find in modern terms the safeguards he knew were necessary to make liberty conspire with equality in a system of legitimate authority, or the energies that he knew were needed if men were to act collectively for public ends and not sink into a retreat to a small circle of family and friends, fearful of freedom's threats to their material welfare and public order. Americans, he thought, had mingled the passions for freedom and welfare, "hitherto" escaping the perils he foresaw.[29] One hundred and forty years later he would have had to deal with deeper doubts.

Appendix:

A Note on the Ages of Converts in the Great Awakening

Only three towns have been closely studied with reference to the age of converts during the Awakening: Andover, Norton, and Middleborough—all in Massachusetts. Andover was not a revival town and only in Middleborough was the minister an enthusiastic proponent of the revival. Recent "saint"-counting in Middleborough indicates that 27.4 per cent of the Awakening's new male converts were under 21 years of age and 45.2 per cent were between 21 and 30. In Norton, a revival town without a prorevival minister, there were more saints between 21 and 30 (57 per cent) and fewer under 21 (14.3 per cent). Before the Awakening the average age of the male convert in the town of Norton was nearly 40 and only 21.6 per cent of the converts were under 30. In Andover during the revival years, female saints averaged about 5 years younger than before the Awakening, and they were usually not yet married. Young people in the early eighteenth century in America were likely to live under the parental roof into their twenties. We may infer that tensions regarding parental rule, particularly given the stress on "family government," would make for what we would consider a rather extended adolescence.

I have culled these statistics from historical essays seeking to find evidence for changes in the life cycle or looking for economic "causes" so that New Light Calvinism can be seen as a temporary substitute for worldly success in a time of closing economic opportunities. I think, however, that they more convincingly support a psychohistorical focus on the role of the Awakening preaching in resolving emotional issues generated by parental rule over the lives of young people. For the statistics see J. M. Bumsted, "Religion, Finance, and Democracy in Massachusetts: The Town of Norton as a Case Study," *Journal of*

American History, 57 (March, 1971), 817–29; Philip J. Greven, Jr., "Youth, Maturity, and Religious Conversion: A Note on the Ages of Converts in Andover, Massachusetts, 1711–1749," *Essex Institute Historical Collections, 108* (April, 1972), 119–34.

An unpublished study of five river towns (Longmeadow, Suffield, Northampton, Deerfield, and Springfield) points in the same direction I have taken. In 1741 to 1742 the mean age of converts in these parishes was about twenty-one, a drop of ten years from the early 1730's, when conversions mainly affected married adults rather than unmarried young people. Kevin M. Sweeney, *Unruly Saints: Religion and Society in the River Towns of Massachusetts, 1700–1750,* honors thesis, history, Williams College (May, 1972), 136. Copy available in library of Historic Deerfield, Massachusetts.

Notes

INTRODUCTION

1. Tocqueville, *Democracy in America,* Phillips Bradley, ed. (New York, 1945), I, 308.

2. *Ibid.,* p. xcix.

3. Letter to Eugène Stoffels, July 24, 1836, quoted by J. P. Mayer, *Alexis de Tocqueville: A Biographical Study in Political Science,* 2nd. ed. (New York, 1960), p. 18. Max Lerner in the most recent English translation of the *Democracy* interprets this remark inaccurately in relation to Tocqueville's free-trade views. The context shows that law, morality, and religion are the specific features involved in the new type of liberalism. Cf. Joachim Wach, "The Role of Religion in the Social Philosophy of Alexis de Tocqueville," *Journal of the History of Ideas, 7* (Jan., 1946), 74–90; and Seymour Drescher, *Tocqueville and England* (Cambridge, Mass., 1964), p. 11, with J. P. Mayer and Max Lerner, eds., *Democracy in America,* tr. George Lawrence (New York, 1966), p. xlviii. Lerner does, however, recognize the importance of Tocqueville's focus on a kind of American civil religion. *Ibid.,* pp. lxxii–lxxv.

4. *The First New Nation: The United States in Historical and Comparative Perspective* (New York, 1963), pp. 95–96, 141, 154–55, 158, 160, 166. William Lee Miller proposes a corollary to Louis Hartz's treatment in 1955 of Tocqueville's observation "that America is born free, and did not have to become so": "America is born Protestant, and does not have to become so." Actually, Tocqueville said Americans were "born equal" (I, 101), but Miller's essay does acutely develop several of Tocqueville's themes. "American Religion and American Political Attitudes," in James Ward Smith and A. Leland Jamison, eds., *Religious Perspectives in American Culture* (Princeton, N.J., 1961), p. 85.

5. "Tocqueville's Duality: Describing America and Thinking of Europe," *American Quarterly, 21* (Spring, 1969), 87–99.

347

6. "The Protestant Movement and Democracy in the United States," in James Ward Smith and A. Leland Jamison, eds., *The Shaping of American Religion* (Princeton, 1961), p. 21.

7. See Alasdair MacIntyre, "God and the Theologians," *Encounter, 21* (Sept., 1963), 6.

CHAPTER 1: THE PURITAN PARADOX

1. See pp. 18, 34.

2. Cf. *The Liberal Tradition in America* (New York, 1955) with Tocqueville, *Democracy in America,* II, 299.

3. *Democracy in America,* I, 32, 36, 44.

4. *Ibid.,* 31.

5. *The Whig Interpretation of History* (New York, 1951), pp. 36, 57.

6. Quoted by John Tracey Ellis, *American Catholicism* (Chicago, 1956), p. 23.

7. *The Protestant Ethic and the Spirit of Capitalism* (London, 1965), pp. 36, 65, 91, 115, 176.

8. See Herbert Luethy, "Once Again: Calvinism and Capitalism," *Encounter, 22* (January, 1964), 26–38.

9. See Robert S. Michaelsen, "Changes in the Puritan Concept of Calling or Vocation," *New England Quarterly, 26* (September, 1953), 315–36. For Cotton on "calling" see Introduction, Perry Miller and Thomas H. Johnson, eds., *The Puritans* (New York, 1938), p. 61.

10. See Bernard Bailyn, ed., *The Apologia of Robert Keayne, the Self-Portrait of a Puritan Merchant* (New York, 1965).

11. *The Revolution of the Saints: A Study in the Origins of Radical Politics* (Cambridge, Mass., 1965), p. 13.

12. *Ibid.,* p. 64.

13. *Ibid.,* p. 13.

14. *Liberty and Reformation in the Puritan Revolution* (New York, 1955), p. 108.

15. *Ibid.,* p. 355.

16. "Religion and Society in the Early Literature of Virginia," in *Errand into the Wilderness* (Cambridge, Mass., 1956), p. 106.

17. See David Little, "Max Weber Revisited: The 'Protestant Ethic' and the Puritan Experience of Order," *International Yearbook for the Sociology of Religion, 3* (1967), 105, 109. The theme is expanded in his *Religion, Order, and Law: A Study in Pre-Revolutionary England* (New York, 1969).

18. *Their Solitary Way: The Puritan Social Ethic in the First Century of Settlement in New England* (New Haven, 1971), p. 172.

19. *Democracy in America,* I, 300.

CHAPTER II: THE CITY ON THE HILL, THE
GARDEN IN THE WILDERNESS, AND THE
GLORIOUS REVOLUTION

1. *Democracy in America,* I, 43–44. For Winthrop see *ibid.,* pp. 42–43.
2. *Ibid.,* p. 40.
3. *The Puritan Dilemma: The Story of John Winthrop* (Boston, 1958), p. 172.
4. "John Cotton on Limitation of Government," Edmund S. Morgan, ed., *Puritan Political Ideas* (Indianapolis, 1965), pp. 175–76.
5. *Democracy in America,* I, 416.
6. On voting rights see George D. Langdon, Jr., "The Franchise and Political Democracy in Plymouth Colony," *William and Mary Quarterly,* 3rd ser., *20* (October, 1963), 513–26; Timothy Breen, "Who Governs: The Town Franchise in Seventeenth Century Massachusetts," *William and Mary Quarterly,* 3rd ser., *27* (July, 1970), 460–74; Emery Battis, *Saints and Sectaries: Anne Hutchinson and the Antinomian Controversy in the Massachusetts Bay Colony* (Chapel Hill, 1962), p. 256; Stephen Foster, *Their Solitary Way: The Puritan Social Ethic in the First Century of Settlement in New England* (New Haven, 1971), pp. 173–79. In Dorchester a Negro maid was a saint. See George Lee Haskins, *Law and Authority in Early Massachusetts: A Study in Tradition and Design* (New York, 1960), p. 87, n. 11.
7. See B. Katherine Brown, "A Note on the Puritan Concept of Aristocracy," *Mississippi Valley Historical Review, 41* (1954), 105–12.
8. "John Cotton on Church and State," *Puritan Political Ideas,* p. 166.
9. *The Social Teaching of the Christian Churches,* tr. Olive Wyon (New York, 1960), I, 342, 331; II, 664, 714.
10. "A Key into the Language of America," in Perry Miller, *Roger Williams: His Contributions to the American Tradition* (Indianapolis, 1953), p. 64.
11. "Mr. Cottons Letter Lately Printed," *ibid.,* p. 98; "A Reply to the aforesaid 'Answer' of Mr. Cotton," *ibid.,* pp. 145, 147–48, 151; "The Copie of a Letter of R. Williams . . . to Major Endicot," *ibid.,* pp. 162–63.
12. "Letter to the Town of Providence," *ibid.,* p. 226; "George Fox Digg'd out of his Burrowes," *ibid.,* p. 250.
13. "The Journal of John Winthrop," *Puritan Political Ideas,* p. 101; quoted by Edmund S. Morgan, *The Puritan Dilemma: The Story of John Winthrop* (Boston, 1958), p. 129.
14. *Liberty and Reformation in the Puritan Revolution,* pp. 334–35.
15. Perry Miller, *op. cit.,* pp. 194–95.
16. "Letter to Major John Mason," *ibid.,* p. 234.
17. "Williams to Daniel Abbot," *Puritan Political Ideas,* p. 225.

18. "Letter to Major John Mason," *Roger Williams,* pp. 233, 235.

19. "The Bloudy Tenet of Persecution," *Puritan Political Ideas,* p. 212.

20. A. H. Lewis, *Critical History of Sunday Legislation* (New York, 1888), pp. 197–99.

21. Frederick B. Tolles and E. Gordon Alderfer, eds., *The Witness of William Penn* (New York, 1957), p. 110.

22. *Ibid.,* p. 75.

23. *The New England Mind: From Colony to Province* (Cambridge, Mass., 1953), p. 167.

24. "John Wise on the Principles of Government," *Puritan Political Ideas,* pp. 256, 267.

25. *The Revolution of the Saints,* p. 302.

26. *Democracy in America,* I, 305.

27. *The Triumph of the Therapeutic: Uses of Faith after Freud* (New York, 1966), p. 9.

28. T. H. Breen, *The Character of the Good Ruler: A Study of Puritan Political Ideas in New England, 1630–1730* (New Haven, 1970), pp. 251–69.

29. *Ibid.,* pp. 164–65. Talking about the "secularizability" of Puritanism misses the point about the non-Puritan sources of the republican tradition and minimizes the substance of the Puritan contribution to it, as Sydney E. Ahlstrom does in defining the Puritan legacy as "a sacrifice to responsible citizenship." See "The Puritan Ethic and the Spirit of American Democracy," in George L. Hunt, ed., *Calvinism and the Political Order* (Philadelphia, 1965), p. 106.

CHAPTER III: THE GREAT AWAKENING AND THE RISING GENERATION

1. *Democracy in America,* II, 134–35.

2. Frederick B. Tolles, *Quakers and the Atlantic Culture* (New York, 1960), pp. 112–13.

3. See Nelson R. Burr, "Revivalism and its Continuing Influence," in Burr, *A Critical Bibliography of Religion in America* (Princeton, 1961), Parts 1 and 2, pp. 117–48.

4. For the Southern revivalists see H. Shelton Smith, Robert T. Handy, and Lefferts A. Loetscher, *American Christianity: An Historical Interpretation with Representative Documents* (New York, 1960), I, 354–71. See also Wesley M. Gewehr, *The Great Awakening in Virginia, 1740–1790* (Gloucester, Mass., 1965).

5. Robert Pope, *The Half-Way Covenant: Church Membership in Puritan New England* (Princeton, 1969), p. 236.

6. Quoted by Thomas A. Schafer, "Solomon Stoddard and the Theology of the Revival," in Stuart C. Henry, ed., *A Miscellany of American Christianity* (Durham, N. C., 1963), pp. 334, 343.

7. Richard Bushman has explored the family history of Edwards with a psychoanalytic eye in a paper he kindly has shown me, which is even more enlightening than his "Jonathan Edwards and the Puritan Consciousness," *Journal for the Scientific Study of Religion, 5* (1966), 383–96. He argues that the son's tension between proud ambition and fear of God's wrath is also a popular problem in an era of expansion, thus giving Edwards a following.

8. "Covenant of Redemption: 'Excellency of Christ,'" in Clarence H. Faust and Thomas H. Johnson, eds., *Jonathan Edwards: Representative Selections* (New York, 1935), p. 373; "Dissertation Concerning the End for Which God Created the World," *ibid.,* p. 344.

9. "Sinners in the Hands of an Angry God," *ibid.,* p. 163; "Personal Narrative," *ibid.,* pp. 60–61; "Sinners," *ibid.,* pp. 170–72.

10. "Religious Affections," *ibid.,* p. 250.

11. Carl Van Doren, *Benjamin Franklin* (New York, 1938), pp. 136–37.

12. For neglected similarities between Franklin and Edwards see Alfred Owen Aldridge, *Jonathan Edwards* (New York, 1964), pp. 103–4.

13. See Ola Elizabeth Winslow, *Jonathan Edwards, 1703–1758* (New York, 1940), Chap. 12.

14. *Christian History* (Boston, 1743–45), I, 210. These reports of local churches are a valuable but neglected source for the revivals.

15. J. M. Bumstead, "Revivalism and Separatism in New England: The First Society of Norwich, Connecticut, as a Case Study," *William and Mary Quarterly,* 3rd. ser., *24* (1967), 588–612.

16. See Joseph Tracy, *The Great Awakening: A History of the Revival of Religion in the Time of Edwards and Whitefield* (Boston, 1842), pp. 287–88.

17. See note 14 *supra;* Tracy, *ibid.,* pp. 345, 358, 362–63. For the views of the Separates see *ibid.,* pp. 317–18.

18. Cushing Strout, "The Pluralistic Identity of William James: A Psycho-historical Reading of *The Varieties of Religious Experience,*" *American Quarterly,* 23 (May, 1971), 135–52.

19. Her story is told in Edwards's account of an earlier revival in "A Faithful Narrative of the Surprising Works of God . . . in Northampton," reprinted in Vergilius Ferm, ed., *Puritan Sage: Collected Writings of Jonathan Edwards* (New York, 1953), pp. 202–8. For James on neurotic insight see *The Varieties of Religious Experience: A Study in Human Nature* (New York, 1928), p. 25. For Davenport's confession see *Christian History,* II, 237–39.

20. *Varieties,* p. 199; Erikson, *Young Man Luther: A Study in Psychoanalysis and History* (New York, 1958), p. 41.

21. Josiah Stearns, *A Sermon Preached at Epping in New Hampshire*

(Exeter, N.H., 1780), p. 21; Dickinson, *A Call to the Weary* (New York, 1740), p. 43; "A Faithful Narrative," pp. 167–68.

22. "A Faithful Narrative," *Puritan Sage,* pp. 190, 172, 174.

23. *Christian History,* I, 183, 191, 196, 198, 200, 252–53, 255, 261, 371, 399–400; II, 14, 108, 150, 253, 340, 347, 375, 378.

24. *Ibid.,* I, 371, 377, 379.

25. *Ibid.,* II, 390, 414.

26. *Ibid.,* II, 90. On the increase in male church membership in the revivals see Cedric B. Cowing, "Sex and Preaching in the Great Awakening," *American Quarterly, 20* (Fall, 1968), 624–44.

27. *Ibid.,* I, 372, 414; II, 94.

28. Quoted by C. C. Goen, *Revivalism and Separatism in New England, 1740–1800* (New Haven, 1962), p. 167.

29. My calculations are based on data in Edwin Scott Gaustad, ed., *Historical Atlas of Religion* (New York, 1962), pp. 4, 162, 167, and in *Historical Statistics of the United States* (Washington, 1952), p. 25, table B12.

30. "Farewell Sermon," Faust and Johnson, eds., *Jonathan Edwards,* pp. 194–97.

31. For Edwards see *Christian History,* I, 381; for denominationalism see Timothy L. Smith, "Congregation, State, and Denomination: the Forming of the American Religious Structure," *William and Mary Quarterly,* 3rd. ser., *25* (April, 1968), 155–76.

32. *From Puritan to Yankee: Character and the Social Order in Connecticut, 1690–1765* (Cambridge, Mass., 1967), p. 231.

33. Quoted by Carl Bridenbaugh, *Mitre and Sceptre: Transatlantic Faiths, Ideas, Personalities, and Politics 1689–1775* (New York, 1962), pp. 51–52, 132–33, 151, 157.

34. William G. McLoughlin, *Isaac Backus and the American Pietistic Tradition* (Boston, 1967), p. 187. For Baptist ideas on Calvinistic separation of church and state see McLoughlin, *Isaac Backus on Church, State, and Calvinism: Pamphlets, 1754–1789* (Cambridge, Mass., 1968).

35. For a similar point see Sidney E. Mead, *The Lively Experiment: The Shaping of Christianity in America* (New York, 1963), pp. 34–43.

CHAPTER IV: CALVINIST WHIGS AND THE SPIRIT OF '76

1. *Democracy in America,* II, 257, 261, 263.

2. *Ibid.,* I, 56, 47.

3. Quoted by Edwin Scott Gaustad, *Historical Atlas of Religion in America,* p. 21.

4. Josiah Stearns, *A Sermon Preached at Epping in New Hampshire* (Exeter, 1780), p. 21.

5. W. S. Hudson, "John Locke: Heir of Puritan Political Theorists," in G. L. Hunt, ed., *Calvinism and the Political Order* (Philadelphia, 1965), 108–29.

6. William B. Sprague, *The Annals of the American Pulpit* (New York, 1858), III, 290–91.

7. For Rush see J. Kendall Wallis, "Benjamin Rush," in Willard Thorp, ed., *The Lives of Eighteen from Princeton* (Princeton, 1946), pp. 51–67; for Witherspoon see Lyman Butterfield, *John Witherspoon Comes to America* (Princeton, 1953), pp. xiii, 82.

8. Quoted by Alice M. Baldwin, *The New England Clergy and the American Revolution* (New York, 1958), p. 113, n. 22; *ibid.*, pp. 183–89.

9. Samuel West, *A Sermon Preached before the Honorable Council* (Boston, 1776), p. 40.

10. Gordon S. Wood, *The Creation of the American Republic 1776–1787* (Chapel Hill, N.C., 1969), pp. 114–24; *Cato's Letters* in David L. Jacobson, ed., *The English Libertarian Heritage* (Indianapolis, 1965), pp. 89, 162.

11. Alan Heimert corrects the misconception about Mayhew, but turns Bellamy into a New Light version of Mayhew's legendary role, a reversal characteristic of the argument in *Religion and the American Mind: From the Great Awakening to the Revolution* (Cambridge, Mass., 1966), pp. 253–55, 341, 346.

12. *A Sermon Delivered before the General Assembly* (New London, 1762), pp. 19, 25, 38, 42, 34, 9–10.

13. *Patriotism Described and Recommended* (New London, 1764), pp. 6–7, 9, 11, 14, 16.

14. *Ibid.*, pp. 25, 26, 29; cf. Bellamy, pp. 22–23, 26.

15. Quoted by Edmund S. and Helen Morgan, *The Stamp Act Crisis: Prologue to Revolution* (Chapel Hill, N.C., 1953), p. 91.

16. Edward Dorr, *The Duty of Civil Rulers* (Hartford, 1765), pp. 26, 28.

17. *Some Important Observations, Occasioned by . . . the Publick Fast* (Newport, 1766), pp. 47, 23, 5, 19, 21, 31, 40.

18. *Ibid.*, pp. 18, 29.

19. Quoted in Morgan, p. 234.

20. *Ibid.*, p. 254.

21. *The Snare Broken,* in Frank Moore, ed., *The Patriot Preachers of the American Revolution, 1750–1776* (Cambridge, Mass., 1860), pp. 17, 32.

22. *A Discourse on "the Good News from a Far Country"* (Boston, 1766), pp. 8, 19, 20, 31.

23. *A Sermon Preached at Cambridge* (Boston, 1771), pp. 19–20, 33, 61, 35.

24. *Innocent Blood Crying to God* (Boston, 1771), p. 16. For Chauncy see *Trust in God* (Boston, 1770), pp. 35–36.

25. Stephen Johnson, *Some Important Observations,* pp. 60–61; Samuel Stillman, *The Duty of Magistrates,* in Moore, *Patriot Preachers,* p. 269.

26. *Civil State* (Boston, 1773), pp. 8, 11, 21–23.

27. *Two Discourses* (Newburyport, 1774), pp. 15, 9, 20, 44.

28. *Ibid.,* pp. 59, 53, 27.

29. Wood, *op. cit.,* pp. 48–65; Niles, *Two Discourses,* pp. 34, 37, 38.

30. Heimert, *op. cit.,* p. 518.

31. *Liberty Described* (Hartford, 1775), pp. 9, 11, 12.

32. *Ibid.,* p. 10.

33. *Ibid.,* p. vi, 22.

34. "From the Covenant to the Revival," in Smith and Jamison, eds., *The Shaping of American Religion,* p. 339.

35. Anthony Haswell, *An Oration, Delivered at Bennington* (Bennington, Vt., 1799), pp. 7–8, 11–15. Heimert cites this oration as proof that "rural Jeffersonians vehemently denied that the government of the United States had been created through 'contract' or 'covenant' " and stood on the "general will" instead. But Haswell, like the pietists, mingles contractual and Rousseauistic concepts. See Heimert, p. 517.

36. Samuel Williams, *A Discourse on the Love of Our Country* (Salem, 1775), pp. 10, 13.

37. David V. J. Bell and Allan E. Goodman, "Vietnam and the American Revolution," *Yale Review, 61* (Oct., 1971), 28.

38. *Antidote against Toryism,* in *Patriot Preachers,* pp. 188, 193, 214–15, 230.

39. *Nehemiah, or the Struggle for Liberty Never in Vain* (Newburyport, 1779), pp. 37, 39.

40. *Jerubbaal, or Tyranny's Grove Destroyed and the Altar of Liberty Finished* (Newburyport, 1784), pp. 55, 71, 59.

41. *A Confutation of Two Tracts* (Boston, 1774), p. 13; Heimert, *op. cit.,* pp. 506–8.

42. Edward Frank Humphrey, *Nationalism and Religion in America 1774–1789* (Boston, 1924), pp. 64, 423; W. De Loss Love, Jr., *Fast and Thanksgiving Days of New England* (Boston, 1895), 399–409.

43. *A Discourse Addressed to the Sons of Liberty at a Solemn Assembly, near Liberty-Tree, in Boston* (Providence, 1766), p. 6.

44. Williams, *op. cit.,* pp. 15, 22, 14.

45. *An Anniversary Sermon Preached at Plymouth* (Boston, 1778), pp. 78–79.

46. *Divine Goodness Displayed in the American Revolution,* in *Patriot Preachers,* p. 334.

47. *Declaration of Peace,* in *Patriot Preachers,* pp. 360–61.

48. *An Anniversary Sermon,* p. 55.

49. Carl Bridenbaugh, *Mitre and Sceptre,* p. 197.

50. *The Selected Writings of John and John Quincy Adams,* ed. Adrienne Koch and William Peden (New York, 1946), pp. 23, 16, 14.

51. *Mitre and Sceptre,* p. 323.

52. *Ibid.,* p. 203.

53. *Bath-Kol, a Voice from the Wilderness* . . . (Boston, 1783), p. 62.

54. *Pamphlets of the American Revolution 1750–1776* (Cambridge, Mass., 1965), I, 160.

55. *Freedom from Civil and Ecclesiastical Slavery* (Newburyport, 1774), pp. 11, 14–15.

56. *Remarks on a Discourse of the Rev. Jonathan Parsons of Newburyport* (Boston, 1774), pp. 11–12, 14, 32–33.

57. *Freedom from Civil and Ecclesiastical Slavery,* p. 16.

58. *A Sermon Preached before the Honorable Council,* pp. 27, 43–44.

59. *A Confutation of Two Tracts,* pp. 11–12, 16, 65.

60. *Nehemiah,* p. 21.

61. *Bath-Kol,* p. 63.

62. Heimert, *op. cit.,* p. 525.

63. *Peaceable Kingdoms: New England Towns in the Eighteenth Century* (New York, 1970), pp. 241, 254.

64. *Democracy in America,* I, 71, 392.

CHAPTER V: DISESTABLISHMENT IN VIRGINIA: A SYMBIOTIC ALLIANCE

1. *Democracy in America,* II, 24–25.

2. Evarts B. Greene, *Religion and the State: the Making of an American Tradition* (New York, 1959), p. 82; Daniel W. Markwyn, *Disestablishment and the Christian State in the Age of the American Revolution,* diss. M.A. (San Jose State College, 1967), p. 162.

3. "The Contribution of the Protestant Churches to the Religious Liberty in Colonial America," *Harvard Review,* 2 (Winter-Spring, 1964), 67.

4. "Law or Prepossessions?" in Robert G. McCloskey, ed., *Essays in Constitutional Law* (New York, 1957), p. 327.

5. Carl Van Doren, ed., *Benjamin Franklin's Autobiographical Writings* (New York, 1945), pp. 784–85.

6. Letter, Nov. 13, 1818, in Lester J. Cappon, ed., *The Adams-Jefferson Letters* (Chapel Hill, N.C., 1959), II, 529. See George Harmon Knoles, "The Religious Ideas of Thomas Jefferson," *Mississippi Valley Historical Review,* 30 (Sept., 1943), 187–204.

7. Letter to Adams, Aug. 22, 1813, *ibid.,* II, 368; letter to Jefferson, Sept. 14, 1813, *ibid.,* pp. 373–74.

8. Letter to Jefferson, May 6, 1816, *ibid.,* p. 473; letter to Adams, Oct. 14, 1816, *ibid.,* p. 490; letter to Jefferson, Sept. 3, 1816, *ibid.,* p. 488; letter to Adams, Oct. 14, 1816, *ibid.,* p. 491.

9. *Notes on the State of Virginia,* ed. William Peden (Chapel Hill, N.C., 1955), pp. 159–61.

10. For the Virginia struggle see R. Freeman Butts, *The American Tradition in Religion and Education* (Boston, 1950), pp. 45–47; Charles F. James, *Documentary History of the Struggle for Religious Liberty in Virginia* (Lynchburg, Va., 1900), *passim.*

11. Butts, pp. 48–52.

12. *Ibid.,* pp. 53–57.

13. Douglass Adair, "James Madison," in *The Lives of Eighteen from Princeton,* pp. 141–42.

14. *The Rights of Conscience inalienable, and, therefore Religious Opinions not cognizable by Law,* reprinted in *American Christianity,* I, 469–70, 474. For Leland's absorption of Jeffersonian ideas see LeRoy Moore, Jr., "Religious Liberty: Roger Williams and the Revolutionary Era," *Church History, 34* (March, 1965), 12–13.

15. *Memorial and Remonstrance,* reprinted in Anson Phelps Stokes and Leo Pfeffer, eds., *Church and State in the United States,* rev. ed. (New York, 1964), pp. 55–60.

16. "Law or Prepossessions?" *op. cit.,* pp. 327–28.

17. Quoted by Stokes and Pfeffer, *op. cit.,* p. 71.

18. See David E. Swift, "Thomas Jefferson, John Holt Rice and Education in Virginia," *Journal of Presbyterian History, 49* (Spring, 1971), 32–58.

19. See William G. McLoughlin, "The Balkcom Case (1782) and the Pietistic Theory of Separation of Church and State," *William and Mary Quarterly,* 3rd. ser., *24* (April, 1967), 267–83.

20. Article VI, Bill of Rights, in *A Constitution Containing a Bill of Rights, and Form of Government* (Portsmouth, N.H., 1783), pp. 4–5.

CHAPTER VI: DISESTABLISHMENT IN "A COMPOUND REPUBLIC"

1. *Democracy in America,* I, 311.

2. Father John Courtney Murray emphasizes the eight senators who did not accept the First Amendment; Leo Pfeffer emphasizes the majority in Virginia's legislature who did. See Robert G. McClosky, ed., *Essays in Constitutional Law* (New York, 1957), pp. 313, 346.

3. See *The Federalist,* Nos. 10 and 51, for Madison's theory of republican remedies.

4. Quoted by Irving Brant, *James Madison: Father of the Constitution 1787–1800* (Indianapolis, 1950), pp. 268–69.

5. *Ibid.,* p. 240.

6. Joseph Gales, ed., *Debates and Proceedings in the Congress of the United States* (Washington, 1934), I, 451–52; 758–59.

7. *Ibid.,* pp. 759, 784.

8. Charles B. Kinney, Jr., *Church and State: The Struggle for Separation in New Hampshire, 1630–1900* (New York, 1955), p. 100. Livermore himself said that his constituents did not consider the religious amendment important because it only went "to secure rights never in danger." See *Debates and Proceedings,* I, 805. He was most concerned about limiting Congress's tax powers and often differed with Madison on such issues.

9. *Debates and Proceedings,* I, 796, 948; *Journal of the First Session of the Senate of the United States of America* (Washington, 1820), pp. 70, 88. The whole process is closely recounted in Stokes and Pfeffer, eds., *Church and State,* pp. 92–100.

10. *Debates and Proceedings,* I, 758.

11. Stokes and Pfeffer, *op. cit.,* pp. 60–61.

12. *Memorial and Remonstrance,* reprinted in *ibid.,* p. 56.

13. Mark DeWolfe Howe, *The Garden and the Wilderness: Religion and Government in American Constitutional History* (Chicago, 1965), p. 28. Though he confuses Huntington (Conn.) with Livermore (N.H.) at one point, he valuably suggests that the Livermore wording about preventing Congress from making laws "touching religion" was actually a *narrowing* of Madison's phrasing because it was meant "to respect state law when it happened to sustain a religious enterprise." See pp. 22–23.

14. *Church and State in the United States,* pp. 247–48.

15. *Democracy in America,* I, 313.

16. *Ibid.,* pp. 308, 312.

CHAPTER VII: POPULAR REVIVALS, THE ART OF ASSOCIATING, AND MAJORITY TYRANNY

1. *Democracy in America,* II, 11, 98.

2. See Seymour Drescher, "Tocqueville's Two *Démocraties,*" *Journal of the History of Ideas,* 25 (Apr.–June, 1964), 201–16.

3. See my "Tocqueville's Duality: Describing America and Thinking of Europe," *American Quarterly,* 21 (Spring, 1969), 87–99.

4. *Democracy in America,* II, 6, 107, 110.

5. *Ibid.,* I, 263, 266.

6. *Ibid.,* p. 261.

7. George W. Pierson, *Tocqueville and Beaumont in America* (New York, 1938), p. 286.

8. Quoted by Charles A. Johnson, *The Frontier Camp Meeting: Religion's Harvest Time* (Dallas, Texas, 1955), p. 134.

9. William Warren Sweet, *Religion in the Development of American Culture 1765–1840* (New York, 1952), p. 145.

10. Quoted from James Finley, *Sketches of Western Methodism,* by T. Scott Miyakawa, *Protestants and Pioneers: Individualism and Conformity on the American Frontier* (Berkeley, Cal., 1964), p. 58.

11. *Ibid.,* p. 224.

12. Johnson, *op. cit.,* pp. 161, 124.

13. *Democracy in America,* II, 122–23.

14. Sweet, *op. cit.,* p. 165.

15. Johnson, p. 252.

16. *Ibid.,* p. 121.

17. See John R. Bodo, *The Protestant Clergy and Public Issues 1812–1848* (Princeton, 1954), pp. 93–111.

18. See Ralph H. Gabriel, *Elias Boudinot, Cherokee, and his America* (Norman, Okla., 1941) for the whole story.

19. *Protestants and Pioneers,* pp. 191–92.

20. *Protestant Clergy,* p. 117.

21. Quoted in *The Frontier Camp Meeting,* p. 222.

22. Quoted in *Protestants and Pioneers,* p. 201.

23. *Ibid.,* pp. 203 ff. Cf. Donald G. Mathews, "The Second Great Awakening as an Organizing Process, 1780–1830," *American Quarterly,* 21 (Spring, 1969), 23–43.

24. For the Baptists and Johnson see Lynn LaDue Marshall, *The Early Career of Amos Kendall: the Making of a Jacksonian,* Ph.D. diss., University of California (Berkeley, 1962), pp. 216, 256. For Jacksonian ideology see Marvin Meyers, *The Jacksonian Persuasion: Politics and Belief* (Stanford, Cal., 1957). The Congressional reports against giving up the Sunday mail service were written by O. B. Brown, a Baptist preacher who (as if making symbolically the point I argue) lived in Richard M. Johnson's boardinghouse. See Bertram Wyatt-Brown, "Prelude to Abolitionism: Sabbatarian Politics and the Rise of the Second Party System," *Journal of American History,* 58 (Sept., 1971), 335.

25. For the number of churches in 1850 see Gaustad, ed., *Historical Atlas of Religion,* p. 78.

26. *Democracy in America,* II, 9.

27. *Memoirs,* in *American Christianity: An Historical Interpretation with Representative Documents,* eds. H. Shelton Smith, Robert T. Handy, Lefferts A. Loetscher (New York, 1963), II, 22.

28. Quoted by H. Shelton Smith, *Changing Conceptions of Original Sin: A Study in American Theology Since 1750* (New York, 1955), pp. 107, 109.

29. *Lectures on Revivals of Religion,* 6th ed. (New York, 1835), p. 189.

30. *Ibid.,* pp. 203, 351–52.

31. Smith, *op. cit.,* pp. 132–33.

32. Bernard A. Weisberger, *They Gathered at the River: The Story of the Great Revivalists and Their Impact upon Religion in America* (Boston, 1958), pp. 111, 127. Other major studies of the revivalists are Whitney R. Cross, *The Burned-Over District: The Social and Intellectual History of Enthusiastic Religion in Western New York, 1800–1850* (Ithaca, N.Y., 1950); William G. McLoughlin, Jr., *Modern Revivalism* (New York, 1959); Perry Miller, *The Life of the Mind in America from the Revolution to the Civil War* (New York, 1965). I have drawn on all of them.

33. Weisberger, p. 77.

34. Miller, pp. 67, 66, quoting Barnes and Kent.

35. *A Plea for Voluntary Societies* (New York, 1837), p. 23. For the "united front" of evangelicals see Charles I. Foster, *An Errand of Mercy: The Evangelical United Front 1790–1837* (Chapel Hill, N.C., 1966), which is especially good on the English side of it. See also Clifford S. Griffin, *Their Brothers' Keepers: Moral Stewardship in the United States, 1800–1865* (New Brunswick, N.J., 1960); W. David Lewis, "The Reformer as Conservative: Protestant Counter-Subversion in the Early Republic," in *The Development of American Culture,* eds. Stanley Coben and Lorman A. Ratner (New York, 1970), pp. 64–91.

36. Quoted by Miller, *op. cit.,* p. 81. The specific attribution to Theodore Grimké is probably a slip for Theodore Dwight Weld who married a Grimké.

37. Odell Shephard, ed., *The Heart of Thoreau's Journals,* rev. ed. (New York, 1961), p. 34; Emerson, "Self-Reliance," *Essays,* First Series, Standard Library Edition (Boston, 1893), pp. 53–54.

38. Quoted by Leonard W. Levy, "Satan's Last Apostle in Massachusetts," *American Quarterly,* 5 (Spring, 1953), 29. I have condensed his full account of the case.

39. *Democracy in America,* II, 4, 6; for the context of Emerson's address see Conrad Wright, Introduction, *Three Prophets of Religious Liberalism: Channing, Emerson, Parker* (Boston, 1961), pp. 19–32.

40. *Democracy in America,* II, 9, 11, 27–28.

41. *Ibid.,* 41.

42. *The Infidel: Free Thought and American Religion* (Cleveland, Ohio, 1961), p. 128.

43. *Democracy in America,* II, Appendix BB, 368; I, 267.

44. *Ibid.,* I, 307, 265; II, 333.

45. *Studies in Classic American Literature,* in Edmund Wilson, ed., *The Shock of Recognition* (New York, 1943), p. 952. On Deerslayer's

religious upbringing see Susan Fenimore Cooper, Intro., *The Deerslayer or, the First War-Path* (Boston, 1898), pp. xxiv–xxvii.

46. Cooper, *Gleanings in Europe: France,* ed., Robert E. Spiller (New York, 1928), pp. 355–56; *Home as Found* (New York, 1782), p. 261.

CHAPTER VIII: PECULIAR PEOPLE IN THE LAND

1. *Democracy in America,* II, 9.

2. William R. Hutchison, *The Transcendentalist Ministers: Church Reform in the New England Renaissance* (New Haven, 1959), p. 31.

3. *Historical Atlas of Religion,* p. 127.

4. "Some Ideological Functions of Prejudice in Ante-Bellum America," *American Quarterly, 15* (Sept., 1963), pp. 124–25. See also his "Some Themes of Countersubversion: An Analysis of Anti-Masonic, Anti-Catholic, and Anti-Mormon Literature," in Richard O. Curry and Thomas M. Brown, eds., *Conspiracy: The Fear of Subversion in American History* (New York, 1972), pp. 61–77.

5. See John Tracy Ellis, *American Catholicism* (Chicago, 1956), pp. 62–67.

6. See Raymond B. Culver, *Horace Mann and Religion in the Massachusetts Public Schools* (New Haven, 1929); Howard Mumford Jones, "Horace Mann's Crusade," in Daniel Aaron, ed., *America in Crisis: Fourteen Crucial Episodes in American History* (New York, 1952), pp. 91–107.

7. Letter to Mann, May 30, 1852, *Letters and Journals of Samuel Gridley Howe,* ed. Laura E. Richards (Boston, 1906), II, 380.

8. See Vernon Stauffer, *New England and the Bavarian Illuminati* (New York, 1919) for this Federalist conspiracy theory.

9. See Ray Allen Billington, *The Protestant Crusade 1800–1860: A Study of the Origins of American Nativism* (New York, 1952), pp. 390, 411, 416.

10. *Democracy in America,* I, 300–1.

11. See Daniel Callahan, *The Mind of the Catholic Layman* (New York, 1963), pp. 28–48.

12. Ray B. West, *Kingdom of the Saints: The Story of Brigham Young and the Mormons* (New York, 1957), p. 19.

13. Vittorio Lanternari, *Religions of the Oppressed* (New York, 1963), pp. 131–34; Thomas F. O'Dea, *The Mormons* (Chicago, 1957), p. 137.

14. P. A. M. Taylor, *Expectations Westward: The Mormons and the Emigration of Their British Converts in the Nineteenth Century* (Ithaca, N.Y., 1966), p. 157.

15. *Ibid.,* pp. 62–63.

16. *The Mormons,* pp. 164–65.

17. Quoted in *Kingdom of the Saints,* p. 50.

18. Quoted in *ibid.,* p. 74.

19. *History of American Socialisms* (Philadelphia, 1870), p. 23.

20. Quoted in *Kingdom of the Saints,* p. 320.

21. Quoted in *The Mormons,* pp. 171, 168.

22. *Democracy in America,* I, 416.

23. *Ibid.,* II, 261.

24. David B. Davis points out that "in a rootless environment shaken by bewildering social change the nativist found unity and meaning by conspiring against imaginary conspiracies." He also notes in passing that "Protestant ministers played a key role in these crusades against alleged subversion." His acute observations point toward the factor of "republican religion" in *Democracy in America* without actually mentioning it. See his "Some Themes of Countersubversion," p. 77; "Some Ideological Functions of Prejudice in Ante-Bellum America," p. 116. *Supra, n. 4.*

25. Quoted in *Kingdom of the Saints,* p. 25.

CHAPTER IX: THE SIN OF SLAVERY

1. *Democracy in America,* I, 381, 359.

2. *Ibid.,* p. 379.

3. David B. Davis, *The Problem of Slavery in Western Culture* (Ithaca, N.Y., 1966), p. 261.

4. *Ibid.,* pp. 325–26.

5. *Ibid.,* p. 442.

6. *Uncle Tom's Cabin,* Modern Library edition (New York, 1938), p. 181.

7. W. D. Weatherford, *American Churches and the Negro: An Historical Study from Early Slave Days to the Present* (Boston, 1957), pp. 121, 123–24.

8. *Fleuve profond, sombre rivière: Les "Negro Spirituals," Commentaires et traductions* (Paris, 1964), pp. 41, 50.

9. Newman I. White, *American Negro Folk-Songs* (Hatboro, Penn., 1965), p. 51, n. 33.

10. *The Souls of Black Folk: Essays and Sketches,* intro. Saunders Redding (Greenwich, Conn., 1961), pp. 146–47.

11. Cf. *Life and Times of Frederick Douglass* (Hartford, 1881), p. 157 with *ibid.,* Dolphin edition (New York, 1963), pp. 87–88, 15.

12. Quoted by Archie Epps, "A Negro Separatist Movement," *Harvard Review, 4,* no. 1 (1966), 81–82.

13. Carter G. Woodson, *The History of the Negro Church,* 2nd. ed. (Washington, 1921), pp. 125–28.

14. *Ibid.,* pp. 137–40.

15. See Chap. 7, n. 20, *supra.*

16. *Protestant Clergy,* p. 62, quoting Charles B. Boynton, July 5, 1847, Oration.

17. *Ibid.,* pp. 113, 124, quoting John Clark Young, *Address to the Kentucky Colonization Society* (1833), and Nathaniel Bouton, *Christian Patriotism* (1825).

18. *The Varieties of Religious Experience,* pp. 20, 362–63.

19. Quoted by Davis, *The Problem of Slavery in Western Culture,* p. 87.

20. *Millennium and Utopia: A Study in the Background of the Idea of Progress* (Berkeley, Cal., 1949), p. 10. See also Ira V. Brown, "Watchers for the Second Coming: The Millenarian Tradition in America," *Mississippi Valley Historical Review, 39* (Dec., 1952), 441–58; Mircea Eliade, *The Quest: History and Meaning in Religion* (Chicago, 1969), 90–99.

21. *Thoughts on the Revival of Religion in New England* in *Works* (New York, 1881), III, 314. See C. C. Goen, "Jonathan Edwards: A New Departure in Eschatology," *Church History, 28* (1959), 25–39.

22. See Louis Billington, "The Millerite Adventists in Great Britain, 1840–1850," *Journal of American Studies, 1* (Oct., 1967), 191–212.

23. See Thomas F. Harwood, "British Evangelical Abolitionism and American Churches in the 1830's," *Journal of Southern History, 28* (Aug., 1962), 287–306.

24. The phrase is from the title of William Goodell's book (1854).

25. See *The Federalist,* No. 55.

26. Tuesday, June 26. In Convention. *Notes of Debates in the Federal Convention of 1787,* intro. Adrienne Koch (New York, 1969), p. 194.

27. Stow Persons, "The Cyclical Theory of History in Eighteenth Century America," *American Quarterly, 6* (Summer, 1964), 158.

28. *The Problem of Slavery,* p. 119.

29. William Peden, ed., *op. cit.,* p. 161.

30 Quoted by Louis Filler, *The Crusade against Slavery 1830–1860* (New York, 1960), p. 81.

31. *Ibid.,* p. 24, n. 34; p. 31.

32. Quoted by George M. Marsden, *The Evangelical Mind and the New School Presbyterian Experience: A Case Study of Thought and Theology in Nineteenth Century America* (New Haven, Conn., 1970), pp. 72, 104.

33. Quoted by Charles C. Cole, Jr., *Social Ideas of the Northern Evangelists* (New York, 1954), p. 195.

34. Quoted by David B. Davis, "The Emergence of Immediatism in British and American Anti-Slavery Thought," *Mississippi Valley Historical Review, 49* (Sept., 1962), 224.

35. *Ibid.,* p. 229.

36. *The Injustice and Impolicy of the Slave Trade and of the Slavery of the Africans,* 2nd. ed. (Boston, 1822), pp. 5, 38.

CHAPTER X: THE ART OF ASSOCIATING:
THE ABOLITIONIST SECT

1. *Democracy in America,* II, 109–10, 333.

2. *Roger Williams the Prophetic Legislator* (Providence, 1872), pp. 15–16. Cf. his *Justification: A Sermon* (Salem, 1847), p. 14.

3. See Andrew E. Murray, *Presbyterians and the Negro—A History* (Philadelphia, 1966), pp. 103–30; Benjamin Quarles, *Black Abolitionists* (New York, 1969), pp. 68–84.

4. Pierpont later introduced resolutions against the Fugitive Slave Law at the Unitarian convention in 1850. See *Heralds of a Liberal Faith,* ed. Samuel A. Eliot (Boston, 1910), II, 185–92.

5. Bryan Wilson, *Religious Sects: A Sociological Study* (New York, 1970), pp. 36–41.

6. *Democracy in America,* II, 27–28.

7. Leonard L. Richards, *"Gentlemen of Property and Standing": Anti-Abolitionist Mobs in Jacksonian America* (New York, 1970), pp. 145–48.

8. *Fourth of July Address,* in George M. Fredrickson, ed., *William Lloyd Garrison* (New York, 1968), p. 19; *Editorial on Nat Turner's Insurrection, ibid.,* p. 26; *Thoughts on African Colonization, ibid.,* p. 33; *Editorial on Perfectionism, ibid.,* pp. 48, 51.

9. Letter to H. C. Wright, April 1, 1843, quoted by Aileen S. Kraditor, *Means and Ends in American Abolitionism: Garrison and His Critics on Strategy and Tactics* (New York, 1969), p. 254. Garrison was opposing Robert Owen's socialistic ideas.

10. *Editorial on Disunion,* Fredrickson, *op. cit.,* p. 54; *Editorial on John Brown, ibid.,* p. 62.

11. See Lewis Perry, "Versions of Anarchism in the Antislavery Movement," *American Quarterly, 20* (Winter, 1968), 768–82.

12. Quoted by William Goodell, *Slavery and Antislavery,* 3rd. ed. (New York, 1855), pp. 513–14.

13. Reprinted in *American Christianity,* II, 42–48.

14. *The Sin of Slavery and its Remedy,* reprinted in John L. Thomas, ed., *Slavery Attacked: The Abolitionist Crusade* (Englewood Cliffs, N.J., 1965), pp. 16–17.

15. See Ronald P. Formisano, "Political Character, Antipartyism and the Second Party System," *American Quarterly, 21* (Winter, 1969), 683–709.

16. See Carleton Mabee, "A Negro Boycott to Integrate Boston Schools," *New England Quarterly, 41* (Sept., 1968), 341–61; Leonard W. Levy and Harlan B. Phillips, "The *Roberts* Case: Source of the 'Separate but Equal' Doctrine," *American Historical Review, 56* (April, 1951),

510–18; Louis Ruchames, "Jim Crow Railroads in Massachusetts," *American Quarterly, 8* (Spring, 1956), 61–75.

17. See James Brewer Stewart, *Joshua R. Giddings and the Tactics of Radical Politics* (Cleveland, 1970), which portrays Giddings's anti-slavery position as a reintegrating response to career failure, a function religion often plays.

18. Bertram Wyatt-Brown, *Lewis Tappan and the Evangelical War Against Slavery* (Cleveland, 1969), pp. 256, 278. I have followed his account in the following paragraph.

19. Quoted by John Demos, "The Antislavery Movement and the Problem of Violent Means," *New England Quarterly, 37* (December, 1964), 522; quoted by Tilden G. Edelstein, *Strange Enthusiasm: A Life of Thomas Wentworth Higginson* (New Haven, 1968), p. 166.

CHAPTER XI: DAY OF VENGEANCE

1. *Democracy in America,* II, 256; I, 379, 402 f., 416.

2. *Ibid.,* I, 418, 434.

3. Major L. Wilson, "The Free Soil Concept of Progress and the Irrepressible Conflict," *American Quarterly, 22* (Winter, 1970), 769–90.

4. See Mike Thelwell, "Back with the Wind: Mr. Styron and the Reverend Turner," in John Henrik Clarke, ed., *William Styron's Nat Turner: Ten Black Writers Respond* (Boston, 1968), p. 82.

5. *The Varieties of Religious Experience,* p. 426.

6. Thomas R. Gray, *The Confessions of Nat Turner* (1831), in Clarke, ed., *op. cit.,* pp. 105, 113.

7. *Ibid.,* pp. 102–4.

8. *Ibid.,* p. 104.

9. *Ibid.,* p. 105.

10. Quoted by Raymond Weaver, Intro., *Uncle Tom's Cabin or Life Among the Lowly,* Modern Library edition (New York, 1938), p. xviii. For her relation to bondage see Constance Rourke, *Trumpets of Jubilee,* Harbinger edition (New York, 1963), pp. 80–82.

11. Quoted by Rourke, *op. cit.,* p. 80.

12. *Cavalier and Yankee: The Old South and American National Character* (New York, 1961), pp. 307–13.

13. *The Crusade Against Slavery,* p. 210.

14. Letter to Francis Jackson, Nov. 24, 1859, in Henry Steele Commager, ed., *Theodore Parker: An Anthology* (Boston, 1960), p. 265.

15. See Edwin S. Redsky, *Black Exodus: Black Nationalist and Back-to-Africa Movements, 1890–1910* (New Haven, 1969).

16. Quoted by William H. and Jane H. Pease, "Antislavery Ambivalence: Immediacy, Expediency, Race," *American Quarterly, 17* (Winter, 1965), 691.

17. Quoted in Charles H. Foster, *The Rungless Ladder: Harriet Beecher Stowe and New England Puritanism* (Durham, N.C., 1954), p. 122.

18. *History of American Socialisms,* p. 23.

19. See my *"Uncle Tom's Cabin* and the Portent of Millennium," *Yale Review,* 57 (Spring, 1968), 375–85.

20. Quoted in "Antislavery Ambivalence," p. 693.

21. *The Life and Times of Frederick Douglass* (Hartford, 1881), pp. 290, 293, 296.

22. Stephen B. Oates, *To Purge this Land with Blood: A Biography of John Brown* (New York, 1970), pp. 22, 81.

23. *Ibid.,* pp. 196, 208 f.

24. Quoted in *ibid.,* p. 258 (from James Hanway's *Reminiscences*).

25. *Ibid.,* p. 271.

CHAPTER XII: A PEOPLE'S CONTEST AND THE JUDGMENTS OF THE LORD

1. *Democracy in America,* I, 416.

2. *The Life and Times of Frederick Douglass,* pp. 497–98.

3. Quoted by James M. McPherson, *The Struggle for Equality: Abolitionists and the Negro in the Civil War and Reconstruction* (Princeton, 1964), p. 27.

4. Quoted in *ibid.,* p. 35.

5. "Stranger in the Village," *Notes of a Native Son* (Boston, 1955), pp. 174–75.

6. *The Struggle for Equality,* p. 36.

7. See Harry V. Jaffa, *Equality and Liberty: Theory and Practice in American Politics* (New York, 1965), especially Chaps. 5, 7.

8. See Thomas J. Pressly, "Bullets and Ballots: Lincoln and the 'Right of Revolution,' " *American Historical Review,* 67 (April, 1962), 647–62.

9. No. 22.

10. Quoted by William J. Wolf, *The Religion of Abraham Lincoln* (New York, 1963), pp. 99–100.

11. Quoted in *ibid.,* p. 103.

12. See David Donald, *Lincoln's Herndon* (New York, 1948), p. 359.

13. Wolf, *op. cit.,* p. 102.

14. *Ibid.,* pp. 147–48.

15. The story of the "vow" derives from the Secretary of the Navy, reporting a Cabinet meeting with Lincoln. See Wolf, "Abraham Lincoln and Calvinism," in G. L. Hunt, ed., *Calvinism and the Political Order,* p. 147. Lincoln's religious view of the war, Edmund Wilson emphasizes, omits the economic forces at work. See his *Patriotic Gore: Studies in the Literature of the American Civil War* (New York, 1962), pp. 99–130.

16. Lincoln's lack of conventional creed or membership in a church leads both Herndon and Mrs. Lincoln to underestimate the depth of certain Christian beliefs and ideas in Lincoln's outlook. See *Lincoln's Herndon,* p. 278.

17. *The Struggle for Equality,* pp. 406–7, 427.

18. Quoted by Willie Lee Rose, " 'Iconoclasm Has Had Its Day': Abolitionists and Freedman in South Carolina," in Martin Duberman, ed., *The Antislavery Vanguard: New Essays on the Abolitionists* (Princeton, 1965), p. 180.

19. For a critical evaluation of how recent historians have dealt with the conflicting evidence on this issue see Richard O. Curry, "The Abolitionists and Reconstruction: A Critical Appraisal," *Journal of Southern History, 34* (Nov., 1968), 527–45.

20. *Miss Ravenel's Conversion from Secession to Loyalty,* ed. Gordon S. Haight (New York, 1964), p. 460.

21. *A Fool's Errand,* 2nd. ed. (New York, 1879), p. 357.

22. Ralph E. Morrow, *Northern Methodism and Reconstruction* (East Lansing, Mich., 1956), pp. 200, 223.

CHAPTER XIII: THE POWER OF WORLDLINESS

1. *Protestant-Catholic-Jew: An Essay in American Religious Sociology,* rev. ed. (New York, 1960), p. 271.

2. *Democracy in America,* II, 127.

3. *Ibid.,* p. 122.

4. See Cushing Strout, "William James and the Twice-born Sick Soul," *Daedalus, 97* (Summer, 1968), 1062–82. Reprinted in Dankwart A. Rustow, ed., *Philosophers and Kings: Studies in Leadership* (New York, 1970), pp. 491–511.

5. *The Varieties of Religious Experience,* pp. 357, 360.

6. *Historical Atlas of Religion,* pp. 43–44, figs. 32–33; 162, fig. 128.

7. Quoted by Agnes Rush Burr, *Russell H. Conwell and His Work* (Philadelphia, 1917), p. 228.

8. *Ibid.,* p. 393. The book includes Conwell's famous address.

9. *The Varieties of Religious Experience,* pp. 365, 368.

10. *Our Country,* ed. Jergen Herbst (Cambridge, Mass., 1963), p. 239.

11. *Ibid.,* p. 253.

12. *Truths for Today,* reprinted in William R. Hutchison, ed., *American Protestant Thought: The Liberal Era* (New York, 1968), p. 55.

13. Cushing Strout, "Faith and History: The Mind of William G. T. Shedd," *Journal of the History of Ideas, 15* (Jan., 1954), 153–62.

14. Arthur Cushman McGiffert, "The Historical Study of Christianity," in *American Protestant Thought,* p. 71.

15. Willard Thorp, "The Religious Novel as Best Seller in America,"

in *Religious Perspectives in American Culture,* James Ward Smith and A. Leland Jamison, eds. (Princeton, N.J., 1961), pp. 223–24, 229–31.

16. See Cushing Strout, "Personality and Cultural History in the Novel: Two American Examples," *New Literary History, 1,* no. 3 (1970), 423–37, especially 426–32.

17. Willard Thorp sees the novel as the story of the inability of "the old-time religion" to meet a subtle Catholicism, the new learning, and paganism, but it is Theron Ware's inauthentic relation to his faith *and* his doubt that is the source of his trouble. See "The Religious Novel as Best Seller in America," *Religious Perspectives,* p. 229.

18. The best discussion of the liberal Catholic movement in this period is Robert D. Cross, *The Emergence of Liberal Catholicism in America* (Cambridge, Mass., 1958).

19. Intro., Walter Elliott, *The Life of Father Hecker,* 2nd. ed. (New York, 1894), pp. vii, xvi.

20. *The Positive Thinkers: A Study of the American Quest for Health, Wealth and Personal Power from Mary Baker Eddy to Norman Vincent Peale* (New York, 1965), pp. 123–24.

21. *Democracy in America,* II, 134, 31–32.

22. "The Gospel of Relaxation," *Essays on Faith and Morals,* ed. Ralph Barton Perry (New York, 1947), p. 245.

23. See Appendix A in Nathan Glazer, *American Judaism* (Chicago, 1957). I have followed his analysis of the Reform impulse.

24. See Stephen Steinberg, "Reform Judaism: The Origin and Evolution of a 'Church Movement,'" *Journal for the Scientific Study of Religion, 5* (1965–66), 117–29.

25. See David Singer, "David Levinsky's Fall: A Note on the Liebman Thesis," *American Quarterly, 19* (Winter, 1967), 696–706; Cushing Strout, "Personality and Cultural History in the Novel," *loc. cit.,* pp. 433–36; *Democracy in America,* I, 298.

CHAPTER XIV: THE SOCIAL GOSPEL AND THE ARISTOCRACY OF MANUFACTURES

1. *Democracy in America,* II, 161.

2. *Ibid.,* p. 142.

3. See Edward T. Gargan, *Alexis de Tocqueville: The Critical Years 1848–1851* (Washington, D.C., 1955), pp. 46–50.

4. *Democracy in America,* I, 325.

5. No. 10.

6. See Cushing Strout, Intro., J. Allen Smith, *The Spirit of American Government* (Cambridge, Mass., 1965), pp. xliv–xlviii, lii–liii.

7. See Fred Nicklason, "Henry George: Social Gospeller," *American Quarterly, 22* (Fall, 1970), 649–64.

8. Quoted from *Equality* by Joseph Schiffman, *Edward Bellamy: Selected Writings on Religion and Society* (New York, 1955), p. 44.

9. *Caesar's Column: A Story of the Twentieth Century,* ed. Walter B. Rideout (Cambridge, Mass., 1960), p. 169.

10. *Ibid.,* p. 260.

11. See Edwin H. Cady, *The Realist at War: The Mature Years of William Dean Howells, 1885–1920* (Syracuse, N.Y., 1958), pp. 145–54.

12. Quoted by Herbert G. Gutman, "Protestantism and the American Labor Movement: The Christian Spirit in the Gilded Age," *American Historical Review, 72* (Oct., 1966), 89.

13. See Henry F. May, *Protestant Churches and Industrial America* (New York, 1967), pp. 127–29. This reprint has a new introduction. See also Charles Howard Hopkins, *The Rise of the Social Gospel in American Protestantism 1865–1915* (New Haven, 1967), pp. 280–83. (Originally pub. 1940.)

14. *Ground Under Our Feet: An Autobiography* (New York, 1938), p. 73. See Clyde Griffen, "The Progressive Ethos," in *The Development of American Culture,* Stanley Coben and Lorman A. Ratner eds., pp. 120–49.

15. See Jacob Henry Dorn, *Washington Gladden: Prophet of the Social Gospel* (Columbus, Ohio, 1967).

16. Quoted by Richard Dressner from *Christian Socialist* (July 1, 1906) in *Christian Socialism: A Response to Industrial America,* Ph.D. diss., Cornell University, 1972, p. 79. For Bliss's career see also Hopkins, *op. cit.,* pp. 173–83, 262; Howard H. Quint, *The Forging of American Socialism* (Indianapolis, 1953), pp. 109–26, 256–67.

17. Quoted from *Christian Socialist* (Sept. 1, 1910) by Robert T. Handy, "Christianity and Socialism in America," *Church History, 21* (March, 1952), 49.

18. See Dressner, *op. cit.,* p. 75.

19. Quoted by Handy, *op. cit.,* p. 52.

20. Quint, *op. cit.,* p. 261. Quint (as Dressner shows) ignores Bliss's career after the formation of the Socialist Party.

21. Robert T. Handy, *George D. Herron and the Social Gospel in American Protestantism, 1890–1901,* Ph.D. diss., University of Chicago, 1949, pp. 37, 126–27, 147, 149.

22. *Ibid.,* p. 177, n. 1.

23. *Christianity and the Social Crisis,* ed. Robert D. Cross (New York, 1964), pp. 59–60.

24. *Ibid.,* pp. 323, 331.

25. *Ibid.,* pp. 402, 408, 410–11.

26. *Ibid.,* pp. 285, 376, 272, 279.

27. *A Theology for the Social Gospel* (New York, 1917), p. 273.

28. *Christianity and the Social Crisis,* p. 279.

29. Quoted by Vernon Parker Bodein, *The Social Gospel of Walter Rauschenbusch and Its Relation to Religious Education* (New Haven, 1944), p. 72.

30. Letter to Mrs. Joseph Steffens, Dec. 31, 1909; copy shown me through the courtesy of Harry Stein, who develops the social-gospel aspect of Steffens in his dissertation in progress, American Studies, University of Minnesota.

31. Clyde Griffen, "The Progressive Ethos," *op. cit.,* p. 125.

32. Hopkins, *op. cit.,* pp. 316–17.

33. Quoted by Arthur S. Link, "Woodrow Wilson: Presbyterian in Government," in G. L. Hunt, ed., *Calvinism and the Political Order,* p. 170.

34. Ryan tells his own story in *Social Doctrine in Action: A Personal History* (New York, 1941); see also Francis L. Broderick, *Right Reverend New Dealer: John A. Ryan* (New York, 1963); Aaron I. Abell, *American Catholicism and Social Action: A Search for Social Justice 1865–1950* (New York, 1960).

CHAPTER XV: THE GREAT CRUSADE FOR PROHIBITION, WOMAN SUFFRAGE, AND THE WAR

1. *The Puritan Ethic and Woman Suffrage* (New York, 1967), p. 115.

2. Quoted by Grimes, p. 135.

3. See Grimes, pp. 124, 128, 133, tables iv, v, vi.

4. See Paul Carter, *The Decline and Revival of the Social Gospel: Social and Political Liberalism in American Protestant Churches, 1920–1940* (Ithaca, N.Y., 1956), pp. 21–22.

5. S. J. Mennell, "Prohibition: A Sociological View," *British Journal of American Studies, 3* (December, 1969), 168.

6. James H. Timberlake, *Prohibition and the Progressive Movement* (Cambridge, Mass., 1963), p. 135.

7. *Democracy in America,* II, 201.

8. Susan B. Anthony and Ida Husted Harper, quoted by Grimes, *op. cit.,* p. 94.

9. *Democracy in America,* I, 304.

10. *Preachers Present Arms: A Study of the War-Time Attitudes and Activities of the Churches and the Clergy in the United States, 1914–1918,* Ph.D. diss., University of Pennsylvania (Philadelphia, 1933), pp. 55, 248.

11. *Ibid.,* pp. 138, 135, 213, 214–16.

12. *Democracy in America,* I, 306.

13. William R. Hutchison, "Cultural Strain and Protestant Liberalism," *American Historical Review, 76* (April, 1971), 411.

14. *Democracy in America,* II, 27–28.

15. Abrams, p. 73.

16. H. C. Peterson and Gilbert C. Fite, *Opponents of War 1917–1918* (Madison, Wis., 1957), p. 138.

17. *Ibid.,* pp. 213, 219.

18. *Democracy in America,* II, 253, 263, 257; I, 266–67.

19. *Ibid.,* II, 269.

CHAPTER XVI: A CATHOLIC NATIVE SON IN A "PURITAN CIVILIZATION"

1. George M. Stephenson, *A History of American Immigration 1820–1924* (Boston, 1926), p. 126. For a recent summary of ethnocultural-political scholarship see Robert P. Swierenga, "Ethnocultural Political Analysis: A New Approach to American Ethnic Studies," *British Journal of American Studies,* 5 (April, 1971), 59–79.

2. David G. Farelly, " 'Rum, Romanism, and Rebellion' Resurrected," in Peter H. Odegaard, ed., *Religion and Politics* (Rutgers, N.J., 1960), pp. 36–40.

3. Ruth C. Silva, *Rum, Religion, and Votes: 1928 Re-examined* (University Park, Penn., 1962), p. 2. I have used her figures for proportions of Catholics and foreign-stock whites in the states.

4. Donald J. Bogue, *The Population of the United States* (Glencoe, Ill., 1959), pp. 351, 354, 365; *Census of Religious Bodies, 1926* (Washington, 1929), pp. 293–95, table 25.

5. The Marshall-Smith debate is reproduced in *Religion and Politics,* pp. 49–74. For Smith's statements see *ibid.,* pp. 63–64.

6. "The Catholicism of Al Smith," *Men of Destiny* (New York, 1927), p. 41.

7. Quoted by Edmund A. Moore, *A Catholic Runs for President: The Campaign of 1928* (New York, 1956), pp. 131, 48–50.

8. Kenneth K. Bailey, *Southern White Protestantism in the Twentieth Century* (New York, 1964), pp. 94–95.

9. Silva, *op. cit.,* pp. 22–23, table C.

10. For Minnesota see Lucy S. Dawidowicz and Leon J. Goldstein, *Politics in a Pluralistic Democracy: Studies of Voting in the 1960 Election* (New York, 1963), p. 53, table 15; p. 56, table 16. For North Dakota I have calculated from maps in Michael Paul Rogin, *The Intellectuals and McCarthy: The Radical Specter* (Cambridge, Mass., 1967), pp. 108, 124; and from county returns given in Eugene E. Robinson, *The Presidential Vote 1896–1932* (Stanford, Cal., 1934), pp. 268–92, table ix.

11. For the New York vote see John H. Fenton, *The Catholic Vote* (New Orleans, La., 1960), pp. 75, 82, tables 18, 24.

12. Samuel Lubell, *The Future of American Politics* (New York, 1952), p. 34.

13. *Al Smith and His America* (Boston, 1958), p. 188.

14. *Democracy in America,* II, 27.

15. *Politics in a Pluralistic Democracy,* pp. 86–87.

16. *Religion and Politics,* p. 160.

17. *Democracy in America,* I, 302.

CHAPTER XVII: CRISIS THEOLOGY FROM THE CRASH TO THE BOMB

1. See Francis L. Broderick, *Right Reverend New Dealer: John A. Ryan,* p. 242; Samuel Lubell, *The Future of American Politics,* pp. 142–44.

2. See Werner Cohn, "The Politics of American Jews," in Marshall Sklare, ed., *The Jews: Social Patterns of an American Group* (Glencoe, Ill., 1958), 614–26.

3. See Donald B. Meyer, *The Protestant Search for Political Realism, 1919–1941* (Berkeley, Cal., 1960), pp. 174–75; Ralph Lord Roy, *Communism and the Churches* (New York, 1960), p. 87, 442, n. 1.

4. Edgar Kemler, *The Deflation of American Ideals: An Ethical Guide for New Dealers* (Washington, 1941), p. 34.

5. Quoted by Paul A. Carter, *The Decline and Revival of the Social Gospel,* pp. 176–77.

6. David O. Moberg, *The Church as a Social Institution: The Sociology of American Religion* (Englewood Cliffs, N.J., 1962), p. 151.

7. Carter, p. 222.

8. Meyer, pp. 381, 383, 385.

9. Ward quoted by Meyer, p. 197; Spofford and Fritchman quoted by Roy, pp. 330, 361; Davis discussed by Roy, pp. 177–78; AYC and churches discussed by Roy, pp. 99–101.

10. "Sects and Churches" (1935), Reinhold Niebuhr, *Essays in Applied Christianity,* D. B. Robertson, ed. (New York, 1959), pp. 38, 40.

11. *An Interpretation of Christian Ethics,* 4th ed. (New York, 1935), p. 95.

12. Walter Lowrie's *Our Concern with the Theology of Crisis* was published in 1932. For the "Kierkegaardian" character of continental influences see Sydney E. Ahlstrom, "Continental Influence on American Christian Thought since World War I," *Church History, 27* (Sept., 1958), 3–19.

13. *Leaves from the Notebooks of a Tamed Cynic* (New York, 1957), pp. 60, 222–24, 166–67.

14. *Does Civilization Need Religion? A Study in the Social Resources*

and Limitations of Religion in Modern Life (New York, 1927), pp. 18, 41, 44, 78, 128, 187–88, 229, 242.

15. "The Weakness of the Modern Church" (1931), *Essays in Applied Christianity*, pp. 71, 74, 75, 76.

16. *Moral Man and Immoral Society: A Study in Ethics and Politics* (New York, 1932), p. 61.

17. *Ibid.*, pp. 62, 29, 59.

18. *Ibid.*, pp. 190, 229, 199, 277.

19. *Ibid.*, pp. 81, 252–56.

20. "The Christian Church in a Secular Age," *Christianity and Power Politics* (New York, 1940), pp. 210, 215

21. See Donald B. Meyer, *The Protestant Search for Political Realism*, p. 261. Meyer sees the shift as an escape from the dilemma posed to Niebuhr by the relative success of the New Deal liberalism, challenging his own pessimism. No society and no individual can overcome the "vicious circle of sin," he asserts in "The Test of True Prophecy," *Beyond Tragedy: Essays on the Christian Interpretation of History* (New York, 1937), pp. 105–8.

22. Editorial, *Radical Religion, 5* (Winter, 1940), 5, 10.

23. Cf. "Idealists as Cynics," *Christianity and Power Politics*, p. 79, and "Why the Church Is Not Pacifist," *ibid.*, p. 20.

24. "Christian Moralism in America," *Radical Religion, 5* (Winter, 1940), p. 20.

25. *An Interpretation of Christian Ethics*, 4th ed. (New York, 1935), pp. 187–88, 194.

26. Cf. "A Critique of Pacifism," in D. B. Robertson, ed., *Love and Justice: Selections from the Shorter Writings of Reinhold Niebuhr* (Philadelphia, 1957), pp. 243, 246, and "Why I Leave the F.O.R.," *ibid.*, p. 257.

27. Editorial, *Radical Religion, 4* (Winter, 1938), 3–4; "The War and American Churches," *Christianity and Power Politics*, p. 42.

28. Cf. *Moral Man and Immoral Society*, p. 74, and "The War and American Churches," *Christianity and Power Politics*, pp. 43–46.

29. "Germany and the Western World," *Christianity and Power Politics*, pp. 47, 59–61; David Paton, "The Christian Socialist Movement in England," *Radical Religion, 3* (Fall, 1938), 21–26.

30. Editorial, *Radical Religion, 3* (Fall, 1939), 3.

31. "Christian Faith and Natural Law," *Love and Justice*, p. 53; "An Open Letter," *ibid.*, p. 270.

32. "Airplanes Are Not Enough," *ibid.*, p. 190; "The Bombing of Germany," *ibid.*, pp. 222–23.

33. Robert C. Batchelder, *The Irreversible Decision 1939–1950* (Boston, 1961), pp. 181, 189.

34. "The Atomic Bomb," *Love and Justice,* p. 233.

35. Batchelder, pp. 185–86.

36. Most notably, Father John C. Ford, a Jesuit moralist, attacked obliteration bombing in *Theological Studies* in 1944. Batchelder, pp. 178–80. His grounds were traditional ones: killing noncombatants intentionally is equivalent to murder, an old Christian view on war.

37. "An Open Letter," *Love and Justice,* p. 268.

38. "The Confession of a Tired Radical," *Love and Justice,* p. 120.

39. Batchelder, pp. 177, 182–83.

40. Quoted by Batchelder, p. 251.

41. "The Response of Reinhold Niebuhr," in Harold R. Landon, ed., *Reinhold Niebuhr: A Prophetic Voice in Our Time* (Greenwich, Conn., 1962), p. 123.

42. Quoted by Canon Harold R. Landon, "Discussion," *Reinhold Niebuhr,* p. 116.

43. "Christianity and Politics in Britain," *Love and Justice,* pp. 82–84.

44. Alasdair MacIntyre, *Secularization and Moral Change* (London, 1967), p. 63. For the statistics see p. 60.

45. "Pious and Secular America," *Pious and Secular America* (New York, 1958), p. 11.

46. Preface, *Leaves from the Notebooks of a Tamed Cynic,* p. 13.

47. *We Hold These Truths: Catholic Reflections on the American Proposition* (New York, 1960), pp. 283–85.

48. *Moral Man and Immoral Society,* p. 263.

49. *The Children of Light and the Children of Darkness: A Vindication of Democracy and a Critique of its Traditional Defense* (New York, 1944), p. 185.

50. Joseph Adelson, "The Political Imagination of the Young Adolescent," *Daedalus, 100* (Fall, 1971), 1034–38.

51. *The Federalist,* No. 55.

52. *An Interpretation of Christian Ethics,* p. 93.

53. On Niebuhr's relation to Dewey see Arthur M. Schlesinger, Jr., "Reinhold Niebuhr's Role in American Political Thought and Life," in Charles Kegley and Robert Bretall, eds., *Reinhold Niebuhr: His Religious, Social and Political Thought* (New York, 1956), reprinted in Schlesinger, *The Politics of Hope* (Cambridge, Mass., 1962), pp. 97–125.

54. *The Varieties of Religious Experience,* pp. 163–65, 362, 364, 377, 375. The Jamesian analogy is surprisingly ignored in the commentary on both men, probably because James is relatively nonpolitical.

55. *Ibid.,* p. 367.

56. Quoted by Ralph Barton Perry, *The Thought and Character of William James* (Boston, 1935), II, 315. Niebuhr means by "pragmatism" not a philosophical doctrine but an adjustment of moral principle to the

specifics of changing circumstances. See *Reinhold Niebuhr,* ed. Landon, p. 122.

57. Editorial, *Radical Religion, 4* (Fall, 1939), 1.

58. Hans J. Morgenthau, "Niebuhr's Political Thought," Landon, ed., *op. cit.,* p. 109; "The Response of Reinhold Niebuhr," *ibid.,* p. 123.

59. *Leaves from the Notebooks of a Tamed Cynic,* p. 18; Morgenthau, p. 99.

60. This aspect of Niebuhr's thought is emphasized by Walter LaFeber, *America, Russia, and the Cold War, 1945–1966* (New York, 1967), pp. 40–41, 195–96, 258–59.

CHAPTER XVIII: THE WINDING WALL OF SEPARATION AND THE NEW PLURALISM

1. *Hamilton* v. *Regents of the University of California,* 293 U.S. 245 (1934). See Philip B. Kurland, *Religion and the Law of Church and State and the Supreme Court* (Chicago, 1962), p. 40.

2. *Cantwell* v. *Connecticut,* 310 U.S. 296 (1940).

3. 310 U.S. 586, 596 (1940).

4. *Id.,* at 602, 606.

5. David R. Manwaring, *Render Unto Caesar: The Flag Salute Controversy* (Chicago, 1962), pp. 163–86.

6. *Board of Education* v. *Barnette,* 319 U.S. 624 (1943). Manwaring's analysis is excellent.

7. *Id.,* at 653.

8. *Notes on the State of Virginia,* ed. William Peden, p. 224.

9. *Reynolds* v. *United States,* 98 U.S. 145 (1878).

10. *Board of Education* v. *Barnette,* at 659.

11. *Murdock* v. *Pennsylvania,* 319 U.S. 105, 109 (1943).

12. *Martin* v. *Struthers,* 319 U.S. 141 (1943).

13. *Murdock* v. *Pennsylvania,* at 130; *Douglas* v. *Jeannette,* 319 U.S. 157, 179 (1943).

14. *Board of Education* v. *Barnette,* at 662.

15. See Kurland, *op. cit.,* p. 243.

16. *Board of Education* v. *Barnette,* at 661, 665.

17. *Everson* v. *Board of Education,* 330 U.S. 1, 39 (1947).

18. *McCollum* v. *Board of Education,* 333 U.S. 203, 244 (1948).

19. *Bradfield* v. *Roberts,* 175 U.S. 291 (1899); *Quick Bear* v. *Leupp,* 210 U.S. 50 (1908); *Cochran* v. *Louisiana State Board of Education,* 281 U.S. 370 (1930).

20. Mark DeWolfe Howe, *Cases on Church and State in the United States* (Cambridge, Mass., 1952), pp. 87–88.

21. Anson Phelps Stokes and Leo Pfeffer, eds., *Church and State in the United States,* rev. ed. (New York, 1964), pp. 434–35.

22. 330 U.S. 1, 18 (1947).

23. Robert F. Drinan, "The Constitutionality of Public Aid to Parochial Schools," in Dallin H. Oaks, ed., *The Wall between Church and State* (Chicago, 1963), p. 59.

24. 333 U.S. 203, 209 (1948).

25. 343 U.S. 306, 313–14 (1952).

26. *Id.* at 325.

27. Donald E. Boles, *The Bible, Religion, and the Public Schools,* rev. ed. (New York, 1963), pp. 196, 211.

28. *Piety along the Potomac: Notes on Politics and Morals in the Fifties* (Boston, 1964), p. 43.

29. 333 U.S. 203, 238 (1948).

30. See John Cogley, ed., *Religion in America: Original Essays on Religion in a Free Society* (New York, 1958), pp. 30–31, 47–50, 90–92.

31. Quoted by Martin E. Marty, *The New Shape of American Religion* (New York, 1959), p. 81.

32. *Ibid.,* p. 87. For Herberg see *Protestant-Catholic-Jew: An Essay in American Religious Sociology,* rev. ed. (New York, 1960).

33. "The New Pluralism: From Nostalgia to Reality," *Commonweal, 78* (Sept. 6, 1963), New York, 528.

34. Lawrence H. Fuchs, *John F. Kennedy and American Catholicism* (New York, 1967), p. 183; Arthur Hertzberg, "The 'Establishment,' Dogma and the Presidency," *Commentary, 30* (Oct., 1960), 277–85.

35. Philip E. Converse, Angus Campbell, Warren E. Miller, Donald E. Stokes, "Stability and Change in 1960: A Reinstating Election," *American Political Science Review, 55* (June, 1961), 272–73, 276.

36. Xavier Rynne, *The Third Session, The Debates and Decrees of Vatican Council II September 14 to November 21, 1964* (New York, 1965), pp. 29, 254–61.

37. Theodore H. White, *The Making of the President 1960* (New York, 1961), Appendix C, p. 392.

38. "The 'Catholic Issue,'" *New Republic,* Supplement, "Catholics in America" (March 21, 1960), p. 11.

39. Hertzberg, *loc. cit.,* 283.

40. Saul Brenner, "Patterns of Jewish-Catholic Democratic Voting and the 1960 Presidential Election," *Jewish Social Studies, 26,* no. 3 (1964), 169–78.

41. "The New Pluralism," *loc. cit.,* p. 527.

42. Quoted by Daniel Callahan, *The Mind of the Catholic Layman* (New York, 1963), p. 185.

43. "The New Pluralism," *loc. cit.*

44. "Church and State: How High a Wall?" *Commentary, 42* (July, 1966), 26.

45. 330 U.S. 1, 232 (1947).

46. See Boles, *op. cit.,* pp. 247–49; Philip B. Kurland, "The School Prayer Cases," in Dallin, ed., *The Wall Between Church and State,* p. 144.

47. 343 U.S. 306, 319 (1952).

48. Quoted by Boles, pp. 99, 101.

49. 333 U.S. 203, 217 (1948). Frankfurter, J., concurring.

50. Arthur Gilbert, "Religious Freedom and Social Change in a Pluralistic Society: A Historical Review," in Donald A. Gianella, ed., *Religion and the Public Order 1964* (Chicago, 1965), pp. 113–15.

51. Seymour Martin Lipset, "Some Statistics on Bigotry in Voting," *Commentary, 30* (Oct., 1960), 288.

52. Quoted by Kurland, "The School Prayer Cases," *op. cit.,* p. 147.

53. *Engel* v. *Vitale,* 370 U.S. 421, 431–32 (1962).

54. *Id.,* at 436.

55. *Id.,* at 430.

56. Quoted by Kurland, "The School Prayer Cases," *op. cit.,* p. 174.

57. *Schempp* v. *School District of Abington,* 177 F. Supp. 398 (E. D. Pa. 1959).

58. *Abington School District* v. *Schempp,* 374 U.S. 203, 222.

59. *The Bible in the Public Schools,* Arguments in the Case of *John D. Minor et al.* v. *The Board of Education of the City of Cincinnati et al.,* Superior Court of Cincinnati (Cincinnati, 1870), pp. 414–15.

60. Paul G. Kauper, "Schempp and Sherbert: Studies in Neutrality and Accommodation," in Donald A. Gianella, ed., *Religion and the Public Order 1963* (Chicago, 1964), pp. 3–40.

61. Mark DeWolfe Howe, *The Garden and the Wilderness: Religion and Government in American Constitutional History* (Chicago, 1965), pp. 165–67.

62. *We Hold These Truths,* p. 65.

63. *Ibid.,* p. 152.

64. 343 U.S. 306, 313 (1952).

65. Concurring in *Engel* v. *Vitale,* 370 U.S. 421, 437, 443–44 (1962).

66. A. D. Mayo, "The Work of Certain Northern Churches in the Education of the Freedmen, 1861–1900," *Annual Reports of the Department of the Interior,* Report of the Commissioner of Education for the Year 1902 (Washington, 1903), I, 295.

67. See Dean M. Kelley and George R. LaNoue, "The Church-State Settlement in the Federal Aid to Education Act," in Donald A. Gianella, ed., *Religion and the Public Order 1965* (Chicago, 1966), pp. 110–60.

68. *Tilton* v. *Richardson,* 91 S. Ct. 2091, 2095 (1971); *Lemon* v. *Kurtzman,* 91 S. Ct. 2105, 2112 (1971).

69. Brennan, William, J., dissenting in 91 S. Ct. 2105, 2132; Douglas, J., dissenting in *Board of Education* v. *Allen,* 392 U.S. 236, 255 (1968).

70. New York *Times,* Nov. 23, 1969, and Nov. 8, 1964.

71. *Ibid.,* Nov. 9, 1971. On the civic religion in America see Robert N. Bellah, "Civil Religion in America," in William G. McLoughlin and Robert N. Bellah, eds., *Religion in America* (Boston, 1968), pp. 3–23. The voluntary and silent features of the prayer amendment were added at the last moment to aid in gathering votes.

72. Quoted by George W. Pierson, *Tocqueville and Beaumont in America* (New York, 1938), p. 298.

73. *Democracy in America,* I, 314.

74. *Church and State,* Report of the Archbishops' Commission (London, 1970), pp. 106, 110. By 1969, however, the American figure had declined by seven percentage points from 1958's high: 63 per cent for Catholics, 37 per cent for Protestants. John Deedy, "Religion," New York *Times,* February 1, 1970.

75. *Church and State,* pp. 74, 79. The dissenter was Valerie Pitt.

76. Alasdair MacIntyre, "God and the Theologians," *Encounter, 120* (Sept., 1963), 3–10; MacIntyre, *Secularization and Moral Change,* p. 69.

77. *Torasco* v. *Watkins,* 367 U.S. 488 (1961).

78. See Peter R. Saladin, "Relative Ranking of the Preferred Freedoms: Religion and Speech," *Religion and the Public Order 1964,* pp. 149–72.

79. *Sherbert* v. *Verner,* 374 U.S. 398 (1963) ; *United States* v. *Seeger,* 380 U.S. 163 (1965). See John H. Mansfield, "Conscientious Objection— 1964 Term," *Religion and the Public Order 1965,* pp. 6–7.

80. *Democracy in America,* I, 303.

81. *Ibid.,* p. 420.

CHAPTER XIX: MODERN PROPHETS IN BABYLON

1. See Ralph Lord Roy, *Apostles of Discord: A Study of Organized Bigotry and Disruption on the Fringes of Protestantism* (Boston, 1953), pp. 11–25.

2. Philip Horton, "Revivalism on the Far Right," *Reporter, 25* (July 20, 1961), 25–29; quoted from *The Blue Book of the John Birch Society* by Cushing Strout, "Fantasy on the Right," *New Republic, 144* (May 1, 1961), 13. In 1964 Welch revived the conspiracy theory of the Illuminati, used by clerical Federalists to smear Jeffersonians. See Seymour Martin Lipset and Earl Raab, *The Politics of Unreason: Right-wing Extremism in America, 1790–1970* (New York, 1970), pp. 252–55.

3. Roy, *op. cit.,* pp. 239, 242.

4. Quoted by Martin E. Marty, *Righteous Empire: The Protestant*

Experience in America (New York, 1970), p. 257. See William G. McLoughlin, *Billy Graham: Revivalist in a Secular Age* (New York, 1960).

5. David Danzig, "The Radical Right and the Rise of the Fundamentalist Minority," *Commentary, 33* (April, 1962), 295. For conflict between ultraconservative laymen and liberal clergy in the McCarthy period see E. V. Toy, Jr., "The National Lay Committee and the National Council of Churches: A Case Study of Protestants in Conflict," *American Quarterly, 21* (Summer, 1969), 190–209. The former were led by a Sun Oil Company executive who eventually turned toward the John Birch Society.

6. *Stride Toward Freedom: The Montgomery Story* (New York, 1958), p. 101.

7. *Ibid.,* pp. 97–99.

8. *Moral Man and Immoral Society,* pp. 248, 243, 252, 241.

9. *Stride Toward Freedom,* pp. 50–51.

10. *Ibid.,* p. 89.

11. On King as a Christian prophet see John W. Rathbun, "Martin Luther King: The Theology of Social Action," *American Quarterly, 20* (Spring, 1968), 38–53.

12. Alphonso Pinkney, *The Committed: White Activists in the Civil Rights Movement* (New Haven, 1968), pp. 41, 147.

13. Gary T. Marx, *Protest and Prejudice: A Study of Belief in the Black Community* (New York, 1967), pp. 26, 100, 203 n. 7.

14. See David L. Lewis, *King: A Critical Biography* (New York, 1970), Chap. 9.

15. *Ibid.,* pp. 384–85.

16. Jeffrey K. Hadden, *The Gathering Storm in the Churches* (Garden City, N.Y., 1969), pp. 136–37. A favorable view was not a function of frequent church attendance.

17. *Where Do We Go from Here?* (New York, 1967), p. 143.

18. See Seth M. Scheiner, "The Negro Church and the Northern City, 1890–1930," in William G. Shade and Roy C. Herrenkohl, eds., *Seven on Black: Reflections on the Negro Experience in America* (Philadelphia, 1969), pp. 92–116.

19. Marx, *op. cit.,* p. 26, table 18.

20. See, for example, the essays in John Henrik Clarke, ed., *Malcolm X: The Man and His Times* (New York, 1969) for this estimation.

21. Some 72 per cent of sympathizers with black nationalism also thought that riots helped. See Marx, p. 115, table 70.

22. For the rhythms of this repeated question see Lewis, *King,* p. 292.

23. "God's Judgment of White America," in Clarke, ed., *Malcolm X,* pp. 286; "Malcolm X Talks with Kenneth B. Clark," *ibid.,* p. 178.

24. See E. U. Essien-Udom, *Black Nationalism: A Search for an*

Identity in America (Chicago, 1962), Chap. 5; C. Eric Lincoln, *The Black Muslims in America* (Boston, 1961), Chap. 4.

25. "Definition of a Revolution," *Malcolm X,* pp. 275, 278; *The Autobiography of Malcolm X* (New York, 1965), p. 300.

26. *The Autobiography,* p. 293.

27. *King,* pp. 268–69.

28. Leverett House Forum, Mar. 18, 1964, in Archie Epps, ed., *Malcolm X and the American Negro Revolution: The Speeches of Malcolm X* (London, 1969), p. 139; Harvard Law School Forum, Dec. 16, 1964, *ibid.,* p. 174.

29. Cf. "*Playboy* Interview: Malcolm X," *Playboy, 10* (May, 1963), 59, and Harvard Law School Forum, *op. cit.,* pp. 164, 175.

30. For an insider's view of student black separatism at Cornell University see Cleveland Donald, "Cornell: Confrontation in Black and White," in Cushing Strout and David I. Grossvogel, eds., *Divided We Stand: Reflections on the Crisis at Cornell* (Garden City, N.Y., 1970), pp. 153–204.

31. Cf. Harvard Law School Forum, Mar. 24, 1961, Epps, ed., *op. cit.,* p. 120, and Ruby M. and E. U. Essien-Udom, "Malcolm X an International Man," in Clarke, ed., *op. cit.,* p. 263.

32. "Some Reflections on Negro History Week and the Role of the Black People in History," in Clarke, ed., *op. cit.,* p. 323.

33. "*Playboy* Interview," *loc. cit.,* p. 60.

34. *The Autobiography,* p. 346. Carl Ohmann also notes analogies with Franklin, as well as with Puritans, in "*The Autobiography of Malcolm X: A Revolutionary Use of the Franklin Tradition,*" *American Quarterly,* 22 (Summer, 1970), 131–49. George Breitman believes that Malcolm X became a socialist in his last year. See *The Last Year of Malcolm X: The Evolution of a Revolutionary* (New York, 1968); the *Autobiography,* however, asserts that the "only true world solution today is governments guided by true religion—of the spirit. Here . . . I am convinced that the Islamic religion is desperately needed, particularly by the American black man." *Autobiography,* p. 375.

35. Marx, *op. cit.,* p. 111, table 68.

36. *Democracy in America,* I, 373.

CHAPTER XX: THE NEW SECULARISM AND THE NEW PLURALISM

1. *Democracy in America,* II, 23.

2. *Ibid.,* I, 304; II, 26–27.

3. *The Religious Factor: A Sociological Study of Religion's Impact on Politics, Economics, and Family Life,* rev. ed. (Garden City, N.Y., 1963),

pp. 365–66. Anchor Books also issued a revised edition of Herberg, *Protestant-Catholic-Jew* in 1960.

4. Gibson Winter, "Methodological Reflections on 'The Religious Factor,'" in Richard D. Knudten, ed., *The Sociology of Religion: An Anthology* (New York, 1967), p. 53.

5. Joseph R. Washington, Jr., *Black Religion: The Negro and Christianity in the United States* (Boston, 1964).

6. Hadden, *The Gathering Storm*, p. 138.

7. *Ibid.*, p. 204, table 71.

8. *Ibid.*, p. 74, table 25; pp. 82–83, tables 30, 31.

9. *Democracy in America*, I, 300; *The Gathering Storm*, pp. 95–96, 134–35, tables 54–55.

10. See the criticisms in Richard L. Rubenstein, "Cox's Vision of the Secular City," in Daniel Callahan, ed., *The Secular City Debate* (New York, 1966), 129–44. In his reply to his critics Cox looked to the Marxist Ernst Bloch, with his philosophical emphasis on the future, because only the future could both define and transcend history, thus becoming a surrogate for God in a demythologizing age. "Afterword," *ibid.*, pp. 199–203.

11. "The 'New Breed' in American Churches: Sources of Social Activism in American Religion," in McLoughlin and Bellah, eds., *Religion in America*, p. 380.

12. See Emil L. Fackenheim, "On the Self-Exposure of Faith to the Modern-Secular World: Philosophical Reflections in the Light of Jewish Experience," *ibid.*, pp. 203–29; Milton Himmelfarb, "Secular Society? A Jewish Perspective," *ibid.*, pp. 282–98.

13. Sister Marie Augusta Neal, "Catholicism in America," *ibid.*, pp. 317, 324. See her *Values and Interests in Social Change* (Englewood Cliffs, N.J., 1965), p. 159, for evidence that the New Breed in Boston's Catholic clergy occupy staff positions not in direct line of command to the diocesan parish system.

14. "Eugene Schallert, S.J.," in James Colaianni, *The Catholic Left: The Crisis of Radicalism within the Church* (New York, 1968), pp. 112–15; Richard A. Lamanna and Jay J. Coakley, "The Catholic Church and the Negro," in Philip Gleason, ed., *Contemporary Catholicism in the United States* (Notre Dame, Ind., 1969), pp. 164, 169, 192.

15. Francine du Plessix Gray, *Divine Disobedience: Profiles in Catholic Radicalism* (New York, 1970), p. 57; Daniel Berrigan, *No Bars to Manhood* (Garden City, N.Y., 1970), p. 49.

16. *Divine Disobedience*, pp. 90, 155. See also James Finn, "American Catholics and Social Movements," *Contemporary Catholicism*, pp. 142, 144.

17. Intro., *The Trial of the Catonsville Nine* (Boston, 1970), p. ix.

18. *No Bars to Manhood*, p. 199.

19. Quoted by Gray, *op. cit.*, p. 208. He is, however, repeating Daniel Berrigan's formulation. See Philip Berrigan, *Prison Journals of a Priest Revolutionary*, ed. Vincent McGee (New York, 1970), p. 120.

20. William G. McLoughlin, Introduction: "How is America Religious?," in *Religion in America*, pp. xxi, xi.

21. *Democracy in America*, II, 256, 263.

22. Peter Berger, *The Sacred Canopy: Elements of a Sociological Theory of Religion* (Garden City, N.Y., 1967), p. 133.

23. Seymour Martin Lipset, "Religion and Politics in America," in Robert Lee and Martin E. Marty, *Religion and Social Conflict* (New York, 1964), p. 119. Lipset convincingly argues that secularity has been a persistent trait of American religion since Tocqueville's day, rather than being a recent development or merely the product of role specificity, accentuated by urbanism and industrialism. See *The First New Nation: The United States in Historical and Comparative Perspective* (New York, 1963), pp. 151–59, 168. On problems in using the term "secularization" see Larry Shiner, "The Meanings of Secularization," in *International Yearbook for the Sociology of Religion* (Cologne and Opladen, 1967), III, 51–59.

24. See Conrad Cherry, "Two American Sacred Ceremonies: Their Implications for the Study of Religion in America," *American Quarterly, 21* (Winter, 1969), 742–45, for Robert Kennedy's funeral rites. His conclusion, however, that the "national faith" has "worked its way even further into the public life of the nation," identifies religion with any unifying social ceremony. But this procedure rules out secularization by definition.

25. Richard E. Morgan, *The Politics of Religious Conflict: Church and State in America* (New York, 1968), p. 126.

26. *Democracy in America*, II, 145, 36–37; I, 315, 325, 329.

27. *Ibid.*, I, 13.

28. *Ibid.*, I, 247.

29 *Ibid.*, II, 330, 142.

Index

74 75 76 77 10 9 8 7 6 5 4 3 2 1